FICTIONS OF JUSTICE

This compelling volume takes up the challenge of documenting how human rights values are embedded in a new rule of law regime to produce a new language of international justice that competes with a range of other religious and cultural formations. It explores how declarations of "justice," like "law," have the power to bury the normative political apparatus within which they are embedded, thereby obscuring the processes of their making. The book demonstrates how these notions of justice are produced as necessary social fictions – as fictions that we need to live with. By examining the making of the Rome Statute for the International Criminal Court in multiple global sites, the application of its jurisdiction in sub-Saharan Africa, and the related contestations on the African continent, the author details the way that notions of justice are negotiated through everyday micropractices and grass-roots contestations. Among these micropractices are speech acts that revere the protection of human rights, citation references to treaty documents, the brokering of human rights agendas, the rewriting of national constitutions, demonstrations of religiosity that point out the piety of religious subjects, and ritual practices of forgiveness that involve the invocation of ancestral religious cosmologies. By detailing the rendering illegible of certain justice constructs and the celebration of others, the book journeys through the problem of incommensurability and the politics of exclusion in our social world. In an attempt to pay attention to the diverse expressions of justice within which theories of legal pluralism circulate, the author ends by calling for a critical transnational legal pluralism. This approach takes seriously the role of translation and the making of fictions of meaning as they play out in unequal relations of power.

Kamari Maxine Clarke is a professor of anthropology at Yale University and a research scientist at the Yale Law School. Her areas of research explore issues related to religious nationalism, legal institutions, international law, the interface between culture and power, and their relationship to the modernity of race and late capitalist globalization. Her recent articles and books have focused on transnational religious and legal movements and the related production of knowledge and power. They include *Mapping Yoruba Networks: Power and Agency in the Making of Transnational Communities* (2004) and *Globalization and Race: Transformations in the Cultural Production of Blackness* (2006). Her forthcoming titles are *Testimonies and Transformations: Reflections on the Use of Ethnographic Knowledge* and *Mirrors of Justice: Law and Power in the Post–Cold War Era*. Professor Clarke has lectured throughout the United States, Canada, and parts of Europe, Africa, and the Caribbean on a wide range of topics. She is Director of the Center for Transnational Cultural Analysis and Chair of the Yale Council on African Studies.

CAMBRIDGE STUDIES IN LAW AND SOCIETY

Cambridge Studies in Law and Society aims to publish the best scholarly work on legal discourse and practice in its social and institutional contexts, combining theoretical insights and empirical research.

The fields that it covers are: studies of law in action; the sociology of law; the anthropology of law; cultural studies of law, including the role of legal discourses in social formations; law and economics; law and politics; and studies of governance. The books consider all forms of legal discourse across societies, rather than being limited to lawyers' discourses alone.

The series editors come from a range of disciplines: academic law, socio-legal studies, sociology, and anthropology. All have been actively involved in teaching and writing about law in context.

Series Editors

Chris Arup
Monash University, Victoria

Martin Chanock
La Trobe University, Melbourne

Pat O'Malley
University of Sydney

Sally Engle Merry
New York University

Susan Silbey
Massachusetts Institute of Technology

Books in the Series

Diseases of the Will
Mariana Valverde

The Politics of Truth and Reconciliation in South Africa:
Legitimizing the Post-Apartheid State
Richard A. Wilson

Modernism and the Grounds of Law
Peter Fitzpatrick

Unemployment and Government:
Genealogies of the Social
William Walters

Autonomy and Ethnicity:
Negotiating Competing Claims in Multi-Ethnic States
Yash Ghai

Series list continues after the Index.

FICTIONS OF JUSTICE

The International Criminal Court
and the Challenge of Legal Pluralism
in Sub-Saharan Africa

Kamari Maxine Clarke

Yale University

CAMBRIDGE
UNIVERSITY PRESS

CAMBRIDGE UNIVERSITY PRESS
Cambridge, New York, Melbourne, Madrid, Cape Town, Singapore, São Paulo, Delhi

Cambridge University Press
32 Avenue of the Americas, New York, NY 10013-2473, USA

www.cambridge.org
Information on this title: www.cambridge.org/9780521717793

First published 2009

Printed in the United States of America

A catalog record for this publication is available from the British Library.

Library of Congress Cataloging in Publication data

Clarke, Kamari Maxine, 1966–
Fictions of justice : the international criminal court and the challenge of legal pluralism in
sub-Saharan Africa / Kamari Maxine Clarke.
     p.   cm. – (Cambridge studies in law and society)
Includes bibliographical references and index.
ISBN 978-0-521-88910-0 (hardback) – ISBN 978-0-521-71779-3 (pbk.)
1. Legal polycentricity – Africa, Sub-Saharan.   2. International and municipal law – Africa,
Sub-Saharan.   3. Religion and law – Africa, Sub-Saharan.   4. Criminal law – Africa,
Sub-Saharan.   I. Title.   II. Series.
KQC105.C58   2009
342.6708 – dc22   2008052909

ISBN 978-0-521-88910-0 hardback
ISBN 978-0-521-71779-3 paperback

Dedicated to the late Chima Ubani,
Nigerian human rights leader,
killed under controversial circumstances

CONTENTS

PREFACE

"Eine Idee deren Zeit gekommen ist [This is an idea whose time has come]!" exclaimed Mr. Heimler,[1] a diplomatic host at the New York City–based German Mission to the United Nations (UN). He had taken his place at the speaker's platform to express appreciation for the establishment of the International Criminal Court (ICC) – the first permanent international tribunal with the jurisdiction to try those who commit the worst crimes against humanity. With a room full of people from various countries, and with characteristic diplomatic resilience, he explained, "Today, July 1, 2002, the ICC has come into force as the first permanent international court responsible for adjudicating crimes against humanity, war crimes, genocide, and, when defined, the crime of aggression." He continued, "As you know, this was no small feat. Today the ICC stands as an expression of the will of two-thirds of the world's nations, representing the shared dream of universal personhood."

After establishing the profundity of the moment – the achievement of legal precepts emanating from an international text holier in its supranational institution because it was seen as being untouched by the *tainted* hands of potentially corrupt governments – the German diplomat began welcoming ministers of ambassadorial offices from around the world. He acknowledged a range of diplomatic staff, legal advisors, political analysts, representatives from nongovernmental organizations (NGOs), and guests, then invited us all to share with him the satisfaction of witnessing the realization of two visions of international justice: an institutional dream and a moral dream, both connected to achieving individual freedom for all. He honored those who, in the hope of bringing to fruition the institutional dream, had been involved in the UN Diplomatic Conference held in Rome, Italy, in July 1998. In celebrating this journey, he spoke of the multiple levels of networking, governmental negotiations, lobbying, and advocacy efforts that had been carried out by states, as well as by more than a thousand NGOs from around the world. These efforts, he explained, had later led to the requisite ratification of the Rome Statute, establishing the ICC by sixty like-minded states, thereby signaling another victory in the struggle for international human rights.[2] Unlike human rights instruments (e.g., the UN Human Rights Council, Inter-American Court of Human Rights, European Court of Human Rights), often seen as "soft law" and lacking "teeth," the Rome statute and its antecedents were seen as "hard law," "clean" forms of justice that emanated from treaties, conventions, and various supranational texts as opposed to human rights declarations or principles. They were the only international adjudicatory mechanisms with the institutional potential to actually exert force on a rogue government, a warlord, or a perpetrator of crimes against humanity. This was seen as a victory for the institutionalization of the *Rule of Law!*[3]

Those listening with me in the audience on that celebrated day were told that the second dream, the moral dream, represented the ideal of the universal rights of victims. With the help of the ICC, victims of the worst crimes, regardless of national citizenship, would now be able to access justice and compensation from the world community. Embedded in a language of protest against national sovereignty, which was represented as stunting human progress, the message of the spokespeople for the ICC was one of the moral good of widespread entitlements for all the world's members, an imperative for the prosperity of humankind.

This day, like many others, was fueled by the seduction of human rights rhetoric and its link to the "rule of law" as the new mechanism by which world peace could finally be achieved. Speeches by subsequent guest speakers resounded with similar themes. Various state diplomats and NGO representatives assured us that in making possible the success of the ICC, they were pledging to further the dream that humanity would one day be free from all forms of criminal violence. They proclaimed their institutional and moral commitments to precepts of fairness and equality for all, concluding that world peace was possible along this particular path to justice and through international cooperation among states. In so doing, speakers drew from a line of thought that has its roots in the Western Enlightenment political philosophy of John Locke, David Hume, and Jean-Jacques Rousseau – a line of thought that includes the idea that the equality of all humans is promised by the progression from state sovereignty to its eradication. Such conceptions of "human rights" and "rule of law" presume that in the process of guaranteeing freedoms and classifying rights and entitlements, all peoples will come to share similar visions for what true liberty and equality should be. Such conceptions also presume that the struggles that result in the

commission of the "worst crimes against humanity" are without reason or historical motivation, that in contemporary democratic regimes
there exists a level playing field for democratic governance, and that all
people strive for the same goals of individual agency and freedom. These
are among the presumptions that this book is dedicated to challenging.
It explores the ways by which paths to "justice" are actually vigorously
produced and become contested domains. They are neither universally
embodied in a uniform conception of individual rights nor do they exist
as one of many pluralities of justice-making domains. Rather, justice-
making domains are made in increasingly complex regimes of truth
that circulate in transnational forms of connectivities and exclusions.
Understanding how they become acceptable as "justice," as normative
mandates through which institutional victories are celebrated, involves
understanding their creation not simply in "local" contexts but in the
uneven transnational relations through which justice is shaped.

Based on more than six years of data collection in five world regions and
including insights gathered during observations of the making of the
Rome Statute of the ICC, the research for this study comprises a multisited and transnational ethnography in a post–Cold War, post-9/11
context. My analyses detail the ways by which cultural representations
of the universality of human rights and the rule of law inform particular
legal measures, as well as the ways by which cultural interpretations of
justice contravene those rationalities and, instead, inform other insurgencies. By examining the historical and political imaginaries underlying the forms of utopianism that shape a world of emergent human
entitlements, I ask how people envision a world of hope and justice
and examine the convergences and divergences in those constructions.
In this regard, I trace various micropractices and their instruments of
justice-producing regimes – their regulatory structures, procedures of
reasoning, governmental strategies, interpretive and moral priorities,
and political economies of practice – and examine how they contribute
to the shaping of practices that structure the spectacularity of justice tribunals and of various other religion-based judiciaries, such as
Islamic Sharia courts, as well as of Ugandan truth and reconciliation
ceremonies.

I began this project in 1998, during the cresting wave of truth and
reconciliation commissions and ad hoc tribunals, including the International Criminal Tribunal for the former Yugoslavia and the International Criminal Tribunal for Rwanda. I was inspired by the prospects for

global change suggested by NGOs and by the shift toward international institutions as supplemental to mechanisms of civil and economic governance. To understand the accelerated development of the budding international criminal law movement, I decided to document the making of the ICC. From 1998 to 2006, I attended diplomatic meetings at the UN Preparatory Commissions (known as PrepComs) in New York City, as well as related UN Assembly of States Parties meetings in The Hague. In an attempt to understand the imparting of new legal knowledge, I attended a range of training courses for domestic criminal lawyers in The Hague and various other European sites (in Ireland, France, the United Kingdom), as well as NGO-driven human rights trainings in Banjul, The Gambia; Montréal, Canada; and in Lagos and Abuja, Nigeria. These programs provided an opportunity to observe the making of new brokers of the law – prosecutors and defense attorneys, judges, and freshly minted graduates of law and politics who converged to engage in what was a significant retooling of legal knowledge and resources. These transnational meetings and interactions led to new articulations of rights transported to local sites, but their presence was not always welcome or easily integrated into local formulations. It was these local and national forms of friction with transnational spheres of justice making that were of special interest to me in African contexts because of their engagement with reforming violence-laden regions through the threat of international law. Yet it was clear that there existed incommensurate relationships that were difficult to articulate outside of the problematic hierarchies of Western knowledge. It was also clear that even the transnational logic that shaped the moral and ethical underside of justice aspirations was, at times, so divergent that understanding difference meant going beyond legal pluralism and, certainly, well beyond relativist thinking. This was not simply because of the unequal spheres of power operative in international lawmaking but also because these justice-making spaces are today so transnational that their justice aspirations often represent trajectories that are themselves shaped by international institutions, diasporic communities hoping to revive traditional mechanisms, and various philanthropic agendas to train and support local infrastructures. The revitalization of the truth and reconciliation rituals in Uganda, known as *mato oput*, is one such example; the return of Islamic criminal Sharia in Northern Nigeria is another.

In an attempt to understand these transnational forms of connectivity to seemingly "local" practices as they relate to the making of "traditional" justice, I spent the summer of 2002 in Nigeria, documenting the revival of Islamic Sharia, and parts of the summer of 2007 in Uganda, exploring the revival of northern Ugandan traditional justice forms. It became evident that understanding the revival of these seemingly "traditional" practices, especially as they were being deployed in the face of the encroachment of international criminal justice regimes, meant understanding claims of Ugandan and Nigerian membership in larger transnational institutions, imaginaries, and political economies. In the case of Nigerian challenges over incommensurate conceptions of justice, it meant rethinking not only the relationship of Islamic revivalists to the secular state but also that between prominent Nigerian advocates for the criminal Sharia and their aspirations of membership in a larger world of Islamic devotion and justice technologies. At times, this reality made the revitalization of the criminal Sharia in Nigeria even more radical than their various Islamic contemporaries in Pakistan, Egypt, and Iran. Faced with these transnational aspirational forces, Nigerian NGOs working on rule of law projects became even more inventive and insistent on the significance of instituting particular forms of universal human rights principles in Nigeria. In Uganda, it meant rethinking the webs of NGO and donor streams being deployed to support the strengthening of Ugandan judiciaries and traditional mechanisms in a bid to develop grassroots solutions to deep-seated problems.

I spent the second part of the summer of 2002 in The Gambia, West Africa, attending the African Commission for Human and People's Rights and collecting data from interviews with various commissioners, claimants, and NGO participants about the challenges of implementing human rights principles in war-torn and transitional regions. This experience made clear that the language of individual and human rights central to many of the European human rights training sessions I had attended the summer before (together with a range of national prosecutors and defense attorneys interested in becoming international criminal prosecutors) was quite differently conceptualized in African contexts. The differences ranged from varied articulations of the rights of the citizen to their understandings of the duties to the community and to the preservation of "traditional culture." These conceptions were as locally articulated and as internationally shaped through institutions such as the African Commission on Human and Peoples' Rights as they were by Joseph Konrad's 1902 desire to distinguish and render primitive and unchanging *African* ways from those of the *West*. This dynamic is similar to what V. Y. Mudimbe (1994) referred to as the "idea of Africa" and what Achille Mbembe referred to as *African self-making*. Today, however, the "idea" of Africa is that of a repository of "holistic and pure cultural practices" that is in need of preservation or intervention, faced with an even more aggressive claim to cultural, traditional, and religious rights. Ironically, these assertions, in some cases articulated as "duties to preserve their culture and community," are even more pan-African and transnational in their aspirations than those in the Global North. But, like the rise of the rule of law movement, the revival of "traditional" justice mechanisms is part of the same processes of constructing the ideals of justice through which to build a more equitable world. What distinguished these various human rights movements in African regions from those in Europe and America is what characterizes the central intervention of this book – a different power of mobilization, international influence, and general fields of possibility, and a difference in access as a result of political inequalities.

In an attempt to make sense of these inequalities, I returned to Nigeria during the summers of 2003, 2004, and 2005 in search of an understanding of legal plurality in relation to its manifestation in various social disparities. I traveled among Islamic religious communities in the Nigerian north and worked with and among various people attempting to reform the new Sharia criminal codes. During this three-year period, as I also documented the simultaneous growth of the international criminal law movement, violent strife between Christians and Muslims and the reinstatement of the strict Sharia penal code led to widespread global attention to the controversies of cultural differences – often represented by the press as "Islamic barbarism" in the administration of criminal justice. Visiting the newly instituted Sharia courts, with new jurisdictional powers over criminal matters, I journeyed with Nigerian Muslim human rights lawyers and members of various networks of human rights NGOs working on the defense of what they referred to as "victims of the Sharia" – men and women awaiting amputation of limbs for theft or death by stoning for the crime of adultery.

In attempts to understand further these multiplicities of justice in the context of uneven fields of transnational power in other African regions, I conducted surveys in northern Uganda and hired a team of researchers that worked with me to interview stakeholders of the peace negotiations in the Ugandan north – victims of war, refugees, judicial–spiritual leaders, and perpetrators of violence – struggling to make sense of the ICC presence and what that meant for brokering peace in the region. Finally, I collected preliminary data in the Democratic Republic of the Congo (DRC) to understand regional struggles and the consequent violence there that had led to some of its countrymen being the first charged by the ICC's lead prosecutor with various crimes against humanity. With the ICC and the Charles Taylor trial before the Special Court for Sierra Leone and the Thomas Lubanga Dyilo trial underway, my research team and I attended hearings in The Hague to make sense of the significance of the rule of law as it was playing out in sub-Saharan African contexts of violence and displacement.

Yet, as I collected data, it became clear that the ICC paradigm, increasingly prominent on the world's stage, was at odds with the struggles over sovereign decision making in such a large part of sub-Saharan Africa, and that violence around the world seemed, if anything, to be on the increase. It also became clear that the mission of the ICC was not necessarily to end violence by providing the mechanisms for redistributive justice, but to execute punishment, thereby setting in place a symbol for the deterrence of unjustified killing. As I began writing, the networks of violence as constituted by rebel factions and the disenfranchised continued throughout the world. ICC investigations into crimes against humanity focused not on the networks that enable and foster such violence – the complicity of transnational arms dealers and oil barons engaged in resource extraction – but on local cases, local sites, and individual people held responsible for the mass violence committed by a community of actors. This ranged from violence in Uganda, the DRC, the Sudan, and the Central African Republic. During the course of this writing, the controversies over ICC jurisdiction and the violence in Uganda and the Sudan became central to the identity of the court. Now, as I complete this work, violence around the world has grown exponentially and includes Israeli bombings of innocent Palestinians in the Gaza and Palestinian acts of violence against undeserving members of the Israeli public; America's occupation of Afghanistan and Iraq; ongoing state-sponsored capital punishment in America and a rise in the general prison population[4]; Islamic uprisings and their related fatwas that call worshippers to fulfill their duty and defend the Prophet Muhammad; and suicide bombings not only in Israel, the Middle East, and Pakistan but also in the United States, the United Kingdom, Spain, Kenya, Somalia, Tanzania, and Turkey. These events make clear that violent contemporary struggles and their forms of adjudication and procedures for procuring justice are deeply constituted

within sociohistorical, cultural, economic, ideological, and praxeological constellations within which power is brokered internationally and
globally. Today, these struggles reflect conflict over resources, land, and
politics that is closely related to control over the power to declare "just
wars" as reflective of legitimate acts of violence, to interpret the meanings of justice, and, when all else fails, to impose the spectral force of
law or the divine claims of authorial religious dictates.

Thus, it is becoming more important than ever to recognize the
changing legacies of imperial forces – from colonial forms of external
occupation to self-regulating forms of governmentality – and to examine
their inconnections to the ways in which emergent justice regimes are
legitimized and managed alongside violence in ways that exceed articulations of pluralism. It is here – in the sometimes tiny spaces between
the making of justice and the making of violence – that some of those
who were once victims of colonial rule are increasingly becoming participants in the defence of sovereign power and the search for *traditional*
answers. As this book explores, despite its claim to end impunity, it is
critical to understand that ICC international intervention as the solution to African violence is seen as problematic by many on the African
continent who would normally be supportive of the ICC. Those unhappy with the court's African focus are often identified in the rule
of law literature as anti-human rights or as misguided. However, the
validity of their concerns about the ICC – chief among them that such
prosecution stops short of addressing the root causes of violence – makes
this project even more intellectually radical, in that it insists that we
explore how it could be that a literature on the rule of law and human
rights can be so uninterested in grappling with such root causes in the
first place.

I am not suggesting that, because of the shortcomings of the ICC–
human rights movement and its inability to address root forms of social
inequality, we should abandon their various projects altogether; surely,
in the midst of violence, torture, pain, loss, and death, initiatives that
provide deterrents and aspire for redistributive measures leave open the
possibility for imagining a new world. Nevertheless, we can do it better.
What is necessary is a critical approach to rethinking the growth of
the rule of law movement from a range of social locations – not just
through the deterrence of crime by instilling the fear of prosecution
or the reform of "Third World" African, Iraqi, Ugandan, Afghani, or
Islamic religious-based constitutions. Just as important is a rethinking

of criminal responsibility in relation to those countries that are making arms available to warlords or the way we understand rule of law secularism and the implications for the ways that its products travel or do not travel. It involves reorienting our own locations in the production of knowledge – and rethinking even the terms of brokering "justice," interrogating how it is defined, articulated, and sometimes not rendered visible. In mainstream articulations of justice – shaped by the history of the liberal project, built alongside national state formations – the making of justice is the making of institutional interventions to repair infractions against society after the commission of crime. Seen in relation to the ICC context, it is acts of violence and their criminal classification and legal mobilization that enable such justice making. In Ugandan Acholi contexts, justice involves similar attempts to classify the infraction and mobilize the forces – spiritual and corporal – necessary to produce reconciliation. Yet as this book demonstrates, the production of "justice" is a process through which social fictions are made. Through this process, its making may conform to our aspirations and our imaginaries, but it may also offend them. Although it often becomes manifest as an objective truth, it is actually an effect rather than a stable entity. Its effects can guide what is socially possible, but through its exclusions, it can also be productive of social disenfranchisement and thus of violence.

This book is about apparitions of justice, fictions of justice – the transnational processes of mounting, circulating, sustaining, and contesting its invocation with a victim in the shadows. The reality of justice as socially produced in these conditions does not make it less real. Its study highlights the material effects of its powerful constructs in motion, making it more important than ever to detail the way its normative underpinnings are produced. Thus, inspired by the reality that today there is tremendous diversity in the legal structures of "justice" on the African continent, the reality is that the little untouched village that inspired so much of the scholarly approaches to cultural relativism of the past, and that continues to drive legal pluralism of the present, is no more. The modernity of transnational justice making is "at large," and Islamic Sharia revivalism, Ugandan *Acholi*, and Rwanda *Gachacha* reconciliation mechanisms, often celebrated as "traditional," are as much a product of modernity as they are of local imaginaries. By questioning how we balance the claims of cultural, ethnic, and religious rights against the claims of international justice making and by asking whether international human rights actors further aggravate locally circumscribed problems, even as they intend to engage in capacity-building initiatives, my hope is that scholars and practitioners, leaders, and political visionaries will articulate revisionist instruments through which to broaden the scope of current approaches to the rule of law. This involves recognizing the extent to which they are both products of transnational processes and, therefore, require complex transnational solutions. In this regard, I write this book with the hope that the human rights moral principles that shape emergent rule of law formations can be deployed to reorder the contemporary foundations of capitalist globalization that are part of the root causes of violence that international tribunals are called to punish.

ACKNOWLEDGMENTS

I am fortunate to have conducted this research at such an opportune moment, and in this context, I must acknowledge that no book is written alone or based on a uniform set of experiences. The people and roads informing this work represent an ongoing journey and not an endpoint. The framework for this book took shape while I was doing course work at the Yale Law School, and it was completed during a generous one-year sabbatical leave from teaching at Yale University. There is a luxury that accompanies the writing of any book, whether accomplished at one's leisure while on sabbatical or while entrenched in teaching and other administrative obligations. This luxury can be construed as the power of time – that is, the ability to isolate events and analyze them without having to expend the bulk of one's time on matters of mere survival. In my case, writing such a book under the auspices of one of the world's leading law schools compels me to make explicit the luxuries of deconstructing and critiquing – in contexts so distant from the violence with which the book is centrally concerned – the problems with justice and human rights institutions. It is precisely within such spaces of privilege, spaces from which the export of human rights norms originate, that we must reflect on the realities of inequality and the limitations of those norms, for which the points of departure are often epistemologically different from those elsewhere.

There are many people at the Yale Law School whom I must thank for their input and feedback on this project. First, Michael Reisman was central in encouraging me to pursue the study of international law in an effort to make sense of the deep meanings related to the reorganizations of the "New World Order." I thank him for his encouragement, support, and provocation. Others at the Yale Law School were similarly supportive, and I thank them for their direction and teaching: Jack Balkin, Amy Chua, Marjan Damaska, Oona Hathaway, Harold Koh, Judith Resnik, Peter Schuck, James Silk, and James Whitman. I am appreciative of the students of the Islamic Reading Group, as well as those whose communities I entered, for their support. Special thanks to those who engaged with me and sustained me intellectually during my time there: Emelia Arthur, Don Braman, Ben Deporter, Dan Gordon, Amy Kapczynski, Anita Khandelwal, Kapil Longani, Diane Marks, Amanda Mills, Adilson Moreira, Annelise Riles, Galit Sarfaty, Reva Segal, Julie Suk, Abdul Tejan-Cole, and Alex Turkeltaub.

For permission to reprint versions of chapters from this book, I thank the *Loyola of Los Angeles International and Comparative Law Review* (Chapter 1), Cambridge University Press (Chapter 3), and *Anthropology News* (part of Chapter 1). I also thank those in the many institutions in field sites far and near who sustained and nurtured me with ideas, time, and – in various African locales, in particular – formidable food, which nursed me back to good health during bouts of malaria.

Hauwa Ibrahim has served as an important interlocutor, and I thank her for her generosity, graciousness, and ongoing insights. I also thank her paralegal staff and junior barristers, especially Muftahu Bello, as well as the officers of the Sharia courts, for their ongoing engagement and generosity. I am appreciative of various members and staff of the Nigerian Civil Liberty Organization for their unlimited time and accommodation, both in the office in Lagos and on the road as we traveled to various sites for human rights training. Benson Olugbuo, Mary Kabogoza, and the staff of the Coalition for the International Criminal Court and their Ugandan- and Nigerian-based branches, the Nigerian Coalition for the International Criminal Court, and the Ugandan Coalition for the International Criminal Court were also exceptionally generous in including me in their various deliberations over a two-year period. They facilitated my participation in many UN Preparatory Commissions and many Assembly of States Parties sessions at the United Nations, and they put me in touch with people in their networks as I traveled on missions in various African countries and collaborated with NGOs in providing legal analysis and ICC implementation strategies.

Trainers with Human Rights Watch, Human Rights First; United Nations Educational, Scientific, and Cultural Organization; and Amnesty International on missions to various West African countries were similarly helpful. I thank them for their assistance through what has been a complex and multisited maze of global interconnections. I am appreciative of the helpfulness of the facilitators of training courses for the ICC and other international human rights organizations, especially the International Criminal Law Network in The Hague, the Institute for Human Rights and Development in Africa in The Gambia, and the Irish Center for Human Rights at the National University of Ireland,

Galway. My deepest appreciation goes to various stakeholders of the African truth and reconciliation commissions – Kenneth Attafuah, with whom I consulted in Ghana; Father Mathew Kukah of the Oputa Panel in Nigeria; and Abdul Tejan-Cole, then a mobilizer around the establishment of the Special Court of Sierra Leone.

No relational research project that extends over a five-year period and requires acute attention to a range of important numbers, dates, and sources can do without research assistants of exceptional precision and dedication. I was fortunate to have had some of the best research assistants and collaborators that a scholar could ever dream of – on both sides of the Atlantic Ocean. Special thanks go to Femi Adewole, Omolade Adunbi, Maggie Ahn, Dayo Ajayi, Bamidele Aturu, Lucia Cantero, Evon Clarke, Feyi Koya, Melanie Markowits, Nadia McLennan, Sylvia Mullins, Joseph Ongwech, Tina Palivos, Terry St. Denis, and Kristina Weaver, as well as to the wonderful editors of particular sections of the book: Kathryn Chetkovich and Michael Gnat. Special appreciation for making such assistance possible goes to the Yale University Junior Faculty Fellowship, as well as the Yale Senior Faculty Fellowship. These two grants provided me with the sabbatical leave from teaching that enabled me to complete both the research and writing of this book. I am also grateful to Ian Shapiro and the MacMillan Center for International and Area Studies at Yale for their generous support, and to the Whitney Humanities Center, the Griswold Fund, Gustav Ranis, and the Ford Foundation Crossing Borders Initiative for funding different aspects of this project. I also thank my colleagues in the Anthropology Department, who offered intellectual support as I ventured into new terrain, as well as the critical feedback to steer me back to the concerns appropriate to a social scientist, as opposed to an international lawyer. I am additionally appreciative of their abundant engagement with this book at various stages of completion. Special thanks go to Lieba Faier for her multiple readings of the manuscript, from start to finish, and her commitment to the spirit of its argument. I am particularly grateful for her incisive criticism and generous suggestions during the last stage of this writing. For their critical engagement of earlier drafts, I also thank the following colleagues and graduate students: Omolade Adunbi, Ann Allison, Muff Andersson, Lee Baker, Sandra Bamford, Hugh Baran, Barney Bate, Ian Baucom, Elena Baylis, Paul S. Berman, Nneka Black, Guillaume Boccara, Devika Bordia, Sean Brotherton, Annie Bunting, Jennifer Burrell, Mihri Cakir-Inal, Lucia Cantero, Hazel Carby, Lawrence Cohen,

Marie Dembour, Chris Dolan, Cheryl Doss, Beth Drexler, Jim Ferguson, Silvia Fernandez, Moira Fradinger, Ilana Gershon, Mark Goodale, Bill Hanks, Thomas Blom Hansen, Rebecca Hardin, Ariana Hernández-Reguant, Susan Hirsch, Gavin Hood, Serene Jones, Csilla Kalocsai, Toby Kelly, Michael Lambek, Michael Levin, Darryl Li, Tania Li, Ralph Litzinger, Atreyee Majmunder, Bill Maurer, Michael McGovern, Sally Merry, Elizabeth Mertz, Donald Moore, Hudita Mustafa, Laura Nader, Diane Nelson, Pashington Obeng, Leslye Obiora, Obiora Okafor, Jacob Olupona, Aihwa Ong, Tina Palivos, Charles Piot, Dhooleka Raj, Maria Sidorkina Rives, Doug Rogers, Todd Sanders, Nancy Scheper-Hughes, Alissa Trotz, Ludger Viefhues, Laura Wexler, Robin Whittaker, Brackette Williams, Richard Wilson, and Eric Worby.

I also want to thank the anonymous reviewers for their insightful comments and my colleagues at the various institutions at which I presented arguments from this book: the University of California, Berkeley, Department of Anthropology; Boalt Hall School of Law, also at Berkeley; the University of California, Irvine, Department of Anthropology; the International Center for Ethics, Justice, and Public Life at Brandeis University; the Human Rights Institute at the University of Connecticut, Storrs, as well as the Women's Studies Program there; the Department of Anthropology at Southern Connecticut State University; Harvard University; University of Pittsburgh Law School; The National University of Ireland, Maynooth; the York Centre for International and Security Studies and the Osgoode Hall Law School, both at York University, Toronto, as well as the Social Sciences Division's Law and Society Program and the Department of Anthropology there; Duke University; Yale Law School; Wesleyan University; the University of Toronto Faculty of Law; the Department of Religion and the Institute of Human Rights at Emory University; Columbia University; and the many interlocutors at the American Anthropological Association, the African Studies Association, and the Law and Society Association meetings.

For assistance in final editing and production, I thank Mary Paden and Elizabeth Budd of Aptara Inc., who helped turn the manuscript into a book.

My appreciation additionally goes to those whose life and struggles taught me firsthand the potential power of social justice movements. Ellen Barry, Angela Y. Davis, Gina Dent, Cassandra Shaylor, Julia Sudbury, and members of Critical Resistance, Oakland chapter, as well as the members of various African human rights communities that welcomed me into their circles: Omolade Adunbi, Kenneth Attafuah, Kayode Fayemi, Father Mathew, Sindi Médar-Gould, Russell Mzembe, Benson Olugbuo, Rafsanjani, and Chinwe Uwandu. To those readers working on the front lines of humanitarianism, national and international law, and human rights advocacy whose perspectives have not always been in sync with mine but whose inspiration to work against odds has fueled my critical passion, I am also grateful.

Such transnational and multisited research includes work in countries in which transitions from military to democratic rule have been volatile. This fact often made my research difficult for my family and dear ones, and I am grateful for their support and patience, which has made this work possible. A special thank you, finally, to Herbert Williams, Viola Clarke, and Ronald W. Crooks, whose ongoing support continues to drive this work. I alone am responsible for its shortcomings.

INTRODUCTION: THE RULE OF LAW AND ITS IMBRICATIONS – JUSTICE IN THE MAKING

PROLOGUE: THE INTERNATIONAL CRIMINAL COURT AND THE DEMOCRATIC REPUBLIC OF THE CONGO

In November 2006, the International Criminal Court (ICC) – in pursuit of the quest for justice – began its first-ever hearing before the Pre-Trial Chamber. Thomas Lubanga Dylio, the accused, was charged with using child soldiers to commit violent murders. The prosecution presented him as the alleged leader of a Congolese militia responsible for ethnic massacres, torture, and rapes in the eastern part of the Democratic Republic of the Congo (DRC).[1] Jean Flamme, the lead defence attorney for Lubanga at the time, countered by characterizing his client as a nonviolent man, a shepherd who wanted to lead his flock to peace and whose principal goals were to secure ethnic reconciliation and the equitable distribution of natural resources within the DRC.[2] Lubanga "is a patriot," Flamme contended. "He is a man who wants to defend his people." Portraying Lubanga as a pacifist politician, Flamme maintained that tribal conflict in Congo's "lawless" Ituri region was so violent that people were often hacked to death and sometimes even eaten in the years before Lubanga managed to forge peace in 2003. Lubanga was described as having "entered the political realm by chance in a country that was in chaos. . . . [H]e was considered a man who was able to put an end to the violence." According to Flamme, the reality was that Lubanga, by advocating equitable distribution of Congo's vast mineral wealth, had upset powerful business opponents in both Congo and neighboring Uganda. "The people of the Congo are poor; the country,

1

however, is rich," he said. "He wanted the wealth of the Congo to belong to the Congolese people."[3]

While crafting the accused as an innocent subject whose fate was shaped by poverty and nationalist sovereign opinion against competing business interests in the region, Flamme also asserted the importance of protecting Lubanga's rights and claimed that the prosecution's case was based on flimsy evidence. For Flamme, the prospect of Lubanga on trial represented the advent of the newest and most intolerable kind of justice – what he called "NGO justice."[4] He asserted that much of the prosecution's case was reliant on NGO (nongovernmental organization) research studies and that "NGO justice" was produced through highly biased data fuelled through donor-sponsored agendas. He went on to criticize this evidence as deficient in rigor and objectivity, thereby asserting the absence of a case against his client.

Together the ICC's prosecution and Flamme's defense exemplify the kinds of display that constitute international justice as it is performed and contested on the world stage today, particularly in relation to countries throughout the Global South. Within those performances, however, a conceptual incommensurability concerning how to define the victim and justice often surrounds questions for determining the responsibility of those who actually kill, as well as the socioeconomic and political conditions under which such death occurs.

The actual trial began on January 26, 2009, but a number of stays on the legal proceedings had delayed an earlier commencement. On June 13, 2008, a stay on the proceedings was ordered in the case of *The Prosecutor v. Thomas Lubanga Dyilo* when it was determined that it was not possible to secure a fair trial. The accused was released and transferred back to the DRC five days later.[5] No finding of guilt or innocence was reached. The court decided that the prosecution's case was built on evidence from the United Nations (UN), procured through agreements of nondisclosure. At the time, the prosecution could not change the nondisclosure agreement, which restricted the sharing of evidence and disabled the defense in building its case. However, the judges and defence lawyers were eventually granted access to the evidence by the United Nations, and the trial of Lubanga began some seven months later.

In the unfolding of the pretrial hearings as well as the trial itself, the terms of determining guilt and innocence were built on notions of personal criminal responsibility that linked Lubanga as head commander to the murder and rape of thousands of people. The defense attempted to point to root causes of violence in Ituri, such as challenges of poverty and sovereign control of the wealth of the land, but the prosecution's case surpassed such considerations. Instead, it attempted to assign guilt to a single person – Thomas Lubanga – identified as having orchestrated widespread violence in the region. One consequence of the increasing power of international justice in these contexts is its ability to use statutes, codify laws, and establish new transnational procedures to set new terms of engagement within which defendants, lawyers, and prosecutors reclassify evidence and articulate crime in legally relevant terms. This reclassification of responsibility has had the effect of sublimating root causes of violence, reassigning accountability to those few high-ranking leaders in sub-Saharan Africa who are seen as responsible for mass violations. These terms are circulating within new international forms of jurisprudence in which state and nonstate actors operate within reconfigured forms of governance. New legal mechanisms are being constructed for assigning guilt, and new procedures for victim protection are emerging beyond the domain of the nation-state. An example of this is the individualization of criminal responsibility, otherwise known as "command responsibility,"[6] which, in cases of mass crimes against humanity, is a way to reassign violence committed by many to only a few key leaders, so that commanders bear most of the responsibility. In *Prosecutor v. Lubanga Dyilo*, it was Lubanga Dyilo's designation as chief commander, and thus his responsibility for mobilizing mass murder that was at issue, rather than the root causes of the resource-related struggles. Concerns about larger sociopolitical factors contributing to resource extraction and violence were relevant only insofar as they facilitated the identification of people mobilizing as a result of such conditions. In the second half of the book, in which I deal with other attempts to construct and deliver justice under generalized conditions of neoliberal and postcolonial governance, we see that, like international criminal institutions, the key problematic of governance contributing to the revival of the radical criminal Sharia in the northern Nigerian states had to do with competition over the popular control of power – the challenges of democracy in relation to the distribution of resources.

In this contemporary period of free-market competition over resources, market demands for coltan and oil in the regions addressed in this book, for example, highlight the core intervention: that the rise of neoliberal governance and international institutions, as well as the return to traditional justice systems (Islamic Sharia and various Ugandan truth and reconciliation traditions) as answers to violence through the protection of the victim, fail to engage in productive political action. Rather, this current period of growth in regimes dealing with international and local justice marks one in which violence is increasingly viewed in terms of individual rather than collective guilt and justice is articulated through the achievement of a guilty conviction. This convergence of the guilt of key perpetrators and the defence of the victim actually represents the fiction of justice today – the reassignment of criminal responsibility to the individual and the myth of legal pluralism as a viable way to address violence through both international and national mechanisms.

In a landmark speech in support of the ICC, Kofi Annan said to a packed audience, "To the survivors who are also the witnesses and to the bereaved we owe a justice that also brings healing. Only by clearly identifying the individuals responsible for these crimes can we save whole communities from being held collectively guilty. It is that notion of collectivity which is the true enemy of peace" (July 2002 speech at the United Nations). This approach to reassigning guilt committed by a collective to an individual is central to today's global rule of law movement and is narrativized in some of the most effective ways. But what is important is that this articulation of criminal responsibility in the defence of the victim has had the opposite of its intended effect by producing what Jacques Raniciere (2004) has called *disembodied political subjects* that allow agency to be reassigned to the institutionally powerful in their name.

The establishment of the ICC has been heralded as the answer to global violence. It emerged against the historical backdrop of the recently independent states in Africa and Latin America and the emergent states of Asia, as well as a range of justice-making projects that include nonjudicial truth and reconciliation commissions, reconfigurations of traditional justice mechanisms, and other international criminal tribunals and courts. In the last decade of the twentieth century, more than twenty-five quasi-judicial truth and reconciliation commissions and a range of ad hoc criminal tribunals were set up worldwide; notions of truth reconciliation and forgiveness became the mechanism for addressing systemic violence and transitioning societies into nonviolent democracies. Thus, before the establishment of the ICC, various ad hoc extranational tribunals had become familiar players on the world's stage, contributing to a widespread and growing corpus of international criminal law. These justice-making bodies included United Nations

Security Council tribunals, such as the International Criminal Tribunal for the former Yugoslavia (ICTY), which led to the 1999 indictment of Slobodan Milošević, and the International Criminal Tribunal for Rwanda (ICTR), which established crimes of the Rwandan genocide. Other international courts have included the Special Court for Sierra Leone (SCSL; known as a hybrid court that functions independently using international treaty provisions), the Iraqi Special Tribunal for crimes against humanity,[7] and the recently established Extraordinary Chambers in the Courts of Cambodia (ECCC, 2006). These justice mechanisms being pursued alongside the rise in more circumscribed religious and "traditional" spheres, I explore in Part Two of the book, have re-emerged to compensate for some of the most gruesome effects of neoliberal intervention of our time – perceptions of predatory imperialist resource extraction competing with a more populist assertion of resource control. And while legal pluralism, as a way to deal with judicial difference, has been heralded by scholars as having the answer to the diversity of justice approaches that emerge from the fall out of such violence, the question before us is not simply that of judicial diversity. The key problematic to be addressed by this book has to do with the uneven competition over resources and power and the ways that these differences are articulated, put in friction, and at times rendered incommensurate even in seemingly parallel judicial capacities.

In what is to follow, the book moves beyond basic anthropological relativist principles on human rights that see culture as enacted differently in different places or legal pluralism that views law and its various forms of social regulation as simply manifestations of social difference that must be understood in culturally specific terms. Rather, it posits the array of liberalist values and their colonial and postcolonial, post–Cold War spread as embedded in the same micropractices of freedom in the Global North that constitute related forms of violence elsewhere. In other words, various Northern neoliberal values are not just conceptually "different"; they are also mutually constituted and operate within discursive constellations that are able to reflect and refract different core values in different ways (Clarke and Goodale 2009). These processes try to capture and shape other relations, and their success is justice's viability as an apparition (see Coutin, Maurer, and Yngvesson 2002), as a myth, as an illusionary site of aspiration, of fiction, of securing the perception of political and civil rights for its citizenry.

As a political project, international justice regimes have succeeded in laying the foundations for this illusion of justice. However, the *failure*

5

of liberalist conceptions of justice is in their apparitional quality and their inability to guarantee economic and social equality to all – a principle that runs contrary to the very nature of the capitalist project itself. By exploring the associated circulation of international treaties that are being propelled by NGOs, this book articulates the limits of and challenges to the liberalist human rights project that aims to choreograph the management of life without attention to those who are sacrificed in the process.

I call for the development of a new analytic domain within which we can dissect the workings of the emergent rule of law movement. In so doing, international rule of law tribunals provide mechanisms for understanding one of the most radical types of politicization: the interrelationship between the specter of justice – the victim – and the spectacularization of the law in such a way that produces a representational domain in which performances on the world stage are institutionalized through the ethical cultivation of human rights principles and the crowding out of others.

The foregoing complexities are explored through the workings of what is popularly referred to as "international justice" and its interface with human rights violations in Nigeria, Uganda, the Sudan, and the DRC. In the midst of exploring the operationalization of ICC mechanisms, I interrogate the relationships among individual, state, regional, and international legal practices – that is, how various forms of law travel, how they are taken up, resisted, recalculated, and at times incongruently located alongside everyday life. At the intersection of global and more circumscribed legal formations are culturally constituted conceptions of justice that shape the ways that people express their understandings of appropriate forms of recompense. These more circumscribed practices are neither merely shaped by transnational relations nor are they merely translated by local agents into vernacularized forms. Rather, there are multiple domains of interconnection through which notions of law and justice travel and within which its forms of logic and reasoning are packaged. As will be seen, some of these outcomes take shape in mutually convergent ways. However, where religious conceptions of ancestral land ownership, for example, are seemingly incongruent with particular conceptions of liberalist personhood and property, or in cases in which the introduction of the imagery of the "victim to be saved" represents a necessary component for humanitarian intervention, there exists a dueling, sometimes incongruent, set of relations that require that we engage their meanings within the specific contexts of power in which they are constituted and made real.

In the end, the goal of this book is to show that the logic of neoliberalist legalism exists alongside multiple processes by which justice conceptions are procured, borrowed, and made intelligible. When there appears to be struggle over jurisdiction or the production of juridical guilt or innocence, neither declaring the problem as a simple conflict of laws nor insisting that one approach should simply trump another (e.g., ICC justice versus that of "traditional" truth and reconciliation mechanisms) is enough. The Rome Statute and its language of secular objectivity and universalism – its image of freedom and fairness for all of humanity and its discourses of nonpartisan and secular sensibilities, for example – represents a language of freedom with an ontology that reflects "Western" religious roots that have traveled and become hegemonic in a range of contexts (Tsing 2005). The key is in understanding the arena of the political as a space of unequal contests within materially unequal spheres of power. Because of this inherent unevenness, it has taken somewhat longer to grasp many of the phenomenal corollaries. Political predicaments long identified, often exclusively, with postcolonial African states (e.g., their diminished capacity to regulate successfully their own economies, the constraining dictates of international financial institutions) have now played out more visibly across the globe. State contraction, the erosion of social safety nets, the demands for flexibility in forms of work and sociability, large-scale privatizations of social goods and utilities on one hand and enterprises and security operations on the other, the diminished capacity of states to discipline their citizens by means of consent – these widespread transformations witnessed in political systems of various kinds have made aspects of Africa's "exceptional" crises seem suddenly mainstream. Such phenomena have played out across much of the globe, in distinct social contexts and with distinct cultural and political consequences.

The inequality of power among a range Africa's people threatened by war is emblematic of the continent's marginal status but reflects similar enmeshments of local and global dynamics. If the resulting formations render contemporary Africa an "alternative" form of modernity, another example of pluralism, then various Africanist scholars have been early forerunners to the insight that there exist nothing *but* alternative modernities, nothing but alternative legal domains: every region is a product of particular local and translocal histories, including those at the center of global economic and political power. Yet those formations

celebrated by some scholars as "global," such as the rule of law, are neither "global" nor the result of a series of isolated events that have led to
an uncontested union of universal practices. They do not represent an
empirically "better" system of human protectionism of care and do not
reflect the continuity of an evolutionary goal toward the betterment
of society. Further, it would be incorrect to assume that the promise
of individual protections exists within some political, historical, or
economic conditions and not others. Rather, the growth of democratization and rule of law embodies a spectacularization that works through
historical formations of the secular to craft its micropractices as
ordinary, yet hegemonic. As a result, the conceptual alliances of these
formations within relations of power reflect an ease of association that
produces an ordinariness that is often taken for granted as "natural."

The exports of these hegemonic forms are not totalistic and do not
always succeed in establishing new norms (Tsing 2005). Rather, they
also engage in disjunctural encounters that, at times, are incompatible
with various tenets of liberalist personhood and, thus, produce divergent
spaces of justice making, the meanings of which are relevant in different
spheres of power. Different agents engage in different practices within a
range of cultural histories and meanings, and within this context, individuals choose how they want to live within particular sociopolitical
spheres (W. Brown 2004:456). This space of the sociopolitical sphere
is the space of agency, which produces the effect of freedom in multiple
domains. However, significant studies of justice, as well as related studies
regarding the emergence and growth of international law movements,
have tended to argue that human rights and rule of law activism are
paramount because their calling is derived from a transcendent truth,
that they carry with them an ultimate set of principles for humanity, or
that the justice they derive from international adjudication is founded
on fairness and judicial diversity (Ignatieff 2001). These scholars often
argue that human rights secure agency, autonomy, and individual protections from an abusive state or individual power, enabling people to
protect themselves from injustice and to gain empowerment to choose
their life options. These liberalist conceptions of individual personhood
are shaped by a political economy of human rights that draws its power
from ritual spectacles funded through donor capitalism and positioned
within new biopolitical bureaucracies comprising governmental and
nongovernmental organizations.

However, to enter into a discussion about civil and political rights
and freedoms without considering the conditions necessary for cultural

and economic security is to locate a starting place for rule of law instrumentalities in what Derrida (1992) would call its *mystical foundations of authority*, a notion he used to disrupt the idea that seemingly "secular" formations celebrating the absence of religious moralities are themselves mystical constructions. In disrupting the fiction of law, he located both the religious and the secular as social fictions and then articulated notions of justice not as an answer but as an ongoing process. Applied here, Derrida's concept of mystical foundations clearly calls into question the "transcendency" of any truth from which human rights and rule of law activism might derive and their assumed "natural" supremacy over other domains of "justice" making.

ANTECEDENTS TO THE ICC – THE FORMER YUGOSLAVIA, RWANDA, AND SIERRA LEONE

Yugoslavia: Milošević and the ICTY

On May 27, 1999, ethnic Serbian President Slobodan Milošević of the Federal Republic of Yugoslavia (FRY) was indicted for ordering the death of thousands of ethnic Croatians. This act by the ICTY marked the first time in the modern period when a head of state had been denied immunity and prosecuted in accordance with powers drawn from an international convention. It represents one of the most radical modifications of the concepts of both criminal responsibility and territorial jurisdiction in modern criminal law.

Unlike the precedent-setting Nuremberg and Tokyo military tribunals, the ICTY is a nonmilitary court that was established in the midst of an ongoing violent conflict, making it difficult to collect evidence and execute warrants successfully. The indictment that led to the release of arrest warrants followed the widespread massacre of thousands of Croatians as a result of what was believed to be a Serbian ethnic-cleansing campaign. As a result, more than 300,000 Kosovo Albanians fled to neighboring Albania and Macedonia, with many thousands more displaced within Kosovo. From March 24 to June 10, 1999, NATO forces carried out a bombing campaign against the FRY. Justified as a form of humanitarian intervention to protect Kosovo Albanians from the military of the FRY, its irregular militias, and Serbian paramilitary police forces, the bombing led to the death of thousands of Croatians and Serbians.

By April 1999, 850,000 people of predominantly Albanian ethnicity had fled their homes, and this mass exodus of Croatians and Albanians formed the basis of United Nations war crime charges against Slobodan Milošević and other officials deemed responsible for directing the Kosovo conflict. In analyzing the Albanian exodus, the pro-Serbian side has tended to claim that the refugee outflows were the result of mass panic generated by NATO bombs. For its part, the anti-Serbian side has tended to blame Serbian security forces and paramilitaries for emptying towns and villages of their Albanian inhabitants by forcing them to flee their homes or risk execution.

To attend to such violence, in which state actors and their commanders were seen as complicit, the key legal proceedings were not carried out within the juridical powers of the Yugoslavian state. Instead, the UN Security Council passed Resolution 780, creating a commission of experts to investigate possible violations of humanitarian law in the former Yugoslavia. Upon hearing the commission's findings, the UN Security Council passed Resolution 808 to legalize the establishment of an international criminal tribunal that would investigate and prosecute crimes allegedly committed in Kosovo, Croatia, and Bosnia and Herzegovina. The charges ranged from violations of the laws or customs of war (Article 3 – murder), four counts of crimes against humanity (Article 5) in Kosovo, nine counts of grave breaches of the 1949 Geneva Conventions, thirteen counts of violations of laws or customs of war (Article 3) in Croatia, ten counts of crimes against humanity (Article 5), and in Bosnia and Herzegovina two counts of genocide and complicity in genocide (Article 4); ten counts of crimes against humanity involving persecution, extermination, murder, and imprisonment; eight counts of grave breaches of the Geneva Conventions of 1949 involving willful killing, unlawful confinement, etc.; and nine counts of violations of the laws or customs of war. The subsequent passing of Resolution 827 on May 25, 1993, created the ICTY (Cryer 2005:52–4).

The first years of the Milošević trial represented the beginning of a remarkable experiment in international humanitarian and criminal law, a body of law previously rooted in international customs that lacked the power to bind states. At stake in the ICTY project, the cost of which since 2002 has exceeded $100 million a year,[8] was nothing less than the operationalization of international criminal law. When I observed parts of Milošević's defense during the summer of 2002 in the UN courtroom in The Hague, it was clear that his objections to the tribunal rested on his resistance to the transformations of conventional rules of state sovereignty. Milošević repeatedly refused to submit to the court's authority. Beginning his defense with a vengeance, he stood before the international tribunal and steadfastly argued against its legitimacy, questioning the indictments against him and the ad hoc nature of the procedural and substantive laws.[9] The accused, as both defendant and lawyer, continually objected to the force of law that had suspended the sovereignty of the Yugoslavian nation-state – the state of which he was, technically, the reigning president – and had instead created the ICTY as an international body with supranational jurisdiction.

During the next two years, the prosecution presented its case by attempting to establish Milošević's criminal responsibility.[10] Armed with a new vocabulary of growing international clout, the prosecution attempted to pin the blame for the 1990s Balkan conflicts on Milošević and his top agents. By linking the defendant's alleged actions (ordering the deaths of many through a chain of command or enacting willful negligence) to his knowledge of the death of thousands of ethnic Croatians, the prosecutor applied the extraterritorial reach of law to new ICTY substantive definitions of crime.[11]

The prosecution's evidentiary displays included images of mass graves accompanied by exhaustive descriptions of the rape and killing of defenseless victims and the decimation of large segments of the population. The prosecution's lawyers argued that Milošević was guilty not because he actually carried out these mass killings himself but because, under Article 7(3) of the ICTY Statute, he was responsible for the acts of his subordinates: "If he knew or had reason to know that the subordinate was about to commit such acts or had done so and the superior failed to take the necessary and reasonable measures to prevent such acts or to punish the perpetrators thereof,"[12] he was culpable for the thousands of victims whose suffering continued to haunt the proceedings.

What I am highlighting through discussion of this first case are the struggles over justice making through the reconfiguration of state sovereignty, the power of which is felt more through its effects than its embedded social relations. In this light, Milošević – the commander seen as both enabling and not preventing the death of hundreds of thousands of Croatians – was tried for new crimes on the international stage through a new classification of legal responsibility that marks one of the key discourses of this book: the way that emergent forms of justice are being articulated through the individualization of responsibility. Milošević's protest was shaped by his outrage at the court's disregard for national sovereignty and his disbelief in the legitimacy of applying such legal assertions in international contexts. In this light, he ridiculed what he saw as the absurdity of using a supranational body to hold a president responsible for the acts of anonymous rebels.

Amid contestations over the legitimacy of the international trial, the defense and prosecution engaged in the construction of two dueling moral regimes of justice. One side insisted that justice was possible only through the supranational conviction of Milošević and his commanders, by which command responsibility could be used to set precedents in the establishment of a new corpus of international law. The other side, inspired by Serbian nationalist sentiment, insisted that it was only Milošević's release and his return to power that would enable justice to proceed.

Although Milošević died in international custody and his case was therefore dropped, more than five years of hearings produced a complex range of results, including an ongoing debate about the possibility of victims' justice being served through the creation of international tribunals and the plight to end impunity. The ICTY trials are still underway at the time of this writing, with cases pending against other members of the Milošević regime; its advocates continue to assert the triumph of the rule of law in what can be seen through the ways that Daphane Brooks defines *spectacular performances*: "the stylized alternate forms of cultural expression that cut against the grain of conventional social and political ideologies." In this book, the rule of law movement – a term in which the "rule of law" is often capitalized by its advocates to emphasize its authoritative and spectacular quality – is shown to deploy human rights discourses through a spectacularity that involves the abjection of the "victim" and the rescue of humanity from abhorrent violence. Following Brooks, I show how this is done through a technique that rewrites a predominant master narrative. Further, for the emergent movement, the master narrative is state sovereignty; for Islamic religious advocates, the narrative that is often dismantled is that of a particular type of individualism that assumes that the rights-endowed subject is the only type of subjectivity. Thus, the chapters that follow examine the innovations of grassroots legal activists, human rights activists and NGO workers (Chapters 1 and 6),[13] donors and humanitarian workers (Chapter 1), religious and "traditionalist" priests and judges (Chapters 2, 3, and 5), and international court judges and lawyers (Chapters 2 and 3), showing how they, as innovators of "justice," work with and through spectacles of suffering in order to assert a particular type of politics. Yet, as I show, embedded in these performances are often disembodied victims who represent specters of suffering. It is this imagery that makes the work of these actors morally necessary but also troubles the fiction that their performances uphold. For without a victim, their moral – and thus institutional – power would be weakened. The victim is both central yet marginal to the justice project itself.

Key to my exploration of the various innovators engaged in the production of spectacular justice performances is their deployment of micropractices that balance the moral fortitude of legal intervention with the necessary precondition of having a victim to defend. These micropractices include speech acts that revere the protection of international rights; citation references to treaty documents; the brokering of human rights agendas, through which international donor funding is secured; the rewriting of national constitutions, through which international treaties are domesticated in national constitutions; demonstrations of religiosity that make visible the piety of religious subjects; and ritual practices of forgiveness that involve the invocation of ancestral religious cosmologies. The practices that produce these effects work through their ability to construct and reinforce truth regimes in various ways. Following Ann Stoler (1995), building on Michel Foucault (1972), such truth regimes work through domains of knowledge and have the power both to reveal and to conceal understandings about our social worlds. The production of knowledge about what constitutes justice represents one such example of an extraordinarily powerful truth regime with the authority to withhold the very power of life itself. However, what is critical in the way that justice is made real is its concealment of other justice narratives or its monopoly of symbolic and enforced power to exercise the authorial meaning of justice – the fiction of justice.

Rwanda: Akayesu and the ICTR

Concurrent with the violence of the former Yugoslavia, between April and June 1994 an estimated 800,000 Rwandans were killed in what have come to be regarded as some of the most intimate and horrific forms of violence ever documented. The majority of the dead were ethnic Tutsis, and the majority of the perpetrators of violence were ethnic Hutus.[14] On November 8, 1994, the UN Security Council created the ICTR to be located in Arusha in the United Republic of Tanzania and to have jurisdiction over adjudicating tertiary crimes committed in Rwanda between January 1 and December 31, 1994.[15] The leading decision of the ICTR was in the case of Jean-Paul Akayesu. In this case, which began in 1997, Akayesu was represented as responsible for maintaining law and public order in his commune in Taba. Approximately two thousand Tutsis were killed while he was in power, and the killings in Taba were described as being so brazen and widespread that Akayesu must have known about them. Further, the prosecution argued that Akayesu had never attempted to prevent the killing of Tutsis in the commune or to call for assistance to stop the violence. Displaced civilians were murdered on communal premises, and many women were forced to endure multiple acts of gang rape and other forms of sexual violence. Because he failed to prevent the sexual violence, beatings, and murders, Akayesu was portrayed as having encouraged these and other forms of violence on or near the communal premises. These accusations – coupled with the sanctioning of the direct killing of Tutsis – led to Akayesu's criminal conviction before the ICTR. His trial and conviction presented a ritualized articulation of guilt that communicated a message about the power of the court throughout the continent and the world.[16] Among many messages was the critical role of the court in securing "victim's justice," a role seen as fulfilled despite the death of thousands. The commanders who engineered and enabled genocide were narrativized as most responsible, whereas those collectivities that killed, the international clients who sold the thousands of machetes to mercenaries, and the international communities who chose not to intervene were held unaccountable. The first cases of the ICTR were critical in establishing the international crime of genocide and in furthering the notion of individual criminal responsibility as simply pertaining to one "who planned, instigated, ordered, committed or otherwise aided and abetted in the planning, preparation or execution" of any of the crimes enumerated by the Statute of the Tribunal.[17]

As of September 2008, thirty-two accused persons have received judgments following their trials before the ICTR, and an additional four judgments following recently concluded trials are pending. An additional nine trials involving twenty-five accused persons are still scheduled, with judgments expected by the end of 2009. As of this writing, seven detainees are awaiting trial.[18] The spectacularity of international justice performances are seen in their ability to go beyond the limits of national courts and responsibilities that were formerly considered the domain of sovereign states and in reassigning responsibility on the basis of growing international conventions. The innovators rewrite the master narrative of state sovereignty in light of the abhorrence of genocide. These international justice mechanisms represent the tribunal's juridical attempts to define, discipline, control, and regulate related international processes while increasingly responding to the challenges of globalizing forces. The work of the court in Arusha was heralded by many in Rwanda – international law advocates, civil servants, government officials – who saw it as constituting a critical step toward the end of impunity in Africa. By working alongside various supranational agencies and international NGOs to recast the responsibility for punishing crimes that cause the greatest human suffering, these innovators are calling for a reclassification of the relationships among states, nonstate actors, and ordinary citizens.

Yet, given the absence of an effective intervention long before the need for international adjudication, others, such as a young businessman I interviewed while in Rwanda, criticized the court as a "hypocritical institution concerned with justice long after the opportunity to truly achieve it."[19] This statement is central to the rethinking of justice in this book and provides a prism for considering the way that even spectacular international tribunal innovations require the existence of a tragic spectacle of suffering – the specter of a victim representing the condition of oppression in need of salvation.

Sierra Leone: Charles Taylor and the Special Court for Sierra Leone

In Sierra Leone, on Africa's west coast, another spectacle of international justice embedded in rule of law micropractices is currently under way. It relates to conflict that occurred in Sierra Leone from 1991 to 2002, during which extreme acts of violence were inflicted on civilians by rebel groups known as the Revolutionary United Front (RUF) and the Armed Forces Revolutionary Council (AFRC). Widespread violent acts included murder, mutilation, amputation, torture, rape, abduction, and the conscription and use of child soldiers. In 2000, the United Nations intervened and, with the participation of the Sierra Leone government, established the SCSL on January 16, 2002.[20] As an adjudicatory institution, the Special Court holds the mandate to prosecute persons who bear the greatest responsibility for serious crimes committed since November 30, 1996. It represents another international presence established to end impunity. This Special Court functions as a new adjudicatory mechanism for human rights abuses committed during the Sierra Leone armed conflict, in which the nation's governmental leaders were implicated in the violent actions of rebel groups.

To date (September 2008), the court has indicted thirteen people for war crimes, crimes against humanity, and other violations of international humanitarian law. These are Charles Taylor, Issa Hassan Sesay, Augustine Gbao, Morris Kallon, Moinina Fofana, Allieu Kondewa, Johnny Paul Koroma,[21] Alex Tamba Brima, Ibrahim Bazzy Kamara, and Santigie Borbor Kanu (indictments against Foday Sankoh, Sam Bockarie, and Samuel Hinga Norman were dropped after their deaths). Of the ten still indicted, nine are in the custody of the Special Court. The trials have been placed into three groups (Taylor's stands alone and is being tried in one of the ICC court rooms in The Hague): the Civil Defense Forces trial for Fofana and Kondewa started on June 3, 2004, and concluded, after appeals, on May 28, 2008; the RUF trial for Kallon, Gbao, and Sesay began on July 5, 2004 (a judgment by the Trial Chamber is expected in early 2009; and the AFRC trial (Brima, Kamara, Kanu) began March 7, 2005, and concluded, following appeals, on February 22, 2008.[22]

The Special Court innovators also deploy particular mechanisms for ritualizing justice through the "theatre" of the rule of law. The trial of Charles Taylor, the former president of Liberia accused of having assisted rebel forces in Sierra Leone, is a case in point. Taylor has been indicted on a range of charges for commanding the murder, violence, rape, and mutilation of hundreds of civilians and is said to have supported and financed Foda Sankoh's RUF with the goal of destabilizing Sierra Leone in order to monopolize access to its diamond resources. His arrest on March 29, 2006, in Nigeria and transfer to the SCSL on the same day highlights the ongoing micropractices involved in preserving the power of the law to provide fairness and justice to those whose fate lies in its hands. However, through its enactments of the technicalities of law, its advocates see themselves as engaged in the victim's justice.[23]

These four courts (the ICC, the ICTY, the ICTR, and the SCSL) – international in both scope and reach – have attempted to redefine the meaning of justice through the prosecution of only a few individuals, further setting in place a conception of the individualization of criminal responsibility pursued in the name of the victim. Further, because only a few who are responsible for such crimes have ever been tried and prosecuted by a national court, an international court, or a military tribunal, such mechanisms are seen by their various advocates as representing institutional correctives that will bring into international adjudicatory spheres a spectacular example-setting agenda. And in so doing, it produces a social narrative about vicarious liability – common in many contexts across legal systems. But in international criminal contexts it does not displace responsibility for lower-ranking individuals who also committed crimes that are often being adjudicated in national courts; it merely coexists with them promoting a narrative that spectacularizes the mission of the court – that leaders are to be held responsible for the most serious crimes of violence enacted by those who serve them; that impunity can no longer exist under the reign of international rule of law. In this regard, one of the things that the law does well is to bury the normative political apparatus through which legal norms are constructed. Thus command responsibility represents a new construct whose social context is being obscured by its attention to perpetrators in name of victims everywhere.

By examining the ways that law and justice are anchored in processes and concepts that often erase their normative underpinnings, this book explores the way that law, whether funnelled through secular or religious mechanisms, obscures the conditions of its making. In so doing, it produces notions of justice, of international human rights, of traditional or religious authority, that make its labor invisible. As an apparition, it is the labor from various micropractices that has the effect of displacing human action and replacing it with what is deemed the appropriate symbol of justice. In this case, the apparition or the fiction is made real through the figure of the victim – a victim to be saved by the rule of law, a victim around whom collective guilt is made visible and reassigned to those seen as bearing the most responsibility for mass atrocity. The possible ellipsis is the often violent processes of producing the fiction: the creation and codification of a regime of truth that concerns itself with some crimes and not others and that celebrates the achievement of punishment and its symbolic potential to deter future crimes rather than addressing some of the contests at the heart of violent struggles.

THE ICC AND COMPETING NOTIONS OF JUSTICE IN SUB-SAHARAN AFRICA

With the signing of the 1998 ICC treaty known as the Rome Statute and its coming into force in 2002, a new mechanism for assigning guilt was concretized. The ICC, located in The Hague, The Netherlands, as one of many institutions engaged in the growth of the rule of law movement, is distinguished from its antecedents by innovators of the court through its status as the first permanent and independent international criminal court[24] and operates not in UN-based courtrooms but in its own buildings. As grand structures for the production of justice, the court is legitimated by a new institutional treaty order. Yet, its jurisdictional reach and its associated liberalist principles have prompted negative responses from a wide array of agents. Some object to its claims of universalism and bids for widespread international judicial control; others disagree with its case law; others are committed to the return of national sovereign principles.

As a regime working toward the implementation of punishment for crimes against humanity, war crimes, genocide, and the crime of aggression,[25] the court's much-vaunted "end to impunity"[26] has characterized its moral discourse as working to end rather than support violence against humanity. However, within various international legal networks, state and nonstate actors are engaged in signing and ratifying a range of treaties by expressing their commitments to the rule of law, but also through their instrumentalization of membership in a global community of aid, alliances, and diplomatic negotiations. They were also engaged in a critical preliminary act: the identification of the crimes to be included under the subject matter jurisdiction of the court. In the decision-making process, it was the Prepatory Commission for the crimes to be included under the jurisdiction of the ICC that was engaged in the establishment and codification of the elements of crime. This decision-making process is key to the negotiation of the ways that we understand the court's stance on criminal responsibility in the first place. As we shall see in Chapter 1, these processes take shape within fields of interaction being propelled as much by various pro–human rights neoliberal agendas as by as their contestations.

The court's supporters have been managed by a growing cosmopolitan elite: legal experts, private interest groups, and members of international organizations engaged in the establishment of institutions and what Mark Goodale (2008) has called the production of technocratic instrumentalities through which to protect and maintain life – the development of human rights documents, the production of normativities and laws. Its contesters have been varied, ranging from states that resist the court's jurisdiction (e.g., the United States, Sudan, Uganda,[27] China, India, and Russia) to nonstate actors – freedom fighters and rebel groups, Islamic religious resisters, and a range of persons objecting to the court's seemingly political agenda, its focus on Africa, and the timing of its interventions.

As of fall 2007, the ICC has pursued investigations in four regions, all of them in Africa: the Central African Republic, northern Uganda, the

DRC, and Darfur, the Sudan. Late in May 2007, the prosecutor for the ICC announced the opening of an investigation in the Central African Republic, focusing on the commission of rape and a range of sexual violence crimes. In northern Uganda, arrest warrants were issued in 2005 for five of the commanders of the Lord's Resistance Army (LRA), three of whom are at large, two dead. Relating to cases concerning violence in the DRC, the trial of Lubanga for crimes related to recruiting child soldiers was the first case before the Pre-Trial Chamber to arise out of the prosecutor's investigations there. Three other Congolese (Bosco Ntanganda, Germain Katanga, and Mathieu Ngudjolo) have been charged with crimes related to using child soldiers in attacking civilians in early 2003; the pretrial hearings of *The Prosecutor v. Germain Katanga and Mathieu Ngudjolo Chui*, and *The Prosecutor v. Bosco Ntaganda* are ongoing at the time of this writing, early 2009.

In Darfur, the prosecutor issued arrest warrants in May 2007 against two Sudanese men, and, with the support of the United Nations and the UN–African Union force in Darfur, he hopes to execute arrests. In July 2008, the prosecutor presented evidence that the president of Sudan, commander-in-chief of the Sudanese armed forces, Omar Hassan Ahmad al-Bashir, had planned, ordered, and commissioned the crimes of genocide and crimes against humanity through his alleged recruiting and arming of the Janjaweed militia, which for more than five years was known to have caused the death of over 300,000 in the region. A warrant for al-Bashir's arrest was officially requested[28] in early 2009 and issued on March 4th, 2009.

However, not only is the ICC engaged in battles over their legitimate jurisdiction, but the problem is that the reassignment of the guilt of thousands of people to a single chief commander and a few of his top aides neither ends violence nor captures adequately the complicity of multiple agents involved in the making of war. In most of the Africa-based cases, the basis for justice in war-torn regions is founded in the grassroots call for brokering peace first and then setting in place postviolence structures for rebuilding. How are we to extrapolate the meaning of criminal responsibility for violence interpolated on the world stage, and thus justice itself, when the root causes of violence in various postcolonial contexts are underlain by histories of colonial subject formation, contested governance and boundary-making dictates, foreign resource ownership and extraction in the midst of poverty, and unresolved conflict – all contributory factors to the ongoing conflict in so many of the recent African civil wars? This backdrop has no adjudicative relevance in the ICC. Instead, with its establishment, there has been a widespread and unproblematized consensus that African cases targeting high-ranking African leaders should be the first before the court, and this is where the ICC has put much of its investigatory and prosecutorial energy. In all the ICC-identified situations in sub-Saharan Africa, the problem for the prosecutor has had to do not only with questions of the admissibility of evidence but also with the legitimacy of assigning to a handful of people the murders committed by thousands. It is this conception of individualization of criminal responsibility that is being deployed to transform the terms of complicity in international justice regimes and that is providing a new, although contested, moral economy of victims' rights writ large. However, there are often incommensurabilities in not only what justice is, but also who is a victim.

FICTIONS AND SPECTERS OF JUSTICE

Justice and *victims* are two words that are often articulated in the literature and, outside of it, without clear conceptions of their meanings and under what conditions those meanings may change. They are often invoked as terms that represent a given set of understandings, yet they are often resignified and imported into other fields of meaning and power and used with knowing resolve. Both terms are far from uncontroversial, in fact, because they are manifest in different ways in varied locales and embody different constellations of practice and expression.

Tim Allen's most recently published book, *Trial Justice: The International Criminal Court and the Lord's Resistance Army* (2006), explores the histories and contemporary politics of the ICC intervention in Uganda. He provides incisive discussions about the kind of robust engagement with the ICC that is needed to procure "justice" for northern Uganda's victims, thousands of whom have been displaced by war and many of whom have lost family members or have suffered amputations of hands, arms, legs, or lips. Allen locates viable justice in the ICC's adjudicatory mechanisms rather than the range of quasi- and nonjudicial mechanisms available to the people of Uganda. For him, justice for "victims" in northern Uganda is possible only through ICC intervention. As he indicates in his conclusion, "Too many wars go on for too long as it is. Other strategies to resolve them have frequently been shown to fail" (2006:180). Trial-based justice – the book's namesake – is what he sees as the most effective mechanism for producing "justice" in Uganda.

Susan Hirsch's beautifully written book, *In the Moment of Greatest Calamity: Terrorism, Grief and a Victim's Quest for Justice* (2006), takes us through her emotional journey as she struggles to make sense of the meaning of personal and political justice in the context of post-terrorist bombings in Tanzania in 1998. Widowed as a result of her husband's death during the bombing at the U.S. Embassy in Tanzania, Hirsch articulates the challenges involved in creating a space for victims' justice. Although disenfranchised through her loss, she, a victim of loss, asserted her will and objected to the use of death penalty violence as an appropriate form of recompense, of justice in the 2001 U.S. terrorist trials in New York. This stance highlighted for the reader the precariousness of justice's techniques and the various trajectories in which it can be found.

One such technique is the invocation of suffering and violence as a qualifier for action. When pronounced on behalf of a deceased victim or in the name of a widow, the language of justice can do a particular type of work through the affirmation of loss. The pursuit of justice invoked through privileging claims of victim subjectivity is a technique that manifests aspirations of justice as both real and justified. Yet, as I show in the pages to come, there is no monopoly over the construction of the category of victimhood. People enter and depart from its constructions from time to time. In fact, those persons who suffer loss directly might be as victimized as those persons in societies whose conditions of desperation and disenfranchisement sometimes and unfortunately drive them to violence in the first place – either in retaliation or through exploitative action (see the discussion of political Sharia in Chapter 5). However, to assume that certain persons embody the definition of "victim," even as they walk in and out of various empowered social spaces, only highlights the ways that fictions actually work. What I am saying is that discourses about victim's justice can create the conditions in which the notion of the "victim" can function as a modality for the pursuit of justice. Hirsch is not simply the embodiment of a victim per se. As shown in her book, she is someone who has suffered a great loss, but she is also someone for whom suffering has come to constitute her moral authority around the appropriate forms of punishment and thus the preconditions for her pursuit of justice.

Yet, there are many differences in the ways Allen and Hirsch construct their preconditions for justice. For example, they disagree on the pursuit of state criminal adjudication for widespread terror. Allen, writing within an ongoing context of violence in northern Uganda, is resolute with his dismissal of various alternate and traditional forms of reconciliation as justice producing. Allen cites the traditional Acholi ritual of *mato oput* as more contemporary than traditional, as constructed, and as problematically revived. The irony here is that the ICC seems to be immune from his critique of human interference – as if the international court, with the power to adjudicate cases outside the African continent, is without self-interest, social invention, or political influence from elsewhere.

For Hirsch, state-based criminal adjudication opens up spaces for understanding values in our social worlds for those in the pursuit of justice, but the death penalty as a manifestation of one expression of justice remains for her an unacceptable means to achieve that goal. However, as a "victim," what justice is remains a domain to be defined within the individual quest for social reconciliation. Through her comportment, dress, and speech acts, as well as her participation in the 2001 trial, Hirsch engaged in the production of a personal narrative through which justice seemed more tenable:

> The critical task is to push aside the specter of that horror [the terrorist bombing] by focusing on what a more harmonious social existence might look like and how we might achieve it. From my view, this would require imagining vibrant pluralistic contexts, where diverse groups interact in a dynamic coexistence of multiple beliefs and values. . . . Having the patience to project that vision before us in the moment of greatest calamity, and to keep it prominent in our thoughts and goals in the aftermath, would guide us toward productive and just responses. (2006:263–4)

This aspiration for a form of justice in the midst of social difference is important: it is in the making real of the aspiration that the power of social change lies. More centrally, it involves recognizing that the terms of the aspiration must be negotiated, amended, and compromised; through that process, new fictions will be derived to meet the memories of our past and the needs of our pluralist social worlds.

In making sense of social fictions, Jacques Derrida (1992) introduces the concept of *spectrality* to disrupt notions of ontological presence and linear notions of history – the "specter" is the past, returning contingently and repeatedly in new guises and incarnations, which we must in some way learn to recognize and live with. Elsewhere Derrida (1994) writes of cohabitations – haunted houses – where different specters uneasily appear and reappear. He sees the present as always haunted by an unsettling past and thus never existing unto itself; rather, it is always present alongside that which precedes it. This concept is useful in understanding the ontological presence of different justice regimes sometimes conceptually incommensurate within particular contexts, but it can also be broadened to explore the way that those regimes are engaged in the spectacularization of adjudication through which the ontological linkage is to a victim whose mission they protect and whose purpose exists as a necessary precondition for justice. This linkage between the spectacularization of justice through the specter of the victim represents a critical spectrality of suffering that has a real presence in the world but that is not real in an ontological sense. However, the corporality of suffering or the affective experience by an embodied subject – such as the victims of Northern Uganda, a widow whose partner was killed, a mother whose child was decapitated, or the witness whose lips and limbs were amputated – represent a politics of suffering that can be narrativized to incite various types of justice through a range of means. The current trend in international criminal law is to deploy the specter of the victim in order to spectacularize the significant import of international intervention. The consequence, at times, is the incommensurability of the logic that made violence possible in the first place.

Interrogating Legal Pluralism, Mapping Justice through Power
Recognizing the spectacularization of justice through the defense of the victim, how do we understand the corporality of suffering and assign the terms for justice in the midst of diverging conceptions of what justice is? In the pages to come, I suggest that the key involves first recognizing that the process involves the creation of new fictions – new aspirations that are inclusive and willingly negotiated over time. Second, the process of translating across difference is important while making sense of the sociohistorical bases on which those tenets are related. Third, it requires reconciling the relationship between our assumptions and our acts: the conditions out of which we make sense of the world and our actions within it. These processes involve recognizing that those who enact violence on others need to be held responsible for that violence and then negotiating the proper domains for such accountability. This notion of the appropriateness of venue, form, and technique of "justice making" is the site of difference, of struggle, because it reflects our cultural conceptions of legitimate and illegitimate actions. In determining the meaning of justice, it is critical to ask how the institutional possibilities, including particular mechanisms such as the ICC, have come

about as the appropriate domain for justice making. Further, what does it tell us about the appropriateness of that domain for political life? In the end, if justice as a fictive construction represents aspirations, and if aspirations are imagined and can be enacted, then social agents can participate in the building of a more equitable social world that reflects the conditions necessary for the fiction to be embodied through the good life.

This book examines those multiple trajectories of human rights principles operating within new rule of law institutions and insists that we approach conceptions of justice in two lights: both as collections of intertwined social processes that reflect cultural and political spheres of meaning and as conceptual spheres that are, at times, disjunct and incongruent. To understand the complexities of adjudicative difference, legal difference, new jurisdictional practices, and the place of Africa and Africans in the growing international rule of law movement, we need to move beyond conceptions that overlook histories of disenfranchisement, that make it difficult to understand the divergent ontologies at play. In the scholarly literature, comparative legal pluralism has been used to understand such forms of adjudicatory difference but has not always been able to articulate the related challenges of inequality that shape the expression of justice and the exercise of law.

Legal pluralism came of age in the field of legal anthropology as an intellectual tradition that grew out of cultural relativist influences in an attempt to recognize the existence of differing legal systems. Holding that multiple legal spheres, which may be equal but are in conflict with each other, must be seen as legitimate in a world of vast variation, it promoted the analytic coexistence of law in multiple domains. The problem with accepting diversity in law as the end point, however, is that it does not help us make sense of the exercise of legal and political power – the power to mobilize, the power to name – in the contemporary realities of transnational connectivity. Such pluralist theories of coexistence do not reflect the real-world effects of hegemony in which competing senses of law are embedded in competing moralities of personhood or religiosities that continue to shape other traditions and be transformed in the process. Rather, the key points are the effects of justice making and the ways that the specter of the victim is deployed in uneven relations of power.

Justice making, as an effect, represents domains of negotiation, communication, collaboration, cohesion, and domination made manifest through action. It is a domain that represents a political struggle for power. The resolution is the contested terrain that we call politics. Through micropolitical interactions within different spheres of legal power, justice is produced. Thus, justice is mediated within the domain of politics and is actually an outcome of struggle. This is the space of justice making – political struggles to attain power through which to control the terms of engagement, to mobilize action, and to resignify meaning. It is the ability to enact sovereign power not simply through law, governmental statehood, or international regimes, but also through individual inactivity, acceptance, and alliance in which preemptive action can be taken without the suffering of a victim.

The contemporary expansion of the rule of law movement and the rise of the defence of the "victim" at all costs reflects various powerful phenomena working in tension. One involves the way that particular neoliberal moral values are gaining global traction through the efforts of governmental and nongovernmental institutions and organizations to provide those who have been socially marginalized with spaces from which to make justice claims. These mechanisms of legal entitlement presume secular rather than religious, democratic rather than monarchic, as the means through which justice will be achieved. By insisting on a legal distinction between the public and the private and on a politicolegal arrangement requiring "religion" to be limited to the private domain (Asad 2003) and divine kingship to be rendered a vestige of the past, such rule of law projects are often constructed as representing the victory of secularism. This narrative of secularism as the only legitimate form of democratic governance gains traction alongside particular ideologies of modernity and moral individualism, with its freedom-of-choice guarantees and presumptions of the universality of personhood.

Another supplemental influence in the current international rule of law movement is the economic force of neoliberal capitalism. As one of many policy trajectories within which human exchange and value is shaped, it has been widespread since the 1970s, when it was imposed onto a range of developing countries by powerful financial institutions such as the International Monetary Fund (IMF), the World Bank, and the Inter-American Development Bank. Neoliberal capitalism has had the effect of deemphasizing governmental (and nongovernmental) intervention in national economies and privileging instead free-market methods that liberate business operations. Informed by laissez-faire economics and working through international institutions such as the World Trade Organization (WTO), the World Economic Forum, the International Convention on Labor (ITO), and various free-trade treaty agreements, as opposed to relying on direct government intervention to apply multilateral political pressure through labor politics and collective bargaining, neoliberalism has served to open foreign markets to corporate colonization.

Critics have argued that the consequences of this program throughout sub-Saharan Africa and Latin America include unfair competition, the erosion of workers' rights, and the escalation of resource-related struggles that are often refracted through religious and ethnic conflicts. In postcolonial African states, neoliberal expansionism suggests a renewal of an earlier-told narrative: management policies around export-driven growth being developed with the support of global institutions including the World Bank, the IMF, and other lending institutions. The ongoing trend is one in which rich corporate interests supported by market democracies are working alongside international organizations to shape new economic values and practices in the Global South. These new global economic alliances are making it increasingly difficult for postcolonial states to maintain economic independence and political autonomy, particularly in resource-rich areas. Instead, in sub-Saharan Africa, response to the changing market has led to increasing paramilitary contests over resources, and thus to increasing militarization and sectarian violence. It is in this context that the construct of international justice might represent competing domains of justice making. However, as with the differences in ideas of legitimate adjudicatory authority in the earlier ICTY and ICTR cases, in those that deal with different conceptions of rights and personhood in Islamic revivalist renditions of Sharia in Northern Nigeria or revived truth and reconciliation approaches in Uganda, it is more than just pluralist constellations around which jurisdiction is contested or simple challenges to international definitions of crime. The incommensurabilities of lawmaking in spheres of authority and power are also relevant to the fictions of justice.

Incommensurabities in Religious Truth Regimes

On February 27, 2006, the ICC accepted a formal accusation against the Islamic Republic of Iran filed by an Iranian NGO attempting to gather evidence against members of the Iranian regime for indictment of crimes against humanity, war crimes, and genocide. Accusing the ruling Iranian theocracy of gross violations, the NGO submitted thousands of written statements, eyewitness reports, tapes, and videotapes by Iranians who had been jailed, tortured, and discriminated against under the laws of the Islamic Republic on the basis of Islamic Sharia. The videotapes show evidence of implementation of the Islamic law of *qesas* (retributive punishment): stoning and amputation of the hand and foot. Although Iran has signed the Rome Statute, the current government refuses to ratify the statute unless its leaders are guaranteed immunity from international prosecution. They argue that the actions taken by the regime and its leaders are automatically validated by Islam and do not answer to any authority other than Allah.

Among rebel groups vying for the sovereign management of their regions, such as the LRA in northern Uganda or militia protagonists in the Sudan, alternative trajectories in the form of social protest have taken shape. Through rhetorical claims to replace secular constitutionalism with various biblical or Islamic doctrines, the LRA is engaged in new formations in the name of justice.

The Sharia courts of Nigeria, discussed at some length in Chapters 5 and 6, pose a similar challenge. Sharia courts – judicial institutions presided over by a Muslim judge to adjudicate legal disputes in private, civil, and criminal and public matters – are seen by many believers as representing the will of Allah through the application of Islamic law. The recent implementation of the criminal Sharia law in twelve of Nigeria's thirty-six states has raised the question of whether the Sharia's approach to criminal sentencing – amputation, lashing, death by stoning – should be taken as examples of cruel and unusual punishment or as culturally normative practices. In a nation-state deeply divided by its relatively equal numbers of Muslims and Christians, the Nigerian controversy over the Sharia has led to philosophical and practical debates about justice more generally. What kinds of social act should be criminalized? What are the appropriate analytical means by which one should assess practices as legitimate or illegitimate? How should people be punished in a diversely complex society of cultural differences? Who has the right to decide? Democratically elected or independently established judicial bodies? Divine prophets or impartial international activists?

CONTEXT AND SCOPE OF THE BOOK

By documenting how innovators engaged in rule of law movements produce a new language of international justice that sits uneasily alongside a range of other formations (e.g., human rights, religious revivalism, national sovereign control of resources), this book explores how notions of justice are negotiated through everyday micropractices and grassroots contestations of those practices. However, I am not privileging international spheres of justice making. It is clear that actors in the Global North are not the only ones who can enact decisions or create social fictions around which justice is played out. Various Nigerian, Ugandan, and Sudanese agents are engaged in national state struggles over international jurisdiction, and various Islamic or "traditional" forms of justice are deployed in hegemonic ways. Instead, I show that notions of justice and its accompanying discourse concerning "victims," have the power to enact extraordinary fictions that imbue them with the status of the real and thus enable them to create real effects in the world. In this context, I examine the enactments of these fictions and the ways that they become real within particular regimes of truth and that they call into question other truth constructs.

In this regard, the making of international justice might be seen as a discursive constellation embedded in particular regimes of truth. These regimes are made recognizable through modes of democratic governance around which narratives about what justice is and how it should be achieved are shaped. Thus, I focus on these sites of justice making and probe the limits of global analysis, while reflecting on the convergence of religious faith, capitalism, and the making of an individual-centric rights framework. What I show is that this convergence has led to the mobilization of various contestations; religious fundamentalism is a case in point. By producing a countermorality through which religious governance is brought into the "secular" life, this countermorality provides both a discursive and corporeal modality through which people narrativize their claims.

Perhaps the most consequential example of religious contestation is over the right to take a life. In the case of Islam in its most radical forms, for religious adherents to claim the right to kill (under the fatwa, for example)[29] is to challenge the fundamental power of the state and its monopoly on that right. Further, the act of killing may hold a different meaning for a belief system that does not consider death to be the end of life. Belief in the afterlife makes it possible to view life and death as mere stages of life. Thus, among various Muslims of sub-Saharan Africa, death is politicized in that the destruction of the body becomes an extension of life – life after corporal death. The struggles in which they are involved do not gain their power from the maintenance of individual freedom and liberty alone. Rather, death becomes a means through which "justice" is produced through acts of war or national resistance. The cause of the martyr – for example, the suicide bomber, willing to sacrifice his or her life in the interest of "justice" – is itself a statement about the impossibility of defining justice in rights-oriented, life-preserving terms. In this case, for a Muslim martyr, the act of killing may involve both the sacrifice of giving up one's own life on behalf of others and the taking of others' lives in the interest of a different conception of "justice." For where violence against, or even the death of, some individuals is actually "justice" for others, the rhetoric of justice represents multiplicities with meaning that is elusive at best. Their adherents often intend such death practices to be understood as purely spiritual acts. In reality, they also reflect particular claims to power and governance – the power to manage the terms of life, a quest that may be embedded in an ontology of the afterlife. Through such examples, we see how both the "secular" and the "religious" are deployed as domains of knowledge through which particular truth regimes are constructed and, in the case of this book, the basis for articulating justice is secured. Thus, when victims, prosecutors, defendants, scholars, and others make pronouncements concerning violence as religiously or ethnically motivated, it is important to recognize the ways that these invocations are part of a discursive arsenal of what Paul Zeleza refers to as contemporary claim making.[30] This means understanding that the complex web of social locations and political affiliations represents the various ways that people compete for power.

Claim making about justice, victims, religious violence, or sovereignty may well be the justification mobilized to protect against political marginalization or even state violence, but this is not a problem of "religion" or false consciousness. Rather, it is a problem of inequality in the sociopolitical field and the ways that various persons mobilize institutions and categories of power to craft their causes. In fact, this mobilization may at times be conducted using violence in the name of freedom. Yet what is at issue can often be the way that local histories of religious mobilization – or, say, of resource extraction – are undergirded by particular formations of imperial capitalism, in which those formations came to dominate contemporary global politics and disseminate particular visions of democracy and rights as the terms for global engagements. Such is the reality of violence in the DRC, where paramilitary competition over resources is at the heart of the arming of child soldiers and the creation of war zones out of villages. There, as here in the United States, individuals' responses to their transforming circumstances are shaped by locally understood meanings, histories, and interests, which create, in turn, new sites and vehicles for action – new social movements or forms of claim making, reconfigured sites of solidarity and attachment, or new fantasies of success and recognition. In particular places in contemporary sub-Saharan Africa, some of these new forms have led to overwhelming destructiveness, others to new sites of sanctuary and identity. Some call the ethos of neoliberalism and human rights into question, whereas others embrace and channel its promises through reworked conventions of hierarchy or sociality.

These new social forms are not traditional, externally determined, or entirely predictable in advance. They represent a technology of daily life in which agents use tools of mobilization to gain power and access to resources. However, at times, these new social forms are so imposing that they crowd out vernacular approaches and foreclose them before they are brought into being.

Modeling the Spread of "Human Rights" and the "Rule of Law"

Over the past ten years, one of the leading questions to preoccupy studies of the rise in international justice institutions has been how to make sense of their different approaches to legal systems and their changing forms in many areas around the world. In the quest to come up with solutions to violence, phrases such as "the spread of human rights" and "the globalization of the rule of law" have become central explanatory categories to describe the movement of human rights in quite unrestricted ways. These terms suggest the existence of a morally superior domain, especially in relation to other cultural and religious practices that may be seen as running parallel to it. These presumptions are not only empirically misleading but are also not analytically useful.

With the increasing analytical and scholarly work on the multiple domains of human rights and justice principles, today there are three popular models used to explain the deployment of various human rights universals in a range of geographies. One model, *norm internalization*, emerged in the late 1990s and early twenty-first century to explain the ways that the emergence of human rights principles could be universalized through both voluntary and involuntary means. This norm internalization model, popularized by Harold Koh (1998) and Margaret Keck and Kathryn Sikkink (1998), adopted horizontal and vertical forms of circulation to address a mechanism to improve the universality – and thus enforcement – of human rights. According to their model, the circulation of human rights works with a "top-down" dissemination of human rights norms through the horizontal importation of treaty resolutions from one state to the other. This is followed by the vertical incorporation of treaty norms through a "trickle-down" mechanism through which citizens would eventually internalize the human rights aspirations codified into international treaties. Carrying with it a presumed moral imperative through which the globalization of new human rights universals represents a necessary intervention to rid the world of violence, this model requires the internalization of dominant norms by citizens along with various levels of mobilization. As outlined by Koh, who was at the time preoccupied with providing a mechanism for the widespread circulation of new liberatory norms, this model assumes that people will internalize human rights norms once states legislate their commitments to these principles.

In response to this top-down approach, the second model – the process of *vernacularization*, which was prominently articulated by Sally Merry (2006a) and further clarified by Goodale and Merry (2007) – highlights the export of human rights norms globally and examines their interaction with local conceptions, what Merry refers to as "the vernacular" (2006a:1). By interrogating the reshaping of a set of "core" meanings within "culturally resonant packaging" (ibid.:137), Merry and others engaged in this approach (e.g., Annelise Riles, Mark Goodale) are committed to exploring, through the intersections of connection, the ways that international legal and human rights institutions are structured through fundamental dilemmas that lead to gaps between "global visions of justice and specific visions in local contexts" (ibid.:103). Through the vernacularization of dominant renditions of law, the encounter between international and more circumscribed discourses reflects the movement of ideas beyond the contexts from which they originally emerged (ibid., 2006).

The third model – the *encounter* model – is best articulated by Anna Tsing, using the concept of "friction," a metaphor of globalization that presumes globality through connection: "the grip of worldly encounter" (2005:1). It is further articulated through the conceptualization of cultural "encounters" in the work of Lieba Faier (2009). In such frictional encounters, ideas embodying multiple conceptual approaches come together, and – through difference, misunderstanding, and negotiation – otherwise disparate formulations are reworked and, at times, clarified.

These three models of the development or spread of practices taken to be (or that become) universal provide a window into different forms of widespread circulation in the midst of social complexity. In the first, a form of mobilization in which the force of change is buttressed by a moral hegemony aims to instill cultural change through top-down legislative change, eventually leading to the production of new norms. The second and third complicate the presumptions about the internalization of norms articulated by Koh and others. Although I draw on aspects of all three models in various contexts, my goal is to go beyond the tendency to attribute processes related to the ICC movement to the widespread globalization of human rights, which works to imbue on local peoples everywhere a discourse that reflects a liberalist conception of criminal responsibility. Rather, what becomes important is detailing the different social logics that shape varied understandings of personhood and justice, which include or exclude particular forms of consideration. In this regard, various political contestations, as well as incommensurate fields of meaning, need to be explored within the fields of power in which they operate (also see Strathern 2004; Povinelli 2001, 2002).

Merry's argument (2006) is concerned with demonstrating the complexities of making local meanings out of global forces, and thus her book focuses on demonstrating the workings of culture in the localization of meanings. Similarly, Tsing is so committed to showing the ontology of universals, and the ways that they are made through interconnection and various forms of engagement and disagreement, that she focuses on the language of encounters to demonstrate how meanings are not simply internalized but negotiated through complex forms of convergence and difference. Where both intervene into debates that presume unmediated internalizations of liberalist values by local peoples, they are necessarily committed to demonstrating the processes by which meanings circulate and are renegotiated in different ways. However, although I explore forms of negotiation, vernacularization, and friction in the making of the rule of law movement, my intervention points to cases in which convergence and negotiation are not an option, when meanings of justice are so incommensurate that they cannot be understood in terms of each other because they are defined against (or in contradistinction to) each other. I thus consider how certain relations are governed by a *politics of incommensurability*. I suggest that these cannot be explained in terms of particular forms of norm internalization or straightforward attempts to supplant vernacular forms, nor can they be understood as simply vernacularization or even as an emergent relation of "friction."

Limits to the Models

Because all three models assume that people are collaborating or working together in a given endeavor, they do not help us make sense of refusals to cooperate, to connect, or to enter into a joint project, nor of drastically different conceptualizations of personhood, crime, and justice – spheres so divergent and powerful that they at times foreclose the conceptual basis on which each is conceived. For example, in spaces of international justice making in which fields of liberalism set the standard for protecting individual rights, certain cultural understandings of justice and power in various parts of sub-Saharan Africa are often foreclosed before ever being brought to bear on international rule of law conceptualizations, into friction, in the first place. The hegemony of the making of governable subjects in international and increasingly regional domains involves a different sphere of conceptualization, intervention, and power relations. In the DRC case involving Thomas Lubanga, the inadmissibility of socioeconomic and historical contributors to violence in the assignment of genocidal guilt is an example of conceptually duelling fields of meaning relation. In this case, it is not that the global circulation of competing approaches rub together (Tsing) or lead to a rearticulation of the vernacular (Merry). The two conceptualizations of the transnational would have to be within more equal fields of power for these spheres to be viably put in contact. To explain this point further, another case in this book describes the logics of freedom through the story of the pious Nigerian woman, famously known as Amina Lawal, who was convicted of adultery under Sharia law and initially acquiesced to her death (see the opening of Chapter 6). Set alongside the model of the rights-bearing subject of secular human rights movements in the Global North, there are analytic limits to which Lawal's conceptualizations of personhood can be understood as simply intersecting with those of human rights activists.

International justice understood as a domain of regimes of truth highlights not only the power of the conceptual knowledge fields within which the individualization of new forms of criminal responsibility are constructed and made real but also the pervasiveness of the quest to produce "justice" in relation to expectations of individual subjectivity of the victim. Popular liberalist human rights conceptualizations of subjectivity are often understood in relation to the temporal present. As noted earlier, other conceptions of personhood presume life after death as an extension of life itself. Such differences make it difficult to put these presumptions about life (and freedom) into conversation with other conceptions of life; they call into question the temporality, as well as the governability, of life beyond the reach of the state. However, divergent fields of conceptualization are not the difference that makes the difference; in incommensurate relationships, it is critical to make sense of disjuncture, because the individuals involved also live within uneven spheres and mobilize resources, often in an attempt to lay claim to contemporary domains of power.

In understanding how these new legal conceptual fields travel, detailing the ways certain concepts are easily mapped onto other conceptual grids or superimposed onto other vernacular forms, rendering them unintelligible (or "uncivilized"), this book tracks the micropractices related to the making of various truth regimes. It explores the making of the knowledge regime known as the "rule of law" and explores its interface with other legal forms that operate in related but different conceptual fields. The claims of religious advocates or the demands of rebel groups vying for the sovereign management of their resources are examples of competing truth regimes and are raised to ask questions about the ways that incommensurate understandings of justice can enact powerful inclusions and exclusions. In this regard, the question that this book explores is the following: How might we rethink different patterns and conceptions of law that take seriously the powerful role of international institutions, mapping new and different connections while highlighting those relationships that do not always connect or that are rendered unintelligible? The lessons from recent sociopolitical theory are instructive in understanding diverse regimes of law, their effects, and the complex ways they circulate. Take, for example, the following incommensurabilties in which international justice is being called into question through challenges over the management of victims and the vying for jurisdiction over the means of punishment and terms for peace.

Challenges to the Fiction of the Rule of Law as Supreme Justice
During the first few years of the ICC's existence, controversies resulted from two central issues: the primacy of international law over national law – along with the related preference for achieving justice through criminal prosecutions as opposed to amnesties or truth commissions – and the general rejection of the ICC as a result of competing religious, political, or cultural positions on appropriate ways to measure criminal responsibility. As the world's first permanent court with a specific jurisdiction to prosecute individuals who are responsible for genocide,

war crimes, crimes against humanity, and crimes of aggression, the ICC claims personal jurisdiction over all persons living in states that have ratified the Rome Statute.

The goals of the ICC involve ensuring that high-ranking government officials who commit crimes against humanity are apprehended and prosecuted through an international body working in conjunction with states that have both signed and ratified the Rome Statute. The statute is often heralded by its advocates for revolutionizing the ways that people understand states' responsibilities to "humanity" (art. 1). It thus creates a new relationship between international and national forms of justice, emphasizing that the ICC "shall be complementary to national criminal jurisdictions."[31] However, its preamble also identifies the international, rather than the national, as the principal unit for acting out of humanitarian concern, establishing the court "with jurisdiction over the most serious crimes of concern to the international community as a whole" (¶9). These principles are further detailed in Article 17, which reiterates the ICC's complementary jurisdiction while ensuring that national courts retain initial jurisdiction.

As used in the statute, "complementary" is meant both to represent a nod to the primacy of the nation-state and to ensure that the standards of international adjudication are used as the ultimate measure of justice. In practice, however, the relationship between the international and the national spheres of governance is highly volatile (Schabas 2001:1–20) and is leading to ongoing forms of resistance.

In July 2005, the independent prosecutor for the ICC issued five arrest warrants accusing Joseph Kony, Vincent Otti (d. October 2006), Okot Odhiambo, Dominic Ongwen, and Raska Lukwiya (d. August 2006) of crimes against humanity and war crimes.[32] However, Ugandan law also has a provision for amnesty that contravenes the arrest of these men. In response, the "traditional justice" approach known as the *mato oput* has been proposed as an alternative to the jurisdiction of the ICC. In keeping with the terms of *mato oput*, Vincent Otti, the deputy commander of the LRA, has expressed readiness to ask forgiveness for wrongs he committed against the Acholi people. The problem is that despite the willingness of the Ugandan government to enter into amnesty peace talks with members of the LRA, an amnesty offer from Ugandan president Yoweri Museveni will not be binding so long as the ICC indictment remains in force. In other words, Ugandan sovereign power might not be authoritative enough to protect the will of Ugandan deliberations – even with the support of the African

Union, the declaration of which insists on the protection of African cultures, peoples, religions, and traditional practices. (The Ugandan case is explored in detail in Chapter 3.)

Another example involves struggles over jurisdiction between the Sudan and the ICC. On June 1, 2005, the lead prosecutor for the ICC, Luis Moreno-Ocampo, "decided to initiate an investigation in relation to the crimes committed in Darfur." He hoped to engage the ICC in prosecuting a small number of top officials for genocide, systematic torture, enforced disappearance, rape, destruction of villages, and pillaging of households – actions that appeared to have led to the forced "displacement of approximately 1.9 million civilians."[33] State officials in Sudan have signed the Rome Statute of the ICC; however, its governing bodies have not yet ratified it through their executives. The position of the Sudanese officials, therefore, is that because Sudan is not yet among the official States Parties of the ICC, it does not have a duty to relinquish jurisdiction to the court. Although the Sudanese government has insisted that it will not engage in the extradition of its citizens to be adjudicated in "foreign" courts, in keeping with UN Security Council Resolution 1593, the government has established a Darfur Special Criminal Court with its own rules, jury, and venue to adjudicate cases related to the Darfur crisis.[34]

U.S. Contestations of the ICC

Interestingly, the "solutions" from the West to violence and injustice in sub-Saharan Africa have historically called for rigid economic mandates – prescribed by the international lending institutions on which postcolonial African states have been financially dependent – that measure "progress" using indicators not always in keeping with the cultural rationalities of the regions in question. However, after Islamic militants flew two airplanes into New York's World Trade Center on September 11, 2001, the language of justice and human rights became even more pronounced, and the invocation of religious and cultural rights more circumspect. The goals of turning African countries from potential "breeding grounds for terrorists" into new "democratic regimes" and eradicating "military coup syndrome" – goals stipulated by various economic mandates such as the World Bank's Structural Adjustment Programs of the 1980s and 1990s[35] – have spurred an increasing trend toward what I call the *tribunalization of African violence*. These various forms of tribunalization were popularized with the spread of truth and reconciliation commissions. International tribunals have come to represent normative forms of international justice regimes in Africa, becoming hegemonic models for justice. This method of "justice making" through the construction of the rule of law has formed the backdrop for contemporary encounters with human rights, democracy, and "secularism," in addition to a range of other trajectories of justice. Further, whereas the United States has become a supporter of internationalist paths of justice for other states, it has insisted on its own military sovereignty to pursue its "War on Terror," all the time assuming that particular "Western" or "international" paths to justice are more viable than "local" ones.[36]

One of the most powerful and publicly vocal of those nations challenging the scope and jurisdiction of international law has been the United States, specifically the administration of President George W. Bush. Although the United States, along with other states, quite publicly refused to sign the Rome Statute when it was presented at the UN, President Bill Clinton eventually did sign it on December 31, 2000[37]; however, following a series of disputes over the language of the statute, on May 6, 2002, Clinton's signature was nullified by the January 20, 2001 transfer of power to President Bush. This action was during a period when the United States was engaged in a multipronged campaign against the ICC to protect U.S. nationals from the possibility of politically motivated prosecutions. The first set of actions taken by the Bush administration to shield Americans from ICC jurisdiction was to engage in bilateral immunity agreements (BIAs) with states worldwide.[38] With provisions that guarantee the immunity of U.S. military personnel, current or former government officials, U.S. employees (including contractors), and nationals by prohibiting signatory states from surrendering them to the ICC,[39] these agreements effectively remove Americans from the jurisdiction of the court. These BIAs thus further enlarge the spaces of management from institutions to individuals and, through the establishment of blanket immunity, place them above the law. In exchange for granting this freedom from governance, states receive financial compensation and U.S. military assistance. The fact that African countries, many of them under the jurisdiction of the ICC, are both signing these immunity agreements *and* ratifying human rights treaties highlights the complexity of political interactions operative in these spheres of governance.

The second set of U.S. actions involves the adoption of two pieces of legislation: the American Service-members' Protection Act (ASPA) and the Nethercutt Amendment. The ASPA, passed by Congress in

August 2002, contains provisions restricting U.S. cooperation with the
ICC and making American support of peacekeeping missions largely
contingent on achieving immunity for all U.S. personnel – ultimately
granting the president permission to use "all means necessary" to free
U.S. citizens and allies from ICC custody (prompting the nickname
"Hague Invasion Act").[40] The Nethercutt Amendment, originating in
the House of Representatives, was passed by the Senate and then signed
into law by President Bush on December 8, 2004. It prohibits foreign aid
to countries that have ratified the ICC treaty but not signed a bilateral
immunity agreement with the United States.[41]

A third set of actions in which the United States was the setting
up of military tribunals in a range of countries or participating entities,
through the UN Security Council, in the erecting of ad hoc tribunals
such as the ICTY and ICTR. Regarding the Iraq Special Tribunal[42] that
tried former president of Iraq Saddam Hussein, among many others, the
United States did not work through the ICC; rather, it collaborated
with the new Iraqi government and helped not only to set up a criminal
tribunal but to hire specialists to rewrite the country's constitution and
rebuild its institutional infrastructure. The trial of Hussein rocked the
international scene and represented a justice mechanism parallel to the
ICC. The first legal hearing in the Hussein case, transferring custody,
was held before the Iraqi Special Tribunal on July 1, 2004. Broadcast
on Iraqi public television and through widespread satellite, this hearing
marked Hussein's first public appearance since his arrest by U.S. forces
in December 2003. On July 18, 2005, he was charged by the Special
Tribunal with the 1982 mass killings of the inhabitants of the village
of Dujail.[43]

The first days of the trial, which began on October 19, 2005, were
tumultuous, as the legal defense team continued to call into question
the legitimacy of the court by storming out and rallying against Chief
Judge Amin and the tribunal. This disruption notwithstanding, the
trial proceeded, and a judgment was eventually handed down. Saddam
Hussein, unprotected by claims of national sovereignty, was hanged
on December 31, 2006. His surrender, trial, and death represented the
triumph of American unipolar power, not the spectacularity of the rule
of law writ large.[44]

Similarly, the revival of Islamic formations in a range of African
states can also be seen as a response to the perceived encroachment of
the hegemony of the secular human rights politics of the West. The
declared nonparticipation of states in various treaty regimes, the ICC

among them, might be seen as another response to the problems with the norm internalization model, which is accompanied by the growing insistence that "globalization" and integrated economies are the only alternatives for states in the Global South. These contestations are not simply contemporary protests, however. Haunted by particular histories and fears, as well as protections from potential threats, they actually stand in for past and present aspirations and responsibilities. They represent the social politics of humanitarianism, the goal of which is to protect the "victim" in the quest for "justice."

This book considers the fundamental effects of justice when the force of its making is manifest in various uneven power relations. The issues at hand are central to the various regimes of justice, including those that sit adjacent to one another, those that encroach on and dominate others, and those that are so incongruent that they must be understood in different terms. This analytic domain requires that we uncover the theatre of human rights and rule of law as it intersects with daily life and makes visible its social fictions within imbricated relations of power. In this era of growing internationalism, it is instructive to consider the evolving concept of justice through both its institutional growth into a kind of spectacularism and its relation to the divergent domains that are redefining the limits of state power.

States have not become irrelevant, and we are not living in a postnationalist or postreligious era. International justice making is not universally welcomed or accepted everywhere; a range of justice trajectories are taking shape in complexly divergent and transnationally allied formations in which justice as symbolic of human aspirations is made real through social fictions. What is needed is a complex mapping of the various transnational webs of influence and power that makes real various approaches to justice but that highlight the ways that those domains are unevenly shaped. The second part of the book allows us to see the effects of these uneven formations – the ways that the modernity of internationalism and the rights-bearing individual are incorporated (Koh 1998), rub up against other forms (Tsing 2005), are strategically negotiated (Merry and Goodale 2007), and also diverge and exist in a space of incommensurability.

ORGANIZATION OF THE BOOK

Part One of this book, "Multiple Domains of Justice," maps the formations of secular human rights developments by detailing the rise

39

of the rule of law movement that followed the Cold War. Part Two, "The Politics of Incommensurability," exposes the controversies over such formations by examining competing vernacular forms and understandings of justice. I explore various ICC-related contestations as well as contemporary developments connected to the spread of neoliberal commitments and the disregard for those practices – religious and spiritual, for example – that do not fit neatly into liberalist genealogical logics.

Chapter 1 examines the role of nongovernmental agents of the ICC who, like previous intermediaries from the Global South – the early African Christian converts, translators, and members of the literati – are participating in the development of new international spheres. Here I begin by taking a look at a relatively new class of actors driven by global democratization movements and the rapid deregulation of capital markets in an attempt to map the multiple domains of justice-making alliances taking shape in the contemporary rule of law movement.

Chapter 2 highlights a range of contestations and forms of incommensurate relations by examining the first case before the ICC (discussed at the beginning of this chapter). It explores the expanding supranational jurisdiction of the international justice community and the ways in which international law has constructed narratives of conflict and violence that perpetuate its power and justify its own mandate. Through an examination of the child soldier, I argue that although the international justice community purports to focus on and involve the "victim," the process fundamentally denies victims agency and authority and instead needs the figure of the victim to execute the moral work of "justice procurement."

Chapter 3 explores the relationship between international criminal law and alternative quasi-judicial mechanisms of justice as they are playing out in contemporary Ugandan "traditional" reconciliation rituals. The goal of this chapter is to demonstrate how challenges over cosmologies of justice – in this case, represented by ICC prosecution versus national amnesty plans – entail challenges over national sovereignty and point to the incommensurability of justice in action.

As I show in Part One, the work of international human rights institutions is being contested by a range of states and competing actors who are both happy and unhappy with the mission of the court, the codification of crimes, or the presumptions about individual subjectivity. These challenges have centered on reactions to the hegemony of universalizing a particular moral economy of rights derived from the cultural, ethnic, and religious contexts of the Global North. It is with these challenges – the "secular" and "religious" – that Part Two of this book is largely concerned.

Chapter 4 focuses on instances of religious violence in Nigeria and addresses the ways that international law and the secular nation-state have become entangled in Islamic revivalism. By exploring how the "genocide" category of the Rome Statute is embedded in different spheres of authority and by marking the relations of incommensurability with radical Islamic interpretations of the political crime, the chapter details how the language of law facilitates particular exclusions and points to the tensions that arise among Islamic religious governance, the secular nation-state, and the international human rights economy.

Chapter 5 continues with questions of religion in Nigeria to examine the implementation of the Sharia legal order in the Nigerian postcolonial state as an example of a challenge of legal pluralism. In this regard, it explores a set of relations that remains undertheorized in the anthropology of religion literature: the micropolitics of acquiescence in relation to the politics of Sharia implementation. In trying to understand a different logic within uneven competitions over power, I ask: Why do those critical of the uneven application of Islamic power nonetheless choose to submit to its religious-judicial judgments? I use a praxeological method to understand the micropolitics of submission to the courts as an instance of performing "proper" actions that are both politically and spiritually meaningful. This example highlights the ways that incommensurate approaches to justice are played out in quite consequential ways and highlights the limits of relativist or pluralist approaches in dealing with social inequalities.

Finally, Chapter 6 explores competing notions of justice and the controversies over interpretation among feminists engaged in the anti-Islamic Free Amina Lawal case. Investigating intersections between the morality of human rights and religious organizing, the chapter considers the implications of the new wave of international rule of law discourses in centralizing the work of global social movements while putting it in conversation with other rationalities that highlight faith, piety, and the performance of the preservation of life after death. The book closes with an epilogue that calls for a critical transnational legal pluralism that takes seriously the role of translation and the politics of difference as understood in uneven and incommensurate relations of power.

PART ONE

THE PRODUCTION OF LIBERALIST
TRUTH REGIMES

CHAPTER 1

CONSTRUCTING FICTIONS: MORAL ECONOMIES IN THE TRIBUNALIZATION OF VIOLENCE

Understanding the *tribunalization of African violence* and the rise and expansion of the rule of law campaign in sub-Saharan Africa involves asking how various factors have led to conditions such that it is Africa and not Europe, the Sudan and Uganda and not the United States, for example, that are subjects of the ICC. Asking why Africa and in what context, rather than simply asserting the need for the implementation of human rights norms, allows us to focus on the ways that human rights principles travel, how they are transmitted, propelled, anchored, and in the end, how they bury the normative political apparatus that constitutes them as distinct.

Significantly, although the idea for the International Criminal Court (ICC) was presented not long after World War II, any such plans were deferred because of the Cold War. At the close of the Cold War, a growing arms trade began to fuel African conflict zones in which rebel groups were vying for regional power. The literature on civil wars in the region (Rwanda, the Democratic Republic of Congo [DRC], Ethiopia and Eritrea, Sierra Leone, Liberia, and Nigeria; e.g., Collier and Hoeffler 1998; Abdullah 2000; Hirsch 2001; Ross 2004) establishes histories of violence and struggle in which it is often the regulatory forms of resource control that are ultimately at issue. The problem: throughout the 1990s, in regions such as Rwanda, Sierra Leone, the Ivory Coast, the DRC, and Uganda, many resource-related conflicts and their resolutions, despite obvious connections to global trade circuits, found little international support – especially compared with the significant international brokering at the end of the Cold War and the formative international justice interventions at the end of World War II.

The contemporary rule of law movement coincides with a particular shift in the spread of human rights liberalism that is marked by the end of the Cold War, highlighting this moment as the historical break that must be understood alongside the rise of a post–World War II human rights regime. The phenomenon of interconnected state obligations and duties that gave rise to the moral impetus of international law – and by extension the ICC – was the moral force of human rights. Driven by the desire to punish World War II war criminals, international law took shape in the modern era, and by the late 1980s, it was expanding exponentially with the growth of global capital, and ultimately the rise of new institutions of social organizing – primarily nongovernmental organizations (NGOs).

The end of the Cold War has led to attempts to interlink the globalization of both capitalism and the secular neoliberal state. The concurrent rise of the rule of law movement, with its demands on particular kinds of rights-endowed subjectivity, has led to what I refer to as a *human rights economy* in which the micropractices that are deployed to produce a moral and institution regime of rights protection is actually fuelled by an political-economic industry that propels its formation and shapes it logic. This reality of the central place of political economy in the formation of human rights is critical to the way that we understand the making of international justice in the contemporary present. For today, the rise of the rule of law as another regime of knowledge and truth is fundamentally connected to an even more intertwined economy, which, although interconnected with human rights, is directly related to struggles over the management of Africa's violence through a complex moral sphere to protect the "victim" but is driven by the quest for justice made possible through donor capitalism. Thus, this new sphere of internationalism is certainly about victim's justice but must be understood through an ontology of the management of postcolonial African resources, the place of Europe's declining colonial power, and American and Asian capital in the new "scramble for Africa."

Interestingly, at the end of the first decade of the twenty-first century, the situations and cases before the ICC have involved transregional struggles for resources that are sometimes articulated through local histories and meanings yet often are recast as merely ethnic and religious violence. There are issues at hand, however: the unequal distribution of wealth and the failure of the state to provide what Jim Ferguson (1999) has called *expectations of modernity*. The same colonial infrastructures that put in place the conditions of possibility for the unequal distribution of capitalist power and privilege throughout sub-Saharan Africa in the contemporary present is the same infrastructure that contributed to the plunder of its resources in the nineteenth and twentieth century. Today, in this post-independence era, these inequalities are still manifest in various antigovernment struggles for resource control on the African continent. In this regard, it is worth taking a closer look at what the shift to the rule of law has come to mean and at the way it is being produced in the African context in the wake of the collapse of the former Soviet Union, which created a political vacuum in Africa – one that has affected the conditions for resource struggles in the Middle East and in West, Central, and East Africa.

FROM COLONIALISM TO THE NEW SCRAMBLE FOR AFRICA

The first "scramble for Africa" was part of the European colonial rush of the 1880s, with African colonies created and ownership claimed to engage in the extraction of their resources. Today, with the temporal end of both European colonialism and the Cold War, at the height of neoliberal capitalism, a new scramble for Africa has begun in which local, national, regional, and international interests – in particular, the dramatically increased economic presence of both China and India – are competing for regulatory control of Africa's vast mineral resources. From the mining of coltan in Central Africa to the dumping of millions of tons of toxic "e-waste" along Africa's coasts each year, these extraction and disposal activities are crucial nodes in interlinked markets and in cycles of computer production. New competitors – African and non-African alike – are inserting themselves in African locales, and international market forces remain an integral aspect of local power formations and of new sites of territorial and occupational identity. In Ituri, DRC – the site of violence addressed in the first case before the ICC – it was competition for lucrative gold mines and control over trading routes that contributed to a significant amount of the violence in the region. It is the presence of resource struggles that shape and fuel the regional conflicts so often perceived, outside Africa, as atavistic ethnic clashes. These conflicts, in turn, provoke still other local–global interrelations: from the sale of firearms to African warlords, to the intervention of humanitarian workers, to the curious U.S. military presence in Africa through its AFRICOM (United States Africa Command) – a new hybrid alliance between the U.S. Department of Defense and African governments, created to promote both "security" and "nation-building" throughout the continent.[1] These manifestations of the international linkages are shaped, in turn, by long-standing histories of interaction that further blur the boundaries between internal and external dimensions of the continent's newly evolving competition for governance.

These contemporary struggles have involved the management of extra-state paramilitary forces, mercenaries, and independent security forces working alongside international corporations. With increasing struggles over the management of violence, we are seeing a growing industry of militarization in various sub-Saharan African states, leading to some of the most violent deaths since World War II. The twenty-first century's two most visible new "global" presences in Africa – the new scramble for Africa and AFRICOM – are indeed significant and transformative presences. Both of these provocative new entities, Asian and American, have been perceived alternately as new forms of colonization and as new vehicles of deliverance. Yet among the most disastrous consequences of the increasing conditions of war and resultant displacement has been not only the large numbers of civilian deaths but also the movement of people – victims, perpetrators, civilians – from less affluent to wealthier countries, leaving behind war-torn villages, cities, and regions. The impact of such violence thus extends beyond the boundaries of a conceptualized detached continent. It has extended to bring international legal solutions to deeply global socioeconomic questions.

In this chapter, I explore how the moral economy of the ICC "rule of law" movement is being shaped by particular technocratic instrumentalities that have evolved through various forms of contestation, state interests, and justice-making initiatives – specifically, how and for whose benefit a global elite of liberalist lawyers and policy makers are setting the moral and political agenda for addressing violence and, in doing so, engaging in micropractices supported by a larger and increasingly expansive political economy of the rule of law. This merging of morality, practice, and economy is developing truth regimes by which particular forms of legal knowledge are made recognizable and others increasingly incommensurate. In this regard, I depart from assumptions about the universality of human rights or theories that insist on the spread of the rule of law as simply a matter of norm internalization (Koh 1998). Instead, by exploring the realities of circulating local knowledge forms and how they sometimes exist as unconnected, or how, following Lieba Fairer (2009), they "come into productive relation" with other

knowledge forms – becoming incorporated, vernacularized, or obfus-
cated – I seek to investigate several matters. First, what is the political
and economic context within which the tribunalization of African violence is taking shape? With the implementation of criminal tribunals as
a key international mechanism to address contemporary violence, how
and why are various court advocates engaged in the individualization
of criminal responsibility in regions beyond their authority? Then, by
detailing the limitations of this project, I map how ICC projects are
part of a production of a global elite engaged in the work of naturalizing
notions of good governance, transparency, and the rule of law. I end by
demonstrating how justice regimes being negotiated on the ground are
brokered by international donor capitalism.[2]

In making sense of the perceived power of the rule of law's moral
fortitude in relation to the apparitional quality of the economic basis
of various NGOs, I explore its forms of agency and the conditions
of possibility within which such conceptions of "justice" are brought
into being. In considering nongovernmental forms of advocacy that
are responsible for a new ethics of morality, it is useful to understand
disparities in the implementation of human rights principles that are
embedded in rule of law discourses. Too often such disparities are left
out of discussions about how, exactly, an international court, operating
outside the power of a particular state, achieves its moral power. The
extent to which we understand how new adjudicatory techniques are
being vernacularized or marginalized will allow us to make sense of those
knowledge regimes that are never brought into productive relation and
why this is the case.

MORAL ECONOMIES AND PRAXEOLOGY

It has been well established in the literature that a new human rights
regime is taking shape and, in particular places, is forming the basis for
the expansion and vernacularization of human rights principles (Merry
2006a). The ICC, the ICTY, the ICTR, and the SCSL[3] – all components of this rule of law regime – are gaining power through the
burgeoning field of international humanitarianism. However, a regime
demonstrating an additional reach of the law – that is, new international extradition agreements – is now taking shape through the ICC
with the execution of particular liberalist micropractices. Like democracy and forms of liberal governance requiring that the government
participate in the functioning of the economic or social worlds of its

citizens through the maintenance of human life, liberalism has been concerned with the well-being of citizens, and its expressions have come to represent the maintenance of the personal autonomy of well-articulated political communities. A long lineage of scholars (Kant, Locke, Heidegger, Horkheimer and Adorno, Gramsci, etc.) has debated how we are to understand liberty and freedom in relation to the extent to which government is and should be involved in the functioning of daily life. By the late 1970s, it became clear through the work of Michel Foucault, among others, that the very issues of liberty and freedom seen by those scholars as the right of the individual were actually mythic constructions. Instead, individual action – and agency itself – represented a form of governmentality by which the liberalist idea of personal freedoms maintained its power through the illusion of individual agency (see, e.g., Foucault 1994). Thus, the very idea of individual choice gains its power not through its existence but through the concealment of the role of institutional forms, the social life of which resides in the way we organize the everyday – our way of speaking, our way of seeing, our silences, our moral precepts, and our definitions of justice. This intervention has highlighted the problem with agency as emanating from the individual and has reshaped the relevance of modern institutional governance in terms that maintain the illusion of autonomy of rights.

By the early twentieth century in a range of Northern states, agreements between citizens and their governments involved the protections of entitlements to rights that were based on the presumption of a social contract. This idea of a social contract also asserted itself as the vehicle for granting rights, adjudicating law, and taking and maintaining life. The language of freedom and rights and their related protections were popularized in the West by two key documents, the fervor of which led to the post–World War II building of the human rights movement: the 1948 Universal Declaration on Human Rights (UDHR) and the 1966 International Covenant on Civil and Political Rights (ICCPR; in force 1976).[4] These two documents set out to establish negative rights through which government intrusion into the "private sphere" could be prohibited, and they would lay the groundwork for making states accountable for the consequences of their ill-founded actions. However, the irony of these two moments for the emergence of modern human rights is the reality that, in the midst of such formations, states in the Global South were still engaged in anticolonial struggles; their mobilizations toward self-determination thus took shape outside of this movement (Okafor 2000). Today, however, the modern human rights–rule of law movement has claimed governance over those violent struggles in the South and is being constituted through them.

EMPOWERING "JUSTICE," JUSTIFYING POWER

The international justice literature, vast and growing, has tended to emphasize the expansion of jurisdiction and the coming into being of a new rights agenda without much attention to the particularities of the practices that make new norms possible (Henkin 1990; Bass 2001). The rise of an elaborate rule of law moral sphere with the mission of protecting the victim has led to conditions for complex encounters, circulations, and innovations and among some advocates has produced a narrative of individual criminal responsibility. This narrative is being propelled through particular interactions, alliances, influences, and contestations. This process does not happen through a unidirectional, top-down, Western, hegemonic imposition. New work in anthropology, international law, and development studies has offered complicated accounts of interactions in the circulation of law in multiple directions, with international law at times being generated from below.[5] Following Sally Merry (2006a), among others, we have many analyses of how local actors "vernacularize" or transform (or even subvert) human rights norms for strategic purposes. Scholars have also provided more nuanced discussions about the roles of NGOs and human rights elites, with studies emphasizing the plural sources of norms to which these actors respond and participate in shaping. Understanding the micropractices involved in constructing particular moralities of criminal responsibility is crucial to understanding the dynamics at play. In this regard, I borrow from theories of *praxeology* – the science of human action – as a way to understand how the cultivation of the ethics of human rights, as well as other values, are produced through liberalist micropractices.

The use of praxeology helps one recognize that it is not individuals' articulations of their goals and actions that are central to any understanding but the process of "doing" that foregrounds the meanings of the practices thus achieved. This approach points to the ways that micropractices enable the internalization of values, what Pierre Bourdieu (1977) popularized as *habitus*. It allows us to understand how they constitute the locus of understanding mainstream political and international movements, including those whose formations are not commensurate with the liberalist principles central to the rule of law.

These micropractices, whether in Africa or elsewhere, include the legal presentation or defense of a case (or both) as an extension of national or international justice on a larger scale, the display and circulation of human rights documents by international NGOs, the forms of oration through which particular moral economies are circulated, the grant-proposal writing and negotiation of donor funding for the brokering of human rights projects, and the various forms of acquiescence that are part of the display not only of religious subjectivity but also of particular forms of liberalist subjectivity. Through their referential power, they reflect that which embodies the fiction under construction. For example, the treaty domestication processes index judicial treaty acts and through that process makes real the spectacular force of law. This is the site for the making of international justice writ large: the act of linking particular micropractices with founding moral values that, through their authorial embodiments, are exported elsewhere and sometimes imposed, strategically vernacularized, or set alongside divergent values. Through the ethical cultivation of ideas of justice, rights, and a discourse of victim rights, the technical production of international treaties that transmute into legal rules is becoming a site of encounter and conflict or a domain for the inconceivability (Povenelli 2001) of social viability. In fact, at times such treaties bump up against significant contestations that either deny their legitimacy or undermine their ability to enforce their laws. Through the praxeological execution of micropractices, then, international criminal justice reflects competing moral economies of justice, and the shaping of these concepts, that sometimes justify interventions and attempt to crowd out vernacular forms of justice making.

Moral economy is a phrase often used to describe the interplay between moral or cultural beliefs and economic activities. I invoke it here to highlight the imbrication of not only various forms of religiosity but also particular ways that rule of law principles circulate through presumptions of the rights-bearing subject as a universal model of subjectivity to be replicated throughout the world. In the literature, the concept of a moral economy that is based on fairness and justice is often seen as generally operable only in small and interconnected communities in which webs of mutual obligation form the basis for exchange. Economists have often related the concept of a moral economy to the balance of economic power (Powelson 1998). Such an approach indicates the ways that economic factors are balanced against ethical norms in the name of social justice. In these contexts, principles of mutuality operate to promote the maintenance of these social networks and shape the basis for assigning value to services and various goods. They acquire force through informal forms of practice and the circulation of notions of appropriateness; in some cases, they may eventually become aligned with the force of law.

In anthropology, the literature on moral economy has emerged through the work of James Scott (1976) and has been further extrapolated by a range of anthropologists. Scott extends political economy analysis to the religious and moral spheres, showing how this ideology could be used as a method to resist authority. By connecting economics and anthropology to the interplay between cultural mores and economic practices, Scott and others have come to use the notion of moral economy to describe the different ways in which custom and social pressure shape various economic actors to conform to traditional norms. For my purposes here, however, such traditional uses of moral economy do not fully capture what I mean by the moral economy of the rule of law and the ways in which we might understand it in the context of how ICC innovators address violence and work toward ending impunity in sub-Saharan Africa. Here, the moral principles reflect interventions on behalf of victims in the pursuit of justice – what I call *justice talk* – and represents a more discursive circulation of moral values. These values have their roots in the expression of suffering and the deterrence of future violence, but in the development of this moral sphere, there is actually a resultant concealment of the underlying factors of violence and what it would take to end it. This complexity of the underside of justice talk has not been the focus of rule of law movements. Instead, by focusing only on political and civil rights, the burgeoning rule of law movement is, in effect, operating alongside another specter – not only the specter of the victim (to be taken up in the next chapter) but also that of capital-driven interventions, which, in sub-Saharan Africa, are only lightly regulated by governments. The concealment of capital-driven violence and a capital-driven rule of law movement has more to do with the organized circulation of moral imperatives to protect victims as articulated in public domains than with the assumption that a political and economic structure actually exists to constrain economic action from overcoming morality. In other words, the role of neoliberal capitalism, which has contributed to the competition over resources and related violence, has, in various places, also succeeded in constructing a notion of victims' justice as a moral product not always visible as a contested narrative. Instead, justice talk as a discursive practice is performed in an extraordinariness, a spectacular expression, that further accentuates its power and makes its meaning relevant to social aspirations for change. This extraordinariness is profound – from the extradition of DRC nationals to a European-based court sitting in The Hague, to the authoritarian robing in black and display of a panel of six judges from around the world to hear a case about violence in a region from which none of them originated; from the judgment of guilt and punishment of stoning to death in a local Sharia court to the ritualization of forgiveness in a Ugandan reconciliation ceremony. For the ICC, it is the founding moment in which nation-state ratification and the related signatures and parliamentary and congressional processes are performed.[6] For Islamic justice, it is the declarations from the Prophet Muhammad's sacred texts and ritualized interpretation that highlight the spectrality of justice. These acts, as extraordinary as they often become, are constituted through micropractices, the enactments of which are embedded in daily, mundane expressions of power and inequality.

Yet international legal movements such as the ICC are also, in the eyes of some, facing a crisis of legitimacy because the very places embedded in widespread violence – places where populations have been decimated and national judiciaries are most in need of repair – are also the domains most in need of interventions that address root causes, which these movements often do not provide. In the midst of failures to address the causes of death regimes, the brokers of these life- and death-generating formations – freedom fighters, children, adults, international institutions – participate in unequal relationships through which to rearticulate the terms for justice. Facilitating this widening of the management of life and death, the imagery of Africa as a place of suffering has further propelled new forms of intervention that have made possible supranational jurisdiction, enabling the arrest and adjudication of nationals from "elsewhere." These new instrumentalities for the technical production of a new basis for justice, such as the Rome Statute for the ICC, are at play and are deeply embedded in power relations that, at times, circumvent the commensurability of justice making in international spheres of interaction. One such ICC-based example is the conceptual formation of the statute crimes.

Ontologies of ICC Notions of Criminal Responsibility
The court's focus on mass violence draws on the most explicit forms of criminal responsibility in which only those persons responsible for

executing death can be held politically responsible. This attention to individualized responsibility for guilt draws on Western liberalist thought in its assignment of individualized guilt and its construction of self-reflective images of justice and freedom for all of humanity. It does not provide a forum for rethinking of the root causes at the core of violence in sub-Saharan Africa or an interrogation of the political economy of state power of those under the jurisdiction of the court (Uganda, the DRC) versus state powers outside its reach (the United States, China, Japan, India, and Pakistan, for example). Rather it is the discourse of liberty and freedom through adjudicatory action that prevails within the mission of the court – root causes of violence are only collected as histories for establishing mitigating circumstances (also see ICTY documentation of causes of violence in the former Yugoslavia). As such, liberalism, popularly identified as a doctrine that is political in nature and committed to the maximization of individual liberty balanced with the maintenance of that liberty against a state, provides the framework through which such forms of justice operate. This framework operates to secure life for the majority but also concedes to the death of others outside of its purview, outside of its primary responsibility. The ICC operates within this domain and seeks to protect the victim by deterring future perpetrators. However, in reality the basis on which mass violence is often perpetuated is not preventable through the threat of international adjudication. These various struggles, some of which are resource struggles, represent fights over the political economy of sovereign control of national resources – the conditions of which are sometimes the sacrifice of life itself.

With a life-protecting mission to adjudicate the "most serious" of mass crimes against humanity, the ICC was formed with the signatory power of 120 nation-states in support of the Rome Statute of the ICC, and its eventual ratification by 60 of the 120 (Schabas 2004:18, 20). By July 1, 2002, the ICC had entered into force (ibid.:19), asserting that those states that had both signed and ratified the statute had placed themselves, and any of their nationals (especially high-ranking officials) deemed responsible for large-scale atrocities, under the jurisdiction of the court.[7] Through its judicial formation, the court became the first permanent international body empowered to adjudicate individuals for four categories of offense: war crimes, the crime of genocide, crimes against humanity, and the crime of aggression (when defined).[8] The statute, a comprehensive text that established the ICC and determined its composition and function,[9] borrows its presumptions of criminal liability from precedents established at the end of World War II (Gurule 2001–2:2–3; Schabas 2004) that address the aftermath of violence. The crimes selected for inclusion in the ICC's jurisdiction were the result of several years of negotiation. The original 1954 version of the Code of Offences was based on the laws and legal principles codified in the Geneva Conventions (1864–1949) and the Nuremburg War Crimes Trials (1945–1949).[10] Later versions of the draft continued to incorporate laws and principles based on treaties, tribunals, and customary laws covered under *jus cogens* rather than codifying new practices into the statute. In 1981, the International Law Commission (ILC) resumed its work on the draft "Code of Offences against the Peace and Security of Mankind" (hereafter, Code) at the request of the United Nations (UN) General Assembly.[11] By 1989, representatives from Trinidad and Tobago requested that the ILC resume the process of establishing an international criminal court to deal with the major drug-trafficking issues in the region.

However, over the next few decades, the process of creating the ICC passed through several phases of negotiation and refinement. The ILC used government reports as input for the drafting process and created the comprehensive Draft Statute for an international court. In 1994, it presented a draft for the establishment of the ICC to the UN General Assembly, which established the Preparatory Committee to advance the process the next level.[12] The Preparatory Committee met six times over the course of two years (1996–1998) during which time it received feedback from national delegates, government reports, NGOs, and intergovernmental organizations. Once the revisions were completed, it was presented to a diplomatic convention and ultimately resulted in the Rome Statute of the ICC in 1998.

The UN General Assembly established another Preparatory Commission to review and refine the document through the adoption and ratification process. This commission convened ten times between 1999 and 2002 during which time it prepared the Rules of Procedure and Evidence and the Elements of Crimes for the Court.[13]

In 1991, at the forty-third session of the ILC, the commission adopted a draft code, which defined the following crimes: aggression; threat of aggression; intervention; colonial domination and other forms of alien domination; genocide; apartheid; systematic or mass violations of human rights; exceptionally serious war crimes; recruitment, use, financing, and training of mercenaries; international terrorism; illicit traffic in narcotic drugs; and willful and severe damage to the environment.[14]

In 1995, the special rapporteur omitted six of the twelve crimes in the subsequent draft created at the forty-seventh session. The crimes that were omitted included colonial domination and other forms of alien domination; apartheid; recruitment, use, financing, and training of mercenaries; willful and severe damage to the environment; international terrorism; and illicit traffic in narcotic drugs. The special rapporteur presented several justifications for the omission during the session in a topical summary report to the UN General Assembly. If the court were to gain universal acceptance among nations, it would have to avoid crimes that were too controversial or widespread.

A number of delegations expressed support for the special rapporteur's recommendation to limit the list of crimes against the peace and security of mankind to those which were difficult to challenge – namely, acts that were so serious, they would unquestionably fall into the category of crimes against the peace and security of mankind. Many expressed the view that the commission needed to strike a balance between legal idealism and political realism, and the special rapporteur's approach was commended as appropriately leaning toward the latter, as likely to facilitate the work of the committee, and as justified in view of the lack of consensus on certain crimes in the draft code. Bearing in mind that the aim of the code was to make possible the prosecution and punishment of individuals who had perpetrated crimes of such gravity that they victimized mankind as a whole, it was remarked that it seemed sound to reduce the list to a "hard core" of crimes, making it easier for the draft Code to become operative in the future, possibly in conjunction with the establishment of a permanent international criminal court.[15]

The report also stated:

> This restrictive approach would avoid devaluing the concept of crimes against the peace and security of mankind, that crimes incapable of precise definition or which had political rather than legal implications should be left out and that the six crimes proposed for deletion, however reprehensible, had no place in the Code and could only impede the preparation of a generally acceptable instrument.[16]

Those in support of the omissions presented specific justifications against the inclusion of the crimes, such as the claim that colonial domination no longer existed and was therefore not an issue. The opposing opinion argued that

> recent scientific progress had led to the opposite conclusion, and that, for example, the exploitation of new sources of wealth was expected to be reserved for a few countries having the requisite financial and technical resources. It was also observed that, while most of the crimes which the Special Rapporteur had proposed for deletion reflected practices that no longer existed, deterrence considerations justified the inclusion in the Code of practices which might reappear.[17]

Those who opposed the omissions were dissatisfied with the outcome of the debate and suggested it should continue at greater length. The opposition argued that these crimes "constituted serious offences against the human conscience and threats to the peace and security of mankind"[18]; therefore, "there was no justification for excluding from the draft Code serious crimes such as intervention, colonialism, apartheid, mercenarism and international terrorism."[19]

The general opposing position argued that

> the Special Rapporteur had been obliged to select the incontrovertible crimes to be included in the Code on the basis of the reservations or views of a small number of States, which were not representative of the international community's position, since the majority of developing countries had failed to submit comments on the draft articles adopted on first reading.[20]

Other justifications that were made for excluding particular crimes included "the view that the disappearance of the symptoms of apartheid was no reason for apartheid to be excluded from the Code, which should include acts because they were criminal in nature and not exclude them because they were no longer likely to occur."[21]

The counterargument to this position argued that

> although apartheid as such had ceased to exist, the problem of "institutionalization of racial discrimination" still persisted in some parts of the world and that consideration should be given to the Special Rapporteur's proposal to include a general provision that would apply to any system of institutionalized racism by whatever name in any State. It was suggested that consideration should be given to including not only racial discrimination, but also economic, political and cultural discrimination as a crime. It was also suggested that the continued existence of situations of institutionalized racial discrimination should be addressed as systematic violations of human rights rather than as a separate crime.[22]

Later debates regarding terrorism and drug trafficking occurred during the Preparatory Committees. For example, India and the Russian Federation proposed the inclusion of acts of international terrorism based on the widespread and vast destruction that result in serious cases. Representatives from Austria, Sweden, Malaysia, the Republic of Korea, the Netherlands, and the United States argued that treaty-based crimes, such as terrorism, should be adjudicated at the national level. The representatives from Lebanon, Pakistan, Libya, and Qatar emphasized the distinction between terrorism and struggles for self-determination and national liberation. In particular, the representative from Pakistan raised the point that "colonial and occupying powers had always sought to suppress liberation movements by designating their activities as 'terrorist.' Foreign domination itself was a form of terrorism."[23] Ultimately, after decades of debate, the crimes that were covered under the jurisdiction of the Rome Statute were reduced to four from the twelve previously defined in 1991 draft. The result was that only "the most serious crimes" of concern to the international community were to be included as admissible crimes.

In the end, the crimes classified as the "most serious" were those that involved mass death and widespread killing of such gravity that they were threats to peace and security of the international community. Thus, the crimes that came to occupy the moral and legal concerns of the court were those dealing with explicit forms of mass violence – akin to the forms of violence being perpetrated in sub-Saharan Africa and Latin America at the time. As mentioned, as of the adoption of the Rome Statute for the ICC in 2002, the crimes under its jurisdiction as outlined in Articles 5 to 8 included genocide, war crimes, crimes against humanity, and the crime of aggression.[24] These crimes are described as being managed by the ICC as an independent institution rather than by individual state powers.

Yet, much of the literature on power, rights, and entitlement explores notions of power through the advancement of the idea of government and its exercise. This scholarship has maintained the need to locate sovereignty in the state, the practice of which was related to that of imposing power on the individual. In *Discipline and Punish*, Michel Foucault (1977) disturbed the foundations of sovereignty by recentering them in the disciplining action of the individual. In the first volume of his *History of Sexuality*, Foucault (1978) explored the workings of modern forms of governmentality in which power circulated not through the state itself but through various forms of capillary power. His analysis examined how power is shaped by what Foucault termed *biopolitics* (1978:140) – that which is concerned with population as a political and scientific problem. As such, biopower acts on the population in a preventive fashion and works to optimize life chances. It operates in the West through surveys for the prevention of epidemics and scarcity, and through Foucault's prism, it was governments that participated in the regulative mechanisms that work toward the maintenance of human life. The sphere of biopower is especially critical in contexts in which life is sustained by means of an economy of rights that operates through a complex constellation of the moral right to life and the political obligation of the state to protect its citizens from undue harm that might result in death. However, in the context of the rise of international criminal crimes managed by contemporary global forms of practice and regulatory action, how are we to understand the inability – and at times refusal – of the postcolonial state to participate centrally in such forms of biopolitical practice alongside their overrepresentation in international criminal court proceedings? In sub-Saharan African contexts, it is what Achille Mbembe has called *necropolitics* (Mbembe 2003), which, alongside paramilitary regulatory power, involves a more dismal administration of life and death and which extends well beyond the state into the realms of international institutions and NGO governmentality and represents a supranational management domain of determining who can live and who must die. However, these contemporary institutions in sub-Saharan Africa, while fostering new models of legalistic and technocratic management, are neither successfully diminishing the militarization of communities through illegally imported arms nor resolving ethnic crises brought into being by earlier colonial demarcations. Rather, in the regions under examination, their human rights consciousness is emerging within an economy of violence, and the ultimate expression of their adjudicatory power is their capacity to dictate who may live and who must die – a function significantly explored by scholars as the fundamental basis for sovereignty (Agamben 2005). Yet the response to African violence within ICC-liberalist circles has not begun with the necropolitical challenges on the continent. The responses of the international rule of law regime has involved setting in place a permanent institution to punish those commanders responsible for the gravest crimes against humanity and to make possible the protection of living "victims" after extreme suffering. This justice agenda exists within multiple webs of state participation and transnational regimes of economic mobilization.

At the base of my intervention are questions regarding how Foucault's biopolitics is still relevant in these nodes of transnational interconnection, in which it is neither the state nor the individual alone that is engaged in forming the basis for the crafting of the individual, the citizen. The links among big donors, big institutions, and big NGO mobilizations offer insight into the ways that divergent conceptualizations of justice are being crosscut in these justice-making encounters, propelled by mechanisms in many sub-Saharan African states that are not always life producing. As we shall see by the international management of crime, death and its management are integral ways of managing the protection of life, of victims, in the emergent ICC–rule of law regime underway.

The shift in governmentality in the postcolonial state is akin to Mbembe's (2003) necropolitics: new spatial demarcations of the state of exception in which the most brutal mobilization of the African war machine, connected to international moral and political economies, produces death as well as the management of those whose lives are chosen to be saved – barely. For those who are subjects of poverty and neglect represent the living dead – the dispensable whose political status has been reduced to the condition of "bare life" (Agamben 1998) and whose value is relevant only insofar as humanitarianism requires an object to be saved. Escape from violence, both economic and political, through illegal and difficult forms of migration sometimes results in death or forms of life so devoid of palatable existence that they can be called "bare." Like biopolitical expansionism, the necropolitical sphere is best understood in terms of international, national, and individual use-values of the bodies of these living dead, which provide the discursive material for particular forms of intervention.

By recasting the domain of biopower in terms that are intertwined with African political landscapes, we see how international institutions, their treaty bodies and the NGOs who mobilize change in alliance with these institutions are one such interventional force. This is made visible in no better place than throughout the African continent, where its diverse national citizens remain dedicated to mobilizing particular types of advocacy networks or intellectual production through which to manage human bodies. This trend toward the microcultivation of instrumentalities for the maintenance and documentation of life (i.e., *biopolitical techniques*) is often legitimized through justice talk – a practice in which the narrative that African states are corrupt and thus we must intervene in the interest of victims is most vibrant (for further exploration, see Chapters 2 and 3).[25]

THE COSTS OF "JUSTICE" TALK

The post-1989 period has been one in which various states – with varying success – are being enlisted to sign on to international treaty bodies and participate in the growing world of global governance. In an attempt to achieve neoliberal mandates and manage "insurgencies" by "rebel groups," various international rule of law NGOs are playing key mediating roles in working with states to maintain the biopolitical mandate of liberalism. This mandate entails a style of governance that involves the regulation of populations through the exertion and impact of political power on all aspects of life, including the application of emerging technologies toward the welfare and maintenance of all forms of life.[26]

However, rule of law mechanisms are produced extranationally and at great expense. To be a member of the ICC, states must pay an annually assessed, scaled fee[27] and spend hundreds of thousands of dollars flying personnel to meetings and hiring consultants to work on legal documents; in addition, they are encouraged to donate to the victims' fund on a yearly basis.[28] The cumulative costs of the ICTR (established 1994; trials began 1997) were projected to be just over a billion dollars by the end of 2007;[29] the ICTY's cumulative budget for 1993–2007 (hearings began late 1994) was $1.47 billion.[30] Operating costs for these two tribunals in 2006–7 were roughly $270 million apiece.[31] The ICTR and ICTY, like the ICC, are mainly funded by assessed contributions from member states, supplemented by ad hoc donations. In a December 2007 ICC press release announcing the "programmed budget for 2008, the Assembly approved a budget totaling €90,382,000 and a staffing level of 679. It also decided on the Working Capital Fund for 2008 in the amount of €7,405,983, the scale of assessment for the apportionment of expenses of the Court, and the financing appropriations for the year 2008."[32]

In addition to the costs involved in establishing and operating these courts, specific funds have been created to pay reparations to the victims of the crimes being tried. Recently, in September 2008, the Board of Directors of the Trust Fund for Victims (TFV) announced "a global appeal for €10 million to assist 1.7 million victims of sexual violence within the jurisdiction of the International Criminal Court."[33] Shortly after the call for contributions, Denmark responded with a contribution of €500,000 to initiate the fund, which will be "in addition to the euro 3 million (US$4.2 million) earmarked this year for reparations to war victims and for community rehabilitation projects as part of the court's regular budget."[34] Although funds have been donated or earmarked, the process involved in distributing the reparations is lengthy and likely will leave victims without a payment for years.[35]

Such new funding mechanisms have led to the growth of NGO governmentality and represent the development of what David Trubek (2006:84) has called the "project of markets." As he argues, they are part of the campaign of export-driven growth dependent on private foreign investment that today propels the internationalization of human rights through rule of law enforcement mechanisms. It is partly the economic forces involved in establishing "justice" that are establishing a new terrain for the development of a moral economy of the rule of law, especially in African and Latin America.

Indeed, the market of NGOs has led to a multi-million-dollar industry, a *political economy of the rule of law*. Today, when various states are unable to furnish the services they once did, NGOs have been enlisted to provide those services in their place – and international corporations, donors, and states have been called on to fund the non-governmental (or even governmental) elite engaged in making the rule of law a central justice force in the world. NGOs in international criminal law networks thus work alongside international donors and national governments to engage in the dispensation of services and advocacy, the spread of international justice institutions, and the support of new forms of governmentality, such as the ICC. In their quests for coordination and "capacity building" (i.e., general upgrading of performance ability), ICC NGOs are working in tandem with international and national organizations as well as governmental ones to direct advocacy projects and ratification campaigns for the implementation of treaties.

INTERNATIONAL NGOS AND THE COSMOPOLITAN ELITE

Who are the people who are carrying out the work of NGOs, and what are the conditions that have spawned and continue to support these increasingly powerful institutions? In his well-known work

"Cosmopolitans and Locals in World Culture," Ulf Hannerz argues that world cultural formations are created through the increasing interconnectedness of people in varied localities (Hannerz 1990:237). Arguing that contemporary globalization has brought a large number of people into contact and that territorial cultural practices that were once distinct are today increasingly entangled,[36] Hannerz uses the term "cosmopolitan" to describe persons who travel around the world and possess "a willingness to engage with the Other" (1990:238).[37] The willingness to become thus involved and to achieve competence in navigating the cultural practices, values, institutions, and languages of "the Other" is central to the cosmopolitan elite who make up the participants in international rule of law brokers – activists, legal advisers, and consultants – working to establish the rule of law as the basis for international justice. The interests that tie these individuals to their elite enterprises are varied – shaped by professional ambitions, corporate economic interests, a personal desire for travel, idealistic aspirations for world peace, a commitment to the moral project of human rights through rule of law mechanisms, or a combination of these.

The mobility of these actors and their knowledge products marks an important change in the political organizing that has accompanied and facilitated the massive decentralization of capital accumulation worldwide. The postcolonial and post–Cold War mobilizations of ethnic and national groups have fundamentally reorganized global political spaces, in which postcolonial representatives from NGOs in Africa, India, South and East Asia, Latin America, and the Caribbean now work alongside predominantly white middle-class American and European men and women. Simultaneously, rapid advances in information and transportation technology, as well as the forms of linkage of new forms of communication, have changed the ways in which various types of governance are being administered and articulated. These processes have served to justify a fragmented social landscape embedded in profoundly uneven and contradictory articulations of capital, labor, market, and other rationalities. The global rise of human rights and rule of law NGOs reflects the development of a strand of political mobilization that has, in some places, produced even a Southern cosmopolitan elite[38] armed with the language of democracy, access to donor funding, and flexible national loyalties – actors willing and convinced of their abilities to generate programs to address failures in state governance. Whether in India, London, Lagos, or Port of Spain in the Caribbean, they are engaged in transnational treaty negotiations in which they lobby various officials, attend UN human rights meetings, and participate in the negotiation, documentation, and monitoring of governments. Already armed with bachelor's or graduate-level degrees from Ivy League American or historically prestigious European universities, many update their knowledge with additional training in Geneva, London, The Hague, Galway, or New York, as well as regional training sites on every continent. Engaged through volunteerism or middle-wage employment, these young (late twenties to early forties) human-rights professionals – lawyers, legal scholars, policy makers – are brokers of a legal "science" that entails local reporting of human rights abuses and the crafting of official documents (protocols, treaties, and constitutions) toward the production of a rule of law regime. Generally at the early stages of their careers, they are part of the development of a new class of cultural intermediaries at the center of the internationalization of cooperative networks. Kenneth Anderson (2000) has referred to NGOs as fundamentally "campaigning organizations." Unlike community-based organizations (CBOs), which tend to be more locally constituted and focused, with less access to transnational donor capital and a more limited membership base,[39] NGOs tend to target broader social and political issues and constituencies through a wider mandate that does not directly benefit the NGO staff.

The expansion of human rights and rule of law advocacy has involved the development of an analytic community of legal experts whose "science" has been established by the rule of law and whose conviction has been propelled by both a moral project and an economic engine driving democratization in the Global South. Having trained as international lawyers, international consultants, and business advisors, these professionals seek donor support to fund the writing of legal documents, such as treaty protocols and constitutions, and act as advisors in the implementation and amendment of national documents. Many of these intermediaries are engaged in producing and reinforcing new regimes of internationalism that are invested in the predictability and legibility of governments and markets. These new actors in international human rights arenas are characteristically eager to act and willingly mobile in their professed service of humanitarianism on behalf of both civil society and governmental officials. The consequent output – training manuals, constitutional research, briefs, and case law – is designed to inculcate the value of democratic stability and the threat of international prosecution for offenders of that mandate.

NGOS ON THE RISE: THE COALITION FOR THE ICC

In the first five years after the signing of the Rome Statute in 1998, there was an ICC-centered explosion of "scientific" investigations into the histories, politics, and legal systems of those peoples affected by crimes against humanity, war crimes, and genocide. This project was spearheaded by the ICC's Office of the Prosecutor but propelled by a network of thousands of NGOs engaged in the work of treaty adoption and compliance.

The primary shadow organization and key support mechanism behind the development of international criminal law has been the Coalition for the International Criminal Court (CICC), an organization that began with twenty-five member NGOs in 1995, three years before the adoption of the Rome Statute. Now having a membership of more than two thousand regional and international NGOs, the CICC works alongside the ICC and its member states to accomplish the passage of the Rome Statute in as many states as possible. Its membership includes such humanitarian powerhouses as Amnesty International, Human Rights Watch, Human Rights First (formerly the Lawyer's Committee for Human Rights), the International Bar Association, and many other less well-known organizations. Through the creation of regional networks of local and foreign participants, and with a language of juridical obligation, the coalition's participants facilitate the analysis of national constitutions in respective regions.

Today, fostering the consequent statute implementation campaigns, constitutional reforms, and documentation and circulation of human rights violations, the CICC and other large-scale NGOs work to ensure that the ICC priorities of human rights and international law are reflected in the practices of member states. With a secretariat in New York City, the CICC has offices throughout the world – in the Middle East; East, West, and South Africa; Latin America and the Caribbean; Western and Eastern Europe; and East and South Asia. The Moroccan Coalition, the Nigerian Coalition, and the Ugandan Coalition for the ICC are a few of the centrally active CICC-affiliated NGOs on the African continent engaged in the documentation of various state-based knowledge. Although the CICC is known for not taking public positions on ICC issues, it clearly works – in the areas of research, advocacy, education, and networking – toward the achievement of ICC goals.

Both the NGOs and the CBOs that constitute the CICC and partner networks employ techniques of democratic liberalism in reconceptualizing a society free of violence and offering universal entitlements for all. Using legal analysis techniques, NGOs and CBOs are engaged not only in the pragmatics of legal reform but also in the production of "local" knowledge databases, comparative documents, and various resources and tools designed to aggregate "scientific" knowledge about the regions being "served." On the CICC Web site (www .iccnow.org), for example, is a country-by-country database that serves to educate readers about the history of various regions; provide information on trainings, meetings, and international summits and events; and make tools available to assist in the legislative drafting process. These tools include a compilation of downloadable pieces of legislation from states around the world for the purpose of comparison, public education instruments such as public service announcements and videos, Web links to other resources for advocacy work, a downloadable "how-to" kit to assist civil society groups in their ICC campaigns (with advice on informing the media, planning events, conducting outreach to governments, etc.), tips on forming networks, exemplary draft legislation from countries that have successfully ratified and implemented the Rome Statute, and scholarly articles on ICC ratification and implementation. The CICC Web site also provides country updates and stimulates activities of member NGOs by targeting particular nation-states as the "country of the month." This Universal Ratification Campaign funnels resources into particular national coalitions each month and then provides reports on their local efforts, including press conferences and NGO meetings with national and international politicians and jurists.

Such empirical forays involve the documentation of state-based histories, the determination of constitutional status, and the setting of agendas for state-by-state treaty implementation, efforts that are expanding the basis of ICC jurisdiction by bringing national constitutions into compatibility with the Rome Statute. How is this done? The process of legal incorporation is being driven by a new form of modern capital that has its interests in regulating particular practices. In their attempts to implement international treaties and doctrine, NGOs have become more important than ever to facilitating the spread of global capitalism. This has occurred not simply through an ideological mission to secure rights for all on the basis of humanity; rather, it has necessarily involved the capitalistic circulation of donor funding that is producing new and entrepreneurial forms of capital support to some of the leading and most recent graduates and professionals from a range

67

of countries. Many of the cosmopolitan human rights activists working with and for the CICC develop the cultural capital to join international human rights and justice institutions and are hired to conceptualize, run projects, broker funding, implement the goals of donors, and spend minimal amounts of time engaging in the type of biopolitical forms of state-building projects that might otherwise promote the development of state capacities. Instead, they provide translations of "local" contexts into packages that can be incorporated into "global" discourses (often inundated with justice talk – legalistic or even moralistic jargon – and circulated predominantly in English, French, and Spanish), rendering legible to international bodies the vulnerabilities of nation-states throughout the world.

International and local trainings, the circulation of information, the mechanisms for advocacy and treaty ratification, and the construction of user-friendly Web sites are just some of the techniques fundamental to the development of what has become the biopolitical management of ICC-driven human rights. These new technologies of knowledge generation have guided the development of a new international domain dependent on the viability of its supranational disciplinary institutions. Further, all of this is accomplished "on the ground" through the euphemistic discourse of "capacity building," one of the critical tools used by ICC NGOs working toward Rome Statute treaty implementation. In this regard – and as Foucault (1977) reminds us – knowledge formations are shaped by disciplinary technologies rooted in institutional power.

The new ICC biopolitics, the supranational management of the life and death of the victim, however, is engaged in the creation and expansion of particular principles with a mission that extends beyond the nation-state and requires recognition of the sanctity of democracy. The mechanisms deployed for the establishment of this particular knowledge regime have implications for how we understand late-twentieth-century democratization movements, the interventionist policies of powerful nations, the widespread upheaval of communist regimes – and, for our purposes, the birth of the twenty-first-century transnational criminal law network.

Funding pools, with Northern donors, are among the large and growing web of international linkages through which NGOs (and collaborating CBOs) are interconnected, and many members of Southern NGOs continue to be conflicted about the realities on which human rights agendas, priorities, and strategies are decided and enforced. The

following controversy over Morocco's cultural notions of immunity versus those required by the Rome Statute for the ICC is a good example
of cultural differences that represent incommensurate regimes of truth
and governance within which the political economy of the rule of law
is imbricated.

High Stakes and Big Ideas: The Rule of Law in Morocco
In response to a question from reporters about why Morocco has not
ratified the Rome Statute, Morocco's then-Minister of Foreign Affairs
and Cooperation, Mohamed Benaissa, indicated that the Rome Statute
contradicts the essence of Morocco's constitution and legal system
because it offers widespread immunity to its king and high-ranking
leaders, whereas Article 27 of the Rome Statute insists on the irrele-
vance of the official capacity of the leader as the basis for immunity.
Asserting that Morocco had signed the Rome Statute as a first step
toward ratification, the coordinator of the Moroccan Coalition for
the ICC, Hicham Cherkaoui, countered the minister's statement by
insisting that there was no real contradiction between the Moroccan
Constitution and Article 27 of the Rome Statute. Cherkaoui emphasized, "Actually, Morocco is in violation to its commitment to the ICC
and . . . the Moroccan diplomatic representatives should affirm international criminal justice values by attending to actual events related to
the international criminal justice."[40]
Claiming that the king of Morocco has a sacred capacity and enjoys
an absolute immunity, Benaissa then reasserted the primacy of Moroccan constitutionalism and the (Moroccan) political and religious duty
to respect it. "Chapter 23 of the Moroccan Constitution states that the
King's capacity is sacred and should not be violated. The purpose of
the immunity is to enable the King to perform all of his duties without
any obstruction. Indeed, this form of immunity contradicts Article '27,'
which renders problematic all immunities of official capacities."[41]
To this, NGO activist Cherkaoui responded:

> I am greatly surprised, because such [a] response might have been acceptable
> in 2000 before Morocco signed the Rome Statute. But coming six years
> after signing this Statute, this response indicates that Morocco has not only
> violated its international commitments as [a] member in the Human Rights
> council, but has also neglected the recommendation of the Committee of
> Equity and Reconciliation to ratify the Rome Statute. The Minister of the
> Foreign Affairs should know that 104 states have ratified the Rome Statute
> even though they had the same legal and constitutional obstacles.[42]

He later expanded on the immunity question and on the need to con-
temporize older legal forms:

> [T]he older immunities model served a given purpose but it is not meant
> to facilitate and guarantee that he [the King] escapes from punishment if
> he commits genocides, crimes against humanity, or war crimes. These are
> crimes that the president of the state is not expected to commit. These
> crimes do not fall within the official duties of any member of the parliament
> or government officials, thus, such crimes are not covered by the immunity.
> If we look at this issue from this point of view, we will find that there is
> no contradiction between the Moroccan Constitution and article 27 of the
> Rome Statute.... [T]here are many legal and constitutional obstacles and
> difficulties, but they can be overcome like many states did – if Morocco
> has the political will of Morocco to first ratify the Rome Statute and then
> harmonize its national legislations. Constitutions are not sacred documents.
> They can be amended in accordance with the needs of the society.

Like the friction (in Tsing's terms) between the United States and
the officers of the court,[43] this dialogue between the minister of foreign
affairs and the NGO advocate is typical of the kind of interchange that
has accompanied efforts to achieve the jurisdictional reach of the ICC.
Through such complex and intensive efforts to convert critics into
advocates, NGOs are playing a central role in mobilizing governments
to ratify the Rome Statute. These efforts are in turn making possible
the rapid norm-generating machinery of the ICC in which new rule
of law initiatives and human rights articulations are being posited as
"universal" – the ultimate moral basis on which international tribunals
are able to push beyond not only the limits of various types of monar-
chy and religious governance identified as antiquated by many in this
movement but also beyond the limits of the state. These reconfigurations of state governance highlight the problematics at the center of
the cultural life of rule of law liberalism: the regulating of a nation's law
and its subjects according to key extranational liberal commitments to
rule of law principles.

The CICC and State Constitutions: Rome Statute
Implementation in Africa
With the goal of ensuring the universality of the Rome Statute, the
primary objective of many of the activists engaged in CICC organizing
is to ensure implementation of the Rome Statute in as many countries
as possible. As of 2008, 146 countries had signed the Rome Statute

of the ICC, and 108 nation-states from every continent, including three permanent members of the UN Security Council (France, Russia, and the United Kingdom), had also ratified the Rome Statute, with Madagascar, Suriname, and the Cook Islands being the most recent.[44] With more than three-quarters of the world's states as signatories to this treaty, the challenge today, then – as far as moving the jurisdiction of the court forward – centers on whether the statute is compatible with national constitutions. When states ratify a treaty and incorporate it into domestic law, they agree to the interface between international law and national constitutionalism. As NGO advocates often articulate, including an interlocutor with the Nigerian Coalition for the ICC whom I rename here "Henry" has argued with conviction, "for the ICC to execute its ideal duties fully, member states *must* [emphasis mine] fulfill their obligation to incorporate the terms of the statute into their national laws"[45] (interview in Nigeria, July 2005).

In this regard, most nation-states have one of two approaches to international treaties built into in their constitution. One approach, used by such states as Germany and Sweden, follows the norm of the self-executing treaty: In these cases, signed treaties are automatically incorporated into national law, and no further legislative changes are required. The second, more frequent type of constitutional structure allows for the applicability of treaties only if they are legislatively incorporated.[46] In this latter case, the treaty is not expected to have a domestic effect until implemented by domestic legislation.

Once implemented, the treaty itself is not technically the law; rather, it is the implementing legislation that represents the effective law. As of November 1, 2007, of the ninety-nine states that require domestic legislation to ratify the Rome Statute, fewer than forty had enacted such legislation. For states engaged in the treaty implementation process, progress is slow and involves multiple levels of advisory review, presentation, revision, and debate. This is as much a political exercise as a legal one, and it produces many cautionary warnings and heated debates about how to safeguard national interests while upholding international ideals.

This reality is well illustrated by several African cases (one of which I explore in Chapter 3).[47] NGOs and African states were active during the ICC Preparatory Conferences of 1996–8 and continue to play key roles in the growing membership of the ICC. Senegal was the first country in the world to deposit its instrument of ratification of the Rome Statute, doing so on February 2, 1999, and by mid-2006, twenty-six other African states, out of a total of a hundred states that were member states parties, had done so. In 2008, there were four investigations being conducted by the prosecutor for the ICC, all in African countries: the DRC, Uganda, Sudan, and the Central African Republic. Despite the ongoing contestations over the sovereignty of these countries to try their own cases, the various regional bodies, such as the African Union, outlined a 2004–7 Strategic Action Plan that called for the participation of African countries in the ICC through the ratification of the Rome Statute.

Notwithstanding this apparent support for the ICC, as of September 2007, South Africa was the only African country to have fully implemented the Rome Statute. Through the networking strategies of the CICC, several regional coalitions of rule of law NGOs (e.g., the Nigerian Coalition [NCICC], the Zambian Coalition, and the Uganda Coalition [UCICC] for the ICC) have been created since 2002 to work with African states toward implementation. The NCICC, for example, continues to be a central actor in pressuring West African governments to ratify international treaties and implement codes of the statute. However, like its Ugandan counterpart, the NCICC has not succeeded in achieving implementation of the Rome Statute in its home country.

Spurred by the current investigations into criminal responsibility of perpetrators of violence in Uganda and the DRC, many African NGOs have expanded their mandate from direct implementation to include the coordinating work of ensuring that state laws are compliant with international treaties as they are gradually implemented. However, these efforts remain in the realm of securing political and civil rights for people who are victims of the various crimes enumerated by the Rome Statute. Their only means of securing economic rights and provisions for their people is in the realm of victimhood: the Victims Trust Fund[48] is set aside to protect the rights of victims and support those whose perpetrators have been found guilty by the court of law.

Thus, states ultimately carry the constituent power for reform of their own laws to further the political and civil protection of the rights of their citizens; but ensuring that state laws are compliant with international laws involves providing expert analysis and assistance in the rewriting of national bills. The CICC is centrally involved in this project in Uganda, for instance, where it works closely with a local coalition of Ugandan human rights NGOs and those that constitute the UCICC. The CICC has set up a Ugandan coordinator for East Africa, who is working alongside the CICC and the UCICC to achieve legislative implementation of the Rome Statute. To attain this goal, the UCICC has required tremendous financial support from international donors and the help of lawyers and other human rights brokers to work with local members of Parliament to rewrite the national bill to be presented to the Ugandan Parliament.[49]

The signing and ratification of the Rome Statute, like the adoption of many other human rights–motivated treaties, is less a function of the profundity of the "buy-in" of the rule of law than a result of the reconfiguration and retooling of global capital institutions. Today, the financial resources being brokered with international lending institutions are increasingly linked to state compliance with international rule of law and human rights standards. Significant donor funding has therefore shifted from supporting governments to supporting independent NGOs. This move has also had implications for how we understand the embodiment of different forms of governmentality in postcolonial Africa today; but the relevant point is its unself-conscious concealment of the process of constructing a moral economy around which it circulates in uneven relations of power.

DEVELOPING AFRICA – FROM THE OUTSIDE IN

Extraction and the "Public Good"

The history of "benevolent" involvement in Africa far predates the rise of NGOs. Long before European colonialism in sub-Saharan Africa, secret societies such as clan groups and religious formations were a central vehicle for community organizing. As far back as the late 1870s and 1880s, African development associations existed throughout the region, and these local associations continued into the colonial period. With increasing urbanization and colonial influence in the late nineteenth and early twentieth centuries, however, Christian missions and Islamic associations with international ties began to assume greater control over providing education and various health care services. By the mid-twentieth century, colonial enterprises in collaboration with private corporations and nonprofit foundations – with wealth garnered from commodities and industries including steel manufacturing, computers, and car insurance – began engaging in widespread resource extraction while articulating the mutual benefits of such ventures as involving the redistribution of wealth for the "public good."

In the interest of continuing their mineral extraction efforts, various corporations assisted in defining national agendas in the countries where they worked. This meant that while promoting a positive corporate image, initiatives that were billed as being for the public good were in fact self-serving strategies for pushing through changes that would enhance their abilities to make money off the resources of the countries (Michael 2004; Barnes 2005). For example, mining has long played a key role in African economic development. Southern African countries such as South Africa, Namibia, Zambia, Angola, Zimbabwe, and Botswana – states rich in natural minerals, holding many of the earth's mineral reserves, including gold, cobalt, and platinum – have over the years provided corporate investors with many resource extraction opportunities. In the fourteen-state Southern African Development Community (SADC), the mining industry contributes roughly 60 percent of foreign exchange earnings, 10 percent of GDP, and 5 percent of employment. Eight of SADC's member states derive 22 to 90 percent of their foreign exchange directly from mining and mineral exploitation,[50] and these economic resources have gone into sustaining social services in the public sector – building roads, maintaining national railroad services, shipping and import sectors, and educational technical training institutions. However, the environmental costs of large-scale mining in regions have been substantial, with long-term ecological and monetary effects ranging from problems of land conversion and degradation to habitat conversion and groundwater pollution.

Land and environmental issues in Africa are also becoming increasingly important because the main gold belt where surface gold mining is being conducted is mostly located on former indigenous lands and cropping zones and is increasingly encroaching on the agricultural regions. Once this land is mined, its uselessness for agriculture is irreversible. These various effects of mining have been widespread throughout sub-Saharan Africa, leading to large volumes of waste and, in some cases, chemical pollution that have devastating effects on regional ecosystems.[51] Such consequences of environmental degradation have lead to significant economic profits and, in some cases, a small amount of profits channeled into sustaining local services through various NGOs and CBOs of the region.

During later periods in the twentieth century, oil production in Africa became significant in corporate and governmental management. Today, with the recent discovery of crude oil reserves in Sudan, East Africa may well become a crude oil exporter like all other subregions of Africa.[52] Oil drilling and investment capital have been key factors in Africa's economic growth. However, these oil resources have also contributed to environmental degradation and civil conflict. To prevent the return of civil strife, or to prevent its inception, growing numbers of African states are working with international organizations such as Amnesty International, Human Rights First, and Doctors Without Borders to establish institutional systems that promote investment in social services. The government of Chad, in collaboration with the World Bank and various nonprofit NGOs, has been working to channel its oil revenues so as to benefit the indigent and not only large corporations. The challenges, of course, have involved determining exactly which sectors of society should benefit from oil profits.[53] This decision making has varied from the participation of states, international organizations, international monetary institutions, and various NGO forms of governance.

Reconfigurations of State Practices

By the late nineteenth century, the state had become the primary field of governance in Western Europe, and the protection of its sovereignty central to the welfare of its citizens (Hansen and Stepputat 2005). This (co)dependency relied on the unifying construction of a nationalism that was itself based on the imagining of a common ancestry or "culture." This period also saw the development of regimes of multiply tiered nation-states, differently connected to colonies and territories, for which explicit state laws designated the limits of what could take place within state boundaries.

Along with the ongoing spread of colonial occupation of new territories came differently tiered relationships of power and various hierarchies of governance. The system of governance yielded multiple systems of rule by locating people differently based on their relationship to European imperial power. This produced "citizens" and "subjects" and, through various hierarchies, shaped the formation of "subject-citizens" (Mamdani 1996). In colonial states, either the laws of imperial powers prevailed alongside "traditional custom" or the politics of plunder enabled the management of violated bodies that did not matter to the crown. Such forms of governance shaped the basis for the crafting of not only particular types of subjects but also particular hierarchies of belonging. These hierarchies were often ordered within the hegemonic production of national identity and forms of religious morality, nationalism, and racial purity that underlay different human hierarchies of scale.

Nevertheless, it is not the complexities of state making that is often rehearsed in telling the story of state sovereignty (or its reconfiguration).

Rather, contemporary human rights literature has tended to trace a genealogy that describes the nineteenth century as a period in which the interference of one state in the affairs of another state, in order to assist the enforcing of obedience to a governing authority, was a moral dilemma – one that, through discourses of universal protections, later gave international human rights institutions their power to intervene. Accordingly, we are today the inheritors of a widespread trend toward the internationalism of legal jurisdiction over the punishment of violence, the choreography of "peace," and the everyday management of life and death. Yet this discourse of internationalism has historically obscured – and even facilitated – the persisting inequalities among nation-states.

Having fought ten civil wars in the past two decades – many rooted in mineral resource management, ethnic strife, and religious politics – the majority of new innovations in international courts and tribunals can be found on the African continent. The signing of international treaties is increasingly economically linked to democratic restructuring mandates. African states that have signed and ratified treaties such as the Rome Statute are actually experiencing a form of governmental reorganization that some have seen as the weakening of their capacities to protect their borders, manage their populations, and control their markets and currencies (Hansen and Stepputat 2005:32). However, this is taking shape alongside the strengthening of regional forms of governance and state attempts to consolidate power for resource control. Indeed, multiple brokers – including postcolonial state actors in Africa and elsewhere – are vying to control the terms of governance that constitute the basis for justice.

Partnering for Public Services

To strengthen the ability of African states to collaborate and protect the needs of their people, partnerships among financial institutions, international organizations, and states have been on the rise over the past thirty years. The Ford Foundation, for example, was one of the largest of these donors working in West Africa, its mission reflecting another set of strategies for which hoped-for gains in capacity building were often undermined by the depths of national poverty in various regions. The foundation's first grants, beginning in 1958, were made in the public service sector and involved a commitment to the training of professionals out of their central West African office in Lagos. Between 1958 and 2005, more than six hundred individual and institutional grants amounting to US$250 million had been awarded to various institutions interested in capacity building, good governance, transparency, and development of a politics of *justice talk* among members of urban and rural African *civil societies*.

A major initiative began in 2000 with the Partnership to Strengthen African Universities, a collaboration among the Ford, MacArthur, Carnegie, and Rockefeller foundations that initially dedicated US$100 million over five years.[54] A year later, the Organization of African Unity (OAU) combined two plans for Africa's economic regeneration – one fostered by South Africa, Nigeria, and Algeria, the other by Senegal – into the New Partnership for Africa's Development (NEPAD) with the goal of developing an integrated socioeconomic development framework for Africa.[55] What we see here in the new century is the rechanneling of donor funds within Africa – funds that are being used to foster NGO influence. Some of the beneficiary organizations represent some of the largest and more established throughout the continent, and others represent relatively new organizations, the leaders of which are African returnees to their countries of birth from the United Kingdom, Canada, Australia, Germany, France, or the United States.

Today, through an ever-expanding rule of law economy, the constituent power to shape governance is being propelled by other holders of donor capital as well. Various non-U.S. grant-making institutions, especially in Europe, are also prominent in West African philanthropy. For example, Volkswagen of South Africa recently granted ZAR 1.2 million (c. US$161,000), through its Community Trust, to cover a number of students at Nelson Mandela Metropolitan University for four years; the trust has other programs supporting students from preschool up to higher education.[56] The Volkswagen Foundation, in Hannover, Germany, earmarked €1.9 million for cooperative research projects in sub-Saharan Africa.[57] Much of this funding goes to NGOs.

NGOs have also benefited from the "problem" of the postcolonial African state. From the 1960s to the 1990s, African states were riddled with dictatorships and military governments, many of which lacked the ability to implement public programs. They were laden with heavy debts from earlier regimes as well as various economic and political scandals and, in their politically and economically weakened condition, were dismissed by international donors as "corrupt." Furthermore, at times their military officials were themselves the perpetrators of violence against their citizens. As a result, international donors began looking to nongovernmental spheres, such as nonprofit organizations or the private sector, as alternatives to "development" (Michael 2004).

Mortgaging Africa's Future: The Fine Print on Loans

As funds were redirected elsewhere, many sub-Saharan African economies were embedded in serious crises. Official investments were either on the decline or were attached with particular conditions – for example, those of the Structural Adjustment Programs (SAPs) of the World Bank and the International Monetary Fund (IMF), policy-change programs created with the goal of reducing the borrowing country's fiscal imbalances. These lending institutions (jointly known as the Bretton Woods Institutions) insisted on developing countries effecting various "conditionalities" to secure new loans or obtain lower interest rates on existing loans – one such conditionality often being international treaty ratification and implementation. These policy changes have not always contributed short-term benefits to African economies; moreover, the money lent had to be spent in accordance with the overall goals of the loan, and not necessarily the immediate economic needs of the populace. The loans offered were described as promoting economic growth through which to generate household income, which would enable states to pay off accumulated state debt, rising interest rates, and debt accumulation. However, because SAPs open countries to foreign corporate investment – such as factories that exploit cheap local labor and lack of environmental regulation to enhance their profitability – the ongoing influx of investment capital is diverted outside of Southern national economies. The implementation of structural adjustment policies has thus widened the gap between rich and poor and produced worldwide deindustrialization, creating a mirroring "community" of economic refugees even as the rise of financial, service, and informal economic sectors pump wealth into new global cities of elite consumers (Clarke and Thomas 2006).

By the mid-1980s, these new funding strategies were in full swing. With the end of the Cold War in the early 1990s and the success of the United States in "winning" the fight for democracy, increasing numbers of sub-Saharan African governments were in economic crisis because of the withdrawal of U.S. and Soviet financial support. Additionally, the mid-1970s and early 1980s were a period in which some African economies were being pilfered by corrupt governments, and international donors were being called on to support efforts to topple "totalitarian regimes" and support neoliberalism, with its accompanying conditionalities and free-trade initiatives.

In Ghana in the 1970s and 1980s, for example, loans made available to the Ghanaian state focused on increased cocoa production in an effort to foster export earnings, the reduction of budget deficits, and currency devaluation. These economic measures led not only to the development of new leadership under the guidance of President Jerry Rawlings but also to a shift from a socialist economic policy to that of a newly defined form of capitalist economics – and with that, an agreement to accept the terms and conditions under an SAP. Under that SAP, the Ghanaian economy was to expect an approximate growth of 8 percent in export volume from 1987 to 1990. In actuality, and on account of poor external trade and lack of export diversity, economic growth was for a short time negative and averaged less than 2 percent for this period. The consequences included a decline in wages and further deterioration of social infrastructure, such as health and education.

In the Sudan, a country engaged in civil war over the past twenty-five years, the state has undergone several neoliberal reforms mandated by the Bretton Woods Institutions since 1978. As part of Sudan's SAP, the IMF and the International Bank for Reconstruction and Development promoted the exportation of cotton and grain. Business owners were encouraged to buy leases on large parcels of land, and various brokers – against the advice of government agents – cleared the land of all trees and herds and redirected it toward increasing the production of these crops for export. Because local consumption was no longer a priority, this resulted in the underproduction of food, the erosion of once fertile land, and the displacement of thousands of farmers and land laborers. The eventual violent struggles over the control of oil and other resources led the country into civil war. In February 1986, the IMF declared Sudan ineligible for loans and grants because of the government's inability to settle its arrears fund.

NGOs Ascendant: Who Sets the Agenda?

Given the growing impotence of so many sub-Saharan African states to determine their economic strategy without international institutional dictates, by the mid-1990s, African NGOs working in partnership with international NGOs and various transnational corporations had become the popular mechanisms for reaching those most in need of aid, replacing the postcolonial state in this role. "Manageable" in size, NGOs were supported by international donors to pursue democratic pluralism in the political arena through which to emphasize principles of democracy, gender parity, and transparency through a prevailing discourse of "rights talk" and general principles of individualism. These international NGOs, nonelected organizations with budgets as large as a regularly functioning corporation, thus became public intermediaries, increasingly central to the transnational flow of ideas from international organizations to national cultural domains. In a symbiotic way, they furthered the political aims of economic donors of the 1980s and 1990s while benefiting directly from their patronage.

In formal development initiatives, the United Nations has also promoted the role of NGOs. In her book on NGOs in the Global South, Sarah Michael (2004) points out that the "UN's Economic and Social Council [ECOSOC] now grants consultative status on its work to 2,234 NGOs from around the world." Citing Michael Chege's 1999 paper "Politics of Development" and the ECOSOC report of 2003, she compares this number to the mere forty-one NGOs that were similarly involved in UN work in the 1940s. She also notes:

> Even the World Bank, often primarily focused on large-scale development and infrastructure projects, recognizes NGOs as vital to its work. In 1998, 50 percent of the projects it approved incorporated NGO participation, a marked increase from 1973, when only 6 percent of Bank projects involved NGOs. The growth in number, scope and profile of African NGOs over the last thirty years mirrors these general trends among Southern NGOs. Of all the regions of the developing world, it is Africa that has experienced the most marked proliferation of NGOs in recent years – rapidly expanding NGO sectors have been a phenomenon of Ghana after its economic collapse, Zimbabwe after independence, and South Africa after apartheid.

In part because of the purported "weakness" of postcolonial governments, powerful human rights and rule of law NGOs have become recognized and institutionalized in the African development scene. Their members tend to speak from a place of authority on issues that affect indigent communities, and some have been able to influence national and international spheres of public policy by expanding into new geographic sites and engaging in unprecedented partnerships (Michael 2004). The consequence, however, has been that flows of official development assistance (ODA) from Western states to those of the developing world declined by an estimated 25 percent during 1991–2001, with a drop of more than 50 percent in ODA flowing to seven African nations in that period.[58]

As I have shown, the idea of the moral fortitude of human rights and the rule of law is not being circulated by government officials alone. NGOs are playing powerful roles in championing the international struggles for human rights and arguing for the implementation of international law agendas. This is enabled by governmental and nongovernmental donor funding arrangements that have involved the targeting of specific initiatives within donor countries or the allocation of a small amount of donor funds to various international NGOs. Whether giving large amounts or small, all donors have introduced criteria to determine eligibility of potential funding. These criteria, like the terms of SAPs that have debilitated African economies, determine the conditions for funding and the amounts to be allocated to nonproject funds.

Today, with the absence of significant philanthropy originating within the African continent, many of the donors are from the North and continue to offer direct funding to Southern NGOs. Such donor–NGO initiatives became prominent in the early 1980s and have continued to expand. However, this relationship has not always been one of mutually agreeable conditions for agenda setting, for the rise in donor funding has led to a rise in the role of official aid agencies to determine the conditions for the use of donor funds, forcing African human rights advocacy groups to continue to develop projects that these international agencies are interested in funding. Further, where the agencies and NGOs have competing approaches to development, there has been considerable conflict over what NGOs refer to as the *reverse agenda* – the process through which NGOs influence the activities and perceptions of donors and official aid programs.

One pathway that remains invisible is the form of donor procurement known popularly in West Africa as *donor dancing*, in which members of NGOs attract sponsors willing to support particular aspects of an organization's activities and then must submit ongoing reports using the organization's reporting guidelines, mechanisms for documentation and service, and narrative structure to maintain the program.

Donor Capitalism to the Rescue?
What projects are being enabled by the rise in the rule of law economy? What projects are going unfunded? What directions are not being pursued as a result of these collaborations? Such questions lie at the

heart of this inquiry and call for a rethinking of political rights and the mechanisms of morality and global capital that are engaged in the production of international justice. The international spheres of inter-action under scrutiny here reflect not simply viable spaces for the internalization of constitutional rule of law principles but also the locus for the vernacularization and mobilization of justice-making mechanisms in socially and culturally familiar contexts.

One champion of "democratization movements" is the Soros Foundations Network, funded by the Hungarian-born American billionaire George Soros, which since 1984 has offered private grants to support various foundations in the former Soviet Union and Central and Eastern Europe. This network, supported since 1993 by Soros's Open Society Institute (OSI), aims to shape public policy to promote democratic governance, human rights, and economic, legal, and social reform. In Eastern Europe, its network of foundations has helped countries with their transition from communism to capitalism, implementing initiatives (as elsewhere) to support the rule of law, education, public health, and independent media, always working toward building alliances across borders and continents on issues ranging from combating corruption to the prevention of human rights abuses. Soros has also supported projects throughout the Global South. OSI's support of African-based projects, in part through its regional initiatives, is widespread and particular to transitional governance and social health. Further, like the many thousands of donor agencies globally, OSI and the network's foundations collaborate with NGOs to help them with their own projects, contributing funds on a subcontract basis.

The John D. and Catherine T. MacArthur Foundation has been similarly involved in widespread initiatives to defend human rights. It has an office in the Nigerian capital of Abuja and, since 1989, has been offering more grants to NGOs, universities, and independent institutions to strengthen them and help them carry out their various missions. The Bill and Melinda Gates Foundation has played a significant role in NGO development projects by contributing to health improvement in various West African countries, including Nigeria. In addition to the Gates Foundation, the four major private foundations – Ford, Carnegie, MacArthur, and Rockefeller – are among the top two hundred private charitable philanthropic agencies; in 2002, this added up to a total of 57,834 U.S.-based international donor organizations with combined assets of US$364.1 billion.[59] Between 2004 and 2005, giving increased by 10.1 percent among the top twenty-five foundations overall, with the top-listed Gates Foundation disbursing US$1,356,250,292 (up 8 percent) and the Ford Foundation US$516,907,177 (down 1.1 percent).[60]

The United States, Canada, Norway, and Sweden are among the leading bilateral governmental donors that have all channeled substantial funds to local NGOs, with a heavy concentration in South Asia and Africa. These donations tend to fall into three categories. The first is to provide emergency relief to populations in need by offering funds to NGO development projects that are working on the ground to make a difference. The second is to support education and health projects for which the goal is to reach the poor and improve their lives. The third is to support those organizations that can provide aid despite a variety of funding obstacles – especially obstacles introduced as a result of various corrupt governmental practices.

Although historically most of the official donor funds have gone to support the work of NGOs based in donor countries, the majority of those funds that made it to Southern countries supported their salaries. This was because, during the early years, there were few viable and effective indigenous NGOs. Yet over the past twenty years, there has been rapid growth in both the number and the capabilities of NGOs based in the South. Their growth has varied from country to country, but effective Southern NGOs generally emerged earliest in South and East Asia (in countries such as India and the Philippines) and in a number of countries in Latin America (such as Chile, Brazil, and Nicaragua). Only in the past fifteen years has there been rapid growth in the number and importance of indigenous NGOs in Africa, and their influence varies markedly across countries. Although many Southern human rights organizations have quite radical agendas, the majority of legal activists working toward the implementation of the Rome Statute are not particularly radical. Rather, they tend to work in concert with donor agendas and produce spaces for the internationalization of central liberalist commitments to international secular governmentality.

One of the largest human rights organizations in Nigeria, the Civil Liberties Organization (CLO), has been engaged in donor networking since the mid-1980s. Their 2004 budget of more than US$2 million reflects their continued relationships with their long-term funding agencies from around the world, including the Ford Foundation, New York; Germany's Misereor-EZE; Prison Watch International (to fund a South African police awareness project aimed at educating Nigerian police on new rights dispensations); Human Rights First; Action Aid – Nigeria (to fund the CLO legal department); U.S. AID; the British Council; Human Rights Watch – Switzerland; the Danish Centre for Human Rights (to fund human rights training for lower court judges); Amnesty International; and Cord Aid (with a contribution of €150,000 to the Women's Rights Project of the CLO, a media advocacy program).[61] One of the characteristic approaches to developing participatory planning for CLO, as is the case for most NGOs in the South, has involved assessing a gender dimension of all of their programs. Concern with gender has not only been used to shape regional programs in target areas but has also become a standard in donor vocabulary and part of mainstream donor agendas globally. The identification and application of gender and particular approaches to gendered equality are examples of the kinds of agenda and programmatic priority being shaped by external institutions. Moreover, the focus on gender has often set in place particular standards of distinction that are not always relevant: for example, the use of gender priorities that assume the absence of female power in Nigerian Islamic communities has at times involved the misinterpretation of different gendered nodes of power. This might also be contrasted with the refusal by some donors to fund personal loan programs for women and men to help to build farms, and thus new economic means of production – a new innovative set of microcredit programs popular through particular CBO-based projects in a range of African contexts, although most popularly growing in South Asian contexts.

In the early 2000s, the Centre for Democracy and Development (CDD), the most powerful NGO in Nigeria, had an annual estimated budget of US$266,154 incoming funds and $211,378 expended funds; it has recently developed a model for the first NGO conference center and hotel in Africa. As listed in its annual report, CDD – Nigeria's funding comes from: Comic Relief Charity Project, United Kingdom; Commission of the European Union, Belgium; International Centre for Rights and Democratic Development, Canada; International Development Research Centre, Canada; John D. and Catherine T. McArthur Foundation, United States; National Lotteries Charity Board, United Kingdom; Swedish International Development Agency; Body Shop International, United Kingdom; the European Union; Ford Foundation, United States; and Westminster Foundation for Democracy, United Kingdom.[62] This list highlights the range of international donor companies engaged in supporting specific projects that enable particular political rights agendas rather than long-term economic and social goals.

Many of these same donors fund similar political rights projects sponsored by international NGOs such as Amnesty International, Human Rights Watch, and what is now Human Rights First. These "Western" NGOs are themselves linked and indebted to donors who are allowed to participate in the shaping of their priorities in exchange for generously funding their projects. The first was Amnesty International, established in 1961; the largest such organization, as of 2008, it claimed to have "more than 2.2 million members, supporters and subscribers in over 150 countries and territories."[63] Member-based and independent from government, religion, and the political views of individual victims, Amnesty International raises money through pledges and donations; according to its 2006 annual report, its annual expenditures totaled nearly US$54 million.[64]

Human Rights Watch is the largest U.S.-based international NGO with connections to Africa; it posted expenditures totaling US$30,185,486 for fiscal year ending June 30, 2006.[65] An institution for the creation of new mechanisms to monitor and report human rights violations, it began in 1978 as Helsinki Watch; in 1981, New York–based Americas Watch was added, and then Asia Watch in 1985. The Human Rights Watch umbrella organization was adopted in 1988, and by 2000, it had divisions in Asia, Europe, the Middle East, and North Africa. Unlike Amnesty International, which is answerable to its members, Human Rights Watch is supported by contributions from private individuals and foundations worldwide. Like various international NGOs, it does not accept government funds directly or indirectly; however, because it is donor driven, it is not fully independent from the agendas of its donors.

Another prominent human rights organization is Human Rights First. Formerly known as the Lawyers Committee for Human Rights, it came into existence in 1978 and now focuses on building legal institutions and structures to guarantee long-term human rights. During 2007, its annual expenditures were US$31,480,886.[66] By insisting governments use the rule of law to press for greater integration of human rights into the practices and policies of the UN, the World Bank, national governments, and international bodies, Human Rights First works to protest discriminatory policies with international implications.

As this mapping of donors and recipients indicates, there is a growing collaboration between donors and various human rights agendas.

Increasingly, donors are becoming interested in topics that have become central to the human rights agenda: enhancing the status of women; alleviating poverty; and taking action to enhance human rights and democratic processes, strengthen civil society, empower the indigent, and strengthen the organizations to which these members of the disenfranchised belong. These overlapping objectives of donor and recipient agendas provide evidence of a widening group of initiatives in which both are engaged. In the case of human rights agendas, donors are making explicit their stated objectives of enhancing democratization globally and strengthening political and social rights.

Interestingly, the distinction between political and social rights, on the one hand, and economic and social rights, on the other, makes clear the ways that contemporary funding strategies are increasingly drawing on international support and, thus, increasingly engaged in a new form of postcolonial governmentality in which it is not the state per se that is involved in the direct biopolitical shaping of the subject. Rather, through state consent mechanisms (such as treaty ratification and economic terms for reporting donor aid), new international legal institutions are being reshaped and setting new terms for compliance and jurisdiction. In contrast to the Anglo-European liberalist tradition, in which ideas of aid, governance, and trade were once negotiated solely in the realm of the state, the social practices now articulated are being realized through transnational micropractices in which state agendas are being shaped by an extranational sphere of practices that exist in transnationally relevant domains of governance.

Today, with the rule of law at the helm of direct funding initiatives in Africa, increasing numbers of African NGOs are joining funding coalitions and aid networks with other Northern human rights groups, such as Amnesty International and Human Rights Watch, to build widening coalitions to support national implementation campaigns and treaty compatibility goals. As part of this global trend, increasing numbers of African NGO members are traveling from their countries of origin to conferences, seminars for short-term trainings, meetings with potential donors, and job interviews with richer international organizations in search of Africa specialists. Such travel ranges from shorter trips in the interest of developing "capacity building" credentials, to longer-term migration to the "West" with the stated goal of one day returning to the country of origin. This is taking shape through the development of a "sense of economy," in the most direct sense of the term – in which ideologies, practices, and structures of international imperatives are creating linkages as well as making evident the differences in the political and cultural agendas of various African-based rule of law advocates.

CONCLUSION

In this post–Cold War period of increasing United Nations involvement in the production of human rights norms, what is central to understanding the making of rule of law truth regimes is the growth not only of new twentieth-century actors negotiating the terms of economic development, or underdevelopment, but of a new class of actors on the world stage engaged in the production of a particular moral economy of justice: NGOs working on behalf of what they refer to as "civil society." Their fight for human rights is an ideological contest for the establishment of what James Ferguson (2006) has argued is that which grants membership and access to "Western" institutional power – the power of information, the power of capital, the power of mobility. Further, acquisition of such powers depends on the acceptance of certain development and human rights agendas. Through particular agendas set aside to support and maintain human life, and enabled by the growth of a rule of law economy, NGOs are thus participating in the development of a new global biopolitical sphere of human management, which, although mobilized in the name of the victim, is also embedded in a contradictory relationship with death as its underside.

Driven by the rapid deregulation of capital markets, known by the production of free-trade zones and market liberalism, international nongovernmental and governmental organizations have reconstituted themselves to propel interconnections among states, world citizens, and local communities, as well as new visions that promote the individual responsibility of commanders and perpetrators of violence. Characteristic of such groupings of NGOs is the formation of what Peter Haas (1992b:187–8) has referred to as an *epistemic community* in which the growth of a broad-based national and international elite has produced "a knowledge-based network of specialists who share beliefs in cause-and-effect relations, validity tests, and underlying principled values and pursue common policy goals." In this regard, I have examined the ways that these knowledge networks or liberalist truth regimes are tied to "philanthropic" capital and are empowering an elite that is working with a variety of technocratic methods ultimately to protect its donors' interests as brokers of neoliberal capitalism through the spread of ICC-based rule of law. This community of elite actors is also generating a culture of "normative" cosmopolitanism – a political and philosophical discourse of human rights and global justice, of global institutions and individual responsibility beyond the national. Their discourse privileges law and fundamental notions of justice on the one hand, and cultural hybridity and border crossings on the other. However, such forms of elite cosmopolitanisms are operating within a discrepant human rights order that is complicated, and sometimes undermined, by persisting postcolonial economic colonialisms and intricate regional divisions that define social value differently. For justice is made within particular moral economies and is an effect that exists not just through its utterance but also through the enactment of micropractices – ideologies, practices, and technical forms and processes that shape the meaning of justice itself.

How can such an odd combination of morality-driven ambitions and political economy coexist? They do so largely through naturalizing processes and financial webs that wed the rule of law economy to the development of a larger regime of knowledge and power in which the state and multinational corporations come to represent a new ontology of universality. This regime is embedded in the growth of particular market alliances that contribute to presenting a set of relations as if they are universally shared, although this is far from the empirical reality. The mystery of the shifting notion of individual criminal responsibility is in its ability to imbue with magical qualities the allure of victim's rights, so that our values and motivations are based on a notion of rights that is derived through humanitarian protectionism. This discourse of victims' rights as justice is made real through moral cultivation, technical production, and economic and military power. It expresses the unreality of securing economic rights in practice for maximizing life-producing options. Instead, this current enactment of ICC political rights secured under the Rome Statute represents the active construction of conditions for "justice" and their enactment as such. In other words, by focusing on political and civil rights, the neoliberal rule of law project has led to the production of conditions for securing rights in the contemporary arena in a way that has left unaddressed the implementation of economic social and cultural rights as a necessary precondition for rights themselves.

CHAPTER 2

CRAFTING THE VICTIM, CRAFTING THE PERPETRATOR: NEW SPACES OF POWER, NEW SPECTERS OF JUSTICE

The case against Thomas Lubanga Dyilo was the first to be brought before the International Criminal Court (ICC) Pre-Trial Chamber. It also marks the first time an individual engaged in noninternational crimes was brought before an international court solely on the basis of those acts. What were his noninternational crimes? On August 28, 2006, the Office of the Prosecutor of the ICC filed a document containing the charges against Lubanga Dyilo. It outlined three counts of war crimes charges, under the Rome Statute, for which he was being held:

Count 1: CONSCRIPTING CHILDREN INTO ARMED GROUPS, a WAR CRIME, punishable under Articles 8(2)(e)(vii) and 25(3)(a) of the Rome Statute.

Count 2: ENLISTING CHILDREN INTO ARMED GROUPS, a WAR CRIME, punishable under Articles 8(2)(e)(vii) and 25(3)(a) of the Rome Statute.

Count 3: USING CHILDREN TO PARTICIPATE ACTIVELY IN HOSTILITIES, a WAR CRIME, punishable under Articles 8(2)(e)(vii) and 25(3)(a) of the Rome Statute.[1]

According to the evidence, Lubanga Dyilo did not *personally* conscript children into the rebel war. Instead, at the time the crimes were committed, he was acting as president of the Union des Patriotes Congolais (UPC) and the commander-in-chief of its former military wing, the Forces Patriotiques pour la Libération du Congo (FPLC). When the ICC's jurisdiction began, and throughout 2003, FPLC commanders were enlisting, forcibly recruiting, and abducting children into the ranks of the FPLC, using them to participate actively in hostilities in the Ituri district of the Democratic Republic of the Congo (DRC). The prosecution has argued that, in his leadership positions, Lubanga Dyilo played an overall coordinating role in the UPC/FPLC's policy to recruit and enlist child soldiers and that he provided the organizational, infrastructural, and logistical framework for its implementation.[2]

This charge has implications for both the international management and the assignment of responsibility of war crimes, as well as for the moral economies[3] within which such initiatives are being pursued. The ICC is becoming increasingly authoritative in managing global violence on the world scene. In particular, brokers working through the ICC have taken a stand against recruiting child soldiers in national conflicts by establishing what is intended to be a punitive deterrent for future violators.

CHILD SOLDIERS: SPECTERS OF INTERNATIONAL JUSTICE

International perspectives on the recruitment of child soldiers have changed greatly over the past two decades. Although the Convention on the Rights of the Child, adopted in 1989, prohibits the recruitment of children under age fifteen, recruitment has not always been thought to warrant prosecution as a criminal act of individual responsibility. In fact, the then secretary-general of the United Nations (UN), Kofi Annan, expressed doubt about that issue as recently as 2000, stating, "While the prohibition on child recruitment has by now acquired a customary international law status, it is far less clear whether it is customarily recognized as a war crime entailing the individual criminal responsibility of the accused."[4] Article 8 of the Rome Statute, which entered into force on July 1, 2002, explicitly defines "conscripting or enlisting children under the age of fifteen years" as a war crime for which the ICC shall have jurisdiction.[5]

On March 7, 2003, the Special Court of Sierra Leone (SCSL)[6] indicted five leaders of the Revolutionary United Front (RUF) on seventeen counts of crimes against humanity, one of which was the use of child soldiers. That same day, the SCSL also charged three members of the Armed Forces Revolutionary Council (AFRC) with numerous counts, including the use of child soldiers, and Charles Taylor, then-president of Liberia, with crimes against humanity and other serious violations of international humanitarian law, including the use of child soldiers.[7] In May 2004 the SCSL found that an individual can be held criminally responsible for recruiting child soldiers into armed conflict. On June 20, 2007, an SCSL decision resulted in the first convictions of the Special Court: the three AFRC members were found guilty on eleven counts, including that regarding child solders.[8]

Meanwhile, on March 17, 2006, the ICC had charged Lubanga, on the basis of individual criminal responsibility, with the war crimes of enlisting, conscripting, and using actively in hostilities children under the age of fifteen.[9] More than 18,000 children under age sixteen had been released from rebel-backed armed forces or groups in the DRC between January 2004 and May 2006, according to the then-UN Secretary General Kofi Annan's latest report on this issue.[10] Although thousands more have escaped, children remain vulnerable to re-recruitment, rape, and violence.

Yet child soldiers are a particularly problematic category for such international courts, seen not only as perpetrators of murder but also as victims to be rescued by the international justice community. To create the conditions for justice, contemporary international legal institutions such as the ICC must therefore enable the negation of child soldier responsibility, a mission cast as the pursuit of morally appropriate interventions on behalf of the "victim-perpetrator." This imbrication of "perpetrator" and "victim" – thus far, both African – enables the particular pursuit of justice to end impunity. However, when prosecutors accuse someone of using children for grave crimes, they cast into relief and effectively reassign the legal category of responsibility, with far-reaching consequences. In this regard, a new tenet of criminal law has emerged on the world scene, redistributing accountability and redefining those who bear the responsibility for inflicting suffering – such as commanders. This initiative has implications both for the international management and assignment of responsibility of war crimes and for the moral economies within which such initiatives are being pursued.

There are two dilemmas that arise when considering African child soldiers. First, what kind of legal quandary does this identity category pose to the ways in which legal institutions parse responsibility? Second, why *African* child soldiers?

In the first pretrial hearing of the ICC[11] – that regarding *The Prosecutor v. Thomas Lubanga Dyilo* – the victims are child soldiers: children aged ten to fourteen whose alleged participation in armed violence in the DRC has accounted for the death of thousands of civilians and more than twenty thousand combatants but whose identities are hidden from the public throughout the course of the trial. We were told that at the height of the violence in eastern Congo in 2003, approximately 30 percent of militia fighters – more than 30,000 recruits – were children.[12] With this indictment in place, Lubanga was the first suspect to stand trial before the Pre-Trial Chamber's first permanent international tribunal, and much is at stake. This case before the ICC represents a substantive shift in the advocacy of victims and the intervention into the use of child soldiers in Africa.

In considering the trial, I delineate what problems child soldiers present to a court that requires singularly embodied accountability. By detailing the circumscribed forms of speech within the court, my central argument highlights the power of adjudicatory performances, which parse subjectivity through adherence to the strictures of law.[13] I demonstrate that the actual power of the tribunal lies in its authority to define the objects of responsibility and thus acquire the biopolitical power to manage life and death. This is possible through the dual imagery of victims and perpetrators. These victims appear as "ghosts" whose power lies in the symbolic presence of the body being protected. Concurrently, the perpetration of violence justifies international indictments powerful enough to dismantle, isolate, simplify, and reconstruct subjectivities of culpability or suffering.

The reassignment of responsibility, and the micropolitics related to assigning guilt, has reinforced a particular narrative within which allocating blame is judicially assignable and the category of the victim affected in such a way that its relevance is not only incidental but a necessary component of the micropolitical formations of international justice. In this regard, I am concerned with extant notions of subjectivity as they relate to the changing ways in which these regimes parse criminal responsibility – the rebel leaders spreading violence to plunder natural resources, the child soldiers at once both victims and perpetrators.

Departing from earlier explorations of subject making as shaped by state or historical understandings of regional forms of cultural production, I argue that the twenty-first-century human rights production of the rights-endowed subject represents a transformation not only in the rise in individual sovereignty through self-government but also in the ways that particular subjects vie for sovereignty over regional resources through which to control the terms of life itself, the biopolitical domain to let live or die. In view of the widespread escalation of the sovereign power of Africa's rebel groups, these contests have involved the outer limits of governmentality. In response, once-grassroots movements, through a discourse of rights and individualism, are deploying liberalistic commitments to adjudicate such forms of violence, thereby providing the locus and moral rationalities for the restructuring of national adjudication and the participation of international/supranational judicial formations. These new international entities are shaped by an economy of subject formation that draws power from spectacles of victimhood positioned within new bureaucracies that comprise supranatural, governmental, and nongovernmental organizations.

My line of analysis points to a further goal of this chapter: to chart an agenda for the development of critical transnational legal studies that moves well beyond discourses of protecting victims – as if it is always clear who the victims are – but also forces us to ask larger questions about the individualization of criminal responsibility in relation to the contemporary preoccupation with adjudicating African warlords as the central problem behind African violence. This inquiry not only forces us to ask critical questions: Why Africa? Why now? and What does this preoccupation with political rights and the international adjudication of a handful of commanders tell us about the place of Africa in a post–September 11 world? This inquiry also calls on us to ponder how the allocation of blame to Africa's violent perpetrators has come to represent the object of Africa's poverty, the object of Africa's economic instability. Through this frame, it is victims who occupy the space of those to be saved and the reality of Africa's poverty – its root causes of bodily violence – that exist as specters haunting the theater of justice.

The case of Lubanga provides several important examples of the elisions central to the pursuit of international justice and the related ways in which perpetrators are crafted for the production of legal meaning and victims strategically included in proceedings. The ICC risks undermining its own reallocation of responsibility if, as a result of victim testimony, the focus of indictment turns to child soldiers themselves. To avoid this, only particular forms of testimony are invited into the courtroom; other complicating narratives are elided. Although victims appear as ghostly "specters," in these contexts, ghosts are not necessarily dead: they represent memories of the past understood through loss and suffering, a necessary moral platform for the ICC.

In *Specters of Marx* (1994), Jacques Derrida argues that to be rendered visible and intelligible, the authorial presence of specters must be embodied. For Derrida, institutions – and, for my purposes, legal institutions – provide the context within which specters manifest. They carve out spaces for ordering new grammars of participation, choreographed through rules of procedure and evidence that enable particular forms of knowledge to be paraded, whereas others are obscured (Derrida 1994:6). The mandate of the ICC's Rome Statute is legitimatized through the figure of the victim. However, this very process of legitimization serves to dissolve the victim's corporeality, leaving a residue – akin to a specter or ghost – something that is not physically "real" but that haunts the proleptic possibility of justice because its history – as lived in the present – is so powerfully horrific. These ghosts of the past-under-construction represent the making of fictions of justice in the international sphere. As a result, new forms of governance are embedded in one of the most radical types of politicization, the making of a new reality of justice rendered visible through the absence – the disappearing – of the old.

THE ICC AND THE TRIBUNALIZATION OF AFRICAN VIOLENCE

As a response to atrocities in a postwar climate, the ICC was developed through an international treaty regime to stop crimes against humanity from going unpunished. Backed by the adoption of the Rome Statute, a comprehensive treaty that established the ICC and determined its composition and function,[14] the ICC came into being on July 1, 2002, when the statute came into force.[15] The statute's presumptions of criminal liability borrow from post-WWII precedents.[16] Modifying the state's role as the final arbiter of justice, the statute supplements state adjudication functions with those of the independent ICC, through which cases under the court's subject matter jurisdiction can be pursued (Gurule 2001–2:45; Schabas 2004).

By both signing and ratifying the statute, a state places itself, and any of its nationals (high-ranking officials, in particular)[17] deemed responsible for imputing large-scale atrocities, under the ICC's jurisdiction.[18] Because its jurisdiction may extend to both States Parties and non-States Parties, the court challenges earlier conceptions of sovereignty (Gurule 2001–2:12; Schabas 2004:78). In fact, the Rome Statute's

Preamble establishes the precedence of the international domain, not the national, as the unit of humanitarian concern, wherein "the most serious crimes . . . must not go unpunished."[19] Practically, the ICC was designed to address the many gaps in national regulations that characterize the limitations of legal enforcement outside such regulations' jurisdiction (Schabas 2004:14). In fact, the Rome Statute functions on a presumption of complementarity with national governments in which its relevance is viable through the lack of action (investigation or adjudication) by a national court.[20] Thus, in the absence of adjudicatory action, the international community – that is, the states under the jurisdiction of the Rome Statute – can assign the right of intervention to the ICC.

As of August 2006, ten situations of violence had been analyzed by the ICC's Office of the Prosecutor for possible prosecution. Two situations concerning violence in Iraq and Venezuela had been dismissed, leaving eight Africa-based situations before the court. Of these, two had proceeded to investigation – one in the Sudan and the other in Uganda; in Uganda, arrest warrants have been issued. As of autumn of that year, five situations were still being analyzed, including in the Central African Republic (CAR) and the Ivory Coast.[21] Those being pursued by the lead prosecutor were in resource-rich locations where structural adjustment and the transition to democracy have involved significant contests over economic planning and control, rule, and legitimacy. These sites are also some of the poorest countries in the world – DRC, Uganda, Burundi, CAR (Ganesan and Vines 2004).

Historically, Africa – especially sub-Saharan Africa – has provided for the "West" a symbol for ineffective governance, and it continues to be represented through a series of "lacks and absences, failings and problems, plagues and catastrophes" (Ferguson 2006:2). "Africa" is portrayed by popular media as "irrational" and "primitive," beset with sectarian and religious violence – an argument constructed through reference to the many incidents of horrific violence that have occurred on the African continent since decolonization. As a result, among many ICC advocates, there is a widespread and unproblematized consensus that African cases should be the first before the court.

This African focus on the part of the ICC, as well as the proliferation of ad hoc tribunals and international legal infrastructures generally, is leading to the tribunalization of African violence as the new space within which justice is articulated through the management and maintenance of human life and in which the restructuring of power and forms of subjectivity are taking shape. Through the institutionalization of newly emergent subject forms ("child soldier," "victim," "perpetrator," "warlord"), the space of the tribunal has transmuted the spaces for recuperating the violation of the victim into domains for the legitimacy of international adjudication. This recuperation, like the highlighting of the actions of insurgents, relocates agency from the state to inter- or supranational agents who, in sub-Saharan African contexts, are setting new terms for the management of violence. The global reach of international law is thus becoming relevant to the micromanagement of daily life: in postcolonial African states, everyday actions and their meanings are being opened up by the expansion of national jurisdiction into international jurisdiction. However, this formation is taking shape within a particular irony of victimhood.

THE DRC, THE ICC, AND THOMAS LUBANGA DYILO: HISTORIES OF VIOLENCE

Before it achieved independence from Belgium on June 30, 1960, the Belgian Congo had been held first as a personal property of King Leopold II of Belgium (Congo Free State, 1885–1908) and then as a Belgian colony. The newly independent Republic of the Congo was soon renamed Democratic Republic of the Congo[22] and then, for a quarter-century, Zaire (1971–97). The DRC is rich in natural resources such as oil, cobalt, cadmium, industrial and gem diamonds, gold, silver, uranium, zinc, iron ore, coal, hydropower, and timber. Between 1998 and April 2004, the DRC housed the deadliest conflict on the African continent since World War II, one that resulted in the deaths of 3.8 million people and the displacement of millions more (International Rescue Committee 2004).[23] At the center of the DRC's ongoing conflicts have been struggles to secure the control of natural resources – including attempts by other states to gain access to the diamonds, gold, timber, and strategically important sites (ports, airfields, roads, and mining centers) in the eastern Congo region. States such as Rwanda and Uganda claim to have been supporting rebels against the DRC government to protect its own territorial interests because these countries had become a route for illegal diamonds and other resources from the DRC. Such struggles, in the context of a relatively "weak" state, highlight the increase in sovereign power among those vying for regional control.

Centered in the eastern Congo and involving nine African nations, the conflict in the Congo basin was sparked in October 1996 when troops of the Rwandan Patriotic Army (RPA) invaded the region that was then Zaire. Coalition leader Laurent-Désiré Kabila entered Kinshasa, the capital city, and declared himself president, renaming Zaire the Democratic Republic of Congo. Due to the conflicts over resources and attempts at strategic positioning, the relations between President Kabila and his foreign supporters deteriorated, and in late 1997, he ordered the departure from the DRC of all foreign troops. This was widely interpreted as an aggressive act and resulted in the offensive mutiny of Rwandan and Ugandan troops.

By July 1999, the DRC was divided into three combative segments: the Ugandan-backed Mouvement pour la Libération du Congo (MLC), which along with Ugandan forces held control of the northern third of the DRC; the Rwandan-backed Rassemblement Congolais pour la Démocratie; and the internationally supported Forces Armées Congolaise. With a military deadlock in place, a cease-fire was proposed and followed by the Lusaka Accord. Parties agreed to the deployment of a UN peacekeeping operation, the United Nations Organization Misison in the Democratic Republic of the Congo (in French, MONUC), the withdrawal of foreign troops, and the launching of an "Inter-Congolese Dialogue" to form a transitional government leading to democratic elections. However, all sides were accused of not following through with the 1999 provisions. President Kabila, for example, was seen as blocking the deployment of UN troops as well as suppressing international political groups.

On January 16, 2001, President Kabila was assassinated; ten days later, he was succeeded by his son, Joseph Kabila, who engaged in a range of peace talks with representatives from the government, the political opposition, civil society, rebel groups, and the Mai-Mai, precipitating the 2001 Inter-Congolese Dialogue, which formalized the Sun City Agreement on April 19, 2002. This was followed by several initiatives: the July 30, 2002, peace deal in Pretoria, South Africa, between Rwanda and the DRC; the September 6, 2002, Luanda Agreement formalizing peace between the DRC and Uganda; the December 17, 2002, "Global and All-Inclusive Agreement" between involved Congolese parties (resulting in the establishment of a transitional government in the DRC); the May 2003 withdrawal of troops by Uganda, intended to result in disarmament and national reunification; and the scheduling in June 2003 of elections in the DRC for 2005–6. As a result of these negotiations, the majority of the DRC is recognized as experiencing relative democratic stability.

Today, the state has established economic reforms leading to new relationships with international financial institutions and donors, as well as to membership in international organizations. The DRC is now a signatory to many international treaties, including the Rome Statute of the ICC. Yet, despite these measures, violence has continued. Throughout 2005, for example, rival militias backed by Rwandan and Ugandan forces allegedly murdered, raped, wounded, and took hostage thousands of civilians in a battle over border trade and gold fields in the region of Ituri, in the northeast. This precipitated violence by Kinshasa-aligned forces – in North and South Kivu, Ituri, and northern Katanga (all eastern border provinces) – whose goal has been the creation of a strong state to control the region's resources. This conflict provides the context for the forthcoming ICC trial of Thomas Lubanga Dyilo.

COMMAND RESPONSIBILITY AND THE SPECTRALITY OF JUSTICE

This book opened with the radically different representations, in the ICC's first-ever Pre-Chambers Trial hearing, of Thomas Lubanga Dyilo, charged with using child soldiers to kill in armed hostilities.[24] The dramatic prosecution and defense in this case, taken together, are an example of the kinds of display performed in (or against) international justice today, especially throughout the Global South. As outlined in the introduction, one result of the burgeoning power of international justice mechanisms in these contexts is the retooling of the state power that accompanies it: new forms of governmentality are emerging as multiple actors work toward the management of justice beyond the nation-state and through the reclassification of individual culpability known in international criminal justice circles as *command responsibility*. Often defined by lawyers as the responsibility of commanders for war crimes committed by persons subject to their control, command responsibility provides supranational technologies of control over violent crimes committed under the jurisdiction of the Rome Statute. It serves as a critical domain for assigning guilt and, as used in new internationalist realms, should also be seen as representing a new form of governmentality for producing the spectacularization of justice.

With their focus on the individualization of criminal responsibility (art. 25), those engaged in the ICC have succeeded in operationalizing

a key concept, command responsibility, that in the twentieth century had been used only in the case of serious international violations
(e.g., in the Nuremberg or International Criminal Tribunal for the former Yugoslavia [ICTY] tribunals).[25] Command responsibility as a form
of legal classification thus has important antecedents in international
criminal law. Article 25, section 2 of the Rome Statute indicates that "a
person who commits a crime within the jurisdiction of the Court shall
be individually responsible and liable for punishment in accordance
with this Statute"; section 3(a) stipulates "whether [committed] as an
individual, jointly with another or through another person." In articulating the commission of crime through another person, the writers
were especially concerned with addressing those who are responsible
for ordering, soliciting, or inducing a crime that occurs or is attempted
(art. 25 (3)(b)). Also included is one who "For the purpose of facilitating the commission of such a crime, aids, abets or otherwise assists in
its commission or its attempted commission, including providing the
means for its commission" (art. 25 (3)(c)). Military commanders are
then specifically included, with provisos, in Article 28. This attention
to individual criminal responsibility as played out in the development of
international criminal courts has popularized this mechanism for assigning guilt. Courts now target those high in the chain of command, seen
as bearing responsibility for the greatest crimes against humanity. Thus,
Lubanga's arrest and indictment by the ICC represent a performance
of a new international order: children's consciousness is brought into
question by the court and their complicity attributed and transferred to
the wrongdoing of one or more adults.

The truth and reconciliation commissions of the late twentieth and
early twenty-first centuries tended to assign victims spaces for narrativizing their devastation, providing a symbolic possibility for democratic transition postviolence. In contrast, the ICC's goal of ending
the impunity of commanders highlights a new relationship between
retributive and restorative justice in which the rule of law, rather than
the politics of compassion, forgiveness, or reconciliation, drives a mission of reassigning responsibility for grave and widespread crimes. Ultimately, it is international judicial intervention that distinguishes mechanisms of power in relation to contemporary forms of violence involving
the enlisting of children and then in turn provides a new mechanism
for reallocating children's responsibility onto perpetrators – command
responsibility, which fosters the ascension of the victim on the world
stage and the sublimation of victims as specters. This procedure has

led to the reassignment of agency for individual acts committed under hierarchies of adult authority, thereby absolving children of criminal responsibility under international law.[26]

Previously, there were two critical moments in the twentieth century when comparable shifts took place. The first involved the major war trials held in Nuremberg and Tokyo after the Second World War. These addressed the principle of individual criminal responsibility for particular violations of international law applicable in armed conflict contexts (Twist 2006). The second moment occurred with the adoption of the four Geneva Conventions on August 12, 1949,[27] in which a specific framework for the prevention and punishment of grave crimes was established for the protection of war victims (Ratner and Abrams 2001). Over the past twenty years, however, the majority of armed conflicts involve civil wars in the Global South, in places such as Cambodia, Iraq, Sri Lanka, and a range of countries throughout sub-Saharan Africa – Somalia, Rwanda, Sierra Leone, Liberia, Uganda, the Sudan, and the DRC (Urdal 2005). Many of these hostilities in Africa have consisted of struggles to control the plunder of natural resources and are buttressed by a thriving underground military economy (Allen 1999; Billon 2001; Mattei and Nader 2008). Through such conflicts, we have witnessed in the twentieth and early-twenty-first centuries the widespread militarization of everyday life – including the production of childhood killing fields.

THE CASE OF THOMAS LUBANGA DYILO AND THE SPECTERS OF THE VIOLATED

On September 8, 2000, the DRC signed the Rome Statute.[28] Ratification on April 11, 2002,[29] placed the DRC in a complementary relation with the ICC and, ultimately, under its jurisdiction. On March 3, 2004, following standard procedure for the reassignment of jurisdiction from the state to the international tribunal, the situation in the DRC was referred by President Joseph Kabila to the ICC's Office of the Prosecutor. On June 23, the lead prosecutor, Luis Moreno-Ocampo, announced his decision to open an investigation into crimes committed after July 1, 2002. Upon the establishment of findings of fact for criminal responsibility, the investigation was followed by the Office of the Prosecutor's issuance of a sealed warrant of arrest.[30]

In early March 2005, Thomas Lubanga Dyilo was arrested in the DRC, and on March 17, 2006, he was transferred from DRC jurisdiction to the ICC. He is now being held in the ICC Detention Centre in The Hague. The ICC's arrest and extradition of Lubanga served as a celebrated day for the court. Like the Nuremberg tribunal victories after World War II criminals were punished, that day represented for advocates of the ICC yet another advancement of justice for the world community.

At the November 9, 2006, opening of the Confirmation of Charges Hearing in the Pre-Trial Chamber,[31] the prosecution announced its intention to prove that Lubanga, a politician purporting to act in the interests of peace, was actually a brutal commander-in-chief of the FPLC. To effectively recast freedom fighter as heartless rebel, the assigned prosecutor announced that the hearing would give the world an idea of the brutality experienced by child soldiers. In so doing, he would rely on various forms of evidence, including the statements of witnesses, official UPC and FPLC documents (some of which had been signed by Lubanga Dyilo), an assortment of video footage, and testimonies from victims.

Luc Walleyn, who with Franck Mulenda legally represented three of the four anonymous victims, opened with a statement regarding their testimony to establish that there existed an armed forces committee in the DRC under the supreme command of Lubanga.[32] In his attempt to highlight the conditions of desperation under which child soldiers were enlisted, he painted a general portrait of the impoverished, displaced, and traumatized families deemed representative of many thousands of victims of the DRC's regime. This testimony provided an image of African misery that pervaded all other allusions to the everyday life in DRC war zones. The strategy was clearly effective: during the evidentiary report by ICC Senior Trial Lawyer Ekkehard Withopf on November 14,[33] tribunal observers representing a range of humanitarian nongovernmental organizations continued to comment on the desperation of African victims and, in particular, child soldiers. However, the majority of witness testimony produced a different effect and was used to highlight Lubanga's power as a commander. For example, one victim stressed the military commands that were in Lubanga's control:

> No-one else took part in the meetings of the military committee which met most often in the evening or at night. Lubanga had limited discussions on military actions to the military committee alone.... The military information was a State within a State. (24–5)

101

In insisting that Lubanga, not the children, was responsible for the violence caused by child soldiers, the witness assured the prosecution that the accused held authority over soldiers who committed human rights violations:

> [N]othing important took place without his authorization. Lubanga con-ducted himself as the Commander-in-Chief of the FPLC. He visited soldiers in barracks in some villages of the Ituri district, presided over the installation of a battalion in Iga-Barriere, a brigade in Aru, the Bule base and the Mandro military camp. At all times he was in military uniform. . . . Sometimes he meted out punishment to his soldiers. For example, he dismissed one of the commanders accused of rape in FPLC in an outpost – a distant outpost. Finally, he led some – he chaired some meetings of the Executive in military uniform – that is, in his capacity as supreme commander. (25)

The rhetorical concerns of this witness' testimony highlighted not the violation of the victim nor the anguish of child soldiers, but the supremacy of Lubanga's leadership. On the same day, further statements insisted that, from the creation of the FPLC, Thomas Lubanga, Bosco Ntaganda, and Floribert Kisembo were among the leaders. As the next witness recalled,

> military operations of the FPLC were planned during meetings of – military planification – meetings which were held two or three times a month. The persons participating were the FPLC commanders, including Kisembo, Ntaganda and others, and the traders as Thomas and Manase Savo, were the leaders. Thomas Lubanga took part in some of the military planification meetings. . . . Thomas Lubanga received reports on the military structure, including the minutes of the planification – military planification meetings, which he requested and received in his capacity of supreme commander of the army, together with regular reports on operations, as he was the coordinator of the FPLC's activities. . . . Thomas Lubanga Dyilo, he himself gave orders to the FPLC officers. (28)

Prosecutor Withopf also related a description taken from a witness who confirmed that Kisembo was one of the top-ranking leaders and that he visited Thomas Lubanga every day in his residence:

> Kisembo's house and that of Thomas Lubanga were just opposite each other and sometimes Kisembo would spend the whole day at Thomas Lubanga's residence. . . . Thomas Lubanga was in touch with Ntaganda and the com-mander of his battalion. . . . [I]f somebody went there in the evening, they would sure find Thomas Lubanga seated at the table with Kisembo, Ntaganda and with the commander of the . . . battalion. (26)

After presenting a range of victim testimonies intended to establish these various chains of command and responsibility, the prosecutor turned to videotapes that had been broadcast on television as public interest documentaries in an attempt to affirm Lubanga's practice of child recruitment. The footage highlighted the involvement of children in a military training camp, featuring boys in uniform with belts of bullets around their necks and assault rifles strapped around their backs. In the first video, a man described the head of the militia as being Thomas Lubanga:

> He [Lubanga] took the control of Bunia with the support of his Ugandan ally. He has a Diploma in Psychology and an army of children underneath his orders and blood on his hands. Those peace processes that we're dealing with, in Africa and beyond, the heads of factions to a greater or lesser extent are warlords and have very Mafioso-type of tendencies. You have to deal with them. You may not want to deal with them and they may have committed all sorts of human rights abuses, but unfortunately you have to deal with them because they are the ones with the power. (34)

Despite the fact that witness testimony overwhelmingly cited the structural evidence for Lubanga's culpability, when in December 2006 I conducted posthearing interviews about the substantive issues related to this hearing, my informants emphasized "the desperation of the victims" and the need to help them. Commentators appeared satisfied that the testimony of victims was used not for the description of victims' experiences but rather for the delineation of actions of adult perpetrators such as Lubanga. As one American woman interviewed shortly after the December 14 hearing put it, "command responsibility is one thing, the desperation of children to join the militia for food and clothes, for just their survival, is another."[34]

Soon after showing the video described earlier, the prosecutor turned to another documentary, titled *The New Killing Fields*,[35] with a narration about Lubanga's guilt: "Lubanga's men had been trying to capture a big gold-mine a few miles north of Bunia. It is greed for Congo's riches that drives this war." Insisting that human rights organizations want Lubanga indicted at the ICC for crimes against humanity, the narrator turned and asked "why the people of Bunia have been murdered with impunity" (36). The video continued with ongoing narrations and images of the suspect interacting with his militia. The prosecutor concluded by summarizing that in the upcoming trial he would reveal that Thomas Lubanga had been involved in the recruitment of children from the early formation of the UPC:

> We will show that this practice, including the direct involvement of Thomas Lubanga Dyilo in it, continued after the creation of the FPLC and, as we have shown, the FPLC was created in summer 2002, it continued throughout the time relevant for the charges against Mr. Thomas Lubanga Dyilo, and we will show that this practice was based on a policy of the UPC and the FPLC to recruit children to participate actively in hostilities.... I draw your attention to the fact that in particular the pattern of recruitment of the children and their use will also form part of the presentation of the individual cases that will be made later on today by my colleagues.... It will become clear that the individual cases of the six children concerned... do, indeed, represent the fate of literally hundreds of children. (50–1, prosecutor's transcript)

Throughout the proceedings, the prosecutor used charts of hierarchical linkages that attempted to locate a connection to Lubanga's command. Testimony after testimony, the narratives described the hundreds of African children recruited to kill their families, and extended communities were converted from complex perpetrators of violence to helpless victims under Lubanga's command. Imagery repeatedly featured children wearing ragged shorts and T-shirts or else parading in camouflaged uniforms. Videotapes were shown in which Lubanga was portrayed accusing people from outside the Ituri region of tribal unrest and insisting, with religious conviction, that when the children finish their training they would receive arms to protect themselves against intruders. As the person said to be Lubanga stated: "[Y]ou will ensure the security of the inhabitants. It is work of great importance before the world and before God" (78).

In looking at the pretrial hearings, we can begin to see just how the triumph of the rule of law is playing out. The Lubanga proceedings before the ICC represents spectacular performances in which a new language of responsibility and a new moral economy of victimhood – the rationale for just intervention – are being articulated and displayed. In their testimonies, witnesses were asked by the prosecutor to map the chain of association of perpetrators of DRC's violence and thus highlight the leaders of the organization. What we see from these pretrial hearings, then, are particular craftings of the child soldier for the purposes of transferring responsibility to another subject – what is referred to in legal circles as the "assignment of culpability." The shift from children as perpetrators to victims was made possible through the demonization of Lubanga's recruitment strategies and the discursive power of the lingering specter of the child victim.

For anthropological inquiry, the process of classifying crime in this way urges us to redirect our attention toward the mechanisms through which the power of international law gains its force. In this case, once command responsibility was legally established, the prosecutors needed only to gesture toward actual violence inflicted on particular victims to demonstrate the commission of a crime. They never named or established the threshold of proof of suffering. Rather, the standard of proof centered around chains of command. The result was the underlying specter of suffering operating like a ghostly, yet necessary, shadow in the courtroom but hardly articulated within the hearings.

However, contemporary legal formations are increasingly involving the interplay among international, national, and local-judicial and non-judicial domains, with the expansion of international tribunals making a new form of justice visible outside of the state and putting the perpetrator in tension with the victim. At times, when the perpetrator is also the victim, as with the child soldier, we see in most explicit terms the horror of the specter alongside the performance of justice as triumph. In these contexts, particular shadows of violence – the violence of poverty, the violence of inequality, the memory of death – exist alongside the performative power of international justice making.

VICTIMS AND THE MORAL ECONOMY OF INTERVENTION:
ICC RULES AND STRATEGIES

The ICC defines victims as "individuals who have suffered harm as a result of a crime falling within the jurisdiction of the court" (ICC literature). The Rome Statute contains what many members of the court see as innovative conditions for victims of accused perpetrators in that they, too, are granted legal representatives to speak on their behalf: "For the first time in the history of international criminal justice, victims can participate."[36] Yet this participation – so critical to the adjudication of crimes determined through command responsibility – is circumscribed in particular, and often prescriptive, ways. Individuals must provide evidence proving they are, indeed, victims of crimes that not only fall under the subject matter of the court but are also relevant to the scope of its proceedings. Applications (filed from the point when the Office of the Prosecutor requests authorization to investigate crimes all the way through the appeals stage) are forwarded to the

Victims' Participation and Reparation Section and to members of the chambers, who then determine whether the claimant is a victim and, if affirmed, they make arrangements for victims' participation in the proceedings. The judges from the chamber are empowered to accept or reject applications.[37] In the Lubanga case, official victims included the African dead and wounded, the families of the dead and wounded, and child soldiers, ultimately those who have experienced physical harm, psychological harm, and material harm.

To apply for reparations, which are authorized by Article 75 of the Rome Statue, those who claim victim status must, following Rule 94 of the Rules of Procedure and Evidence, file with the Registry a written application that contains evidence of injury. For reparations to be awarded, the trial must end with a conviction of the perpetrator and, in so doing, articulate publicly the appropriate reparation for victims or their beneficiaries. The reparations – which may take the form of restitution, indemnification, or rehabilitation of the perpetrator or victim – are payable from the ICC Victims Trust Fund (which may include "money and other property collected through fines or forfeiture"; art. 79). Among other provisions are security and counseling (through a Victims and Witnesses Unit; art. 43(6)), described by the officials of the court as being geared toward the betterment of reintegrating the victim into society and holding perpetrators responsible for their crimes.[38]

These victim procedures serve as mechanisms to support the doctrine of command responsibility that enables execution of the ICC's mandate to end impunity. This doctrine is codified in Article 28 of the Rome Statute, which in subsection (a) imposes individual responsibility on military commanders if they "either knew or, owing to the circumstances at the time, should have known that the forces were committing or about to commit such crimes." Interpreted literally, Article 28(a) adopts the stricter "should have known" standard. As deliberated in pretrial contexts, the language of Article 28(a) is seen by ICC lawyers as interpreted to impose an affirmative duty to remain informed of the activities of subordinates. However, this requirement has already become a point of contention with lawyers.[39] Precedents for establishing the "knowledge" criterion have been based on two competing standards: one involves whether the commander "knew"; the other, whether the commander "had reason to know." The background for understanding whether a commander "knew" about the commission of violence refers to the actual knowledge, which can be established either directly or indirectly through circumstantial evidence. However, the meaning of "had reason to know" is often seen in the case law in relation to whether a subordinate was about to have committed crimes and the commander failed to take measures to prevent or punish such acts.

One of the formative influences for establishing principles of command responsibility in the Rome Statute was taken from an ad hoc tribunal set up by the United Nations on May 25, 1993, to adjudicate war crimes in the former Yugoslavia. The ICTY first considered the scope of command responsibility in *The Prosecutor v. Delalić et al.*, also known as the Čelebići case.[40] The Lubanga Trial Chamber agreed with the Čelebići court that jurisprudence following World War II had established a customary law position that imposed on superiors a proactive duty to remain apprised of the acts of subordinates. However, the Čelebići case reached a different conclusion on the knowledge standard, deciding that commanders have a duty to be "constantly informed of the way in which their subordinates carry out the tasks entrusted to them."[41] By contrast, the Lubanga Trial Chamber insisted that, based on principles of command responsibility, commanders were responsible for taking the necessary measures to fulfill this obligation.

Prosecutorial interests in command responsibility directed the structure of the proceedings in the Lubanga case. Witness narratives were narrowly tailored to explain chains of responsibility through which the prosecution could articulate a connection between Lubanga and his alleged leadership of the FPLC, thereby attributing to him the responsibility for child soldier violence against civilian and military populations. In this process of incorporation and display, the court acts as author. Through its texts, transcripts, images, videos, legal procedures, and performances, the court institutionalizes victimhood in mediated ways that are also familiarly racialized as "African." What is not made explicit, as noted earlier, are the narratives of victim suffering: the child soldier and his or her status as victim are referentially signaled but never present in the substantive presence of the court. Instead, articulated through their legal representatives, the violation of particular individuals and communities is negated and, through its inclusion in human rights and rule of law adjudication, comes to exist as a specter of suffering, a "ghost." Children's histories as killers thus exist as specters of international justice at large; the victim is represented through signs of both vulnerability and violence that haunts the criminal court.

Yet this ghostly presence-via-absence of the victim drives the perceived moral economy of judicial interventions in sub-Saharan Africa.

Through the crafting of particular types of rights-endowed African victims, there is a necessary construction of the commanding perpetrator as warlord – someone who operates above the law and whose impunity cannot be allowed to continue. In the quest to abrogate such practices, the rule of law is being deployed strategically, through the invention and development of a new language of responsibility, the shadows of which are never fully knowable.

This figure of the child soldier might be seen as representing our innermost fears – fears central to the modernity of post-9/11 imaginaries. Fears that "terrorist" violence that could cause such destruction in the United States is actually endemic in Africa – fears that such violence is not only central to the making of the modern West but to the foundational tenets from which we continue to benefit and without which we cannot live. International justice draws its power from the figure of this victim of war – in wars in which the casualties have become part of our collective imagination. This power is consolidated through the demonization of the adult African perpetrator, whose actions, often made in the name of national freedom struggles, are represented as responsible for the decimation of local populations. This tyrant figure is cast against the backdrop of the paradoxically resource-rich and endemically violent "Africa" of the international imagination.[42] Through the systematic elision of the root causes propelling violence, international law has found a concrete Other: a singular perpetrator – a commander directing mass violence, a warlord – whose agency can be severed only through external judiciaries and whose acts of violence are recontextualized within a new political and moral economy based on victim's justice.

At the heart of this reassignment of jurisdiction is a politics of legitimacy embedded in a morality of humanitarianism – humanitarianism in Africa, in particular – highlighting a moral economy of sorts. The "humanitarian" gesture of "reaching out" for "Africa's benefit" is of course not new: it has precedents in the history of African colonialism and the neocolonial projects of development and humanitarianism (Ferguson 2006).[43] This reality explains why humanitarian interventions in the name of *African* child soldiers are possible.

The unfolding regime of international criminal justice represents a terrain within which the supranational domain is brought into being through the management of the power to decide who is victimized (and thus profits) and who is responsible for violence (and is thus punished) – and on what terms. This is what makes the possibility of child soldiers so horrifying: the potential of a child's authority to execute the management of life and death – our life and death – has come to represent the most horrific possibilities for Africa's future, and for that of the world. Yet the law requires the specter of death to enable its moral mission, even as it needs to control the terms of its deliberation and rescue.

As in the case of Lubanga, it is the development of an institutional infrastructure for the victim – and the drive to protect the category of victimhood – that propels this new moral economy of extranational intervention as the new workings of sovereignty. Thus, African victims are central to the processes of international intervention but not to the prescribed resolutions; rather, the figure of the victim exists as a necessary precondition for imagining the legitimacy of the international reach of the court.

HUMANITARIANISM AND THE PERFORMANCE OF INTERNATIONAL JUSTICE

The ICC is heralded by its advocates – judges, lawyers, diplomats, humanitarian workers – as the first international tribunal in which Statute and Rules of Procedure and Evidence[44] includes victims through their testimonies, protections, and safeguards, thereby contributing to the instrumental value of victim suffering (Aldana-Pindell 2002; Bassiouni 2006). Yet beyond their expressive value within an economy of compassion, victims are given no place in the authority of justice making. What this ellipsis masks – and what a critical merger between bio- and necropolitical formations highlights[45] – is that the struggle over human management is deeply embedded in long-standing conflicts over material resources: the fight for control of Africa's wealth in relation to the status of the victim.

The imagery with which the figure of the victim collaborates is that of the Third World sufferer – be she or he the indigent woman or man, the defenseless child soldier forced to bear arms, the raped or violated concubine, the (African, Christian, Muslim, Jewish) refugee, or the internally displaced person. African victimhood is crucial for constructing a moral obligation to punish the adult perpetrator in charge. Moreover, as a consequence of this focus on the perpetrator, the related suffering of the violated is decentered and often overlooked in the final decisions of the court. Instead, with particular liberal-economic regimes of governance using the language of victims' rights and ending impunity to control the terms of engagement, the production of the rights-endowed subject is shaped alongside a discourse of justice and an imagery of the spectacular powers of the international tribunal.

This discourse of justice is illusory and, through its spectacles of lawmaking, shows the actual limits of the law rather than its potential achievements. Here we see that international tribunals are mechanisms for one of the most radical types of politicization: a spectralization of international justice that produces a visual domain in which performances on the world stage are institutionalized locally through the biopolitical workings of the rule of law and more circumscribed forms of individual sovereignty.

Two hundred years after the British abolished their slave trade (1807), it is now the language of "humanitarianism" that embodies the international discourses around human entitlements to life. Through its charge to protect human rights, this mode of justice represents the possibility that victims everywhere, without regard for national citizenship alliances, are entitled to international inclusion and protection. This presumption of rights and protections is materializing alongside the expansion into international domains of the new biopolitics of the postcolonial state, enabled by the erosion of state capacities to build a viable economy for citizens, to command and regulate access to resources in the domestic economy (Mbembe 2003), and to build innovative judiciary mechanisms capable of incorporating indigenous cultural traditions through which to direct future polities. This new internationalized form of governance is subtler than earlier colonial forms yet represents a more tragic set of realities. International institutions work through the law to craft "victims" and "perpetrators" (or, indeed, "victim-perpetrators") within the parameters of legal science (and these individuals themselves participate in such constructions) to perform them, yielding new subjects through which humanitarianism is further legitimatized.

Ethnographic findings that highlight the ways that societies in the "West" have found in "Africa" an "Other" to be manipulated (Ferguson 2006) for their own purposes are not central to ethnographic practice. Instead, studies of regions, especially in the Global South, often require particular forms of relative comparisons and explorations. However, in detailing the ways that international justice-making institutions, such as the ICC, are becoming increasingly hegemonic, it is important to examine the ways that, even in humanitarian advocacy spheres of interactions, new conceptual exclusions are taking shape and rendering unintelligible the very relations that they include. How? They mask as humanitarian inclusivity and involve moral intervention in the name of victims; but these inclusions speak to the externalities of management that are increasingly becoming technocratic and linguistically specific and around which adherents are expected to structure their speech, claims, criticisms, and aspirations. This performance, this theater, linked as it is to a profoundly uneven global political economy, actually serves to undermine the capacity of the postcolonial state to ameliorate material violence. The benevolence of the new internationalism reveals some of the most tragic forms of victimhood – tragic because, despite its biopolitical mission and justice-seeking goals, the ICC's mandate does not involve addressing root causes, preempting violence, and thereby fostering viable life-producing conditions for those who will otherwise likely become "victims."

What we are witnessing, then, is a radical normalization of governance in which particular local forms of knowledge that once shaped the basis for life are measurable through public displays of the rule of law. These justice displays are holding power through what I call, following Derrida, the "mystical foundations of international justice"[46] – the belief that, as a result of a given violation, it is not the regaining of victim loss that will produce "justice" but, rather, the adjudication of the perpetrator and his or her consequent punishment. By focusing on adjudicating and punishing chief commanders engaged in mass violence after violence and not contributing to rebuilding state capacities, the ICC betrays its allegiance to the victims of the latter – that is, it produces a theater of subject making created to construct narratives of justice rather then ameliorating the need for them. As such, it represents the performing of justice in an attempt to make loss and disenfranchisement bearable.

A sense of justice, in these larger international domains, is made possible through the creation of the conditions for the production of justice regimes. That which constitutes justice is enabled not simply through an innate conception of justice but through the workings of international agreements, the state, its judiciaries, and its economies of morality that shape the theater of justice itself. Ultimately, the power of the law represents the institutional authority to make the decision of life over death; but because the institutional structures constituted by the order of the law are distinct from, and reliant on, those that constitute the law, it does not represent power and justice themselves. The law does not have the authority to intercede prior to the actual threshold for establishing justice.

This is the conundrum of justice: the impossibility of ever achieving true recompense in the face of violence and death. Seen in different terms, this structuring of law highlights for us the logic of moral economies in which intervention requires the existence of an infraction through which to perform particular compensatory acts. Hence, institutional authority emerges from the ICC through alliances with state judiciaries and polities, adoption of judiciary forms, and the performance of the (cap)ability to set the terms for what is legally possible in the new world order. These ICC displays of international adjudication represent what Jean and John Comaroff have called a "simulacrum of governance" – a set of rites "staged to make actual and authoritative . . . the activity of those responsible for law and order – and, by extension, an enactment of the very possibility of government" (2004a:819–20).

The generative significance of such international, spectacular movements-in-the-making exists as a kind of self-deception with far-reaching consequences. Movements to establish court authority through the moral imperative to end impunity can never quite redress the horror of loss or evade the incessant reminder that the capture of a commander, or the deployment of command responsibility to reassign guilt, will not end violence. The sources of violence lay elsewhere; they lay in the banality of the everyday and its dramas to control the terms of life and the production of death. These ICC formations entail the complicity of child soldiers; but their reclassification as victims represents a critical innovation in the management of criminal law, providing the grammar that is structuring particular authoritative pronouncements of responsibility by international institutions such as the ICC in a range of sub-Saharan contexts.

WHY AFRICA?

The analysis laid out here suggests a framework for answering the larger question raised in this book: "Why Africa?" In an attempt to understand the role of courts to accommodate complex interactions among international, national, and regional judiciaries as they are increasingly being played out in sub-Saharan African contexts, in what ways do international trials reallocate sites of power? In what ways do they skip over key sites of power through which to reallocate it by performing examples of the spectrality of international justice?

The field of legal anthropology has traditionally examined local explorations of dispute processes and instantiations of justice in more circumscribed, localized contexts. Besides tracking colonial and post-colonial forms of legal expansion, it has not always been able to engage in political analyses that allow us to understand the relationship between culture and power in some places and not others. Following Laura Nader's development of the Berkeley Law Project, one of the most important developments in legal anthropology was that of the significant work by John Comaroff and Simon Roberts (1981), which led to the rethinking of a study of law that focused on rules and a reorientation that set into place contexts for making sense of dispute processes. These approaches highlighted the multiple ways in which societies used law to produce regulatory mechanisms through which to maintain order and stability and attempted to theorize disputes not as anomalies but as central to the practice of the everyday – as central to understanding the contexts through which to understand power relations.

With the development of various approaches to legal pluralism, legal anthropology began to focus on the ethnographic study of Western industrialized legal systems (Conley and O'Barr 1990; Merry 1990; Nader 1990) and various hybrid forms of lawmaking ranging from that of national legal spaces to quasi- and nonjudicial spaces. These forms of investigation recognized that in so-called quasi- and non-judicial contexts, not only was law vibrant through the articulation of norms but that in particular spheres of lawmaking, what was classified as "traditional" law had itself been shaped by colonial reform and various forms of hybrid intervention. Today, it is becoming clear that with the increasingly central role of global hegemonies of "justice talk" in shaping more circumscribed legal contexts, it is more important than ever to consider not simply the plurality of law in its culturally relevant contexts but also how state law penetrates and restructures both normative and nonstate normative orders. As well, we must consider how rule of law activists are deploying such language to produce new forms of practice but also how, in African contexts, these seemingly new types of practices are having dire consequences for the illusory nature of justice. By making central the intersecting global hegemonies as they are playing out in daily negotiations, researchers engaged in understanding the conditions of possibility in which it is

African states that are subjects of the court must develop strategies for mapping the multiple terrains within which images fill silences and engagements are foreclosed before they are ever brought into being. Such presences through apparent absences are necessary components of how particular conceptions of justice become visible. Herein lies the importance of critically engaged interventions in these contemporary realities.

Steps Toward a Critical Transnational Legal Pluralism
It is useful to highlight changes in the new legal order – changes that reflect new legal classifications, rhetorical structure, discourse of rights, and juridical spectacles that involve understanding the politics of life and death through the conditions that shape their representation in the first place. It means exploring the ways that the performance of international justice draws its force from the hypercorporeality of the suffering postcolonial body. It means that we also detail how victims respond to memories of suffering not only for the purpose of healing and reconciliation but also to access institutional structures of compensation and their monetary dispensations. It means recognizing that, despite widespread participation in a treaty regime, not all states enjoy equal membership in the international power play and that the maintenance of racial hierarchies is rarely acknowledged. In this regard, studies of judicial adjudication help to produce social narratives about our social world and are necessary if we are to unravel how discourses about subjectivities and their metonymic powers are operationalized in daily life. However, for legal studies to be useful beyond legal pluralist or doctrinal classifications and applications, we need to explore the constellations of the public imagination that shape the spaces between grammars of violence and core social realities and that explain histories of violence and the related exclusions that haunt those histories.

Today's reality is that in certain African states (Nigeria, Uganda, and DRC, for example), economically, politically, and socially shaped forms of violence are increasingly managed in sites outside the continent; thus, some of the factors shaping the spectrality of justice-making mechanisms are arising elsewhere. Through the accumulated effect of international humanitarian and legalistic procedures, "Africa" is again represented and advocated – like a child whose value and conditions of living must be controlled by adult others. The regulatory mechanisms that shape such legal terrains are hegemonic, coercive, and strategic, and they have led to disproportionate indictments and investigations in African states.

At the dawn of the ICC's history, its special focus on child soldiers and preoccupation with African indictments is a response to and exacerbates stereotypes of an Africa that is politically fragile, legally inept, and economically volatile. The child soldier identity serves, in many ways, as a metonym for childhood. This new example of paternalization heralds the incorporation of the rule of law into the continuing history of institutional protectionism, legal and constitutional intervention, and the management of African resources by new humanitarian regimes. Through particular adjudicatory inclusions, such as the never to be known child soldier, narratives of suffering become secondary to the prosecution of those who are deemed to bear responsibility for crimes under investigation. These processes of ellipsis are already normative in state criminal trials: in both common- and canon-law criminal cases, victims bear little influence except by way of offering witness testimony or offering input during sentencing – despite the fact that the rise in power of international justice institutions is amassed through the claim to champion the cause of the violated. This claim has been broadcast through an acute deployment of the imagery of global victims – woman, child, black, brown, Muslim amputee. Through this imagery emerges a new governmentality, the objects, purposes, and blind spots of which can be analyzed at the sites of new international justice regimes.

In the case of sub-Saharan Africa, the body being defended (and subjugated) is particularly racialized – a black body whose histories of enslavement, war, famine, militarization, and economic failure continue to fuel a Western moral imperative for intervention. The specter of frailty haunts the display of international justice through the figure of the child soldier – a young body who, although possessing a complex subjectivity of perpetrator-victim, is being split, abstracted, and recuperated as defenseless victim. This apparition is central to international authority and cannot exist without it. With the globalization of substantive and procedural international criminal justice institutions, studies of lawmaking and justice-producing domains cannot be isolated from other spheres of control and interaction that go well beyond the state or the materiality of the object, seen or unseen.[47] As I have shown, an examination of the erasures of victims and their material claims to economic control highlights the ways in which the ascension of international criminal justice generates the mystical foundations of its own authority, and thus prevails through the moral foundations of its legal power.

The international management of violence by tribunals intent on ending leaders' impunity has become a privileged solution to the familiar problem of state complicity in violence. Through a process of first destabilizing networks of violence through the arrest of high-ranking leaders and then attempting to vindicate victims through tribunalization, we are seeing the development of a new moral economy of justice in which the international ascension of concerns for the protection of the victim exists by way of the reassignment of perpetrator guilt. In this new governmental context, the sign of Africa has come to represent, in the international humanitarian imaginary, the sign of childhood. Exemplified by the child soldier, it holds the symbolism for the most oppressed and destitute aspects of humanity. It is through this context that the ICC draws its moral fortitude, its force of law.

By exploring the circulation and application of new "bodies of power" involved in the crafting of African subjects, I have reflected on the limits of and challenges to the liberalist project to choreograph the management of life. It is here in the social life of liberalism, its technical production and moral cultivation, that political contestations lie and that the rethinking of the place of Africa in unequal relations of transnational power must begin.

CHAPTER 3

MULTIPLE SPACES OF JUSTICE: UGANDA, THE INTERNATIONAL CRIMINAL COURT, AND THE POLITICS OF INEQUALITY

PROLOGUE: REINSTATING CULTURAL COMPLEXITIES

In an article titled "A Pluralist Approach to International Law," Paul Berman (2007) examined the culturalist work of Robert Cover and his emphasis on decentering the role of the state by examining "norm-generating communities" rather than nation-states, as well as the work of Myres McDougal, Harold Lasswell, and Michael Reisman in their attempts to pay homage to different forms of actors engaged in what he described as norm-generating processes. This focus on social processes came to represent the groundwork for what is known as the New Haven School of International Law, which foregrounded the importance of processes and micropractices central to the production of cultural norms. Berman's intervention set the stage for the successors of the core insights from earlier interventions and turns its focus to the work of Harold Koh and others who insist that a *new* New Haven School is important to effect legal practices in an increasingly complex world (2007a:304). Such a discussion outlines the need for moving from state-centered models to processes that open analytic spaces for understanding changing legal consciousness in a pluralist world.

Coined by Harold Koh, among many, as *law and globalization*, this new New Haven School has taken on the work of Robert Cover. Berman indicates: "Koh again invoked Cover to explain how an epistemic community was formed around a specific interpretation of the Antiballistic Missile Treaty and the ways in which this community successfully pushed the internationalization of its preferred interpretation into U.S. governmental policy" (2007a:310). However, as we can see from Koh's work on the domestication of international law (1997) and his publications on transnational legal processes (e.g., 1996) – in which, says Berman, he combines "the process and policy orientation of McDougal...et al. with Cover's emphasis on multiple norm-generating communities" (2007a:310–11) – Koh's presumptions are centered on the supremacy of international law as the key modality to be expanded and exported globally to transform vernacular approaches and practices so that they are in keeping with new treaty norms. Thus, for Koh, building on Lea Brilmayer among others, it is human rights treaty integration as a horizontal process of incorporation, along with new norm incorporation as a "vertical" process of cultural change, that is critical in the progressive development of human rights principles and rule of law institutions.

Berman, however, in his review of this literature – and in the spirit of redefining the new New Haven School to attend more accurately to legal pluralism – dances lightly around Koh and the new New Haven School's agenda to devernacularize local practices but does not accept it. Thus, Berman, is committed to exploring the cultural complexities enabled through legal pluralist models and willing to work alongside vernacular legal forms that do not necessarily look the same.

With the goal of producing, as he says, "an ever-deepening pluralist orientation" (2007a:311), Berman's interventions point to the multiple ways that various epistemic communities are engaged in various forms of law creation. Accordingly, the work of legal pluralism is playing an increasing role in articulating more precisely the meaning and enactment of legal mandates in local contexts as they relate to how people differently understand justice and rights (Dezalay and Garth 2002). Indeed, legal pluralism has its value. Understanding the politics of postcolonial African states and the various ways that law is deployed differently and produced as legitimate is certainly a good starting point for examining the ways that legal concepts and meanings are imported, as well as the making of justice in transnational contexts. However, transnational legal studies, or global legal pluralism as articulated by Berman (2007b), must move beyond legal pluralism to attend to the complexities of power at play and the ways that force and power cut through even pluralist constellations. These pluralism interventions have often articulated law in quite conventional ways – ways that do not always reflect the workings of structural inclusions, yet cultural exclusions, that often take for granted that plural legal orders operate in equal domains of comparison and social inter-action.

By not making central the particular preconditions under which law is necessarily structured within hegemonic spheres of inequality, such intersecting explorations of legal cultural production eclipse the space of the political. Approaches that downplay uneven relations in the process of lawmaking or the politics of incommensurability surrounding the basis for deriving justice, undermine the relevance of power and hegemony in shaping the conditions of the possible, in shaping the conditions for imagining "justice."

INTERNATIONAL "JUSTICE" VERSUS SPIRITUALLY DRIVEN RECONCILIATION AS JUSTICE

In relation to the incommensurability of uneven justice-producing domains, this chapter examines the Ugandan situation before the ICC, investigating how international intervention has undercut local vic-tims' attempts to come to terms with the region's violent past. It has done this while exploring the competition over the expansion or restric-tion of the political sphere within which these interventions are occur-ring. The particular focus is on conflicting interpretations of justice, the role of various actors (ICC, NGOs, traditional chiefs, perpetrators, and victims) in contests over the ability of the Ugandan state to offer amnesty to its citizens, and the power of the ICC to prosecute Lord's Resistance Army (LRA) perpetrators for war crimes and crimes against humanity.

The Ugandan context raises several important questions for ana-lysts: At what point should the independent prosecutor of the ICC intervene in national contestations? Is national reconciliation alone sufficient? Are judicial interventions appropriate, or are there other ways in which justice for victims might be achieved? In the emergent corpus of human rights–driven international law, the current trend requires states to prevent and punish various crimes against humanity and to restrict the space within which national amnesties can emerge (Laplante 2007). One consequence of the articulation of justice that advocates international law over national law is that it reduces citi-zens in Uganda (and elsewhere) to victims whose very exclusion from political life is the necessary condition for political intervention by international legal regimes such as the ICC. The failure to treat Ugan-dans and other Africans as political agents creates, again, the conditions for seeing Africans as in need of salvation by a benevolent "West." The result is an African population characterized by what Agamben (1998) calls *zoe*, or "bare life" – a condition of extrapolitical, absolute victimhood in which life is reduced to the effort required to satisfy only the most basic needs of existence. (Agamben contrasts *zoe* with *bios:* politically or morally qualified life, the form of life found in a thriving community.)

Bare life exists in tension with another necessary project of the international human rights order: the effort to produce in postcolonial African regions political beings (liberal subjects) who are committed to implementing forms of justice that reinforce the domain of international justice. Such processes of subject (de)construction are often complex and contradictory; local refusals to comply with international legal demands and the creation or implementation of alternative forms of governance can result in their being either resisted or reinforced. In Uganda, this is made manifest in the conflict between international criminal prosecution and national–local reconciliation, highlighting the many unresolved issues of the ICC that are being brought to international attention by NGOs on both sides of the dispute.

On one side of this dispute are those who favor a local solution. Following Article 53 of the Rome Statute,[1] a range of NGOs and legal experts in Uganda, as well as elsewhere, argue that in the "interests of justice," the prosecutor of the ICC should discontinue investigations and arrests in northern Uganda and allow Ugandan peace negotiations to take place. According to this argument, it is only by doing so that moral, legal, and political issues can be effectively addressed in regionally and historically complex situations and that local justice mechanisms can be implemented. On the other side is the lead prosecutor for the ICC and its global institutions, working alongside (now former) United Nations (UN) Secretary-General and various international human rights NGOs, who insist on the refusal of the ICC to comply with national amnesty provisions. Calling amnesties for war crimes and the like an abrogation of international law and even a recipe for disaster – "turning a blind eye to justice only undercuts durable peace"[2] – advocates of this movement have been central to the fight to maintain prosecution-driven justice. In the middle are the more complex and perhaps cynical positions of those who are intent on using the language of international criminal and humanitarian law instrumentally yet may be doing so in bad faith.

Among these are advocates accused of having mastered the basic discourse of internationalism and rule of law to make a living, although they are ultimately concerned with ethnic and family matters, not peace and justice on a national scale.

In interrogating the meaning of a path to international justice, it is critical to explore how, in the context of international criminal law, various understandings of justice overlay and contradict others. Especially pertinent are those paths to peace or justice that fulfill the immediate needs of victims, whereas the rule of law may cause more suffering long before anything resembling peace will be possible. As the legal anthropology literature has shown, diversity in justice conceptions is vast, ranging from differences in the basis for justice and equality (Bohannan, 1957; Gluckman 1965, 1973 [1955]; Kennett 1968; Greenhouse 1986; Rosen 1989; Wilson 2001; Bowen 2003), to differences in how people conceptualize rights (Mutua 2002), to differences in how they understand the duties of the individual to the state versus individual duties to ethnic, cultural, religious, or family groups (Maurer 2004; Moore 2005; Merry 2006b), as well as related differences in the perceived appropriateness of punishment (An-Na'im 1995, 1999). Given this diversity, we should be asking whether the growing expansion of different meanings of justice provides a new language by which people can defend the persecuted or unrepresented in ways not already available to societies. Following this line, we should also ask whether both the human rights movement and the emergent international criminal law movement can provide support for local discourses of justice instead of merely colonizing existing cultural expressions or replacing them with new norms.

Beyond the issue of "justice," the larger theoretical question in a context such as northern Uganda, where victims have been living in extreme poverty in camps for displaced people for more than twelve years, is this: What kind of victims does the ICC require northern Uganda's citizens to be? This line of questioning highlights the ways that ICC mechanisms of political control influence Agamben's *bios–zoe* continuum, in which citizens can so easily come to represent bare life. The process of determining the strategy for maintaining life involves delineating political and moral life, managed by the political subjects of power relations, versus bare life, which exists outside of the realm of the political. It is this differentiation that demarcates which lives "matter" in the eyes of the world and that enables the ICC to claim jurisdiction and intervene.

Despite the grim ramifications of the construction and management of *zoe* and *bios* categories, the victims of northern Uganda's warfare – who have been otherwise excluded from judicial and quasi-judicial proceedings – are now, through NGOs and governmental initiatives, becoming central players in the justice-making process. This inclusion of victims has taken shape as part of a bid toward reconciliation and the laying of new paths toward "traditional" justice. In this process, chiefs and townspeople alike use the language of "rights" and "forgiveness" and – according to Norbert Mao, chairman of northern Uganda's Gulu district, at the heart of the conflict – insist that "justice does not necessarily mean punishment" but is rather part of "aiming for a higher target of seeking a peaceful and reconciled society" in which Uganda can pursue its own ancient reconciliation rituals to end one of longest wars on the African continent.[3] Today, those in sub-Saharan Africa who are victims of violence, refugees of war, and stricken by medical compromises are constantly enmeshed in relational connections that leave them situationally, but never acontextually, vulnerable to change. The Ugandan amnesty approach – rather than treating them as bare-life victims, in the fashion of the ICC – allows them to engage with perpetrators in rituals of reconciliation through which they may reproduce themselves as political beings.

However, as we shall see, whether perpetrators can or should be reintegrated into communities is at issue precisely because victims and their rights have taken center stage. Thus, the dispute among NGOs, the Ugandan government, and the ICC is not simply over the nature of perpetrators and how best to respond to their crimes; rather, it also over the nature of victims and how best to treat them as sociopolitical beings and as sovereign individuals who should be recognized as having the power to decide on the viability of "justice" in their own contexts. This includes whether Ugandans, members of a postcolonial African state, should be able to exercise the power of constitutional self-government to apply the constitutional terms of their Amnesty Act.

THE UGANDAN AMNESTY ACT AND THE DIFFICULTIES OF COMPLEMENTARITY IN ACTION

The Acholi-speaking people of Uganda are from the Luo ethnic group from the districts of Gulu, Kitgum, and Pader in northern Uganda. Popular and local lore describe them as having traveled to northern Uganda from the southern Sudan. By the end of the seventeenth century, they had settled in northern Uganda and set up chiefdoms headed by rulers known as *rwodi*. By the mid-nineteenth century, sixty small chiefdoms existed in eastern Acholiland. During Uganda's colonial period, the British encouraged political and economic development in the south of the country, but the Acholi and other northern ethnic groups supplied the south with manual labor and military might. This military power peaked with the July 1985 coup d'état staged by Acholi General Tito Okello of the Uganda National Liberation Army, ousting President Milton Obote. It ended six months later with Okello's defeat in a military coup led by Yoweri Museveni, the leader of the National Resistance Army, one of several forces that had been engaged in a five-year guerrilla war following Obote's purportedly rigged election in 1981 (Kasfir 1976; Mamdani 1988; Oloka-Onyango 1991).[4]

President Yoweri Museveni, having assumed power nondemocratically in a country fraught with ethnically motivated conflict and political struggle, offered pledges both to restore peace from ethnic strife and to rebuild Uganda's economy. Three successive presidential elections in 1996, 2000, and 2006 confirmed his rule and ushered in a period of relative economic stability.[5] Violence persisted throughout the late 1980s, 1990s, and into the twenty-first century, however, and has continued to affect the northern region. For example, the LRA, formed in 1987 as a popular resistance movement against Museveni's National Resistance Movement government and transformed into a rebel paramilitary group, engaged in an violent campaign across northern Uganda, often spilling over into parts of southern Sudan. A series of cease-fires has been arranged through peace talks that commenced in July 2006.[6]

The LRA, a Ugandan rebel group of predominantly adult militia as well as more than ten thousand child soldiers,[7] emerged from several splinter groups of the former Ugandan People's Democratic Army. It consists of predominantly ethnic Acholi who were displaced by Museveni's 1986 seizure of power and who were angry at what they saw as unfair governance. The leader of the LRA, Joseph Kony – a spirit medium who emerged after his initial success with the growing Holy Spirit Movement – has characterized its goal as replacing Museveni's parliamentary government with an administration that would enforce the biblical Ten Commandments (rather than a national constitution).[8] One UN official in 2003 classified the contemporary violent struggles in Uganda as the "biggest forgotten, neglected humanitarian emergency in the world today," blaming the conflict, which included regular attacks against civilians in northern Uganda, for the deaths

123

of tens of thousands and the displacement of 1.3 million.[9] The LRA has been accused by members of the national and international communities of attacking and abducting some twenty thousand children; looting and destroying civilian property; killing civilians; and torturing, raping, and mutilating girls forced to serve as concubines for senior commanders.[10]

Responding to international pressure to end the northern violence and establish political and economic stability, Uganda signed the Rome Statute on March 17, 1999, and ratified it on June 14, 2002,[11] thus becoming the sixty-eighth member state of the ICC. In December 2003, President Museveni referred the jurisdiction for investigating criminal offenses allegedly committed by the LRA to the prosecutor of the ICC, Luis Moreno-Ocampo.[12] This occurred at a time when the Ugandan government was also drafting a legislative bill to implement the terms of the Rome Statute into national law. Moreno-Ocampo expressed concern that because of a conflict with Uganda's national Amnesty Act, the ICC was unable to investigate effectively LRA crimes committed by the five top commanders in Uganda after July 1, 2002.[13] On July 29, 2004, however, he nonetheless determined that there was sufficient basis to start planning the first investigation of the ICC with the hope of pursuing jurisdiction over the case.[14] In the summer of 2005, indictments for crimes against humanity were prepared by the ICC against LRA leader Joseph Kony and his top five commanders, and arrest warrants were issued under seal on July 8, and unsealed on October 13, 2005.[15]

These indictments have spawned a range of challenges concerning Uganda's sovereign right to resolve the conflict in alternative ways, as well as the right to postpone international proceedings until peace has been achieved. The former is particularly relevant given the parallel and largely irreconcilable reconciliation process that was evolving on the national scene while the ICC investigation was under way. The bill implementing the Rome Statute, submitted to the cabinet for approval on June 25, 2004, failed to remove governmental immunities and amnesties, including the Ugandan Amnesty Act passed by Parliament in January 2000.[16] In late 2005, a Ugandan high court judge issued a ruling pronouncing that amnesty under local law remained available to all LRA rebels, including those indicted by the ICC. On April 18, 2006, the Ugandan Parliament passed an amendment to the 2000 Amnesty Act that excluded LRA leader Joseph Kony and his top commanders from the amnesty.[17] However, on July 4, 2006, Museveni announced that Uganda would grant LRA leader Kony total amnesty as long as he responded "positively" to the Southern Sudan–mediated peace talks and abandoned "terrorism"; the LRA, about to engage in those talks, rejected this offer.[18] Museveni's affirmation of state primacy came after the president, originally an ICC ally, criticized both the United Nations' and the Democratic Republic of Congo's government for failing to capture Kony in the Garamba National Park of Congo and to initiate peace talks with the LRA.[19]

In a country with a violence-ridden past, amnesty has come to be seen by some Ugandan citizens as the best way to rebuild the nation. Especially in the Acholi region, most heavily hit by the recent warfare, the various traditional reconciliation processes of *mato oput* have been seen as complementing the amnesty pardons offered by the state. This path to justice, however, is hardly complementary to that of the ICC.

AMNESTY AND THE "TRADITIONAL" ACHOLI PATH FOLLOWED BY UGANDA

An earlier amnesty bill had been introduced by the Ugandan government in 1998 in an attempt to use pardons for insurgents so as to end what looked like an intractable conflict.[20] Prior to that, de facto and de jure amnesties under the governmental National Resistance Movement had already been offered to various parties and groups/movements that had engaged in rebellion (notably the Uganda People's Democratic Movement/Army [UPDM/A] and the Uganda People's Front/Army [UPF/A]).[21] Regarding the Amnesty Statute of 1987, a landmark in this history, Ugandan lawyer Barney Afako has noted:

> [It] was passed by the National Resistance Council (NRC) [and was] professed to encourage various fighting groups and sponsors of insurgency to cease their activities. In particular, the statute targeted "Ugandans in exile who are afraid to return home due to fear of possible prosecution." Under the statute, four offences – genocide, murder, kidnapping and rape – were considered too heinous to be included under the amnesty. Similarly, the subsequent 1998 Statute also sought to exclude certain offenders from amnesty.[22]

Nonetheless, the 1998 Statute reflected the view held by many Ugandans that subjecting all LRA members to formal prosecution would not offer a valid or effective path toward peace.

Building on the tradition of the Amnesty Statutes of 1987 and 1998, the government adopted a reformed Amnesty Act in January 2000 for Ugandans involved in "acts of a war-like nature in various parts of the country."[23] The 2000 Act provides that

> an Amnesty is declared in respect of any Ugandan who has at any time since the 26th day of January, 1986[,] engaged in or is engaging in war or armed rebellion against the government of the Republic of Uganda by (a) actual participation in combat; (b) collaborating with the perpetrators of the war or armed rebellion; (c) committing any other crime in the furtherance of the war or armed rebellion; or (d) assisting or aiding the conduct or prosecution of the war or armed rebellion.[24]

The amnesty depends on individual application to the authorities for a "Certificate of Amnesty," along with a statement that the person concerned "renounces and abandons involvement in the war or armed rebellion."[25] The Act defines amnesty as "pardon, forgiveness, exemption or discharge from criminal prosecution or any other form of punishment by the State."[26] The granting of amnesty for insurgency-related offences confers an irrevocable immunity from prosecution or punishment within the borders of Uganda (but not outside it). This immunity is underwritten in the Ugandan Constitution and has been established by the Ugandan Amnesty Commission (UAC).[27] Crucially, the 2000 Act promotes "appropriate reconciliation mechanisms in the affected areas."[28] In fact, forgiveness and reconciliation are said to be at the center of traditional Acholi beliefs. Many Acholi believe in the world of the "living-dead" and receive guidance on moral behavior from *jok*, gods or divine spirits, and ancestors. When a wrong is committed, these divine spirits are believed to send misfortune and illness to the community until appropriate actions are taken by the offender and leaders of the clans. Thus, the living-dead are said to play an active role in the world of the living, and an individual's actions can have consequences for the broader community. Thus, justice in this cosmology is a means of restoring social relations. Individuals are encouraged to accept responsibility for their actions voluntarily, and forgiveness, rather than revenge, is stressed.

In the Ugandan Acholi language, *amnesty* is usually translated as *kica*. The term resonates with historically embedded practices. Many people in that region see the mediation of the "traditional" chiefs (*rwodi*) as a particularly appropriate means to resolve disputes in the "traditional ways." The *mato oput*, as it is popularly known (the phrase means "drinking the bitter root" in Acholi), is an Acholi reconciliation ceremony that is performed between two clans following the killing, whether accidental or intentional, of one clan member by another (Finnström 2004; T. Allen 2006).[29] It is the final stage to bring peace between the two clans and follows a period of separation, mediation, and negotiation led by the clan elders.

Beyond the goal of attaining peace between the living clans, the *mato oput* ceremony also has a key spiritual function, that of appeasing the spirit of the person who was killed.[30] Ancestors are often revered and feared in the traditional Acholi religion, therefore efforts must be made to keep them at peace. When a person is killed, the widespread belief is that they are unsettled and may seek revenge on the individual, the clan, and those surrounding the one who killed them. Some believe that the angry spirit may also be vengeful toward the person who finds their deceased body. The Acholi name this type of spirit *cen*, which must be appeased through ritual and ceremony to restore peace in the lives of the killer and those surrounding him or her. The *mato oput* ceremony is an essential practice to make this happen and is presented as a ceremony of the clan group, especially its inner family, in which the perpetrator acknowledges his or her wrongdoing and offers compensation to the victim.[31]

The ceremony is conducted in a variety of different forms, but common characteristics include the exchange of a slaughtered sheep (provided by the offender) and goat (provided by the victim's relatives), and the drinking of the bitter herb, *oput*, by both clans. The ceremony is moderated by elders of the opposing clans, in which a consensus is reached about the event in question, and an appropriate compensation is negotiated for the victim or victim's family. The ceremony culminates in both parties drinking of the bitter herb, which "means that the two conflicting parties accept 'the bitterness of the past and promise never to taste such bitterness again.'"[32]

It is said that "many Acholi believe [*mato oput*] can bring true healing in a way that formal justice system cannot."[33] The point is not to be punitive but to restore social harmony within the affected community. Because of the perception of the ritual's effectiveness as a local form of justice, *mato oput* ceremonies are being supported and institutionalized by governmental as well as nongovernmental organizations throughout the northern region as an alternative path to national and international justice.[34] Since 2001, the district of Kitgum in northern Uganda has regularly earmarked funding for elders to carry out similar atonement rituals elsewhere. Ceremonies have taken place in Pabbo, Gulu district, and others have been planned for different parts of the Acholi region. For example, in a project supported by the Belgian government, the *rwodi* of all the Acholi clans were reinstated and the *lawi rwodi* (head chief) was elected by the other *rwodi* in Pajule. A group *mato oput* ceremony was held in November 2001, which involved roughly twenty LRA combatants, recently returned to the community. The ceremony was intended to demonstrate the support of the wider Ugandan community and was attended by representatives from NGOs and churches, as well as Acholi returnees and government officials, the amnesty commissioners, and senior army commanders.

Many LRA combatants have been forcibly abducted, displaced, or victimized themselves. As a result, there are limitations as to how the formal justice system can recognize these nuances in legal and moral guilt. The traditional Acholi process of reconciliation has been promoted as an alternative to retributive justice and is seen as a means to end the war and reintegrate communities torn by conflict.[35] It was clear from the observations of our research team that the traditional ritual of *mato oput* has been adapted for conflict-related crimes. The ceremonies have incorporated aspects of the justice process, such as truth telling and symbolic compensation. Some people we interviewed spoke of high levels of moral empathy among the Acholi people to explain the need for traditional ceremonies such as *mato oput*. Over the course of our team's travels to document these ceremonies, it was clear that the ceremony was the final act of a long process leading up to reconciliation that culminates in the sharing of the symbolic, bitter drink from which the ritual takes its name.

The first phase involves the separation and suspension of all communications and relationships between the two clans, which acts as a "cooling off" period. It is also intended to prevent any escalation of the conflict. During this period, necessary steps are taken to abide by the legal aspects of committing the crime, such as filing reports with the police. The elders of each clan are also informed of the crime at this time. Initial talks may begin between the clans; however, if they become too heated and unproductive, they are delayed until a later time. Once negotiations begin, the two clans meet to discuss compensation and how to move forward to achieve full reconciliation. This phase may finish quickly; however, in some cases it may last for years. After all the conditions for peace have been agreed on, a date is set for the *mato oput* ceremony.[36]

A *New York Times* feature article welcomed the recourse to "traditional justice" in seeking reconciliation through *mato oput*:

> The other day, an assembly of Acholi chiefs put the notion of forgiveness into action. As they looked on, 28 young men and women who had recently defected from the rebels lined up according to rank on a hilltop overlooking this war-scar[r]ed regional capital, with a one-legged lieutenant colonel in the lead and some adolescent privates bringing up the rear. They had killed and maimed together. They had raped and pillaged. One after the other, they stuck their bare right feet in a freshly cracked egg, with the lieutenant colonel, who lost his right leg to a bomb, inserting his right crutch in the egg instead. The egg symbolizes innocent life, according to local custom, and by dabbing themselves in it the killers are restoring themselves to the way they used to be.
>
> Next, the former fighters brushed against the branch of a pobo tree, which symbolically cleansed them. By stepping over a pole, they were welcomed back into the community by Mr. [David Onen] Acana [II, head chief] and the other chiefs.
>
> "I ask for your forgiveness," said Charles Otim, 34, the rebel lieutenant colonel, who had been abducted by the rebels himself, at the age of 16, early in the war. "We have wronged you." (Lacey 2005)

Not only *mato oput* but also individual cleansing rituals have taken place whenever former LRA members have returned to the community. These rituals involve both the political and spiritual domains of engagement. Through rites of reintegration, then, victims are reunited with ex-combatants both politically and spiritually. Nevertheless, there are many objections toward the use of these traditional methods of reconciliation for conflict-related crimes. Our extensive interviews, conducted in the Acholi regions of Amuru, Gulu, Kitgum, and Pader, yielded three central criticisms of these traditional methods. As also argued by Kevin Ward (2001) and Erin Baines (2007) despite the attractiveness of local justice mechanisms, the following reservations exist:

1. A large number of the crimes committed are outside the jurisdiction of Acholi traditional laws, and the younger generations involved are beyond the reach of traditional customs.
2. The Acholi traditional judicial domain tends to be male-dominated, and thus inadequate for addressing domestic problems related to husbands and wives.

129

3.   The role of Christianity is an important channel for understanding Acholi self-expression of traditional beliefs (Ward 2001) and cannot be understood in its absence.

During our 2007 field visits in the Acholi area, what further complicated our understandings of these "local justice" methods was the precarious role of Christianity in reinventing particular forms of reconciliation rituals. Churches were present throughout the region, especially in the internally displaced persons camps and towns of Acholiland in ways that were unparalleled by any other religious organization. It is clear that the Anglican Church has used traditional beliefs both to explain Acholi grievances to the government and to facilitate the community's own understanding of its suffering (Ward 2001:209–10). And as such, Christian leaders have emerged as a voice for indigenous religious values and have quite seamlessly applied the ideas behind Acholi theology – ideas regarding reconciliation, forgiveness, and truth telling – to the principles of the Ten Commandments (Ward 2001).

A range of organizations is actively participating in ensuring that these revived rituals are integrated into the reconciliation process. As noted by Janet Anderson of the Institute for War and Peace Reporting:

> Northern Ugandan religious leaders and peace negotiator Betty Bigombe, a politician and former international diplomat, have been calling for the ICC to back off in order to give local peace initiatives, based on traditional reconciliation methods, a chance to end the war. The religious leaders, including local Roman Catholic Archbishop John Baptist Odama, allege that the ICC's decision to get involved in northern Uganda's tragedy has undermined their own efforts to build the rebels' confidence in peace talks.[37]

Acholi reconciliation traditions are becoming popularized as a result of the efforts of international development organizations, NGOs, news reporters, and Western researchers sympathetic to local struggles. My findings have also shown that talk of forgiveness is part of a larger discursive process that notably intersects with cultural familiarity and ethnic celebration in the midst of ethnically related violence. When given a choice between Acholi traditions and international displays of 'justice,' most choose that which is familiar, despite their aspirations for intervention from outside. Interestingly, only 2 percent of the five hundred people interviewed seemed optimistic about the peace process.

However, they feared that it would not be successful if derailed by the presence of the ICC.[38]

I am raising these alternative reconciliation methods neither to romanticize traditional forms of justice as reconciliatory in nature nor to suggest that social-healing rituals reflect the totality of people's understandings of justice. Rather, I do so to highlight how the contest over the jurisdiction of LRA crimes is indeed reflective of the politics of friction, in Tsing's sense in understanding competing social practices that exist alongside ICC justice mechanisms. Yet in detailing the ideological – spiritual and secular – differences that shape the power struggles among *mato oput*, Uganda's Amnesty Act, and the ICC with regard to jurisdiction, it is the politics of incommensurability and the inability of competing sides to recognize the conceptual relevance of the others that necessarily divide people's measure of the efficacy of the different justice approaches.

Acholi traditional justice mechanisms represent ritualized public expressions of wrongdoing and corrective measures toward reconciliation that have adapted symbolic meanings to contemporary social circumstances. Although these various justice-making mechanisms provide alternatives to international legal regimes, they are also likely to perpetuate inequalities as well (Nader 2002), especially as increasing numbers of victims – disenfranchised and impoverished – gain access to the political sphere. I met people in the region who have been disillusioned by social rituals that lack judicial power or who were wary of the ability of local people to render fair judgments to women. Some of these were individuals from afflicted villages and communities who argued that some ex-combatants, especially those who do not believe in the power of spiritual redemption, cannot be reconciled using traditional justice mechanisms. Those favoring international and national juridical paths to justice argued that the old systems of traditional justice no longer work in Uganda's contemporary context of "senseless violence."

Others who remain skeptical of the efficacy of traditional justice mechanisms – international NGOs such as the ICC-oriented Victims' Rights Working Group, for example – have lobbied for victims' interests to be taken into account through the exercise of judicial mechanisms, both international and national. This has meant rebutting those advocates like Betty Bigombe who call for peace at all costs. These NGOs have argued that only judicial paths will achieve sustainable peace. For them, the absence of law is the absence of justice and, as such, it will undermine victims' rights and dismiss their suffering as unimportant. As their literature indicates,

> impunity might serve as a quick, short-term solution, but it cannot root out the seeds that led to the conflict nor deter future crimes. Indeed, denying justice can lead to further human rights violations. For example, reports from northern Uganda indicate that amnestied rebels continue to mete out abuses on victims even when they have been released from captivity in the bush.... International obligations to ensure justice for crimes under international law should be upheld.[39]

Not surprisingly, various international NGOs, such as Amnesty International and others that are part of the Coalition for the ICC (CICC), support this position and are working alongside the ICC to block local attempts at amnesty. The net result is that Ugandan pro-peace advocates see themselves as facing the political challenge of having to convince international institutions to respect its chosen path toward peace, while having to put in place processes of justice-based accountability.[40]

Thus, on July 21, 2006, under the guardianship of the government of Southern Sudan, the LRA and the Ugandan government began peace talks in Juba, Southern Sudan.[41] This effort to end the war in northern Uganda reflects a path toward reconciliation that has been seen by all parties as being long overdue. From the start, the Ugandan government demanded that the LRA meet all four of the following conditions: "Renounce and abandon all forms of terrorism[.] Cease all forms of hostilities[.] Dissolve itself, and hand over all arms and ammunition in its possession together with their inventory[.] Assemble in agreed locations where they will be demobilised, disarmed and documented." The Ugandan government then offered, "upon successful conclusion of the talks," to reintegrate ex-combatants into "civilian productive life"; assist with their educational and vocational training, as well as with their resettlement into civilian life; and provide "cultural, religious leaders and all stakeholders" with the resources to allow ex-combatants to engage in social rituals and traditional justice mechanisms, such as *mato oput*, in order to reconcile with their communities.[42]

CHALLENGES AND CONTESTATIONS TO THE ICC IN UGANDA

At the heart of the disagreement between the Ugandan government and the ICC are questions concerning the primacy of international law over national law. For in the case of Uganda, civil war in the north and the economic, social, and cultural rights of its IDPs (internally displaced persons) and its various urban populations remain central to the national debates over appropriate jurisdiction and the ways that governmental action should proceed. Uganda's Amnesty Act, extended to 2010,[43] offers rebels and liberation activists amnesty if they end their violence and engage in the brokering of peace. Some working on behalf of the ICC find themselves at odds with its positions or those of CICC or other rule of law organizations, not always agreeing with their recommendations for action in view of the local implications.

Given Uganda's nationally legislated amnesty, the international court has been condemned by many African NGO advocates, mediators, and academics for intervening in a fragile regional peace process in a way that is bound to make Ugandans even more vulnerable to an LRA backlash. Supporters of the ICC movement, including a number of Ugandan parliamentarians as well as various legal advisors to the president, concerned that the Ugandan Amnesty Act would compromise the ICC's ability to exercise jurisdiction, drafted the Rome Statute compliance bill for treaty implementation to be presented before the Ugandan Parliament in December 2004.

The network of Ugandan NGOs working on treaty compliance, with the help of international experts, in turn developed an advocacy campaign to comment on the draft compliance bill being presented by the parliamentarians. In addition, various international human rights groups commented on the draft bill, highlighting its problems; some did not consider the Ugandan NGOs' strategies for the review of the draft compliance bill to be timely or strategic enough to produce the appropriate results. To present its own analysis, a prominent NGO actively engaged in the CICC produced a twenty-page document that raised concerns about Uganda's International Criminal Court Bill 2004.[44] A later report, offered in the spirit of ensuring the most effective implementing legislation, detailed several criticisms of Uganda's draft bill (as well as those of other states), the most important being in regard to Uganda's Amnesty Act, which the document predicted was bound to cause jurisdictional problems. Other issues included:

> Weak definitions of crimes; unsatisfactory principles of criminal responsibility and defenses; failure to provide for universal jurisdiction to the full extent permitted by international law; political control over the initiation

of prosecutions; failure to provide for the speediest and most efficient procedures for reparations to victims; inclusion of provisions that prevent or could potentially prevent cooperation with the Court; failure to provide for persons sentenced by the Court to serve sentences in national prisons; and failure to establish training programmes for national authorities on effective implementation of the Rome Statute.[45]

The organization not only released its Uganda report to its vast membership but also posted it on its Web site and made a published version available to various Ugandan government offices. This posturing of absolute morality by many international human rights NGOs is not atypical of their commitment to the spread of the rule of law project and actually highlights the perceived hierarchy of agendas in these international contexts.

The Committee on Legal and Parliamentary Affairs, a Ugandan parliamentary commission charged with the task of researching and analyzing the Rome Statute compliance bill, solicited input from various Ugandan NGOs, assembled its facts, and submitted its report to the relevant parliamentary committee on December 14, 2004. Outlining the goals of the bill and identifying problems in it, yet affirming the ICC as the answer to "justice" in postwar Uganda, the committee called on the Ugandan Executive to "give the force of law in Uganda to the Statute of the International Criminal Court" and to "promote universal rights" for all.[46] However, writing with the realities of war in their backyards and the urgency of economic and cultural attention to the most appropriate paths to "justice," the report's authors also acknowledged disagreements over which strategy was best for Uganda's transition from war to peace.

My research into these disagreements revealed that there were three primary, although not entirely mutually exclusive, camps represented in the debates over the ICC–Uganda contestations: those who questioned whether ICC intervention should proceed at all; those who believed that the alternative of the Ugandan Amnesty Act – in which the perpetrators of crime would be offered a pardon, thereby ending the war immediately – might be a better strategy; and those who felt that it was not possible for Ugandans to be objective and, thus, that it was critical for ICC intervention to proceed. Notwithstanding its acknowledgment of the debate over how to proceed, the committee's report endorsed the jurisdictional integrity of the Rome

Statute but warned that the draft bill did not provide for a legally binding procedure for the "harmonisation of the Ugandan national system of laws and procedures, and the traditional reconciliation mechanism, with the Rome Statute."[47] As a result, it proposed several amendments to the effect that the prosecutor for the ICC must not disregard national and traditional mechanisms of justice and must consider processes that were under way before the commencement of the investigations. In short, the existing national mechanisms, based on the existing legal framework and traditional customs, must inform and guide the prosecutor in his decision whether to prosecute. The report also recommended that a new program should be introduced in the bill to provide for alternative accountability procedures that would still meet the standards of admissibility outlined in the Rome Statute.

The differing advocacy approaches of and analytical conclusions reached by domestic NGOs, international organizations, and Ugandan legislators – particularly their disparate levels of respect for culturally shaped and politically relevant justice mechanisms – highlight some of the typical controversies surrounding the ICC and CICC "paths to justice," and their incommensurability in addressing seriously the realities of war and violence, economic displacement, and inequality in the Ugandan landscape. These differences speak, in part, to contradictory agendas between those NGOs committed to working within local contexts and those dependent on international donor imperatives that delimit the power that their own vernacular knowledge forms can have in shaping solutions.

For the ICC and its supporters, the challenges ahead include creating the conditions through which its legal primacy can be established and charting considerations of victims that are in the interests of justice. At the heart of the contestations in Uganda are questions concerning whether the prosecutor for the ICC should pursue investigations and arrests prior to the end of the war in northern Uganda, or whether, "in the interests of justice,"[48] he should deem his findings inadmissible and instead support Ugandan President Museveni's bid for peace.[49] This would enable the Ugandan government to apply its national legislation, the Amnesty Act, and grant amnesty to the perpetrators of crimes against humanity – some of whom were also victims of war – while also applying traditional justice mechanisms to Ugandan paths to justice.

―

In "the Interests of Justice": The Rights of Victims versus the Rights of the State

As discussed in Chapter 2, one of the greatest innovations of the Rome Statute is the central role accorded to victims. As noted in one of the reports from the Office of the Prosecutor (OTP):

> For the first time in the history of international criminal justice, victims have the possibility under the Statute to present their views and concerns to the Court.... The experience of the Court to date proves that understanding the interests of victims in relation to the decision to initiate an investigation is a very complex matter. While the wording of Article 53(1)(c) implies that the interests of victims will generally weigh in favour of prosecution,... The Office will give due consideration to the different views of victims, their communities and the broader societies in which it may be required to act.[50] ... Understanding the interests of victims may require other forms of dialogue besides direct discussions with victims themselves. It may be important to seek the views of respected intermediaries and representatives, or those who may be able to provide a comprehensive overview of a complex situation.... The OTP's activities in relation to Uganda exemplify this approach. The OTP has conducted more than 25 missions to Uganda for the purpose of listening to the concerns of victims and representatives of local communities.[51]

Since the release of the first set of ICC-related arrest warrants, there have been several discussions about the meaning and possible interpretation of Article 53 of the Rome Statute in which considerations of the clause "in the interests of justice" have become a central factor in the admissibility of a criminal case. Article 53, titled "Initiation of an Investigation," describes the substantive rules for an investigation and prosecution of crimes under the subject matter jurisdiction of the ICC. In detailing the initiation of a prosecution, it indicates that "the Prosecutor shall, having evaluated the information made available to him or her, initiate an investigation unless he or she determines that there is no reasonable basis to proceed under this Statute." It then outlines the considerations for deciding whether to initiate an investigation.[52] If the prosecutor determines that there is no basis on which to proceed, then he or she is expected to inform the Pre-Trial Chamber of that decision. The prosecutor is then expected to inform the inflicted state of the findings from the investigation and the reasons for such a conclusion. In determining whether there is sufficient basis for a prosecution,

MULTIPLE SPACES OF JUSTICE

Article 53(1)(c) refers to inadmissibility if there is a determination that proceeding with the prosecution is not "in the interests of justice." However, deciding what is and what is not in the interests of justice remains one of the most underdeveloped and contested concepts in the statute. This is primarily because the concept of acting in the interests of justice extends well beyond the exercise of criminal justice: it extends into political and moral arenas, thereby including many considerations and purposes.

What particular notion of "victim" seems to inform the OTP's commitment to "the interests of justice," and how does the OTP – and international organizations more generally – seem to conceive of the role of state sovereignty? In June 2006, the OTP, responding to questions about the court's political motivations, circulated to various international NGOs and consultants two draft documents that further expanded on the OTP's selection criteria for judicial investigations and clarified the criteria being used by the OTP in pursuing cases. The determinations for cases were described as being shaped by four guiding principles: independence, impartiality, objectivity, and nondiscrimination; however, the most critical were the justifications of decisions to proceed or not proceed with judicial action in "the interests of justice."[53] These determinations require legal analytic tests guided by the purposes of the court as well as larger political determinations that are connected to victim's justice. The legal tests include ending impunity while also guaranteeing respect for international justice and, in so doing, justifying further action that balances the interests of justice in relation to both the gravity of the crime and the interests of the victims to end violence. These tests highlight the considerations for weighing the terms for justice.

In the Uganda case – that of *The Prosecutor v. Joseph Kony, Vincent Otti, Raska Lukwiya, Okot Odhiambo and Dominic Ongwen* – the OTP reported that it had conducted more than twenty missions to hear the concerns of representatives of local Ugandan communities.[54] These meetings provided increased awareness of the differences among victims and their notions of justice and drew investigators' attention to the "dangers" of alternative justice mechanisms. Accordingly, the OTP has continued to express sensitivity to the deep scars that victims of the conflict have endured. Nevertheless, it has insisted that "only in exceptional circumstances will they conclude that an investigation or a prosecution may not serve the interests of justice."[55]

THE OBLIGATION OF STATES TO UPHOLD INTERNATIONAL LAW VERSUS THEIR RIGHT TO RESOLVE DISPUTES IN THEIR CHOSEN WAY

Many developments in the past fifteen years or more point to a con-sistent trend in establishing the duty of states to prosecute crimes of international concern committed within their jurisdiction.[56] This trend is also manifest in the language of the Preamble to the Rome Statute, in which members recognize that "it is the duty of every State to exercise its criminal jurisdiction over those responsible for international crimes" (para. 6). This understanding of the responsibility of states that have ratified the Rome Statute appears to be supported by the UN Com-mission on Human Rights, which has incorporated it in adopting an updated set of principles for the protection and promotion of human rights.[57] As argued by the OTP, the interpretation of the concept of "the interests of justice" should be guided by the objects and purpose of the statute. Accordingly, the pursuit of those (such as LRA perpe-trators) who are responsible for crimes under the jurisdiction of the court, subject to Article 17 of the Rome Statute, is warranted.[58] One of the aforementioned OTP draft documents makes it clear that respect for victims in relation to the "degree of legitimacy and the extent to which serious efforts had been made to respect the rule of law would be among the important factors the Prosecutor may take into account in considering national approaches."[59] In other words, the OTP will seek to work with various persons to ensure the maximum impact.

Human Rights Watch, among a range of other international NGOs, has agreed with the OTP position:

> International law rejects impunity for serious crimes, such as genocide, war crimes, crimes against humanity and torture. International treaties, includ-ing the U.N. Convention against Torture, the Geneva Conventions, and the Rome Statute of the International Criminal Court, require parties to ensure alleged perpetrators of serious crimes are prosecuted. Uganda has ratified each of these in addition to numerous other human rights treaties. . . . The creation of the International Criminal Court and other international crimi-nal tribunals to prosecute genocide, war crimes, crimes against humanity or other serious violations of humanitarian law illustrates the strong interna-tional commitment to justice for serious crimes.[60]

Regarding amnesties, Richard Dicker, director of Human Rights Watch's International Justice Program, asked, "How long can a peace based on this kind of deal last?"[61] To supplement investigation and prosecutions by the ICC, Human Rights Watch recommends that

> Uganda also should conduct meaningful prosecutions in its own courts. . . . [T]he Ugandan government should establish a truth commission or another truth-telling process that would allow people in northern Uganda a forum to speak about the human rights abuses that occurred during the war. This process could work alongside traditional reconciliation measures in which those affected wish to participate.[62]

In questioning amnesty and other traditional justice mechanisms, various representatives from Amnesty International's New York office have argued that amnesties as solutions for peace and reconciliation only lead to undercutting durable peace. A range of local Ugandan NGOs, however, have insisted that the ICC's 2005 indictment of five LRA leaders should not preclude these peace talks from taking place nor obstruct amnesty as one of many "paths to justice." The intervention by a number of international organizations such as Amnesty International and Human Rights Watch is often interpreted by Ugandan NGOs as undermining the local NGO authority. They feel that these differences in strategies and approaches are typical of the micropolitics of collaborations with international NGOs. Various people with whom I developed a close relationship insisted that "this was not unusual."[63] Many argued that one of the ways that Africa has been pathologized in world history has been through the implicit assumption that African societies are unable to address their own problems and are therefore in need of Western interventions. They see this intervention as symptomatic of this bias, highlighting the way that African organizations are often made to comply with the strategies promoted by leadership from the United States and Western Europe.[64] Arguing that international law recognizes Uganda's sovereign right and obligation to resolve conflict peacefully and to address alleged offences, Zachary Lomo, then the director of the Refugee Law Project, and James Otto, director of Uganda's Human Rights Focus referenced the UN Charter as "uphold[ing] the principle of self-determination of peoples."[65] They have also pointed out the "Rome Statute's principles of complementarity and admissibility [through which] Uganda also has a right to assume responsibility for dealing with criminal charges." As they conclude:

> Ugandan efforts to address the tensions between peace and justice are clearly embodied in the Amnesty Law of 2000, an instrument which involved

considerable democratic consultation, was enacted by the Ugandan Parliament, and long pre-dates the ICC's intervention in 2004. Drawing from national procedures and local traditions, the people of Uganda are seeking to complement the Amnesty by developing accountability mechanisms compatible with the twin goals of peace and justice. Further procedures that integrate fact-finding, victim participation, and reconciliation are being actively pursued.

After twenty years of conflict, northern Uganda has an opportunity to work towards a non-violent resolution, an outcome which would allow displaced communities to finally go home and workable accountability options to be brought into focus. In the interests of victims and in the interests of justice, therefore, we urge the ICC and others concerned about northern Uganda and the neighbouring regions to give peace a chance.

Note that on both sides of the debate are questions about what is actually in the interests of victims (or those so deemed). The answer to these questions is central to the reconfiguration of sovereignty today. In the absence of monarchs and absolutist states, and given that we have moved beyond the period of noninterventionist state sovereignty of the early twentieth century, it is clear that the new (transnational) sovereignty must consider "victims" as central.

Victims, the State of Exception, and the New "New Sovereignty"
In *The New Sovereignty* (1995), Abram Chayes and Antonia Handler Chayes argue that the exercise of sovereignty by states in the late twentieth century was characterized by membership in good standing to various international networks. By dismissing approaches to sovereignty that focus on a model of coercive enforcement, they proposed a new "managerial model" (1995:3) of treaty compliance in which the new sovereignty could be described as an "elaboration and application of treaty norms" (Ibid., 123). Accordingly, membership in the international system is made possible through compliance with treaty obligations. Cast this way, the continuing dialogue between international officials and nongovernmental organizations generates much pressure to resolve problems of noncompliance. Chayes and Chayes argue that the new sovereignty no longer "consists in the freedom of states to act independently in their perceived self-interest, but in membership in reasonably good standing in the regimes that make up the substance of international life" (p. 27). Contending that to be competitive and relevant in the world economy, nation-states must submit to impositions of the international system and, in so doing, are accepted into a complex

web of regulatory agreements, the authors suggest recasting the language of sovereignty in more complex terms that articulate the growing networks of obligation connected to international membership.

Although membership in the international order is certainly a critical consideration for how and why national states act, it is also important to recognize that definitions of compliance are no longer being managed solely by the state alone. Complex and undecided relationships between the international and the national (including constitutional provisions and legal norms) characterize the new regime, especially postcolonial African states within it. The struggles it generates over state and international authority are controversial. Multiple international and supranational organizations compete to set the parameters of decisions related to the sovereign decision of how the terms for maintaining life should be established. The inequalities between refugee status and those in positions of privilege are theorized by what Giorgio Agamben (1998, 2005) has referred to as the "state of exception," in which constituent power (the actual power to create government) is seen as being outside of the judicial order and in the realm of an extraordinary state that operates beyond the law.

State of exception describes the authority to suspend the law in the name of an emergency. In the context of ethnic violence, that emergency might be one in which citizens use paramilitary coups to condemn fellow citizens to the status of bare life, using police, army militia, or death squad resources to reduce life to death. The state of exception is also reflected in the power of individuals working through global institutions to manage international justice mechanisms and suspend national-level processes. This is directly relevant to the competition between the ICC and national-level strategies for justice in Uganda because it relates to the power to decide when and with respect to whom the law does or does not apply. For the ICC relies on states to implement its laws by eliminating national laws that conflict with them. This expectation of international supremacy points to the relative power of international courts in relation to states. Although the 120 states that initially signed the Rome Statute of the ICC participated in its development, its writing, and the passing of amendments, cloaked in the universalist language of the ICC are relations of dominance that have privileged particular norms of juridical justice over others. This is because the conditions for inclusion in the ICC already presuppose particular presumptions about the supremacy of international law over quasi-judicial mechanisms. During the UN Assembly of States Parties meetings and the UN-based General Assembly in which the provisions of the Rome Statute were established,[66] politically "weak" states were rarely in positions to overpower "stronger" states. As such, the relations between different types of nation-state and international institutions derive from contests over the power of authority – the power to decide to claim universal jurisdiction and form alliances with international institutions or to implement amnesty laws and defer to state sovereignty.

The path to international justice has thus come to cloak an unequal distribution of power in a language of jurisdiction and membership. This new form of governmentality, in which states in the Global North control the terms of judicial and social compliance for states in the South, highlights what Suárez-Orozco (2005:6) has referred to as the *hyper-presence* and *hyper-absence* of the state – a concept that I articulate here with reference to the ultraexpansion of the statecraft, but not necessarily the state, as a result of the change in governance mechanisms based in networks of international, national, and local spheres of individual and institutional power. Crucially, these networks do not themselves constitute sovereignty. Rather, they work with states and operate through such institutions as international courts and human rights agencies, through which the coordination and determination of new disciplinary principles are mobilized in strategic relation to each other.

Various extranational tribunals have become forums for the development of new paths to justice in African postcolonial state contexts. The management of contemporary forms of violence can no longer be understood as operating through single forms of sovereign power that reflect one path or one hegemonic notion of justice. Rather, the modernity of international criminal law – alongside the work of NGOs that propel human rights imperatives – represents a range of forces that interact with each other and produce hybrid articulations of justice. As discussed in Chapter 1,[67] this supranational sphere of governmentality is being propelled through the legal advocacy of elite cosmopolitans operating within discrepant orders complicated by persisting postcolonial histories of deeply entrenched social divisions. The paradox of sovereignty, therefore, is its ability to make real the notion of the universal in a way that in fact perpetuates the exclusion of certain groups from equal consideration and participation.

Such an approach locates sovereignty not in the realm of everyday people, wherein sovereignty is diverse and diffuse, but in the realm of those who participate in the decision-making process within which suspect rights can be suspended and that process accorded legitimacy.[68] These forms of power lay in the realm of international court regimes, the powers of which represent extensions of some of the most influential nation-states. Moreover, postcolonial state sovereignty does not always trump international legal regimes, which are increasingly forming the model for regulating the contemporary governmental axis. Yet in the process, what we see is the ability of the law to abandon human suffering – to enable the continuation of bare life.

This bare-life status, the reality of those in the modern concentration camp – the refugee camp, the shanty town, the IDP camp – and of those awaiting capital punishment, constitutes the life that exists outside of the law but that international law needs (and claims) to protect. As Agamben (1998) reminds us, in ancient Roman law, the *homo sacer* was someone who could be killed with impunity but whose death had no sacrificial value. This figure, we know, offers the key to understanding political power and explains the "paradox of [Carl] Schmitt's concept of sovereignty" as actually being the *essence* of sovereignty. In that construct the sovereign was the person "who decides on the state of exception,"[69] thereby maintaining a relation to the exception and, in so doing, constituting itself as a rule. Agamben's notion of sovereignty does not move from the domain of the imperial territorial state, and imperial Europe is a trope for understanding sovereignty everywhere (Agamben 2005).

The international criminal law regime reproduces a relation of exclusion in which these various institutions for the production of justice serve as conduits for the normative categories of victim and perpetrator in sub-Saharan Africa.[70] According to this position, "victims" are represented through the jurisdictional claims of the ICC as a category of individuals to be saved by global rule of law institutions. This process, in which international organizations take on concerns on behalf of victims for the purposes of humanitarianism, reflects the limits of international cooperation, highlighting the relegation of victims' agency outside of the political sphere. For in the local realm, victims are included and central to reconciliation and, at times, are part of the state criminal adjudicatory process. In the international realm, however, it is through their very exclusion as political agents, or at least agents whose participation is circumscribed in particular ways, that they are included in victims' protection and compensation programs. They are incorporated into the international political process only by virtue of their symbolic power as dispossessed agents in need of aid.

Although many scholars of sovereignty studies have heralded this age of globalization as an age of international cooperation and respect among different actors – the state, NGOs, and victims – the space for the inclusion of victims and postcolonial sovereignty has not in fact produced the possibility for a new immanent form of genuine justice making. The path to international justice has not surpassed what Partha Chatterjee calls a "public rhetoric of moral virtue" (2005:491) in which a specific set of techniques for the production of democratic consent are deployed to ensure the expansion of the international force of law. As explored in Chapter 2,[71] victims are not expected to interpret or exercise legal power in their own right, other than by testifying in legal proceedings when called on to do so. To some extent, the same can also be said of "perpetrators": they are not expected to exercise the sovereign right to negotiate terms of the peace accords or the type of justice regime they prefer. The new sovereignty represents the power of an international body to declare the exception through the moral imperative of justice and the authority to take on (or take over) the tasks of "educating, disciplining and training" (Chatterjee 2005:496), as well as to determine the terms of punishment.

Even as this new model of international justice is on the rise, a range of new national punishment approaches in the Global North have combined both *retributive* justice models (in which the punishment imposed is seen as repayment or revenge for the offense committed) and *rehabilitation* models (in which society assists the accused in changing his or her behavior), generating new forms of *restorative* justice that emphasize the harm done to persons and relationships rather than the violation of the law (Orentlicher 2007).[72] These approaches, like that of the traditional justice mechanisms in Uganda, focus on both the survivors of crime and the offenders (Pain and Madit 1997; Rachels 1997). They suggest the possibility of enabling the offender to recognize the injustice he or she has committed and to participate in negotiating restoration through community involvement. Many such notions of restorative justice as practiced in the "West" have historically been shaped by Christian values of personal salvation and peacemaking, forgiveness and healing. Secularized in the 1980s and 1990s, these principled approaches have been incorporated in judiciaries in the United States, Canada, and parts of Europe, and they echo a range of nonsecular legal contexts, such as that of Uganda, in which traditional justice is being used to compensate for a failed judicial system. My point here is not that only such restorative justice mechanisms are viable in contexts in which civil war and ethnic hatred have led to the decimation of communities but that the choice of rebuilding and supporting Uganda's judiciary alongside its various traditional restorative justice mechanisms is one that should be considered in the interests of justice as well as peace. The reality, however, is that to speak of the new sovereignty today is to speak of the movement of the force of law, its techniques of coercion and disciplinary mechanisms, but not the foundations that may make a new world order possible. Such a reconfiguration of sovereignty as global and national equality would involve the erasure of various structural violences closely aligned with neoliberal capitalism. This type of liberatory approach to sovereignty opens up for scrutiny new sites of power in which the rule of international law, by suspending the possibility of national jurisdiction (in Uganda this means the application of amnesties), is allowed to determine the relevancy of alternative justice mechanisms. In doing so, the rule of international law too often denies local responses to injustice and treats victims as docile agents in need of salvation. Its moral universals disregard difference and enable the perpetuation of exclusion.

As a far from neutral project, international justice does not operate in an explicitly heavy-handed way through mechanisms blatantly forcing people to submit to its teachings. Rather, the contemporary effectiveness of international criminal law lies in its alluring promise to transcend injustice while obliquely, but effectively, subverting the very inclusions it in fact seeks to protect. These justice hegemonies work alongside a growing regime for the universal establishment of rule of law and represent new pressures toward the supranational management not only of crime but also of new reporting mechanisms that require international organizations to document, account for, and manage the human body in particular ways, in accordance with carefully crafted treaty laws and regulations (see, e.g., the missions of the World Health Organization or the International Labour Organization). The new sovereignty provides rationalities intended to celebrate the utility of contemporary democracy as a viable form of government in the late twentieth and early twenty-first centuries, and their trajectories point to what international law needs to reshape the biopolitical subject outside of the parameters of state institutions.

Through the moral and political force of humanitarianism, invocations of justice as universal contribute to establishing a new moral economy according to particular human rights principles, always clarifying what is legal and illegal, acceptable and unacceptable, and, as such, participating in maintaining notions of the "good life," within "normal" spheres of life relations – the building of a home environment free of violence, the possibility of food and economic resources to sustain education, and the valuing of certain kinds of family life. Such conditions also mark membership in and belonging to the prestige of the global, in which there exists a geography of rights that is already allied with particular global hegemonies.

Today, institutions such as the ICC and its complex web of interlocutors are constituted by the interaction of states, institutions, international and national NGOs, victims, and even rebel groups vying to participate in shaping the law under which they will submit. These various segments represent the new governmentalities central to new paths to international justice and the rule of law. However, the nexus of conflict among social actors and institutions represents a domain in which law is not simply imposed but rather mediated by power relations. As such, it is productive of exclusions that undermine the exercise of the power to choose amnesties versus international adjudication.

The complexities of Uganda's relationship to the ICC bring into focus the power of international law to separate political beings from "victims," thus making the latter the subjects of the court's political control. I end here with a proposition for a general rethinking of core conceptions of sovereignty that would clarify various key paths to international justice by locating these paths as the production not only of justice itself but of the indirect and direct control of the terms by which decisions are made, naturalized, and controlled.

Although national and international contests over lawmaking seem to hold the potential of negating each other, thereby suspending their norm-generating capacities, the reality is that postcolonial African states and African people are engaged in uneven competitions with international legal bodies whose dominance is upheld by those UN member states most powerful on the world scene. In the midst of such uneven social relationships, the ICC does not represent justice in and of itself; rather, it represents the shifting of the locus of the "real" by choreographing processes within which new norms of justice making are reinforcing a dual presence and absence of governance within global spheres of power. This move from the absolute jurisdictional authority of nation-states to the jurisdictional reconfiguration of international bodies to adjudicate international grievances reflects new sovereignties of the twenty-first century but does not constitute their totality. This is because the central issues, and the ones I explore here, are not limited to contests of the rituals of reconciliation versus the rituals of international adjudication over how to treat perpetrators of the worst crimes against humanity. Rather, the central struggles are contests over the place of victims and how best to treat them as sociopolitical beings.

By claiming to work on behalf of child soldier victims – bare-life survivors whose continued existence in that condition is ensured by virtue of their exclusion as political agents – international law claims the power of the decision over what constitutes the life that is to be excluded from the political sphere (the polis). The exercise of this power indexes the true site of sovereignty. It is the new exercise of the force of law – its techniques of coercion and disciplinary mechanisms – that makes possible the new world order of justice and politics. This new sovereignty is not historically constituted from a political authority but presents itself as democratic through the language of international membership and universalism. However, the reality is that it operates through a particular order in which the force of law gains its power through a spectacular theater of humanitarianism.[73] As such, this new sovereignty, superpolitical and brought into being through the politics of virtue and human rights missionization, both creates and preserves a condition – bare life – that it is dedicated to eradicate. It thus represents suffering that it claims to root out.

Of course, human rights–rule of law work continues to be an important ideal in the achievement of global rights and protections against those who take the lives of others in their own hands. However, we need to think more precisely about the meaning and enactment of justice and politics in local contexts – how it should work, whom it should include, and whom it excludes. We must rethink the conditions within which we envisage justice in the first place and expand the basis on which we locate political beings. For it is limiting to assume that "the law" – rule of law, criminal law, national law – is the only way that justice can be achieved, especially because justice itself is not a thing but a set of relations through which people establish norms of acceptability. Following Jacques Derrida (1992:241), the possibility of achieving justice implies the exercise of a performative force and, therefore, the production of an "interpretative violence that in itself is neither just nor unjust." It is a force that places value on or makes legitimate the power to kill, the power to punish, the power to classify crime, and the power to determine who is subject to the law and under what conditions. As such, it is important to examine the mutual-engagement aspects of

147

putting in place enforceable actions that are seen either as legitimate or illegitimate. The "paths to justice" can represent a process rather than an open clearing, and making justice involves incorporating – or else clear-cutting – practices that are circumscribed by particular values, and as a result, are sometimes incommensurate. For these reasons, it is crucial to examine, as I have begun to do here, the struggles over defining "legitimate" paths to justice and the politics of power that make them tenable.

As we shall see in Part Two of this book, the micropractices engaged in the production of the rule of law movement are fundamental to all forms of governance and formal lawmaking. Whether in explicitly religious-based spheres or human rights and rule of law domains, micropractices work to circulate particular principles and norms that set the groundwork for context-relevant "'moral economies.'" By rethinking the relevance of various approaches to rights in other vernacular forms – from those micropractices in northern Uganda, to "NGO justice," to the focus on Islamic moral principles – justice is represented by the ability to produce the truth regime within which its embodiment, often times spectacular, can be enacted as ordinary, as mundane.

PART TWO

THE RELIGIOUS POLITICS OF INCOMMENSURABILITY

CHAPTER 4

"RELIGIOUS" AND "SECULAR" MICROPRACTICES: THE ROOTS OF SECULAR LAW, THE POLITICAL CONTENT OF RADICAL ISLAMIC BELIEFS

In the midst of the expansion of the International Criminal Court (ICC) and its African-based prosecutions, Africa has witnessed rapid religious recomposition in recent decades marked by new scales of religious organization, new directional flows of influence, assertive new theologies, and intensified public presences. This chapter focuses on the ways that different forms of religious ethical value are central to both the human rights principles shaping the rule of law movement and to key revivalist Muslim commitments in other parts of sub-Saharan Africa. Here I examine a particular West African–Islamic politicolegal trajectory and situate it within the recent expansion of the rule of law. At the heart of this chapter is an inquiry into what new tensions are emerging at the intersections of "religious" and political projects. How, I ask, do current radical religious contestations within African polities – or between religious doctrines and secular legal codes – inform wider theoretical and legal debates on the ambiguous conceptual groundings of the "secular"; on rights and duties; and on the presumptive norms of liberalist citizenship central to its production of individual personhood? How does a different rendering of obligation and authority produce a politics of incommensurability that is beyond liberalist recognition?

THE ICC: A MOVEMENT IN THE MAKING

In liberalist circles until the mid-twentieth century, the international notion of "rights" was predominately associated with domestic issues and rested on the nation-state as the grantor and protector of rights.[1]

However, from the second half of the twentieth century onward, the development of international relations and the network of states engaged in the international law regime have attempted to radicalize the basis for the attainment of rights in democratic society. It is well documented that individuals are now popularly identified in the Global North as possessing "rights," human rights, even without state mechanisms in place to always guarantee those rights. By extension, international criminal law has developed as a twentieth-century phenomenon in which the mission involves the end of impunity and, ultimately, of crimes against humanity in an attempt to prevent victims in the future (Schabas 2001).

Agents engaged in the development of the ICC movement have been working tirelessly with local communities to introduce the terms of the Rome Statute. And as detailed in the first half of the book, since 1989, when the end of the Cold War was declared, we have witnessed a conceptual shift in the management of criminal jurisdiction accompanied by a drastic increase in the number of national constitutions being rewritten and international treaties signed against violence, genocide, and war crimes. But as I detailed in Chapter 3, these transformations have led to gaps in the enforcement of new legal principles being negotiated between states and international institutions (Reisman et al. 2004; Clarke, 2007). Although such gaps may suggest that in this age of multilateral membership to treaty regimes, states are not as powerful as they were, the reality is that in modern neoliberal democracies, it is still the authority of the state – its statecraft – and its deployment of law and the economy, that characterize the political legitimacy of the rule of law.[2] Through its central principles of "accountability," "individual responsibility," and the protection of victims as rights-bearing citizens, national and international actors continue to participate in techniques of international management, thereby maintaining hegemony over the classification of various forms of violence.

As the explanation of the formation of modern transnational justice goes, proponents of the ICC argue that, in keeping with the Nuremberg Principles[3] of the Hague Charter – the goals of which were not founded simply on state preservation – the contemporary institutionalization of an international system has become increasingly interconnected. Here, the proponents believe that state actions and rules of enforcement are becoming just as central to the protection of the interests of other states as they are to the protection of the state in question. By attempting to alter the role of the state as the final arbiter of justice, the statute supplements state adjudication functions with those of an international independent body through which cases under the subject matter jurisdiction of the court can be pursued (Gurule 2001–2:45; Schabas 2004).

With its jurisdictional reach into the life of both state and non-state parties, the ICC poses a challenge to former conceptions of state sovereignty (Gurule 2001–2:12; Schabas 2004:78). In its Preamble, the statute establishes the precedence of the domain of the international, rather than the national, as the unit of humanitarian concern, by "[a]ffirming that the most serious crimes of concern to the international community as a whole must not go unpunished and that their effective prosecution must be ensured by taking measures at the national level and by enhancing international cooperation." However, in practical terms the court was actually constructed to address the many gaps in national regulations that currently characterize the limitations of the enforcement of law outside the jurisdiction of national statutes (Schabas 2004:14).

This move toward the interconnected "humanity" of humans, facilitated by the creation of regional and international institutions and treaty-imposed obligations on world citizens, is erecting limits on sovereign autonomy (Shaw 2003:574–6). However, in some contexts, there are conceptual spaces from which the reach of the global is hindered – spaces of incommensurability in which conceptual differences in interpreting crime and violence are buttressed by differences in the spaces of power and authority accorded to God and the state, respectively.

RADICAL ISLAM AND ITS SPACES OF POWER

For millions of Muslims worldwide, the belief in Allah informs cultural practices as well as the structure of political institutions, judiciaries, and the principles underlying everyday notions of justice, duty, and obligations. Those who recognize the authority of Islam accept that, between A.D. 571 and his death in 632, the Prophet Muhammad served as a conduit of Allah by documenting his principles in the Holy Qur'an (Lewis 1992:11–12). Fundamental Islamic principles depart from conceptions of the rights-bearing citizen whose duties are formulated in relation to the state. Instead, the Sharia as a form of Islamic law offers the possibility of adopting particular tenets of faith as the basis for governance. In northern Nigerian contexts, as in the majority of Islamic states internationally, it is the Sharia criminal codes, principally informed by the Qur'an and varied interpretations of it, that provide the legal rules by which Muslims are expected to live (ibid.:25).[4] As such, belief in Allah requires the acceptance of the duties and obligations revealed in Muhammad's message.

The fundamental duties, practices, and beliefs of Islam are understood through what is referred to as the Five Pillars of Islam:

1. the *shahada*, the profession of faith through testimony declaring, "there is no God but Allah and . . . Muhammad is the messenger of Allah";
2. the *salat*, the performance of the ritual prayer conducted at five appointed times of the day – dawn, midday, afternoon, sunset, and evening;
3. the *zakat*, the obligation to share with the less fortunate;
4. the *sawm*, fasting during the month of Ramadan with the goal of abstaining from eating, drinking, and engaging in sexual activity; and
5. the *hajj*, the obligation of making the pilgrimage to Mecca at least once in a lifetime.

Although the Five Pillars represent the religious obligations of Islamic practice, they do not in themselves constitute a complete list of specifically required spiritual duties, beliefs, and standards of conduct. There are, however, obligations, both spiritual and legal, that the Muslim faithful are expected to undertake to show their obedience to God. The spiritual obligations reflect attitudes and states of faith; the legal obligations reflect rules of conduct and codes of law that require a manifestation of the proper spiritual attitude exhibited through practice. The latter outline injunctions for social justice, rules governing daily life, and the means for gaining individual peace and dignity. The list of laws with enforcement powers is extensive. In this light, many obligations are actually spiritual and moral but, in legal terms, also represent codes of social action and rules of conduct according to which a Muslim is expected to live. The ways in which these are put into practice may on occasion confound or disconcert secular, "Western" sensibilities.

LEGAL PLURALISM AND BEYOND

How do we make sense of two seemingly incommensurate traditions that claim to embody practices integral to human rights yet appear substantively different?

Legal anthropologists have been slow to both move beyond relativist and legal pluralist explanations and to study complex transnational legal processes. As a result, they have missed the realities of legal contestation in the international arena. Rather, in the majority of the early twentieth century, anthropologists attempted to understand the logic of cultural norms that are central to localized practices and explainable through cultural difference. These early anthropological approaches to understanding human societies were often based on a view of cultural practices as self-contained and expressed within "primitive" social organizations. This was intended to be a corrective to "Western" schemas of progress that tended to see "other" societies as chaotic, despotic, and incapable of progressing into modernity. The anthropologists' alternative view, motivated by a discourse of cultural relativism in the United States and cultural translation in the United Kingdom, called these universalist schemas into question (Herskovits 1990 [1941]; Goodale 2008b). Scholars such as Franz Boas used relativist thinking to develop frameworks for understanding cultural difference. Here relativism was "enlisted to do battle against racist notions" (Spiro 1978:336) that otherwise explained human difference in terms of primitive mentality. It became a powerful tool of cultural criticism and to develop an emerging vision of the universality of human nature. Similarly, Clifford Geertz (1984) argued for the need to recoup relativism in his 1984 lecture to the American Anthropological Association. Against a popular empiricist insistence that we return to the biology of humankind as the basis for universality, Geertz argued that the "Human Mind" and "Human Nature" could not be understood free of context; this position represented a defense against a type of biological essentialism in which he kept open the spirit of universality. In this regard, Geertz redirected anthropology's focus onto empirical studies of the universalizing articulations of culture. Tracing a genealogy in which the concept of cultural relativism was enlisted not for its defense "but to attack anti-relativism," which he argued represented a "streamlined version of an antique mistake" (Geertz 1984: 263), he proposed "anti anti-relativism" (his lecture's title), thereby making a positive of a negative, as a way to oppose the criticism at the core of anthropology's heritages. The key

155

here is that where relativism was at one time used to perpetuate racism against dominated people, Geertz deployed its language to develop a key tool for cultural criticism to develop an understanding of the possible universality of humanity.

Today, understanding cultural difference within the particularities of its own tradition remains one of anthropology's most important contributions to the complexities of human sociability. However, the late-nineteenth and early-twentieth-century complexities of movement and mixing have made it even more important to recognize the context of cultural formations as well as to detail the ways that they converge and change, are contested, exist in contradistinction to other traditions, and foreclose still others. In this regard, the burgeoning field of transnational legal studies can emerge as a conceptual mechanism for mapping out the ways that various regimes of knowledge travel in complex relations of transnational power and inequality.

With the development of various legal pluralist traditions, legal anthropologists began to focus on the ethnographic study of Western industrialized legal systems (Nader 1972; Conley and O'Barr 1990; Merry 1990), recognizing that, in so-called indigenous legal spheres of lawmaking, that which was classified as "traditional" law had itself been shaped by colonial reform and intervention. Today, with the increasingly central role of the transnational circulation of legal meanings, it is becoming more important than ever to consider both how state law penetrates and restructures older cultural logics (Merry 1992) and how it precludes the possibility of economic conditions of equality for all. In this regard, some studies of legal pluralism have examined international arbitration and reconciliation (Wilson 2001; Dezalay and Garth 2002); others have explored the various ways that the transmission of legal knowledge is spreading globally (Riles 2006), whereas others have ranged from the export of laws and the standardization of constitutions (Koh 1998; Dezalay and Garth 2002) to the vernacularization of new legal norms (Hirsch 1998; Merry 2006a).

However, in keeping with the political commitments to relativism, many legal pluralist accounts have been informed by fairly predictable ideas about what constitutes law, justice, freedom, and individual action. They have tended to be quite proscriptive about what law is, even at times presuming that certain originating concepts and conditions are somehow "natural," or that concepts of justice should be understood only in strictly judicial adjudicatory forms. In some cases, concepts of justice might be so unrecognizable as not to be classified as justice shaped by law at all. The radical Islamic response in Nigeria to the seemingly hegemonic alliance of democracy, individual rights, and Christianity as an injustice that demands different political and epistemological action is a case in point and highlights the challenges for rethinking legal pluralism in sub-Saharan Africa. These African-based examples in the second half of this book point to the realities of the challenges ahead for the development of a culturally effective end to global violence. As will be seen, there are multiple domains of competing spheres of power that shape the ways we understand human duties, self-preservation, just action, and "crime" itself.

SECULARISM, ISLAM, AND INTERPRETING "APPROPRIATE" VIOLENCE

The Response of Religious Revivalism[5]

Nigeria's worst nightmare became reality in November 2002, when conflicts stemming from the controversial Miss World competition to be held in Abuja, the capital in northern Nigeria, plunged the country into fatal clashes between Christians and Muslims.[6] In the midst of already heightened tensions between Christians and Muslims around the revival of the strict Islamic Sharia penal code in Nigeria,[7] an article by journalist Isioma Daniel, printed in the newspaper *This Day*, sparked rioting. In her piece, Ms. Daniel responded to Muslim complaints that the pageant promoted sexual promiscuity and indecency by suggesting that the sacred Muslim leader, were he alive, would have appreciated the pageant. "What would [the Prophet] Mohammed think?" Ms. Daniel asked. "In all honesty, he would probably have chosen a wife from one of [the contestants]."[8]

The social unrest began after the Zamfara State Deputy Governor pronounced a fatwa death sentence against Isioma Daniels in which he proclaimed the reporter's statement an attack on the Prophet Muhammad. A *fatwa* (an authoritative legal opinion given by a legal scholar known as a mufti) represents a call to *jihad* (to strive, to struggle) – that is, a political or military struggle to further the Islamic cause (Esposito 2003). The fatwa had the effect of calling on Muslim worshipers to uphold their moral and legal duty to protect the name of the Prophet against those who offend him.[9]

Qualifying for eternal life, as detailed in the Qur'an, involves many duties and obligations; one such duty is a response to the ritualistic call to defend the Prophet and Islamic faith. Accordingly, the violence that ensued after Isioma Daniel's purported ridicule of the Prophet Muhammad was seen by various members of the faithful as enactments in the exercise of their duty to defend their faith.[10] In the context of an age of "democratization" propelled by the spread of the rule of law and international tribunals, this call on Muslims to defend their Prophet can also be understood as an appeal to the freedom of religion. It represents the will of the Islamic faithful to defend themselves from what was seen as not only the slander of disrespectful journalists but also attacks on their religious practices by officers of the secular state that is obligated to protect them.[11]

Hundreds of northern Muslims armed themselves after Friday prayers at the mosque and engaged in violent action in Abuja, where contestants awaited the commencement of the December 7, 2002, pageant.[12] The violence spread to various northern Nigerian cities, particularly Kaduna, one of Nigeria's most politically volatile cities, located some two hundred miles north of Abuja.[13] Said one Kaduna-based Christian witness, "At around five o'clock Muslim youths came to our homes carrying machetes and chanting 'retribution, retribution.' They came in the morning with weapons and began attacking us." Other witnesses reported seeing people run through the streets, setting everything in their paths ablaze: "People were fleeing in all directions throughout the countryside. The running here and there was confusing and scary."[14] In the end, according to Federal Police statistics, some two hundred people had died, and more than five hundred Christians and Muslims had been seriously injured.[15]

Islam and Sharia, Duties and Obligations

With more than 250 ethnic groups[16] and up to as many as four hundred recognized ethnolinguistic groups (Clarke 2004), Nigeria continues to be engulfed by struggles of competing populations vying for political power. Four ethnic groups are dominant, which comprise two-thirds of the population – Hausa and Fulani in the North, the Yorùbá in the Southwest, and the Igbo in the Southeast.[17] In keeping with divisions along ethnic and language alliances, interpretations of moral and legal obligations of citizens vary dramatically from one part of the nation to another. At the heart of the contemporary contests have been challenges over the basis for legitimate Nigerian governance, including the constitutionality of the recently implemented Islamic Sharia penal code in twelve of Nigeria's thirty-six states (Byang 1988; An-Na'im 1990; Nmehielle 2004).[18] Among the conflicts are questions concerning the right to Islamic rebellion. The problem is that an internal armed conflict, such as an Islamic movement in Nigeria that calls on believers to exercise their duty and obligation to defend their leader, may qualify as a defense strategy for some, whereas in other jurisdictions with different religious and ethnic populations, it may be seen as civilian terror motivated by religious irrationality. Further, from the perspective of international judicial institutions such as the ICC, the application of Islamic governance even within a domain recognized by the Nigerian state may result in an act that would qualify for a criminal investigation, punishable by life in prison. These different opinions about what constitutes crime are at the heart of some contemporary challenges to the notion of international human rights but are not always recognizable as similar responses to addressing social issues.

Instead, many theories have been advanced for the rise of radical global Islamic revivalism and the implementation of Sharia law in various regions around the world, amid the global spread of democratization and respect for rule of law (Venkatraman 1995:1964).[19] Discussions of the international domains of legal authority have emphasized the ways in which expanded global institutions have catalyzed the formation of transnational networks of activists, north–south nongovernmental organizational partnerships, and transborder linkages of a broad spectrum of social movements. Following this analysis, the violence is believed by some to be rooted in Islamic attempts to reclaim political power in the face of perceived losses to increasing democratization initiatives.

What we see with various Islamic revitalization movements, therefore, is a challenge to secular democracies and an expression of dissatisfaction with a political regime fundamentally aligned with an implicitly Christian system (Weber 2001 [1904–5]:3–12, 95–145). The religious roots of Islamic governance in sub-Saharan Africa, in contrast, are explicitly acknowledged and embraced as religious. This kind of narrative often attributes to religion a solely reactive political function and considers "statecrafting" – the making of laws of nation-states and international systems – to be fundamentally distinct from religious practice. However, Islamic revivalism as a response to the perceived hegemony of secular democratization must be seen not as separate from the individual rights movement but as constitutive of it.

The struggle for Islamic sovereignty is deeply connected to the forces of globalization in Islamic "fundamentalism"; however, its responses highlight the intersection of radical Islamic values and neoliberal interpretations of rights. The successful 1979 Iranian revolution against the Pahlavi dynasty led to the emergence of an Islamic government in Iran under the leadership of the Ayatollah Khomeini. This is often credited with providing inspiration to Muslims globally, who saw in Islam a viable alternative to both communism and neoliberal capitalism. In support of this unprecedented event, various groups in different parts of the world added to the celebratory momentum, adopting the slogans of the Iranian revolution, including "Neither east nor west, Islam only."[20] Underlying these claims is an argument that the repercussions of worldwide globalization have included an arousal of cultural insecurity and uncertainty about identities and political control, further resulting in attempts to redefine Islamic practice.

In the sub-Saharan African state of Nigeria, a state not traditionally seen as Islamic, a similar wave of global Islam has engulfed the north since the 1960s. The implementation of Islamic criminal law in the northern states has not been without controversy related to challenges over issues of governance, resources, and the basis of the authority of different forms of rule (Nmehielle 2004:732–3).[21] Analysts of the growth of this type of Islamic revivalism in the Nigerian federation point out that the nation has become more decentralized and that part of this decentralization is in the form of cultural self-determination (ibid.:739). Another explanation views the Sharia as a political bargaining chip, recognizing that the new norms of democratization have been pushed forward by a Christian president from the south, with the consequent loss of the north's historic political influence in the Nigerian federation.

In response to these effects of "democratization," various Muslim political leaders are organizing to assert new forms of autonomy and power, a development accompanied by a rise in parallel social movements. These revivalist countermovements similarly respond to and are shaped by the hegemonic secularization of human rights norms and are producing an ethos of returning to utopian possibilities. This highlighting of the secular goals of religious revivalism is compelling insofar as it directly relates religious-inspired violence to the hegemonic power of the law it seeks to oppose.

Some scholars dismissive of the place of Islamic religion in public life have denied such connections and instead frame the conflict as one of religious irrationality versus modern secular rationality. The Islamic Sharia is presented as an antiquated expression of jurisprudence lacking key conceptions of gender equality and notions of agency, freedom, and autonomy central to neoliberal thought (Dworkin 2000:153–5;

Ignatieff 2001:59–62). By arguing that the development of such Islamic revivalist and religious movements will eventually die out as part of an irreversible evolutionary process of globalization's triumph and that a notion of secularism devoid of religion will necessarily prevail, such scholarly positions presume not only that true individual freedom and autonomy is absent from religious governance but also that the secular is void of religiosity. This is far from the case. Such suggestions of Islamic factional irrationality, underdevelopment, and agential deficits are misleading and produce unsatisfactory understandings of the motivations of certain forms of fundamentalism and the politics of power.

In questioning whether political dissidents should be distinguished from "common criminals," Khaled Abou El Fadl (1998a) outlines three sets of moral and spiritual obligations that highlight how the misunderstanding of Islamic radical logic might yield inequalities in knowledge of Islamic radical action and fields of religious authority and power. The first reflects the intrinsic right and duty of the Islamic faithful to serve Allah and the community. It comprises actions that Abou El Fadl suggests might be seen as legal duties among more radical tenets of the Islamic faithful but are actually moral and spiritual duties held by various Muslims enacted politically to protect the name of the Prophet. The second set pertains to the call on the faithful to form alliances with goodness and protest evil; and the third involves the duty to obey Allah's orders (ibid.:12). Abou El Fadl details the invocation of all three Islamic core principles in accordance with which legal and moral duties are popularly constituted (ibid.:10–12). These duties are not only based on a reverence for the sacredness of life but also refer to the mystical continuity of life, even in "death" (Coward 1997).[22]

Popular Nigerian Islamic beliefs often locate the death of the body as merely a stage of life,[23] as do various Calvinist Protestant principles of life after death that formed the basis for early capitalist practice. Thus, among some of the more radical Islamic adherents, the moral and spiritual obligations enshrined in the intrinsic right and duty of the Islamic faithful to serve Allah and the community move us away from a more liberalist notion of a rights-endowed subject, whose main goal is the protection of the self and its transcendence through allegiance to Allah. One is expected to serve Allah first and the state second. The more orthodox interpretation emphasizes the call for Muslims to obey and support the ruler, thereby placing a premium on the sanctity of unity and the duty of implementing and protecting Islamic order, including the call to "kill contesters to the ruler's power"

(Abou El Fadl 1998a:10). As the Prophet said, "if people see an oppressor and they do not enjoin him [or her] then God will punish all of them" (ibid.:11). This view of duty to a Supreme Being antagonizes fundamental principles of the democratically acting neoliberal subject who is endowed by the state with positive and negative rights. Instead, it focuses on how the individual is to be judged (or punished) because of inactivity as evidence of a failure to resist an oppressor. Thus, one way to interpret the first set of obligations is that the subject who chooses not to resist an oppressor is in violation of his or her moral allegiance to Allah.

Following the Qur'an and Professor Abou El Fadl's explication, if devotees are engaged in an argument, the first course of action is this:

> [M]ake ye peace between them: but if one of them transgresses beyond bounds against the other, then fight ye (all) against the other, then fight ye (all) against the one that transgresses until it complies with the command of God. But if it complies, then make peace between them with justice, and be fair: For God loves those who are fair (and just). The believers are but a single Brotherhood: so make peace and reconciliation between your two (contending) brothers. And fear God, that ye may receive mercy. (1998b:11)

The obligations involving retribution (form alliances with goodness and protest evil) and obedience (obey Allah's orders) highlight the contingency of peace and the primacy of godly authority.

Abou El Fadl details the underlying philosophies that shape these principles of embracing good and forbidding evil through obedience (1998b:12). What is interesting here are the notions of duty and obligation and, ultimately, of culpability as they relate to establishing the rules of conduct of the Islamic faithful.[24] As we can see, when the focus of justice moves from the rights, freedoms, and entitlements of individuals to the duties of the individual and his or her moral or legal obligations to Allah and the community, the basis for understanding what constitutes "legitimate" action and "just" punishment is radically called into question.

"Intention" and the Concept of al-Khuruj

By introducing the competition over religious and legal domains, Abou El Fadl then turns to the concept of al-Khuruj to draw out the difference in calculating intention when the act is seen as a form of moral obligation – specifically, that of defense (1998:13–15). As defined, al-Khuruj is "an assertive act of resistance against the head of the state" or a powerful official or actor, but it is usefully understood in relation to a call to jihad by a mufti or imam endowed with the authority to declare a fatwa to implement the duty of the faithful to protect the leader against "enemies" of Islam (ibid.:13). Although narrowly tailored as an act of demonstrated obedience to the "creator," it can be referenced freely to excuse and reward rebellion against injustice (pp. 14–15). Abou El Fadl explores how al-Khuruj represents a nexus between the offense and the uprising, as the leader or government is prompted to respond to the pressure brought to bear by citizens called on to defend Islamic governance (p. 15). By illustrating how the orthodox rationale locates the Islamic brotherhood as having a duty to aid and support potential dissenters, Abou El Fadl suggests that that duty articulates an obligation of the faithful to support the Prophet (p. 17). Because the fulfillment of the duty to Allah is measured through conduct, here it is the *motivation* of the act that is considered in relation to the action. To explore this as a theory of Islamic legal intent entails recognizing that it is predicated by a range of jurors on sources of self that represent forms of knowledge as unknowable by humankind (Taylor 1989; Messick 2001:151). Like various other religious forms in which the motivations and results of spiritual duty are outwardly attributed to forces outside the individual, the religiosity of selfhood points to differences with liberalist forms of self-making in which it is believed that the self and its motivations are ultimately knowable when adjudicated through the law.

In terms of the philosophy of culpability, "fundamentalist" Islamic interpretations of the Nigerian Sharia have therefore been concerned with first assessing the relevant spiritual as well as social status of the individual accused of enacting, for instance, violence resulting in death.[25] As such, culpability under Islamic law is derived from notions of deliberate intent, quasi-deliberate intent, and indirect causation. A person who is, for instance, a free Muslim (rather than a leader), sane (*akil*), and of age might be seen as responsible (*mukallaf*) for his or her actions and, therefore, culpable of "deliberate intent" (Bahnassi 1982:176). However, when adjudicated in a given Nigerian Sharia court, culpability might instead be bound to intention. This is because the believer would likely be absolved of criminal responsibility if he or she had acted out of religious obligation.[26] Such a notion of intention is determined by attending to both the act and the moral obligation of believers to protect Islam. Where violence is deemed necessary by some – as when a fatwa is issued – the relevant context shifts from that of peacetime to that of wartime, thereby making intention relevant insofar as it relates to the obligation of the faithful to engage in certain actions (Esposito 2003:85).[27]

The ICC and the Concept of Intention

The notion of intent is also relevant to the crimes defined under the Rome Statute: genocide, crimes against humanity, war crimes, and crimes of aggression (as of 2009 still to be defined). The jurisprudence of the ICC is described, by not only state officials but also networks of thousands of NGO representatives, as bringing criminal law to a level of international attention that will revolutionize the ways that people understand the responsibility of states to "humanity," as well as transform conventional conceptions of the codification of crime and determinants of criminal evidence. The ICC is thus setting new norms for what constitutes particular forms of "crime" and what should be the jurisdictional reach of extranational bodies.

The Rome Statute provides a definition of the crime of genocide that matches verbatim the definition in Article 2 of the Genocide Convention.[28] The identical five-point definition can also be found in the International Law Commission Draft Code against the Peace and Security of Mankind,[29] and the statutes of the ad hoc Tribunals for the former Yugoslavia[30] and Rwanda.[31] All three schools of jurisprudence considered here – Islamic as well as the Western European canon and common law traditions – are said to have shaped international law and accumulated large bodies of case law on genocide, widespread ethnic killing, and political rebellions. Their consideration of intention, however, varies.

In "Western" jurisprudence, some but not all crimes require a general proof of intent (Kaufman 2003:318). The measures and assumptions surrounding the notion of intention vary, as do the measures of what forms of intention constitute culpability for criminal action. A persistent dispute in American criminal law has centered on the relevance of a defendant's motive in relation to the extent to which he or she is criminally liable (Binder 2002:34–66). At the heart of the debate is the question concerning whether what is seen as a permissible motive should exculpate someone who has committed a criminal act. The strict interpretation of American criminal law is that proof of intent is rarely made explicit because the motive is seen as irrelevant to the liability of the crime (Binder 2002; Kaufman 2003). Instead, culpability is deduced from the criminal act, and the assumption is that the consequences of the action were intended.[32]

In the realm of international criminal law regarding abuses by high-level state actors distinguished by "intentional and knowing behavior," the Rome Statute requires conceptions of intent that are adequate to gain prosecution of commanders for either ordering a crime or negligence in failing to prevent it.[33] The crime of genocide, for example, borrows from the general principles of Euro-American law and outlines two levels of intent: general and specific.[34]

General intent denotes crimes for which no measure is established: all that must be proved is the commission of the act by the accused party.[35] The authority of proof is drawn from the presumed power of the treaty document. *Specific intent* (*dolus specialis*), a popular concept in Roman-continental law, implies that the perpetrator expressly sought to produce the criminal action.[36] In the international crime allegation of genocide, in which genocide refers to particular homicidal acts committed "with intent to destroy, in whole or in part, a national, ethnical, racial or religious group,"[37] finding guilt involves proof of a more precise, specific intent, which links intention to the mental-psychological knowledge element (known as *mens rea*)[38] with the physical performance of the wrongful act or crime (*actus reus*; Latin for "bad act").[39] Therefore, to prove an accused guilty of the crime of genocide in international law, one must show proof of specific intent, which takes into account both the *mens rea* and *actus reus*, to allow for a calculation of intention that is more precise with reference to the consequence of carrying out one of the crimes enumerated[40] in Article 2 of the Genocide Convention or Article 6 of the Rome Statute.[41]

"Culpability," and how it is designated, is another important principle central to the interpretation of intent in international criminal law. Under common law, it is well established that conspiracy is defined as the agreement of two or more persons to commit a crime (Schabas 2001:103). In most cases, it does not require the actual commission of the crime itself. In the Napoleonic tradition that has influenced canon law, conspiracy tends to be viewed as participation in the commission of or attempt to commit the agreed-on crime (ibid.). Of late, with the development of international criminal law, both European and American principles of law and authority have been used to determine culpability in devising the new internationalist norms. Borrowing from Napoleonic and canon law, the Rome Statute requires an "action that commences its execution by means of a substantial step."[42] In other words, it requires the commission of an overt act as evidence of the conspiracy but imposes no requirement for the commission of the crime itself (ibid.:105). Because the architects of the statute were most interested in linking commanders to crimes committed by their subordinates, the principle of command responsibility has been used to establish culpability, requiring proof of guilt "beyond a reasonable doubt" (Gurule 2001–2:40–1; Schabas 2004:103).[43] As such, command responsibility has recently been codified in Article 28 of the Rome Statute to impose individual responsibility on military commanders for crimes committed by forces under their command and control. The threshold for guilt must establish whether they "either knew or, owing to the circumstances at the time, should have known that the forces were committing or about to commit such crimes."[44]

Competing Spheres of Authority and Power

Taking a pluralist approach to understanding the cultural order and meanings of international criminal law as it is taking shape in The Hague would involve comparing it with another legal system else-where – say, the Islamic political Sharia in northern Nigeria. There, for example, orthodox approaches to guilt among those practicing political Sharia tend to be based on a determination of intentionality (Jackson 1996:200–2).[45] Questions of liability that relate to a crime seen as political (al-Khuruj) in Nigerian Islamic juror circles tend to deploy reasoning that judges action in terms of an implicit obligation and duty to protect Islam. The moral contours of international criminal law, despite the declared secularism that has defined it, emerge from simi-larly religious roots: it is its religious field of authority that can be seen as politically different. The difference between the two legal systems, therefore, should be seen not as based on the false secular–nonsecular binary but rather on the differential authority of kinds of law – that is, a cultural conception that the source of Islamic law begins with the authority of Muhammad as the final Prophet of Allah, compared with the reality that "Western," "international" legal values are the product of Judeo-Christian influences represents its own particular regime of truth. The differences between radical Sharia Islamic movements and the various liberalist political doctrines of international human rights, however seemingly incommensurate, reside in their competing spheres of authority and power. Thus, although their forms of violence may be differently legitimatized and codified within different formulations of law and religion, the important issue is understanding these relations in complex configurations of power within unequal regimes of global power.

Given the related histories of religious influence, this distinction cannot be captured through legal pluralism alone: there is also a relevant politics of secular hegemony in which international law relies on an alliance with the state through the mediation of the Rome Statute. At the heart of law itself are fields of possibility within which people interpret, judge, and, in the end, create obligations from which to act. These obligations shape the domains of authority within which people make complex determinations in both moral and legal terms. It is this problematic from which people choose to act within the options available to them. Here I highlight the role of human agency in mobilizing action responsive to moral or legal obligations and do so by exploring the actions taken in the absence of a hegemonic Islamic state that may enforce sanctions against inaction. Violence, such as the deadly rioting that erupted in Nigeria and led to the relocation of the Miss World pageant,[46] may be seen as a legitimate response to a fatwa in particular fields of meaning and power.

My findings showed that this violence was not seen by many of the more orthodox Islamic practitioners in northern Nigeria as a basis for criminal responsibility under the Sharia. In other words, my research revealed that the acting "dissidents" were actually not seen by the related community of believers as culpable because they demonstrated the legal obligation and duty to maintain the integrity of Islam. The reason the outbreak that followed the previously described calls for jihad – directed against the organizers of the pageant, the journalist Isioma Daniel, and the newspaper office – was in fact celebrated by some as both the intentional fulfillment of a moral, political, and legal duty as well as a form of retribution, and therefore, an "appropriate" response.

Intentionality, understood in relation to fulfilling legal and moral obligations, is critical to distinguish political acts of legal obligation from actions deemed transgressive in the common law, canon law, and the criminal law of the Rome Statute. Located beyond this legal-pluralist approach, however – and at the heart of my inquiry into intention as related to culpability, and especially to command responsibility – is the basis of authority on which various forms of violence may be proclaimed "just." In these various canons of law, unless a declaration of "just war" is called, neither the acting "dissident" nor the commander is likely to be absolved of crimes committed against civilians.[47] Further, because common law *does* recognize the duty of subordinates to carry out orders issued by their commanders, under which an actor might be absolved for following the orders of a superior – comparable to an Islamic believer who heeds the call to jihad – it is clear that the fields of difference are within fields of practice: the speech act (fatwa) as call to violence as a perceived legitimate declaration by a nonstate actor.

Interpreters of the Rome Statute, such as the prosecutor and related officials for member states, have long classified the terms of jihad as illegitimate, thereby establishing the acts as crimes committed in the context of peace and not war (Proulx 2004:1083–4). As such, in relation to charges of crimes against humanity in the Rome Statute, culpability would be measured through the joining of *mens rea* and *actus reus*; the legal question to be posed would be whether the offender – and in the case of the ICC this generally indicates a commander – planned to promote the uprising with the intention of killing (Schabas 2004:280). Although human rights groups in Nigeria did document the Miss World–related violence and the perceived complicity of the imam as a commander to be punished, and submitted it in the form of a complaint to the lead prosecutor for the ICC, it was not pursued because the gravity of the crime was insufficient for further action. However, in interviewing various officers of the ICC, my informants insisted that were this a case to be taken up by the court, the prosecutor would explore whether the acts were carried out as genocide – for example, they would examine whether the violence was committed with the specific intent of destroying a particular group. If the acts were not committed with the intent and knowledge of the commander and various agents of violence and if they were not of sufficient gravity to constitute crimes against humanity or genocide, they might still be prosecuted for unknowingly ordering the crime or for negligence in failing to prevent those under their command from carrying out criminal acts (Schabas 2004:213–14).[48]

In comparing incidents of violence that might emerge within the Islamic Sharia state (Miss World riots) to that of a given secular state (violence in the Democratic Republic of Congo, for example), both the institutional organization and spheres of authority are part of various forms of coercion structured in widespread relations of inequality. Each produces and deploys violence in different ways, but the key difference is in how we understand inequality in relation not only to unequal targets of crime but also to the construction and circulation of notions of legitimacy or illegitimacy. In relation to individual culpability, the distinction to be made would be based on the specific intent to kill a religious group, thereby punishable under the genocide law (Schabas 2004:280). Among the radical Islamic adherents whom I interviewed, neither the crime of genocide nor crimes against humanity would form the basis for inquiry. Rather, judicial differences in classifying the crime and proving intention would result in varying judicial outcomes under Islamic law. However, the key difference is the structure of unequal power between neoliberal, "Western" democracies and "non-Western" states or communities in the international rule of law regime. This inequality means that "Western" states and markets, and international institutions controlled largely by "Western" economic and political agents, are able to enforce their own moral, ethical, and political frameworks, using violence when they deem necessary.

Secular versus Nonsecular Forms of Violence
Liberalist regimes use violence to provide rationales for the laws they make and to ensure the conditions for their enforcement. A major vehicle and justification for this system lies in the key tenet of universality, which, as we have seen through the striking example of U.S. foreign policy, can be enforced militarily when other means do not suffice: a "universal" idea of human rights could be said to have prompted the U.S. invasion of Afghanistan in 2002. Within secular states, differentials in power among segments of the population produce similar potentials for the state to deploy violence in ways that conjoin with the rationalization of rights. The modern, secular-state framework and the international human rights regime, although in competition over issues of sovereignty, in fact function along a continuum in which, in this example, "traditionalist" Sharia duties of jihad or al-Khuruj are pathologized and religion-based violence (such as that termed "terrorist attacks") is seen as barbaric, whereas the violence of the modern secular state – its ability to declare "just" wars of overwhelming destruction – is normalized and even celebrated as furthering the "spread of democracy."

The Sharia, as a religious articulation of a related legal order, also stands in for the greater assertions of state power – to act, protect, and kill legitimately, within relevant spheres of authorial power. Unfortunately, however, the practices of Islamic criminal Sharia in northern Nigeria are often viewed through a lens that envisions what is unlawful in terms of perspectives fashioned by North American and European secular states and actors. Although I am in no way advocating the legitimacy of any form of physical violence as the basis for solving social problems, I am insisting that there is a convergence in the ways that both rule of law and human-rights-infused international/state regimes and overtly religious regimes deploy violence so as to produce social and moral constructions of justice and transgression that are epistemologically constituted and justified. In this regard, national, international, and religious rules of law maintain core principles that operate within regimes of authority that, although they are made to appear distinct, are actually inseparable, sharing in the regulation, not the elimination, of violence. Whether apparently secular or religious, ideals reflect the types of authority we value, the motivations we agree are acceptable, and a force of law that does not necessarily reflect empirical or social truths but exists through the "mystical foundations" of state enforcement. Thus, in the case of human rights and its related norms enshrined in international law, it is the Rome Statute that establishes its authority. The modern nation-state, in turn, continues to claim the power to exercise violence, and to do so in relation to the rule of law. It reflects the violence of legal norms, their social meanings, and the relations of power and authority within which they are embedded.

The classification of particular actions as criminal actions (e.g., genocide) is as political, then, as it is cultural. Classificatory acts represent the authority of particular norms to be represented as legitimate, always supplying a moral dimension. As such, the norms that shape the crime of genocide do not hold power because they represent the democratically derived social contract; rather, they hold power because, in keeping with revolutions of the "West" – such as those of America and France, which absolved themselves from religious persecution or the inheritance of social standing – these twentieth-century legal norms represent a new moral dimension – the human rights treaty as the new social contract of "Western" modernity; the human rights treaty as a truth regime gaining power globally but being deployed to manage violence in the Global South, to name and manage unauthorized violence.

Through treaty doctrine, shared interests are embedded in the enforcement of the duties of the state and protection of the individual. For although the "rights" and forms of "individual autonomy" enunciated in the Rome Statute identify human universality as the scope of entitlements, those rights are more restricted than state entitlements in that they are interpreted as rights that citizens hold as protections against their own governments. Ultimately the authority of international law is an extension of the authority of the state in which rights are enacted (Shaw 2003),[49] and in this regard, international law is increasingly becoming constitutive of the ways in which subjects engaged in neoliberal democracies in the "West" rationalize action. However, also at play – and as seen in the case of the fatwa against Isioma Daniel – are core values embedded in conceptual hierarchies present in the exercise of individual/Muslim obligations to the authority of Allah first, and to state-based democratic principles second. These raise questions concerning the relationships among concepts, theory, and practice and call into question differences between exercising the obligation and duty to act and managing that duty in relation to other obligations and constraints.

In the end, balancing the spheres of authority that shape action and the domain of interpretive agency within which people make determinations allows us to rethink legal pluralism as a way to document the relations of power among international, national, and religiously inspired regimes. This approach allows us to reconceptualize the philosophies of obligation in terms of the contingencies of power; detailing the deployment of that power constitutes the empirical work that can be most useful analytically. For although some states are more successful than others in enforcing their determinants of legitimate violence in relation to widespread democratic principles, all but a few have continued to maintain power through the hegemony of statehood alone.

Secular states continue to draw force from the myth of sovereign authority and its sacred political forms that are being maintained through an illusion of secularism, the logic of legal sanctity, and the force of military and economic power (Asad 2003). The expanding alliance between the secular state and international/global institutions and their shared religious genealogies is only a starting point for comparative explorations into pluralism, not the basis on which dual legal spheres should be understood. Rather – and as Chapters 5 and 6 explore – the violence managed by modern secular regimes, like that of religious revivalist, spheres, calls for a radical rethinking of domination and power within multiple domains.

In considering the complex interactions among new independent institutions, nation-states, and religious organizations engaged in various articulations of governance, it is important to recognize how state functionaries empower international institutions, and the similarities to how religious functionaries empower transnational and regional religious networks. Yet the concepts of secularism and religion have been jointly appropriated but differently legitimatized in liberalist democracies worldwide. Despite the religiosity of "secularism" in the international realm, the Rome Statute presumes a national and

171

international convergence of perspectives on social and human justice under the rule of law, for which the treaty increasingly gives substance as the rational voice of the modern state. Nevertheless, the statute's language of secular objectivity is rooted in "Western" epistemology and its own formations of religion. Its resultant merger of histories of religious rationality and related regimes of power have legitimatized certain forms of legal classification and their punishments. This reality calls for a rethinking of purely legal pluralist reasoning as the basis for understanding the modernity of changing national state, nonstate, and international forms of power.

GENEALOGIES OF "SECULARISM" AND THE POLITICS OF CONSTITUTIVE POWER

The pronouncement that human beings are sacred, as Michael Perry has argued, is "inescapably religious" – even if more often a "merely intellectual affirmation" than a "truly existential one" (1998:11–12) – and yet the tenets of human rights that emerged following World War II established a conception of individual sacredness as a secular principle. With human rights mobilizations based on this principle, a new deeply Judeo-Christian human rights tradition took shape, one embedded in a secularist rhetoric that shaped the nature of neoliberal democracies and their related norms concerning the rights of the human and the authority of the state (Pollis and Schwab 2000:209–13). Underlying and feeding the notion of the "sacred" individual was a fundamental obligation to the state – and a duty to its citizens. Thus, understanding the establishment of rule of law movements and their human rights principles in the twenty-first century involves recognizing the formation of the religious compromise in the West: the transition from explicit articulations of religious governance into secular governance. However, religion and secularism are two distinctly constructed but mutually constituted knowledge forms that Talal Asad, in *Genealogies of Religion* (1993), has long set to rest as conceptual fictions. As fictions, they live in worlds that imbue them with the status of the real and therefore have more in common than not. Thus, the construction of secular–religious distinctions alongside the formation of the democratic neoliberal state and emergent international justice institutions makes explicit the ways that various domains of knowledge and power have been constituted through histories of hegemonic encroachments and contests over various cosmologies.

The basic definition of "secularism" describes a separation of organized religion from organized political power, inspired by a specific set of values (Asad 2003:103). In the early modern period, Jean-Jacques Rousseau first outlined a model for the place of government and law in society (Parsons and Shils 1965:119–25). In it, religion was relegated to the sphere of the social – beyond the terrain of political action. Much of nineteenth-century positivist thought was directed toward the replacement of religion by science (Asad 2003:103). This popular positivist epistemology was heralded by Auguste Comte, who espoused an evolutionary scheme that presumed the modern nation-state would evolve from societies engaged in fetishism to advanced regimes that relied on the rationality of science (Parsons and Shils 1965:646–56). Marxists, too, arguing for the historical inevitability of such an evolution, heralded the increasing "secularization" of thought.

The precursors of what is known as human rights in the contemporary "West" were in fact more "religiously shaped" than various legal positivist thinkers would have had us believe. In addition, the religious origins of the more secular forms of politics that arose in the West were reformulated in a "moral" vocabulary. With roots in Latin Christendom's idea of natural law (*lex naturalis*), which located rules of sociality, the creation, and the proceeds of that creation in a "fixed and invariable relation," the ideational antecedents for modern human rights first appeared as a form of political contestation closely linked to the need to protect one's natural right (property) from the arbitrariness of government power (Montesquieu 1952 [1748]:297–9). The notion of a "natural right," articulated by Aristotle as a right by birth, made it plausible for seventeenth-century theorists, such as John Locke, to invoke natural rights as a principle of individual entitlement that could be used against the relatively lawless structures of the early modern state (Strauss 1953). Locke (1988 [1689]) located freedom as the natural condition of the human, the place of good, in contrast to the modern European nation-state, with its claimed instruments of coercion. Thus, an epistemology and culture of rights emerged as a moral response to the abusive excesses of the state. These nineteenth-century conceptions of human sanctity and natural rights replaced the moral authority of the state as the arbiter of justice and shaped the "moral" basis of early notions of rights that would eventually underlay modern, twentieth-century statehood.

As Talal Asad has outlined in his explication of the development of the modern state, during the period in which religious freedom and tolerance coalesced as dominant values, it became important to develop particular morals that would be tied to the political order of the secular state (1993:206–7). These conceptions were driven by the need to regulate citizens to obey the law and respect the authority of civil government (R. E. Allen 1980:111–12), carving a space for the construction of what was seen as a moral, representative government (Hobbes 1958 [1651]; Macpherson 1962), and the source of these conceptions was found in religious values.

The definitive text on the underpinnings of religious norms in capitalist society is Max Weber's *The Protestant Ethic and the Spirit of Capitalism*, in which he documented fundamental tenets of Protestantism that shaped the cultural logics of capitalism (2001 [1904–5]:95–154). Natural individual freedom would be understood as preserved by a Hobbesian contract, and Weber's work on the Protestant work ethic demonstrates how a social contract not only comes to impel capitalism and the modern state but also manages to efface its own religious heritage through a language of secularism. This genealogy of the modern state and the rights and obligations of the individual since the nineteenth century is instructive in demonstrating that the supremacy of individual rights is far from natural or universal. Rather, it indexes the religious roots of the human (and other living things) as sacred and the development of an accompanying language of rights in a context of coercive state power.

Today, there still exists a range of debates on what it means to be "human" and to whom adjudication of rights should be attached – whether to a spiritual-religious authority or to the state. The literature has long established that the notion of the intrinsic worth, even sacredness, of the individual "human" is a social construct and originates in the fundamental principles of liberalism. Similarly, the notion that humans are "rights bearers" in the modern temporal present can be traced to the epistemological histories of a number of European countries but is not generally accepted worldwide.

In 1215, the Magna Carta established rights as a concession from King John to the barons of England (Howard 1998). The king granted them various liberties, such as the right to wardship and inheritance in return for their duty payment (ibid.). This political negotiation established a social contract between rulers and subjects, and the legal terms for the protection of rights derived from the contract (ibid.:23). By the Middle Ages in Europe, a notion of individual rights was shaped by particular moral standards that were, in theory, articulated as universal, and based on principles of natural law (Parsons and Shils 1965). These principles were not contingent on political concessions (ibid.:87); rather, they derived from the idea that humanity, as sacred, should be protected. With the development of modern conceptions of natural law, philosophers such as Hugo Grotius, Thomas Hobbes, and John Locke expanded on these standards of rights and privileges and developed the ideas that individuals have a general duty to adhere to moral standards and that governments have an obligation to concede to basic terms of the social contact. Accordingly, in the "West," the foundations of the modern state were structured around these developing truth regimes and capitalist conceptions of value that privileged the cultural logics of Judeo-Christianity (Weber 2001 [1904–5]). Weber demonstrated that religious logic was fundamental to the formation of modern capitalist life, and its power was in its ability to render itself invisible yet continue to reproduce itself through daily patterns of exchange. He wrote about the disenchantment of the world as a result of the inroads of modern rationalist ways into traditional social arrangements (ibid.). These eroded the sense of awe and respect for sacred institutions and beliefs and set the groundwork for understanding modernization while not completely wearing away the religious logics of Christian core values.

Over the past decades, the religious roots of law and democracy in the West have been further sublimated by a more secular utterance, that of pluralism and equality as the basis for justice. These conceptions have taken hold through various modalities, including pro-democracy movements in a range of locations and rule of law dictates in postwar contexts. In examining the increasingly overt relationship between religious faith and legal governance in contemporary life, scholars writing about the new face of state power (Habermas and Derrida 2005)[50] have – to follow Weber – articulated increasing forms of secularism as the withdrawal of religious discourse from the public sphere. Yet these modalities have also been met with a more visible countermovement in postcolonial and Islamic contexts in the Global South and Asia – that of the presence of religion in public life. The overt visibility of these forms of religiosity represented a more robust incarnation. Although such religiosity has always been present, it is becoming clearer that its agents have been able to adjust its practices to make them more legible for contemporary relevance and consumption.

Today, following Max Weber's treatise, the formation of secularism involves the entrenchment of cultural values that were deeply embedded in Judeo-Christian religious sanction (Weber 2001 [1904–5]:3–12).

This influence of religious principles shaped the organization of society, the work ethic and its value, and the basis for what constitutes a crime – and, therefore, its punishment, as well as the norms and values enforcing the legitimacy of that punishment (Previn 1996:607; Milligan 2002:137, 146) – through the circulation of capitalist practices that were increasingly closely aligned with early Protestant ethics. Today, their influences remain rooted in the very religious principles that undergird contemporary neoliberal capitalist ethics. Their signs of their influence are expressed in clearly religiously based conceptions of the individual, and thus notions of the human, that came to be aligned with the state's management of the human body.

In various regions of Europe the development of the liberalist position on rights established two basic principles: first, that human beings possess rights to life, liberty, the secure possession of property, and the exercise of free speech – all inalienable and unconditional (W. Brown 2001); second, that the central role of government is to protect these rights. Political institutions were to be judged, therefore, on their achievement of this function. In 1789, the French Revolution led to the widening of this concept with the "Declaration of the Rights of Man and the Citizen."[51] Shaped by British and French colonialism in the seventeenth and eighteenth centuries, what would become the U.S. government enshrined these values in its 1791 Bill of Rights.[52]

Contemporary human rights literature describes the nineteenth-century interference of one state in the affairs of others as a moral question: such interference was neither intended to develop into an alliance of states against others nor to usurp the power of state sovereignty (Henkin 1989). International law – traditionally represented as a set of rules agreed on by countries and meant to govern the relations among them – asserted principles of sovereignty that were embedded in the state. As the narrative goes, the system of territorial sovereignty that had emerged with the European Enlightenment had previously been seen as the domain of the monarch; it had then shifted, after the American and French revolutions, to a political power of the people in a given territory. By the late nineteenth century, fiercely sovereign states had fostered a sense of national belonging, locating individuals in relation to national territory and a shared (if sometimes mythical) heritage. Within state boundaries, explicit national laws held sway. In independent nation-states, these laws were fueled by legal norms for democratic governance on behalf of the rights of the state. In colonial states, however, customary laws existed alongside the laws of the imperial powers, which eventually trumped customary legal regimes at higher spheres of authority. As I shall explore in the next chapter, the development of colonial and post-independence governance in various African contexts involved the careful interplay between various regimes, often attempting political inclusion of customary epistemologies but always being circumscribed by constitutional hierarchies for establishing the steps for legal recourse (Comaroff and Comaroff, 2004a).

In the international sphere, approaches to the belief in the global nature of international humanitarian standards are often seen as linked to the tradition of liberalist idealist thought from which the League of Nations was established in 1920. Although the League lasted only until 1946,[53] its moral underpinnings survived to buttress the theoretical framework of the neoliberal institution that is now the United Nations (Schlesinger 2003:25–8, Shaw 2003:24–31). Liberal universalism has historically proved attractive, for on the surface, the language of liberalism – including its assumptions about individualism and liberty – has ubiquitously become the starting point for any discussion on human rights, democratic practice, or state security and interdependence. It has cornered the general conception of what it means to be a "civilized" society engaged with other "civilized" states on the world stage.

Human rights advocates often point to World War II as the event that accelerated the process of sovereign autonomy. By the end of the war, various forms of national and ideological alliance came to constitute a system that, although constrained by principles of sovereignty, made new international collaborations between powerful states in the Global North more significant. Compared with the period prior to the twentieth century, international law advocated by mostly European states now took a different turn, with questions of international concern becoming more of a focus. Most critically, the newly established United Nations was the central forum organized for international collaboration, with the perceived ability to engage questions of international concern and within a constitutional framework of shared purposes and principles. Although its charter was initially signed by only fifty countries, it was those states through the United Nations that forged the infrastructure for the development of modern international institutions that would become the mechanism through which the principles of the Universal Declaration of Human Rights (UDHR) would become normative (Henkin et al. 1999:286).[54]

"Human rights," a concept that reflects central ideas about the universality of personhood and human equality, assumed its current form with the establishment of the UDHR in 1948 and with the rise of the neoliberal nation-state. In the context of "justice talk" among ICC-NGO adherents, the UDHR is often presented as being the first internationally recognized document to establish certain explicit human rights. These rights – ascribed to all individuals – include not only "life, liberty and security of person" (art. 3) and freedom from slavery or torture (arts. 4, 5) but also certain property rights (art. 17) and less defined "economic, social and cultural rights indispensable for his dignity and the free development of his personality" (art. 22). The declaration's Preamble recognized the "inherent dignity and . . . the equal and inalienable rights of all members of the human family" and stipulated that "disregard and contempt for human rights have resulted in barbarous acts which have outraged the conscience of mankind." The Preamble further declared that the "advent of a world in which human beings shall enjoy freedom of speech and belief and freedom from fear and want has been proclaimed as the highest aspiration of the common people" and established that "if man is not to be compelled to have recourse, as a last resort, to rebellion against tyranny and oppression, that human rights should be protected by the rule of law."[55]

Universalist definitions of the "human" that emerged from UN efforts to achieve consensus around "agreed purposes and principles," such as the UDHR, are indicators of the force of Euro-American influence on the shaping of a dominant ideological principle of human sacredness. Although the determination of the substance of rights and the distinctions between "humans" and "citizens" continued to progress, so did the debates measuring humanity. Three regional initiatives, all of which represented particular amendments to the initial UN declaration, were drafted during the Cold War: the Convention for the Protection of Human Rights and Fundamental Freedoms (aka European Convention on Human Rights [ECHR], 1950), the American Convention on Human Rights (ACHR, 1969), and the African Charter on Human and Peoples' Rights (known as the Banjul Charter, 1981). These declarations asserted particular notions of the individual as a rights-bearing subject but differed in their respective articulations of an individual's rights in relation to his or her obligation to the state.

The European Convention, established during the rise of the Cold War, insisted that "Everyone's right to life shall be protected by law" and "No one shall be deprived of his life intentionally save in the execution of a sentence of a court following his conviction of a crime for which this penalty is provided by law" (art. 2).[56]

The American Convention, created under the auspices of the Organization of American States, declares in its Preamble that the "essential rights of man are not derived from one's being a national of a certain state, but are based upon attributes of the human personality, and that they therefore justify international protection in the form of a convention reinforcing or complementing the protection provided by the domestic law of the American states." In accordance with the UN's UDHR, the American Convention's Preamble also establishes that the "ideal of free men enjoying freedom from fear and want can be achieved only if conditions are created whereby everyone may enjoy his economic, social, and cultural rights, as well as his civil and political rights."[57]

The African Charter on Human and Peoples' Rights goes a step further, committing to the eradication of all forms of colonialism in Africa and stating in its Preamble the need for African states to "coordinate and intensify their cooperation and efforts to achieve a better life for the peoples of Africa and to promote international cooperation having due regard to the Charter of the United Nations and the Universal Declaration of Human Rights." The African Charter also recognizes in its Preamble that the "fundamental human rights stem from the attributes of human beings which justifies their national and international protection," and "that the reality and respect of peoples' rights should necessarily guarantee human rights." It insists not just on the enjoyment of rights for everyone but also on the duties of all to uphold their responsibilities to their communities. In keeping with the American Convention, the African Charter calls for the development of civil and political rights and their fundamental relationship to economic, social, and cultural rights. In marking the colonial and postcolonial status of African states, it also asserts a duty to achieve the uncompromised liberation of Africa, "the peoples of which are still struggling for their dignity and genuine independence," and the necessity of "undertaking to eliminate colonialism, neo-colonialism, apartheid, [Z]ionism and to dismantle aggressive foreign military bases and all forms of discrimination, particularly those based on race, ethnic group, color, sex, language, religion or political opinions."[58] This articulation of duty to the peoples and cultures of Africa differs from the American and European declarations, with their focus on individual rights.

All three declarations emerged from a genealogy of key liberalist values, such as the protection of individual liberty and freedoms that are life-generating, within the bounds of the social contract. Yet with the realities of the "failed postcolonial state" – a state in which central government has become so ineffective that its legitimacy has become eroded and its ability to provide for its citizens compromised – significant economic restructuring through Structural Adjustment Programs and economic liberalization have attempted to bring African nations in line with "Western" neoliberal economies and democracies that further revive the social contract. Indeed, today, sixty years after the UN declaration, among various human rights NGO advocates of the North there is a renewed commitment to liberal values through the language of "human rights" and the performance of "justice talk." This language of rights and justice is best seen in Chapter VII of the UN Charter which outlines two possible criteria under which the use of force is seen as legitimate: (1) through authorization of the UN Security Council and (2) if there is an actual or imminent threat of an armed attack and it is used in self-defense or collective self-defense.[59]

Of late, a third criterion has emerged, one deemed "exceptional" and "controversial": "to avert overwhelming humanitarian catastrophe."[60] These three components reflect mainstream institutional standards, with varying degrees of agreement, for determining the legitimate use of violence by states and their bodies.[61] In the absence of these state-based determinants, forms of force are classified as tyrannical and criticized by human rights activists as "law above positive law." Rebellion is argued to be legitimate, then, only when it is seen as an act aiming to restore state sovereignty or to avert an "overwhelming humanitarian catastrophe" and not when it presents itself as, say, a religious group's response to what it deems unjust and immoral behavior. Yet, what is viewed by one truth regime as lawful may be considered intolerable, and never legitimately lawful, if it contravenes state power or the mandate of human rights.

The UDHR, which gave form to an international vision of human rights, presumes that a convergence will obtain between universal humanism and state-enforced norms.[62] This remains an unresolved tension in the politics of implementing and enforcing international law through state acquiescence. Yet despite contestation and controversy, it is the voice of this treaty, endowed with a secular language of universalism, that currently holds the force of legitimacy in the world of multilateral internationalism.

The final two chapters build on this history but focus on Nigeria-based case studies and their interface (friction) with general international human rights movements directly and indirectly. The next chapter highlights how, when competing truth regimes come into productive relation (Fairer, 2009), the often incommensurate and uneven relationships of Islam to international law make explicit the reality that they exist within complex webs of transnational Islamic and secular power that often undermines the very essence of their logic of practice. In Chapter 6, I demonstrate how, through the use of strategic vernacularization and the procedural compromise of a particular interpretation of various Islamic verses, it is possible to collaboratively rework particular truth regimes toward the greater good.

CHAPTER 5

"THE HAND WILL GO TO HELL": ISLAMIC LAW AND THE CRAFTING OF THE SPIRITUAL SELF

SHARIA-IZATION IN NIGERIA, POST-1999

I conducted research in the Nigerian north during the summer months of 2002–5, a turbulent period of both excitement and anxiety about the successful reestablishment of the Sharia code.[1] Of the range of stories I documented, four concerned the criminal sentence of death by stoning rendered by a judge who had also sentenced six persons to limb amputations as punishment for the Sharia crime of *sariqah* (theft). During the same period, hundreds of persons under Sharia jurisdiction in northern states were sentenced to public caning for varied minor offences such as petty theft, consumption of alcohol, and prostitution. Of special interest to me were those cases in Zamfara State under the lordship of Judge Ghauri, who insisted that he believed the Sharia "was ordained by God."[2] Also in Zamfara State, the judiciary ordered the amputation of the hand of a young boy convicted of stealing a bicycle in January 2000.[3] This youngster, an indigent from a local village, voluntarily submitted to the Sharia proceeding, including the amputation, choosing not to appeal on the grounds that submission to Allah was necessary to gain redemption for his sins.

In another case, a nineteen-year-old awaited his hearing after being accused of theft. The man who was to be his judge told me and a number of reporters the story of another man who a year earlier had been convicted of stealing a sheep and whose right hand had been amputated as punishment. This judge – someone known to have had the most stoning and amputation sentences since Sharia's implementation – claimed that the nineteen-year-old accused of theft said that "as a Muslim, he would submit to the Sharia and whatever sentence that was prescribed."

The judge later told the reporter that the amputation was a positive measure: "When I watched the procedure I remembered what thieves do. The way they break into people's houses. Attack them. Kill them sometimes. I felt this is exactly what they [the convicted] deserve." Now, because of the amputation, the young man, "when he dies, can go to paradise, but not with the hand: The hand will go to hell" (Finkel 2002).

This pronouncement of the hand as symbolic of sin, and of the punishment as a means of atonement, is not atypical. Echoing other popular narratives, the judge explained that "redemption was possible through submission to Allah. The Sharia courts, through their sentencing, serve to facilitate this spiritual sequence."

As he explained, citing a Qur'anic passage, "As to the thief, male or female, cut off [*faqta'u*] their hands as a recompense for that which they committed, a punishment from God, and God is all-powerful and all-wise" (5:38).[4]

In September 2000, a Sokoto Sharia court sentenced another villager to amputation for the theft of a goat, and in early July 2001, the punishment was carried out relatively quickly.[5] In that case, the thief's personal narrative about the possibility of amputation as redemption existed alongside a critique of the motives of institutionalized Sharia. This defendant used the popular label "political Sharia" to question the court's targeting of the poor, girls, women, and the disenfranchised – the politically powerless. Such language highlights a rhetoric of disavowal set in tension with that of faith in God's judgment. It is this duality that I examine here, in an attempt both to highlight the politics of incommensurability at play in secular models of rights and to map the conditions under which the crafting of the "good" Muslim, the God-fearing disciple, is brought into being. Like "secular" constructions of justice, in putatively religious arenas in which agents of the state purport to act on behalf of the citizenry, robustly neoliberal agendas are at play alongside other praxeological expressions. These expressions represent fictions of sovereign power made manifest through practices of faith, one that competes with the postcolonial state to control the terms of authorial legitimacy – the power over the decision to amputate limbs, to take life, to kill at will, as well as the power to control the positive rights of freedom.

Nigeria, a federal republic bordered by Cameroon to the east, Chad and Niger to the north, the Benin Republic to the west, and the Gulf of Guinea to the south, is estimated to have a population of 135 million.[6] Its most volatile political issues have centered around the access to and distribution of oil and other mineral resources by multinational corporations and the increasing violence resulting from religious and ethnic strife.

The post-1999 period represents the first time in Nigeria's post-colonial history that it has experienced an entire decade free of military rule. In 1999, newly elected President Olusegun Obasanjo – a retired Nigerian Army general and the country's onetime military ruler (1976–9) – began a political transition that moved Nigeria from its fifteen-year stretch of ruthless military dictatorship (1983–98) to a new program designed to establish democracy, stability, and a flourishing economy. Working in response to World Bank and International Monetary Fund economic planners, former President Obasanjo's administration enacted trade liberalization measures and drafted an agenda for international and national cooperation; these have resulted in substantive declines in the economic standard of living (Geo-Jaja and Mangum 2003). Indicators have included the loss of many social services, a decrease in currency value, an increase in the prices of imports, and constrained negotiations for land rights and entitlements. These changes have precipitated the search for new politicoeconomic alliances among those citizens who feel their interests are not being met by Obasanjo's administration. Since his 1999 entrée into democratic governance, more than twelve thousand people have been reported dead as a result of religious or sectarian struggles, through which Muslims have attempted to balance management of the state's political and economic resources.[7]

In this chapter, I examine an example of the way that sovereign power and violence have been dispersed historically through the state not only within spectacular performances of punishing bodies but also through the enactment of individual acquiescence. Representative democracy and the rule of law have, therefore, brought their own sets of controversies to Nigeria. In the midst of ongoing economic and social crises, various Nigerians continue to exert pressure for significant political change, seeking new strategies to balance power within a country where different communities are attempting to build a nation reflective of their own socioreligious values. These strategies once took the form of military coups, but they are now manifested in measures such as the recent reintroduction of the strict Islamic criminal code of Sharia (currently implemented in twelve of Nigeria's thirty-six states).[8] This legal system reflects an alternative moral economy, one that both parallels and challenges the federal strategy for crafting a liberal subject governed through democratic constitutionalism. Further, just as the rights-endowed self is constructed through the adjudication of sociopolitical controversy, so, too, does a new identity, that of the spiritually submissive "good subject," emerge through the institutionalization of an Islamic revival – a formation that represents my final example of a manifestation of sovereign power in the postcolonial context.

As we shall see, the public rhetoric describing the implementation of the strict Islamic Sharia criminal code and its punishments does not always reflect a happy marriage between religious practice (Sharia governance) and religious belief (faith), but it often gets constituted as a totality. The complex interplay between practice and belief reveals two discourses regarding the Sharia: (1) that it is the divine code for the Muslim faithful and (2) that its implementation is a response to the (perceived) diminishment of Islamic power in the newly established, Western-allied democratic state. The Sharia is seen as increasingly serving the politicoeconomic goals of politicians attempting to balance power. The terms *political Sharia* and *Sharia-ization* reflect public criticism that aspects of the Sharia have been implemented haphazardly as a response to the hegemony of Christianity and that this has led to procedural irregularities and inconsistencies in application. Despite this recognition of an imperfect administration, religious agendas live through and alongside seemingly secular contexts. They are made intelligible through the crafting of the spiritual self, in which the subjectivity of the defendant in a criminal case is often negotiated through religious submission to Allah in "appropriate" performances of guilt. Justice is measured not through seemingly secular state laws nor the judgments of a "political" Islamic court, but also through the postured piety of the believer – a conception nicely articulated through the work of Saba Mahmood (2005), among others, in which the idea of piety as strategy relocates the image of acquiescence to oppression into a sphere of sovereignty. What I demonstrate in this chapter and in Chapter 6 are the ways that multiple trajectories of subject making live alongside each other and at times intersect with particular vernacular formations that shape social imaginaries, with the power to disperse what is often seen as the sovereignty of the state and relocate it outside of traditional state domains. Here we see how justice and violence

185

live within, alongside, and through the very postcolonial or religiously Islamicized state that formed the basis for its spectral power. Thus, the goals of this chapter are twofold and interrelated.

First, I examine the historical sequence of implementation of the criminal Sharia legal order in relation to the Nigerian postcolonial state as an example of a competing domain of justice. I analyze consequent patterns of inequality to understand the rise of a new context within which the moral circulation of Islamic revivalism is being deployed to run counter to the model of the rights-endowed subject so prevalent with the rise of nongovernmental organizations (NGOs) in sub-Saharan Africa and in which new forms of cultural retooling are taking shape in the name of the revival of religious traditionalism. Second, I explore a set of relations that remain undertheorized in the legal pluralism literature: the micropractices of acquiescence relative to the politics of the spectral implementation of justice regimes seen as legitimate and proper. I seek to uncover why people who are critical of the uneven balance of Islamic power – such as the indigent Muslims invariably accused in Sharia courts – will nonetheless submit to certain philosophico-religious beliefs embedded within changing conditions of governance. In so doing, I explore this space as a site of sovereign power. I investigate belief by focusing on human action, through which Islamic divinity draws its power – not by the relinquishing of "individual rights" in confession but through the crafting of the spiritual self, for whom performing submission is actually an act of accessing the divine. Praxeology – a long established study of practice – is therefore the method for viewing submission to the courts as indicative of inherent values around enacting "proper" behavior in appropriate spaces.[9] Such praxeological mappings of Nigerian Islamic ritual practice – utterances, postures, and so on – involve focusing on deliberate human actions from which one can derive beliefs and rationales. Praxeology enables us to understand submission as reflection of learned exercises that highlight not the passive subservience of potential convicts but the workings of agency and power in the production of both individual redemption and the subjectivity of the pious Muslim, the "good Muslim." As such, these seemingly submissive practices are understood alongside transcendental ritual praxis in which techniques of subjectivity are measured in terms of their success in "acting appropriately." Through such an examination, I explore examples in which various members of the Nigerian Muslim faithful willingly submit to strict punishments under Islamic law, despite the feeling among some that there are other ways to absolve guilt. These practices bring into tension the relation between faith in human obligation to Allah's divine law and acknowledgment that the law (whether international, national, or local) is made manifest through subjective interpretive determinations and applications.

In anthropology, questions of belief in relation to ritual politics have been traditionally collapsed with those of religion. The anthropology of religion has taken shape through a search for the most "primitive" forms of religious and ritual practice, for the structures and function of religious knowledge, for the processes by which people make religious meaning relevant to cultural life and power relations. However, when belief and religion have been linked analytically, scholars have tended to explore the ways that such forms of knowledge are produced and naturalized. What is missing are the mutual spaces of faith, politics, and lawmaking and their relation in post-9/11 economic contexts, in which subjects mobilize religion for political and legal purposes while also engaging in practices that involve the public display of acquiescence. What we have failed to take seriously are the seemingly contradictory ways that religious enactments are made intelligible in postcolonial contexts but how they are sources of exclusion in international and national regimes of liberalist logic.

In *Genealogies of Religion* (1993), Talal Asad recounts how the constitution of the modern state required the forcible redefinition of religion as belief, and of belief as a personal matter belonging to the emerging space of private life. In the eyes of those who advocated a strong centralized state, religion was a threat because it provided what were viewed as uncontrollable impulses contrary to the logic of national citizenship. Contemporary approaches to understanding the relationship among religion, politics, and faith – especially in posttransition, postcolonial states – highlight the futility of disaggregating religion from faith, of dismembering its agency. Through religious coalition building and faith in the word of Allah, the "good Muslim" is often crafted both as a citizen and as an appropriate believer. Not only are such religious agents proactive in what I refer to as these "faith-making projects," but they are artfully and politically strategic in the multiple trajectories within which they engage in crafting their lives.

In the case of contemporary Islamic revivalisms as practiced by many in northern Nigeria, the convergence of Sharia and its faith-based practices are an outcome of a pluralist, contested state shaped by the influence of colonial powers, with their Judeo-Christian moral inscriptions. The Sharia's presence in one-third of Nigeria's states and its uneven victimization of the indigent are commensurate with Nigeria's historical and contemporary struggles over resources and the unequal distribution of power in relation to Christians and Muslims, urbanities and rural dwellers, and agents of the state versus those at the mercy of state functionaries.

MACROHISTORICAL POLITICS AND THEIR ALIGNMENTS WITH POWER

The Early Spread of Islam in Precolonial Nigeria

The introduction of Sharia law first occurred in 1804, when Fulani leader Uthman dan Fodio launched a jihad of conquest throughout Nigeria (Waldman 1965). This was not, however, the region's first exposure to Islam. The ruler of the northern city of Kano is said to have converted in the fifteenth century, when the kingdom of Bornu in northeastern Nigeria was established by the Muslim ruler Ali bin Dunama (r. 1476–1503). Known as Ali Ghazi of Bornu, he was said to have paid regular visits to Chief Imam Umar Masarmba, residing in the area known today as the Middle East, to learn about the Islamic legal system (Bivar and Hiskett 1962). During the reign of Mai Idris Alooma from 1570 to 1602, Islam became entrenched in the northern region and as far south as the city of Ilorin (Davidson 1998).

From the fifteenth through the nineteenth centuries, the Sharia was used intermittently in the settling of civil disputes, including those involving questions of family and personal law. It was applied in deciding criminal cases such as adultery, fornication, and theft, and a system of Sharia was also formed to litigate important land and finance matters.[10] Prior to the sixteenth century, the primary Sharia judicial institution was presided over by a judge – known as a *qadi* (*alkali* among the Hausa in the north [Smith 1964:177]) or *hakim* – empowered to adjudicate legal disputes in both personal cases and public criminal matters. In these traditional Sharia courts, both the plaintiff and defendant represented themselves without the presence of a jury or lawyer/advocate. The *qadi* was responsible for making legal judgments in keeping with the Sharia rules of evidence and testimony.

The spread of Islam did not lead to the universal adoption of Sharia law. The creation of Sharia legal jurisdiction involved the establishment of social relationships among persons governed by the same system of Islamic personal law. In other words, before the territorialization of jurisdiction, personal law formed the basis for jurisdiction. In sections of the south and east of Nigeria, where occult practices and beliefs held sway, the Sharia was not easily assimilated. These underlying distinctions in these regions developed into differences in legal systems, and thus different regional strategies of British colonization.

Changes in Colonial Governance: Vernacularizing the Judicial Reach of Courts

Contemporary Nigerian Sharia is an outcome of a pluralist, contested state shaped by colonial power and the circumstances of decolonization. Under these historical influences, postcolonial regimes have differentially empowered various traditional authorities, in some cases leading to despotic rule and setting the groundwork for the unequal distribution of power. Formations of criminal law in both northern and southern Nigeria are illustrative of the postcolonial contests between Christians and Muslims. In examining these judicial and political landscapes, it is important to understand that the widespread reintroduction of the criminal Sharia has led to the coexistence of two dueling spheres of analysis that are mutually necessary: that of *religion* as a manifestation of politics, and that of *faith* within the sphere of belief and its related performances of self-crafting.

By the nineteenth century, European powers, in addition to competing for Nigerian land and goods, were also vying to control mercantilism along the coasts. Between 1860 and 1862, Britain established its first foothold in the southwestern region of Lagos. This created the conditions for the annexation of Lagos as a British colony. Subsequently, the need to expand trade to the hinterland and to undermine competition led the British to establish direct rule along the entire coastal region – including the Delta ports of Old Calabar, Bonny, and Brass. Such coastal encroachments led to the eventual defeat of the entire southwestern resistance and the British establishment of a Protectorate of Southern Nigeria in 1900. That year also saw the withdrawal of the Royal Niger Company's charter (granted 1886) and the creation of the Protectorate of Northern Nigeria from its territory. This was followed by the 1903 British victory over the Sokoto Caliphate in the Muslim north. These areas were consolidated into one British imperial geopolitical region in 1914, forming the Colony and Protectorate of Nigeria. Lord Frederick Lugard became its first governor general, serving in that post from 1914 to 1919.

Not long after the amalgamation of Nigeria, the British colony was allowed some level of indirect rule (more so in the north). The Native

Court Proclamation of 1900 had directly provided the Eastern (Igbo) region of Nigeria with its own administrative branch, with each component Native Court a political administrative body led by a British official known as the district commissioner (Ekechi 1972). However, the creation of such courts headed by outsiders was not effective, and by 1918, the Native Court Ordinance No. 5 abolished the district commissioner role "in an attempt to make the courts truly 'native'"; later the British changed the Native Courts to "agencies for dispute management" and their name to Customary Courts (Okereafoezeke 2002:163).

In the southwestern region of the colonial state, customary law became the traditional mechanism for dispute resolution in Nigerian communities. There, courts were created and run without statutory authority; rather, state officials with training in the customary laws and traditions of the people, not "legal training," ran the court system. Granted exclusive jurisdiction over all crimes, these occult-derived Customary Courts continued to consolidate moral values and conceptions of sociopersonal and political power.

Lugard's attempts to establish British authority were driven by a belief in the existence of "natural law" protecting procedural rights. Although this enabled the initial continuity of customary law, through the Court of Appeal structure, it also provided the engine for the eventual transformation of the law (Falola et al. 1989; Yakubu 2005:205–6).

Meanwhile, in the northern region, colonial governance contended with another judicial system – administered by the head emir with advice from his executive council – that operated according to its own written doctrine. That is, the Native Court system of northern Nigeria, although comparable to the Customary Court system found in the south, was not one introduced by the British. In the north, Islamic customary courts governed by the Sharia remained the rule of law (Obe 2005:107–8). Thus, in an attempt to negotiate jurisdiction in a diverse ethnic and religiously complex landscape, Lugard allowed for the administration of Muslim law through the modification of procedural strategies that did not contradict the teachings of the Qur'an. Insisting, in fact, on the observance of Islamic customary law, he mandated:

> The High Court shall observe and enforce the observance of customary law which is applicable and is not repugnant to natural justice, equity and good conscience nor incompatible either directly or by implication with any law for the time being in force, and nothing in this Law shall deprive any person of the benefit of customary law. (Lugard 1907:130)

Notwithstanding these concessions to the realm of customary law, for Lugard, the Islamic exercise of criminal law was "repugnant" and its punishments cruel, unusual, or "uncivilized." The later Native Courts Proclamation (1906) gave the Sharia administration not only the power to appoint the emir, who would administer a Native Court of Appeal, but also the mandate to accept a hierarchy of supreme appeal in which particular decisions of execution could not be administered without the review and decision of the Governor (Obe 2005:108). That would change, however, and Islamic law was soon brought into conformity with the basic principles of the Supreme Court of Nigeria.

The structures of authority invested tremendous powers in new chiefs and in new domains of native/customary administration – a situation that Mahmood Mamdani (1996:37) refers to as *decentralized despotism*, with previous forms of power-balancing mechanisms being destroyed in favor of establishing authority in new leadership figures. In southwestern Nigeria, the invention of "paramount chiefs" and new Christian leadership undermined precolonial governance. Similarly, in the eastern regions compromises were made with traditional chiefs redesignated in new spheres of power. In northern Nigeria as well, new "traditions" were invented through the colonial encounter. Unlike the south, however, Islamic governance did not involve direct control of the political sphere. Muslim *qadis* charged with the interpretation and implementation of the Sharia performed functions including economic, administrative, and political tasks – all of which existed in a *social* sphere in which those in power consulted with jurists on matters related to law. These *qadis* served as the mediators between the ruling and working classes and existed as the guardians of Islamic traditions, explaining the decisions of those with economic power to those without it (Abou El Fadl 2003). They served as spiritual intermediaries and led revolutionary struggles in defense of Islam.

The 1914 British amalgamation of the east, south, and northern sectors ultimately set the stage for creation of a Nigerian federation in 1954 under which the predominant system of British common law claimed jurisdiction over criminal matters. With common law and related Christian moral hegemonies beginning to circulate and shape the basis for moral meaning and appropriate notions of punishment, a hierarchical relationship was established between common law and Customary/Native Courts – rendering Islamic and other courts answerable to the High Court of the state and its system of appeals.

191

In preparation for the Constitutional Conference of 1950 in Ibadan, the new Nigerian Criminal Code was drafted; it passed with a declaration of independence in 1960. With independence, the court system changed again – the result, in part, of a realignment of the spheres of law, politics, and religion that colonialism had occasioned. With the institutionalization of the common law system as the ultimate basis for appeal, Sharia courts, Magistrate Courts, and Native Courts were jurisdictionally reclassified, and Nigerian superior courts were established and given the power to transfer and review cases (Obe 2005:115). However, concerns over the juridical power of Islamic law exercised through the Sharia courts as well as the practices of Customary Courts precipitated a constitutional issue.[11] For whereas the older Native Courts, now Customary Courts, maintained the authority to adjudicate according to the substantive principles of indigenous criminal law, the developing mechanism for procedural appeals laid the foundation for new norms that were statute-based.

Up until independence, Native Courts had the power to impose customary punishments on those accused of crimes. Such punishments spanned a range of offenses, and courts were free to impose a fine, imprisonment, or any punishment authorized by native law or custom as long as it did not involve "mutilation or torture, and is not repugnant to natural justice and humanity."[12] This provision, as understood, banned the amputation of hands for the punishment for theft, lashing for fornication, and death by stoning for adultery. With independence, all resident Christians and Muslims were placed under a shared Federal criminal justice system that relied on territory as the basis for determining jurisdiction and jurisprudence based on British common law principles. As such, a new emphasis on unity, "enlightened civility," and nation building set the groundwork for the newly postcolonial state. However, in the north this reorganization of precolonial authority was thought to privilege secular, Judeo-Christian values and ethics over those of Islam – a move that would have deep consequences.

In response to what was viewed as a threat of Christian hegemony after independence, prominent Muslims demanded the return of the exclusive criminal and civil jurisdiction of the Sharia. The Nigerian Federation, adamantly opposed to these demands, cited the Criminal Code Act of 1934, which states: "No person shall be liable to be tried or punished in any court in Nigeria for an offence except under the express provisions of the code or of some Act or Law which is in force in, or forms part of the law of Nigeria" (sec. 4). In southern Nigeria, a region where vernacular practices were becoming increasingly aligned with British Christianity, this meant that some actions that had been criminal offenses under customary or Sharia law would no longer be the subject of criminal sanction under the new statutes. These changes in criminal jurisdiction were approved at the 1957 Constitutional Conference (held in London); but as part of the pre-Conference negotiations, the Minorities Commission was instituted to explore questions about the allowances needed for the intended federation of the three regions (north, south, and east).[13] It was here that Muslim political leaders of northern Nigeria attempted to regain Islamic criminal jurisdiction. Although they were prepared to conform to the new shift in criminal jurisprudence as well as to participate in the justice system, they were emphatically invested in the preservation of the Islamic religion. However, where demands for the maintenance of Muslim jurisdiction of courts were raised, they were often met with criticisms that the Islamic courts were unjust and that the alkali presiding over the court was not impartial regarding non-Muslim litigants.

In an attempt to reach an agreement about the cohabitation of Muslims and Christians in the north under predominantly Muslim laws, northern government representatives sent delegations to visit Pakistan, Libya, and the Sudan to study how they addressed non-Muslim liability in predominantly Muslim states. The results of the findings of those delegations led to the northern government's establishment of a panel of six jurists[14] to consider a system that would include the organization of English, Islamic, and customary law. The six-juror panel recommended a Penal Code outlining provisions for largely non-Islamic regions of the Nigerian north.[15] Upon the presentation and acceptance of the bill in the northern legislature, the Penal Code went into effect in 1960 (Tabiu 2001), giving customary courts the jurisdiction to apply criminal law to those willing to submit to its courts jurisdiction.

The revivalism and recent success of contemporary demands for the extension of Islamic law is connected to this history. Further, Christian fears, in the south, of restrictions on religious practices were met by Muslim attempts to implement the criminal Penal Code, which corresponded to the nation's Criminal Procedure Code but would allow non-Muslims to avoid trial in Muslim courts by choosing, instead, adjudication by a High Court or Magistrate's Court. Instead of achieving simply its intended aim, however, this "opting out" component provided incentive for Muslims to renounce Islam rather than be tried in an Islamic court.[16] This outcome strengthened demands among some for the introduction of the Sharia. The proceedings of the Constituent Assembly, which led to the 1979 Constitution, were also complicated by Muslim demands to set up a Sharia Court of Appeal distinct from the federal Court of Appeal – all features of the new Penal Code of 1960.

The New Nigeria: Secular Democracy and Sunni Islamic Revivalism

With the recent shifts toward constitutional democracy, the rule of law, and a centralized federal system, headed by a Christian president, it has become clear that the power of the Nigerian state is no longer simply embedded in constituent "traditional," Christian, or Islamic societies. Given that the Nigerian state holds a supreme constitution and that the power to make and unmake criminal law is endowed in the life of the statute, the battle to establish a Sharia Court of Appeal for the whole federation has been a contest over the constitutional legitimacy of religious claims. At the same time as the Christian south was gaining political power at the federal level, the leadership in the north was actively working toward regional claims to Islamic Sunni governance. Throughout the 1980s, in the heartland of Sunni Islam in northern Nigeria, a new corpus of Sunni fundamentalism began to take shape with the establishment of the Sharia Court of Appeal in Minna, Niger State.

In 1999, Governor Ahmed Sani, a fundamentalist Muslim who was democratically elected to the governorship of Zamfara State, announced that Zamfara would work toward becoming an Islamic state. Effective January 27, 2000, the state legislature adopted the Sharia penal code as the basis for settling disputes. This intervention reflects the desire to ensure that particular mechanisms of governance are in keeping with Islam's fundamental moral principles. Believed to be "the Path" that embodies the totality of Islamic guidance, the Sharia represents a collection of positive rules as well as a set of principles and a discursive methodology for seeking divine ideals through core Islamic values. Since 2000, eleven more of Nigeria's thirty-six states have followed Zamfara State in the adoption of Sharia penal law permitted under the existing Penal Code.[17] These changes, often represented by adherents as demonstrating religious and political self-determination, also reflect an effort by political agents to secure and balance power as well as to mobilize resources in the quickly transforming economy.

With Nigeria's second consecutive democratic elections in 2004, the religious revivalism of Islamic social movements began to bring to the fore questions about the compatibility of Islamic law and liberalist constitutionalism. Many human rights organizations within Nigeria tend to insist that basic liberalist state laws should be respected and argue that the recently enacted Sharia penal codes violate basic human rights on many levels. By insisting on the constituent right of the state to claim the sovereign power over supreme lawmaking, the field of embattlement for the rights movements has been within particular juridical zones of engagement through which the micropractices of human rights have been at play. For example, according to Article 7, section 1 of the Rome Statute of the International Criminal Court, the "'crime against humanity' means any of the following acts when committed as part of a widespread or systematic attack directed against any civilian population." Subsection (h) adds to the list of violations, "Persecution against any identifiable group or collectivity on political, racial, national, ethnic, cultural, religious, gender, or other grounds that are universally recognized as impermissible under international law."[18] Sharia penal codes are thus said to be in violation of Article 7(1) in that they permit mutilation or execution, discriminate against women, and allow for the persecution of Muslims without due process, and therefore their implementation could be classified as a crime against humanity. Nevertheless, for many Nigerian Muslims, Sharia adjudication is both a political response to conditions of inequality in Nigeria and the region and a means toward crafting a Muslim subjectivity within alternative trajectories of consciousness.

I move now to a discussion of the micropractices of acquiescence and political critique that inform that subjectivity to highlight the ways that understanding such forms of faith-based conviction may run contrary to the shaping of the rights-bearing subject in such a way that its expression is unrecognizable as an equal domain of freedom, of agency.

POLITICS, AGENCY, AND THE CRIME OF ZINA

In January 2001, Zamfara State officials caned a fourteen-year-old girl convicted of fornication because she had borne a child out of wedlock.[19] According to her testimony, her father had forced her to provide sexual favors to three men to whom he was indebted. Instead of prosecuting the three men for statutory rape, in accordance with Nigerian common law, the Sharia court required that the young girl produce four witnesses to corroborate her testimony. Her inability to do this resulted in the Sharia court sentencing her to 180 lashes – 100 for fornication, and 80 for the charge of bearing false testimony. She appealed the sentence. It was temporarily suspended only to be reimposed, although reduced to 100 lashes because of her insistent denials of guilt. She appealed again, this time contesting the propriety of her conviction under Islamic law. This was unsuccessful. In accepting the judgment, the young girl explained that submission to a higher power was the next available means by which justice was possible.

The young girl's case provides one example of a typical form of dualism – that of questioning the propriety of the law while at the same time submitting to it. Despite concerns about the politicization and corruption of their religion, many Nigerian Islamic faithful argue that submission to the will of Allah is their central responsibility as Muslims. This is not inconsequential. The crimes of *zina* (adultery and fornication), which a man and a woman are said to commit if they "willfully have sexual intercourse without being validly married to each other,"[20] entail severe punishment: according to the ordinances in the Sharia penal code in twelve Nigerian states, a man or woman guilty of *zina* shall be stoned to death at a public place if he or she is a *muhsan* (a Muslim now or ever married)[21] or, if not a *muhsan*, publicly punished with one hundred whiplashes.

The Qur'anic verses vary on this issue, and consequently there are a range of interpretations not reflected by the courts. For example, one verse warns: "And come not near to unlawful sexual intercourse. Verily, it is a *faahishah* [a great sin] and an evil way" (Sura al-Israa 17:32). Another passage echoes this but also addresses the prospect of redemption:

> And those who invoke not any other god along with Allah, nor kill such life as Allah has forbidden, except for just cause, nor commit illegal sexual intercourse [*zina*] and whoever does this shall receive the punishment. The torment will be doubled to him on the Day of Resurrection, and he will abide therein in disgrace; except those who repent and believe and do righteous deeds, for those Allah will change their sins into good deeds, and Allah is Oft Forgiving, Most Merciful. (Sura al-Furqaan 25:68–70)

Although both verses highlight Qur'anic warnings against succumbing to *zina*, their implications vary. In the first passage, people are simply warned of the evil of *zina*. The second outlines the possibility for redeeming the soul, both in life and after death, through repenting and performing moral acts. These interpretive variations are further complicated by the tension between belief in human obligation to God's divine law and recognition that the law is made manifest through subjective determination and application. This dilemma is known to Islamic legal scholars as the distinction between the Sharia and the *fiqh* (school of Islamic jurisprudence).

The Sharia is seen as the divine law that exists in an uncorrupted state of being. The Arabic term *fiqh* is used to describe the human attempt to understand and apply that ideal. The Sharia, as divine, is viewed as immutable and flawless, but the *fiqh*, as it is humanly constituted, is seen to be flawed (Abou El Fadl 2003). It is, thus, the *fiqh* – the practice of applying an ideal – that accounts for what is seen as "political" in, or corrupting of, the Sharia. Sharia death penalty cases highlight the complexities of understanding a believer's personal acquiescence alongside public criticism regarding who is prosecuted and why.

Serious complications began in 2002 for defendants Fatima Usman (then a twenty-eight-year-old divorcée with four children) and Ahmadu Ibrahim (a thirty-two-year-old with three children), when their initial sentence of adultery was overturned and converted to death by stoning in a lower Sharia court in Lambata and further upheld in the Sharia Court of Appeal in Minna.[22] As it was explained to me, it was Fatima's father who had reported Ahmadu to the local judge, Abdulrahman Alhassan. The father accused Ahmadu of impregnating his daughter, whose second husband had just divorced her on account of the illicit pregnancy. Fatima's father, himself a struggling villager, insisted in court that Ahmadu must pay him 150,000 naira (roughly US$1,150).[23] The judge then referred Fatima's father to the police station, where statements were taken. The case was brought before the Sharia court judge in Upper Area Court Gawu Babangida, in Gurara local government region. After admitting their relationship, Ahmadu and Fatima were convicted of adultery and each given a sentence of five years in prison or a fine of 15,000 naira for damages. When they were unable to pay, they were remanded to prison.

Once it became clear that the 150,000 naira demanded from Ahmadu by the father was not going to be paid, he went to the Sharia Court of Appeal in Minna and lodged a complaint. Instead of granting him redress, the Upper Area Court judge and the defendants were summoned to Minna. As the trial transcript indicates, Fatima and Ahmadu both submitted to the jurisdiction of the Sharia court and had already offered confessions to having committed adultery. As a result of their confessions, the conviction of *zina* was upheld; but with neither defendant present in court, the sentence was changed to death by stoning.[24]

Initially, after the death penalty conviction, the two maintained their guilt in having had unlawful intercourse. Yet during a series of interviews that I had with the defendants over the course of their trial, they spoke bitterly about the corruption of various villagers and court officials responsible for implementing the Sharia. They argued that they were being prosecuted so that others could become the financial benefactors of their ill fate. It was not until human rights workers, such as Hauwa Ibrahim, intervened and counseled Fatima and Ahmadu, however, that they became willing to challenge their convictions and change their testimony from a declaration of guilt to one of innocence.

Why was the intervention of human rights advocates necessary? What is of interest here is that the case of Fatima and Ahmadu is representative of a widespread acquiescence to the Sharia despite concern that political and economic issues motivate convictions. At microsites of justice making, it becomes clear that even those whom we might see as subjects under (victims of) the Sharia connect their own suffering to substantive notions of transgression that must be redeemed. Contrary to the rights-endowed subject whose guilt is not required for display – who instead performs the role of innocent victim until proven guilty – the culturally acceptable Islamic subject must demonstrate submission before divine law. Repentance and obeisance help to make possible life after the death of the body, as well as social redemption – the making of a proper Muslim.[25]

VERNACULAR JUSTICE: RELIGIOUS POLITICS AND THE POLITICS OF FAITH

In examining the various local, national, and translocal contexts in which people give consent, form alternative alliances, or reject the basis of authority in given domains of power, my intention is neither to flatten differences in authority among state officials, jurists, or the accused, nor to flatten the differences in social equality between Fatima and Ahmadu. Rather, it is to suggest that there are notable differences in social standing and equality between Fatima and Ahmadu and to highlight the acute recognition, flagged by such expressions as "political Sharia," that injustice and suffering underlie such cases. Indeed, among its followers, Sharia revivalism is also accompanied by an explicit anger with the political ambitions of agents of the Islamic state, or – as in Fatima's case – with families seeking economic compensation. The ways in which vulnerable agents negotiate the interplay between religious politics and the politics of faith merit closer attention.

The targets of the revived Sharia machinery in the regions that I conducted fieldwork were not Muslims engaged in corporate theft or office sex in the industrial sectors. Those sentenced were typically the economically underprivileged, who stood accused of sexual crimes for babies born out of wedlock, or of animal or tool theft in villages where poverty levels are such that accused persons cannot afford shoes to wear or food to feed their families. Those in prisons awaiting sentences are indigent boys and girls, young men and women. The accusers, themselves from poor villages, are often interested in remuneration of some kind. For example, in some of the reports of fornication cases throughout northern Nigeria, the fathers of accused women were offering their daughter's sexual services to secure the support of other men. Other cases involved women interested in pursuing vendettas against their husband's mistresses.[26] In the case of Fatima and Ahmadu, Fatima and her father's attempt to secure a marriage with Ahmadu or to secure money from him might be seen as filling the punitive space of Ahmadu's neglect to offer a bride price to the parents in exchange for their daughter. Herein lies the source of Ahmadu's anger. He felt he was being coerced into taking another wife for marriage – a wife whom he could not afford. According to him, had he the money to pay the earlier charge, "the case would not have ever become a case about my disappearance."[27]

Instead, Ahmadu interpreted sexual provocations from Fatima and the follow-up demands for money as reflective of a larger plan to extract financial and moral responsibilities from him. Ahmadu did not intend to take on additional moral obligations and marry Fatima. As detailed in his testimony,[28] Ahmadu agreed that he acted without the intention of marrying, but he attributes his behavior to "Satan," known in Arabic as *junn* – a form of temptation:

> I committed sin; yes, it is true. I was the person that impregnated her without marrying her. . . . In fact, [it] is true because of Allah this matter is true. I committed this offence, and it is me that impregnated Fatima without marrying her, just I like her. . . . I told her that if I marry her my wife will divorce me, we have trust between me and my wife so I cannot divorce her. Your worship, you know it is Satan that brought this, still she did not leave me, every time she will come to me. (Interview 7/15/05)

(For her part, although Fatima concurred that she was guilty of the crime – "True, we have committed this offense with Ahmadu Ibrahim" (ibid.) – she claims that she committed adultery with the intention of marrying him.)

A reading of the defendants' confessions makes explicit the exercise of their faith through their submission of will in a way that reflects the crafting of spiritual subjectivity through an understanding of actions in the world – those seen, as well as those spiritually shaped imaginaries not always easily "provable" in a court of law. In these terms, we see that Ahmadu's responses to the prosecutor's questions continued to highlight the work of Satan in his adulterous action – that he succumbed to such temptation having lost the protection of his good spirits:

> One day she came and there was rain falling and we entered the shop so that to hide for the rain falling. Your Worship, it was here Satan tempted me and sexed her true. I will say since Allah has said that: [he utters prayer in Arabic with eyes closed]. Then I told her you know anyone who sex a woman without marriage, there is no marriage, until if she has done period and seek for leniency. But she still did not stop coming. (Interview July 15, 2005)

In Ahmadu's testimony, Satan is a code word for the Islamic belief in jinne (from the Arabic junn), which refers to both good and bad forces, spiritual beings believed to inhabit the world alongside humans and to interact with them. In this case, Satan represents the impact of bad jinne, the influence of which motivated Ahmadu's sinful act. Seen in this context, his admission of wrongdoing was not a misrecognition of his experiences. For although confession and submission as forms of negotiation did not absolve him of guilt before the law, admission qualified by an insistence that he lacked protection from negative forces locates Ahmadu as a spiritually elevated being within a spectrum of negotiable spheres of redemption.

From this vantage point, Ahmadu is able to shift focus by comparing the quality of his own guilty act with the position of Fatima's father, so possessed by the thought of receiving a substitute for a bride price that he was willing to sacrifice his own kin in pursuit of monetary gain. As Ahmadu explained to me in a follow-up interview (also on July 15, 2005), "Yes, I acted wrongly and the penalty for my actions are death. But I still don't think that I should be punished for it. I have willfully submitted for my wrongdoing. But, those looking for money from me should also submit." Through such complex posturing, outer-worldly spirits who influence personal behavior can be described as

culpable – demons from the secular world who manifest in the material actions of otherwise "good" Muslims. The quote also speaks to
Ahmadu's feeling that *others* should be punished as well (i.e., Fatima's
father), however. Nevertheless, at the heart of the problem was that,
despite an "agreement between Fatima's family and [Ahmadu] that he
would marry Fatima after she had weaned her daughter . . . [he] reneged
on the agreement, claiming that he did not have the kind of money that
Fatima's father was asking for. In a bid to make him pay up, Fatima's
father took the case to court demanding the sum of one hundred and
fifty thousand naira (N150,000) as damages."[29]

As described in the opening section of this chapter, a range of Sharia
prosecutions have taken place in Nigeria since 1999, and in most cases
submission to the punishment – rather than appeal – was the initial response. It is important to recognize how (and why) an accused
person can maintain belief in the law despite competing and contradictory claims. What we see is an acceptance of multiple interpretations of truth, where truth reflects an interplay of the human and the
sacred embedded simultaneously within political and divine spheres.
This manifests within Islam through what I have identified, in the
preceding section, as a distinction between the Sharia and the *fiqh*.
Through interpretation and adjudication, the spectrality of divinity
manifests through, and draws power from, the human subject under
construction.

In this regard, Ahmadu's confession should be seen as a form of divine
obeisance, through which he is engaged in performing the "proper" way
of being in this particular world context. His Arabic utterances further
engage a form of propitiation used to demonstrate adherence to godli-
ness with the goal of undermining the secular evil of the non-Muslim
world. Ahmadu recognized that by confessing, he was acknowledging
his identity as a Muslim and his willingness to submit to higher forces,
to the courts. To understand such a willful confession in the midst
of Ahmadu's insistence that he was being used by others for financial
gain, one must review the rules of conduct that have reinforced this
particular system of behavior, in which submission to God requires
particular types of display.[30] First, the religion is based on both behavior and belief. Pledging one's daily life to God's rules of conduct is
revered, if it is a manifestation of genuine spiritual commitment. The
maintenance of belief in Allah in the face of adversity is meritorious.
Thus, it is important for the believer to exhibit his or her morality
through devout, pious, and upright behavior. These practices are seen

to constitute the submission of the soul to the will of Allah, and it is this that will be considered on Judgment Day when the soul is rendered either suitable or unsuitable for entrance to Paradise. In this case, Ahmadu felt that it was Allah's will that he be held publicly accountable for his relationship with Fatima. Or, as one of the Sharia judges explained to me,[31] "The Qur'an states: 'Those who surrender themselves to Allah and accept the true faith; who are devout, sincere, patient, humble, charitable, and chaste; who fast and are ever mindful of Allah – on those, both men and women, Allah will bestow in alms of that which we have given them.'"

Such a verse captures the spiritual attitudes that individuals are called on to exhibit to gain ultimate redemption on Judgment Day. For at the heart of Islam as practiced in northern Nigeria is the conviction that revelations from the holy book are divine in origin and therefore irrefutable. The demands of faith are often represented as straightforward, thereby requiring only that morality and ethics of submission be maintained – that is, the performance of piety. As a religious doctrine, Islam as popularly practiced in Nigeria is oriented toward praxis, and language is critical, because utterances are central to the theater of submission. In prioritizing the purity of redemption, therefore, Ahmadu's submission of a guilty plea suggests a desire to overcome the presumptions of modern reason and, instead, to betray the modern rationality of the rights-bearing citizen through an admission of faith. Insisting that his transgression reflected the overwhelming and irrational power of Satan, Ahmadu creates the possibility of both spiritual and social redemption. Through the nature of his confession, he performs his faith in an infinite future made possible through the logic of religious practice.

Thus, confession of guilt is not really the *claiming* of guilt. My discussions with Ahmadu suggested that he did not see himself alone as being responsible for his crime. Rather, he pointed to complicity in his weakness and the desire to prevent secular and other evil forces from colluding in his demise. Submission, then, is an attempt to recognize the failure not of the self but of the good forces to protect oneself from the specters of evil, the evils of secular public life. It is an embodied spiritual chorus of complex interrelatedness. As such, faith represents the realm of the knowable; it holds the power to transform sin and reformulate a human life into what is necessary for everlasting life. Faith becomes the knowable, the possible. It is the rationality of such revelations that shapes the basis for praxis. This type of purposive action is in itself an expression of the triumph over irrationality, over the Christian secular that is seen as hegemonic in the Nigerian south. It represents the type of piety that Islamic practice expects of its faithful. Thus, the admission of guilt, the expression of morals, and the submission to Allah all offer paths to virtuousness and redemption. In this context, Ahmadu viewed his submission as a triumph of rationality and his faith as a religious technique for ensuring salvation, in both social and spiritual contexts.

If we acknowledge that the separation between the public and the private is indistinguishable where religion and faith are related, it becomes clear that the moral and the legal are co-constitutive. This recognition enables a further step, moving Islam to another level of expression in which the political is that which allows for subjugation – the political as the eternal. The triumph of the Sharia lies in the ability of religion as politics to produce a perpetual will of submission toward the purification of sinful acts. This mechanism clears the way for the broadening of faith both to compete with politics and, indeed, to become politics writ large.

In reflecting now on the plight of Fatima and Ahmadu – as of January 2009, a stalled case still formally unresolved in Nigerian courts – it is important to acknowledge the complexities of the "self" and its relationship to various cosmologies and social realities. To understand the struggles of those who resist Sharia punishment in the name of obedience to Allah, we must consider their participation in co-constructing "culturally acceptable" subjectivities, co-constructing new fictions. Unregulated individual freedoms, sexual promiscuity, the effects of alcohol, neoliberal restructuring, "political" Sharia, and many more forces are seen as encroaching on the divinity of Islam as it manifests in particular cases of crime and punishment. Recognizing the ramifications of these material forces, individuals negotiate the demands of several interlinked yet competing hegemonies, located at international, national, regional, municipal, and village sites. By understanding how to navigate such complex terrain, defendants such as Ahmadu practice submission in ways that link their personal circumstances to larger power plays in Nigeria, where much is at stake for the future political, economic, and religious autonomy of Muslim states.

Ultimately, it is not surprising that the micropractices at the heart of the theater of justice making – whether international, national, or village-based – is a function of power. When justice making is understood in relation to the power to perform particular forms of subjectivity, of utmost importance are the interactions and contestations of capacities of authority. These include the politics of the decision within which deciding what is or is not appropriate, in contexts that have life-and-death effects, is at stake. The vernacular forms of subjectivity at play here reflect both the informal sovereign who embodies the law itself as well as the sphere of Sharia unconstitutionality as its own originating source of sovereign order.

CONCLUSION

Following Jacques Derrida, religion's "essential relation . . . both to faith and to God is anything but self-evident" (2002: 69). How and why an amputee or convicted adulterer may dismiss the religiosity of the Sharia as being "political" yet honor the conviction that inspires submissive action toward Allah is connected to the subjective construction of "morally appropriate" and "culturally acceptable" practices. It is fundamentally connected to the power to name the victim under conditions of perceived subordination. For just as both judges and defendants participate in the management of crime, so, too, do these people engage in explicitly interpreting authorial texts: translating meanings, assessing applicability, and relating texts to personal style, normative practice, and contextual appropriateness. As I have demonstrated, separating the work that "religion" does from the work that "belief" does is a necessary step in understanding the construction of the subjectivity of a victim or a "good" Muslim; it involves recognizing practices emanating from spheres that may appear contradictory but are in fact related. I have shown how individual acquiescence to religious submission is tied to both the political economy of Sharia macropolitics and the telic quality of spiritual action. Questions of religious faith should be understood, therefore, as existing on the borderlands of both the moral economy of postcolonial politics and the faith-inspired praxis that informs particular disciplinary practices.

The restructuring of Nigeria's political economy to reflect globalizing ("Western") models and priorities has taken shape with increasing centralization of the federal government and the development of a new discourse of "democracy" and individual rights. Religious revivalisms have emerged in response to these changes – and to the accompanying devastation of the Nigerian economy. My larger argument here is that in the midst of uneven power relations and various types of violence – paramilitary, ritualistic changes in the reach of criminal law have brought to the fore a range of trajectories through which different persons assign guilt and responsibility according to a range of cultural logics. In this regard, it is essential to consider how best to understand the ways in which particular people create norms and standards of behavior and, in so doing, to examine not simply what they articulate as the basis for freedom or rights but how they cultivate micropractices that allow them to engage in political contestation, sometimes through acquiescence, all the time narrativizing that which is just within particular regimes of truth.

Throughout northern Nigeria, Islamic fundamentalisms are actively engaged in constructing faith-based subjectivities – some in contrast to the neoliberal, secular, rights-bearing subject, seem submissive and apolitical. In fact, the opposite may be the case. In the expression of freedom, rights, and criminal responsibility, the realities of these differences reflect divergent trajectories in cultivating norms. Sometimes those differences can be strategically undermined and people engage in vernacularizing new forms of meanings; other times differences are embedded in contested encounters that work themselves out through politics. Yet other times, the conceptual bases on which notions of justice are shaped are so divergent that even in their expression of freedom in their own terms, they may be unrecognizable as freedom at all.

In the end, the conceptual challenge is to understand how contemporary competitions over power and authority live on quite robustly within – or even because of – the neoliberal political agendas they seemingly oppose.

CHAPTER 6

ISLAMIC SHARIA AT THE CROSSROADS: HUMAN RIGHTS CHALLENGES AND THE STRATEGIC TRANSLATION OF VERNACULAR IMAGINARIES

SAFIYA HUSSAINI AND AMINA LAWAL

Safiya, as she has been popularly called, was an unemployed and divorced thirty-year-old Muslim mother of four when she was sentenced to death on October 9, 2001, by a Sharia court in Gwadabawa, Sokoto State, in northern Nigeria.[1] She had been found guilty of adulterous involvement (covered by the Arabic word *zina*)[2] with Yakubu Abubakar, an older neighbor. The act had apparently led to Safiya Hussaini's pregnancy.[3] Abubakar denied paternity and was acquitted for lack of evidence. (Safiya would later claim she had been pressured into accusing Abubakar of raping her and that the actual father was her ex-husband.)[4] The trial court judge, Muhammad Bello Sanyinawal, ruled that the defendant had confessed to adultery and was therefore already guilty before the court. As discussed in Chapter 5, the criminalization of adultery remains a central tenet of the new Sharia in northern Nigeria; under Islamic law, the crime may be punishable by death.[5]

BAOBAB for Women's Human Rights, a Nigerian nongovernmental organization whose name was taken from a common baobab tree in the region, had been active in trying to influence Sharia verdicts since 1999, contacted Safiya and mobilized around her case; other NGOs, such as the Nigeria-based Women's Aid Collective, also got involved in the legal process. Safiya's appeal was heard at Sokoto's Sharia Court of Appeal on October 26, 2001. Ultimately her sentence was overturned because of technical and procedural errors; for example, the charge of *zina* had not been adequately explained to Safiya, and Sharia law had not even come into force until the month following her alleged crime. She was acquitted and released on March 25, 2002.

Safiya Hussaini had provided a test case for activists and intellectuals who were interested in critically engaging the Sharia as a threat to the integrity of human rights and a vehicle for the abuse of women and had rallied around her cause.[6] Then, days before the conclusion of Safiya's case, another divorced Nigerian mother became a symbol of the struggle for women's justice.

On March 22, 2002, Amina Lawal, an impoverished, divorced, thirty-year-old Muslim woman, was sentenced to be stoned to death by the Sharia court of Bakori, Katsina State, in northern Nigeria. During this first hearing, and in the absence of legal representation, she had "confessed" to committing *zina*; that is, she admitted to having a newborn child and no husband.[7] (Under the new Sharia penal code, evidence of pregnancy outside of marriage also suffices to convict a woman of adultery.) Yahaya Mohammad, the accused father of Amina Lawal's child, denied having had intercourse with her, and the charge against him was dropped. However, the implementation of her sentence was delayed and the hearing suspended until January 2004, allowing Amina Lawal two years to raise her baby. Meanwhile, led by the Nigerian NGO Women's Rights Advancement and Protection Alternative, and with the assistance of attorneys and consultants secured by BAOBAB, Amina Lawal's lawyers filed an appeal for her on June 3, 2002, at the Upper Sharia Court, Funtua, Katsina State.

An appellate hearing on the matter was held on August 19, 2002. At this hearing, the prosecutor prevailed, and the Upper Sharia Court upheld the lower court's sentence. With Amina being granted, by regulation, thirty days to appeal the decision, her lawyer filed a second appeal, this time with the Sharia Court of Appeal in Katsina. Further attention followed in the wake of the Muslim–Christian riots that erupted in late November 2002, just before the Miss World Beauty Pageant that was slated to be held in Abuja.[8] A variety of international human rights organizations, such as Amnesty International, Human Rights Watch, Fédération Internationale des Droits de l'Homme, and Human Rights First, as well as the British Broadcasting Corporation (BBC), took advantage of the opportunity of the media spotlight to bring the case of Amina Lawal to the world stage.

After three postponements,[9] Nigerians had become politically polarized along religious lines in anticipation of the court's decision, which was finally handed down on September 25, 2003. After hearing the grounds for appeal and reviewing the evidence, the Katsina State Sharia Court of Appeal overturned the conviction and vacated Amina Lawal's death sentence on the grounds that neither the conviction nor the sentence had legal standing.

Safiya Hussaini's and Amina Lawal's legal proceedings took place over a two-year period, and each generated significant public debate over whether the Sharia punishments constituted torture or inhuman and degrading treatment.[10] The juridical appeals processes in both cases were performative spectacles in which the contest was often represented as being between "barbaric Muslims" on the one hand and defenders of human and women's rights on the other – the symbolism favored by multiple networks of feminists from a range of nation-states (including Turkey, Iran, Serbia, India, Canada, the United States, and England). Projecting an image of unity in the name of human rights, hundreds of thousands of women rallied in support of the two Nigerian defendants, circulating Internet-based petitions and press releases (some of them inaccurate).[11] In an effort to bring shame to Islamic legal practices on the world stage and thereby force a reversal of the decision of the judiciary, various NGOs also engaged the global press. This resulted in widespread global media coverage to save Amina and Safiya from what was represented as their imminent and horrific fates.

Nigeria's recent formalization of Islamic criminal laws have had the effect of regulating not only sexual piety but also sexual reproduction – principles long fought over and rights won in North America and Europe. These recent struggles, then, reflect histories of individual freedoms denied and represent a latent moral order of heterosexual women's sexual piety still at large even in the West, but against the root of which gendered tensions continue to be fought. Many international human rights organizations have been at the forefront of critiquing the Sharia code as introducing cruel and unusual punishment, such as stoning for adultery and murder and flogging for lying. The development of this critique has, in turn, precipitated ongoing debates over the incommensurabilities connected with the globalization of human rights and its alliance with "democratic" procedures. As I discussed at some length in Chapter 4,[12] at the heart of these incommensurabilities is the fact that, throughout the twentieth century, liberalism and democracy have fostered a system of advantage based on particular substantive conceptions of individual entitlements and norms that are fundamentally allied with the modern world of rights and individual interests. In the case of Nigeria's implementation of Sharia law, it is also sexual and gendered rights as a sphere of sovereign life that are at play. The ultimate disgust of human rights activists globally with the Islamic judgment and sentencing to death of Amina Lawal and Safiya Hussaini also had a critical gendered political urgency. The issues were connected to the moral economy of the rights-endowed individual and her related sexual rights as the standard for emancipation and individuality (J. W. Scott 2007). In this regard, it is therefore important to recognize the micropolitics of struggle as well as the technocratic patrolling of truth regimes at play in the Global South.

In representative democracies, the "voice of the people" is indeed an important symbol for the expression of individual sovereignty. By participating in not only the voting process but also the making of popular opinion, people believe they are working for the maintenance of fundamental rights that protect their individual and group interests. The tools of democracy have thus been deployed to highlight the right to struggle over freedom and the petition as the publicly expressed "will of the people" mobilized, thereby indexing the notion that the citizens of a nation collectively represent the sovereign. However, in the context of both feminist human rights NGOs and International Criminal Court (ICC) mobilizing structures, the sovereign will of the gendered individual as reflected in the human rights treaty, the statute (the Rome Statute, for example), and the national constitution is being privileged over other subjectivities. Popular feminist and human rights presumptions of mutual interests in both local and global domains are not always straightforward. As I have demonstrated throughout this book, although nation-states have been active in setting up the legal and institutional infrastructures for international global politics, the formal and informal divisions between state and nonstate actors, international norms and local practices, are far less clearly delineated. The implications of a global feminist intervention into a context such as the Sharia controversy are that alternative subjectivities for women and Muslims are neglected or disregarded through the fetishization of the individual, gendered "victim."

In this chapter, however, I explore the ways that performances of sovereignty in the Nigerian postcolony construct a public not through expressions of freedom and liberation in this life but through the threat of violence within which future lives of redemption are lived. To counter the exercise of various related forms of violence over gendered bodies, I examine how the rise of Sharia militancy in northern Nigeria has also brought about new legal strategies of defense against the feeling of an increasing encroachment of a common law–international human rights alliance. By focusing on how to reconcile locally contested practices in relation to their global hegemonic challenges, I explore how the contemporary vocabulary of human rights, articulated through a language of universality, has privileged some principles of justice over others. Indeed, a newly developing literature on formations of secularism and their relationship to the state, human rights, and NGO regimes is highlighting the ways that even the most well-intentioned insistence on the equality of rights represents yet another form of hegemony, which has taken shape within the same trajectory of capitalism, colonialism, and the model of the nation-state (Merry 1996, 2006a; Wilson 1996; Collier 2001; Cowan, Dembour, and Wilson 2001). Such critiques of the rights movements emphasize the need to examine the ways that the modern statecraft – its institutions, forms of governance, techniques of security, and regulations – has extended its epistemic and practical powers into new forms of dominance. One strategy for such an analysis is to examine which particular individuals, communities, and ideologies are either productively excluded from or strategically included within the moral economy of the rights movement, and how. Some constituents of the Islamic faithful represent one such excluded community.

To activists outside Nigeria, a nation already deeply embedded in national and international controversy regarding the classification of particular forms of crime and punishment, the prospect of the female body sentenced to die for a (nonviolent) sexual crime has come to stand for a larger specter of violence against "victims" of an "unjust" law. As evidenced by the global controversies over the trials of Safiya and Amina, the establishment of Sharia criminal courts has, for the democratic and civil subject – the "moral" citizen – come to symbolize the impurity, fanaticism, and illegality of religious state rule. But the differences between Islamic and secular legal procedures are not always as obvious as they might initially seem to the casual outside observer. For example, for most countries, legal reform addresses new international standards, responds to social and economic issues, expands access to justice, or improves court operations. Further, just as legal reform is part of an ongoing, incremental process in secular constitutional governments – one that involves the executive and legislative branches, law reform commissions, nongovernmental organizations, and the public – so, too, is it part of a similar process in Nigerian Islamic contexts. However, the issues at play in the latter are related to the epistemic boundaries on which to articulate that which constitutes "appropriate law" or "an appropriate defence" and, in the context of the modernity of lawmaking, the basis on which Islamic jurisprudence seeks reality and is rendered legible within other domains of enacting law through the fiction of sovereignty itself. Some of these very issues were involved in the case of Amina Lawal.

CASE STUDY: AMINA LAWAL

In building a defense for Amina Lawal, her attorneys first had to dispense with the problem of her earlier confession. During the appellate hearing, they began by arguing that in Islamic law under the Sharia, the accused can withdraw her confession at any time, even at the point of execution. They then represented the state's case as being procedurally flawed. Under the Nigerian Constitution, the burden of proof in criminal cases lies with the prosecution and not the accused. In relation to this threshold of proof, the defense argued that the state's case was vague, lacking details to establish her marital status or to indicate the time, date, or place. They then argued the following points:

1. that the word "adultery," covered by the Arabic word *zina*, had not been explained to the defendant, and her "confession" was therefore not legitimate, because she could not have understood the charges before her;
2. that the appellant had not been allowed to call on witnesses, leaving no basis for her to refute the charges against her; and
3. that because the alleged offense had been committed before the June 20, 2002, revival of the Sharia Penal Code of Sokoto State, one of the most basic principles of law – that there is no crime without law – had been disregarded.

Referencing traditional norms derived from the Holy Qur'an, Amina's lawyers cited three additional defenses. First, under Sharia law, an accused should be given a chance to reform (known as *ihizari*); this chance was not offered to the appellant. Second, following procedures of arrest and the application of *zina* in the Qur'an, individuals should turn themselves in voluntarily when they have decided to confess to *zina*. This means that members of the Nigerian police force should not have entered the house of the appellant and arrested her for committing adultery. Finally, as far as evidence is concerned, pregnancy itself does not represent conclusive proof of adultery. Following Islamic law, according to the *mazhab* Maliki (a mainstream Sunni *fiqh*),[13] a

211

woman can carry a pregnancy for up to five years from the date of her divorce. (This is known as the "sleeping embryo" theory.) Accordingly, if she delivers a child within this five-year period, the child may still be classified as belonging to her first husband. In this case, it was argued that an embryo within Amina had been dormant for over eight years (even though she'd been divorced for less than two years). Said one of Amina's defense attorneys, Aliyu Musa Yawuri:

> The former husband of the Appellant divorced her less than two years ago. According to the presumptions of the law the child belongs to the former husband. Therefore the police have no *locus standi* to arraign the Appellant and the Court has no jurisdiction to hear the case.... [U]nder Islamic law she doesn't have to claim the plea of sleeping embryo. Once the court realized that she was a divorcée the presumption shall automatically apply. Therefore, the court erred in assuming jurisdiction to try her.[14]

Thus, following provisions derived from Islamic cosmologies, Amina's defense attorneys argued against the court's "modernist" interpretation; instead they used, in strategic terms, the more vernacular Islamic logic embedded in the sleeping embryo theory to illustrate that there was actually no proof that Amina had had intercourse with Yahaya Mohammad nor that the child that she bore was his. Rather, calling on a nonliberal teleology of science and the body, they insisted that she may have been impregnated by her first husband – a presumption that it was not incumbent on the defense to prove. In response, the prosecution argued:

> We rely on *fiqh ala Mazahibul Arba'a* vol. V p. 89.... Counsel argued that pursuant to S.36 (1) the prosecution had to prove that the appellant was a *muhsinat*[15] (unmarried [i.e., a divorcée]) and that she was [not] carrying a sleeping embryo. This is not so. She had to plead that she was not a *muhsinat* or that she was carrying a sleeping embryo. Allah SWT[16] in *suratul* [i.e., Sura al-]Qiyama[h] verse 13 [sic; should be 14] stated that "man shall be a clear proof against himself": and the Holy Prophet (SAW) said "he who claims must prove[,] he who denies must take the oath." S.36(5) of the 1999 constitution provides that the accused person shall prove those things which he alone knows.

In other words, even though the court did not recognize the lack of gender equality – an equality promised by the same Nigerian Constitution cited by the prosecution[17] – its ultimate response was to the arguments of both defense and prosecution that eventually recognized the legitimacy of various forms of Islamic logic, such as taking seriously the possibility of an eight-year embryo lying dormant in a woman's uterus.

ENGAGING SHARIA, MANAGING PUNISHMENT

Although disputes as to the validity of the charges against Safiya Hussaini and Amina Lawal constituted an important part of their defense by their lawyers and by international activists, it was the proposed punishment of death by stoning that sparked the greatest controversy.

To "Western" ears, the idea of stoning to death as a legitimate form of punishment may provoke strong responses dismissive of the entire system of Islamic law, or indeed of Islam itself. These responses betray an ignorance of several significant factors, including the debates that are taking place over these punishments within Islamic contexts. Pro-Sharia Nigerian human rights defense teams have participated in debates over the punishment itself, emphasizing the merits of Islamic jurisprudence in general, and have worked strategically to expose certain evidentiary flaws and procedural inconsistencies to challenge these particular cases.[18]

In the pages that follow, I look at the praxeological strategies being deployed by various actors seeking to abolish, resist, or reform the Sharia penal code (SPC) in Nigeria, paying particular attention first to methods employed by international feminists and human rights activists whose ill-informed and, at times, racist representations of the cases under question seriously compromised the ability of local actors to accomplish reform from within Nigeria. As part of a growing human rights economy, these international actors participate in a system that privileges certain values and forms of subjectivity as "moral" and "natural" over others, and consequently employs techniques of change that are empowered by the forces of "Western" nation-states and neoliberal capitalism. As the preceding chapters have demonstrated in greater detail, these techniques of the new international governmentality can have very real material consequences for determining who lives (through international aid and protection) and who dies (through international sanction or military intervention).

This chapter suggests that alternative approaches to "defending" women accused by the Sharia – approaches that could be seen as expressing "core values" of Islamic political vernacular spheres – are already well-developed within Nigeria and are competing for legitimacy within larger fields of national and international domains. Toward the end

213

of the chapter, I detail the more promising efforts of one particular group of Nigerian lawyers working to reform the Sharia "from within" by acknowledging the system's merits, on the one hand, and empha-sizing the constraints imposed by Nigerian federalism, on the other. In my concluding discussion, I critique particular liberalist human rights approaches as being dangerously detached from the realities of the cases of Safiya Hussaini, Amina Lawal, and others like them, and as under-mining the very epistemologies that are the centerpiece of northern Nigerian religious life.

Before moving on to this discussion of the global activism and local reform efforts that have constituted such different responses to the establishment of Sharia courts in northern Nigeria, I begin with a more general look at the "force of law" and the meaning of punishment in religious and secular contexts. Ultimately, I intend to show how a par-ticular Northern liberal fiction of justice – its processes, its strategies – is playing out in various incommensurate spheres of truth. The example details how the human rights intervention at play necessitates a "vic-tim" for the movement to intervene. This time, the victim is the figure of women transgressing the most basic principle of Islamic family life: sexual reproduction.

Cultural Logics of the Sharia

Islamic jurisprudence relies on the Qur'an as the word of Allah and therefore the primary source of legal authority. As the divine source that shapes the understanding of Islamic principles, this text is revered worldwide by approximately 1.2 billion Muslims. According to Muslim belief, the Prophet Muhammad, from A.D. 571 to his death in 632, acted as a conduit of Allah by outlining a life philosophy in the Qur'an. His statements and actions, as recorded through oral traditions (hadiths), in turn constitute the sunna, or "way of the prophet," which has been taken as the secondary body of knowledge that informs Islamic law. Combined with the Qur'an, the hadiths have shaped the establishment of Islam as a philosophy of life guided by principles and laws. Following Muhammad's example through the use of legal reasoning, jurists faithful to Muhammad established the basis for the order of authority known as the Sharia. In respecting the body of law that derives from their beliefs, the prosecutorial team of Islamic jurists in the Hussaini and Lawal cases advocated on behalf of the integrity of the newly implemented Sharia penal code as reflective of the word of Allah. Members of the defense teams, in order to build their cases successfully, therefore chose to engage Sharia jurisprudence from within. This involved arguing that substantive Sharia principles should include (1) equality before the law; (2) equal protection by the law; (3) condemnation of torture, or degrading and inhuman punishment; (4) strict standards of evidentiary proof, as well as various procedural standards; (5) predictability of results; (6) legal certainty; (7) access to justice; and (8) the supremacy of constitutional law. These principles were argued with the recognition of the living nature of law – as an always partial and always unfinished process of adjusting core values to social and political phenomena. As such, they attempted to expand the relevance of Sharia beyond its currently observed limits and, in doing so, forced the court to consider new conceptual fields within which to understand exactly what Islamic Sharia should look like in the Nigerian postcolony.

Interestingly, both sides of the Sharia debate in Nigeria are profoundly shaped by "Western" liberalist ideas. The pro-Sharia position is influenced by the constitutional right to practice religion; the anti-Sharia position is predicated on the lack of constitutionality in failing to privilege separation of church and state as the legitimate basis of the modern nation-state. The pro-Sharia argument for the reintroduction of the SPC and its criminal jurisdiction holds that its implementation in a nation-state as ethnically and religiously diverse as the Nigerian nation is an expression of constitutional pluralism. Reflecting earlier governmental systems in the region, Nigeria has a tricameral system, with an executive, a legislative, and a judicial branch, in which the Supreme Court is the highest court of law. Given that the Nigerian constitution recognizes three legal traditions – British common law, Sharia, and Nigerian customary law – and provides for the establishment of a Federal Sharia Court of Appeal in the Federal Capital Territory of Abuja and of state-level Sharia Courts of Appeal, the 1999 transformation of Area Courts into Upper and Lower Sharia Area Courts in twelve northern Nigerian states is in keeping with the Nigerian Constitution. Further, as a form of Islamic law, the Sharia represents the constitutional right to exercise freedom of religion (art. 38); to deny that right is to deny that freedom.

Opponents of the Sharia courts, including those ICC representatives working against such local instantiations of justice, contend that the Sharia discriminates against women, thereby failing to guarantee equality before the law. Furthermore, at the core of their position is the insistence that, despite its provisions for pluralism, the Nigerian Constitution states that "the Government of the Federation or of a State shall not adopt any religion as State Religion" (art. 10). The Islamic Sharia, as a religious institution, is presumed to be unable to protect civil rights, and its establishment as a part of the legal system is seen to constitute an infringement on the basic tenets of secularist pluralism and the doctrines of international human rights.

Tenets of Punishment

In canon and common law judiciaries globally, national criminal adjudication has been shaped by a combination of retributive, rehabilitative, or restorative justice philosophies – or a combination of these – in which victims have played relatively minor roles in the consideration of punishment and the authorization of the court's power. *Retributive* justice models have emphasized the violation of the law and the need for punishment as a form of deterrence and as repayment or revenge for the offense committed. The accused has often been seen as having a debt to repay to society for his or her wrongdoing and is therefore prosecuted by the state on behalf of society. The *rehabilitation* model has emphasized the need for society to assist the accused in changing his or her behavior. This model has depended on various indicators to predict recidivism, thereby measuring the effectiveness of punishment through its ability to prevent reoffending. The *restorative* model has emphasized the harm done to persons and relationships rather than to the violation of the law. This model has focused on the victims of crime as well as the offenders and has deemphasized the importance of state coercion for the purposes of punishment.

One of the most recent innovations in international criminal law has involved the blending of restorative with retributive justice in such a way that the logic of prosecuting perpetrators has shifted from a focus on the needs or benefits of society at large to a focus on the "victim" or groups of victims to be compensated (or avenged). This shift has involved the reconfiguration of the place of the victim so that the subjectivity of the violated is a factor in the adjudication of the alleged perpetrator, and some form of reparation for the victim's suffering is considered. However, as revolutionary an approach as this may appear, the inclusion of victims in the international sphere represents the crafting, and therefore delimiting, of particular subjects whose violations are to be documented – and whose act of bearing witness and providing evidence is expected to inform a structure of legal proof in accordance with scientific explanations of linear time, rather than the forms of spiritual time evident in Sharia arguments such as the sleeping embryo theory. This model of justice is relevant to this particular set of issues and like ICC trials and the dual inclusion and exclusion of victims, it allows us to ask, What work does the imagery of the place of the victim to be stoned to death do, both in Islamic religious contexts and in the sphere of international human rights organizing?

"Secular" Genealogies of Acceptable Punishment

In describing earlier periods in which explicit religious authority informed the logic of the modern state, Randall McGowan (1989), commenting on the symbolic meaning of forms of punishment, writes:

> The goal of punishment was not simply to deter by imposing the most terrifying form of physical suffering. The violence of punishment was a language employed by authority to write the message of justice. The afflictions suffered by the body of the condemned were a way of representing lessons. A hanging, for instance, was meant to be a frightening example but also an eloquent one, speaking not only the death of the individual but also the divine sources of secular power and the horrifying punishments awaiting him in the next world. The broken body of the condemned represented the restored order of the body politic. Punishments were excessive because they bespoke the disproportion between an individual and the majesty of God and the law. The order and hierarchy that alone made human life possible could be threatened by recalcitrant human nature. God employed the indescribable sufferings of hell as a warning to instruct humanity, and these afflictions were justified not by the severity of the offense but by the character of the infinite authority that had been offended. Human governments relied upon the fear of God, and human punishments were intended to represent the sacred lesson. The violence of punishment pointed to the power and sanctity of authority. (143)

Like McGowan, other scholars who comment on the symbolics of punishment in the early modern state frequently emphasize the importance of terrifying forms of bodily suffering. Michel Foucault (1977), for example, has argued that by imposing the most torturous form of physical suffering, members of the state attempted to deploy punishment as a mechanism for writing terror into the making and exercise of the law. The violence of punishment, the suffering of afflictions by the body, was a mechanism for displaying lessons that reinforced the force of the law. In a similar vein, Walter Benjamin (1986) wrote of the rationale for punishment and its forms, suggesting that the violence of punishment references not only the power of God but also the sanctity of authority. Following this, and in thinking about an amputation or capital punishment by stoning as signaling the force of the law, one might consider the utility of punishment in relation to how it signals the authority of governmental power.

GOOD-WILLED DEMOCRACY: FEMINIST NGOS AND THE ERRORS OF PROTEST

The international campaign of protest against the Sharia was triggered by reports that Amina Lawal had lost her appeal in the Nigerian Supreme Court and had been sentenced to die on June 3, 2003. This was not, in fact, true; in reality, June 3 was the scheduled date of Amina's first *filed* appeal with the Sharia Court of Appeal, Katsina.[19] In rallying support for both Amina and Safiya, the anti-Sharia protests took on a life of their own, often getting crucial facts wrong and ultimately degenerating into a condemnation of Islam as a religion of "cruel and unusual punishment."[20] Other narratives led to charges of "barbaric and uncivilized abuses" of women in the name of religion. The strategy demonized the Sharia as an institution, representing it as void of procedural logic, an agent of patriarchal atrocities against women, and in need of immediate reform.

The many Internet discussions among Nigerian and international users that I monitored from 1999 to 2003 took as fundamentally interrelated the acts of violence against women committed by the Taliban of Afghanistan, by the Iraqi regime, by Pakistani and Indian fundamentalists, and by Nigerian pro-Sharia supporters. Newspaper and telemedia news reports, Internet postings, and television crime dramas further spread the image of the male Nigerian Islamic juror as "unreasonable" and of Muslim women as in need of being saved from his religious laws. For example, in the midst of the controversy around Nigeria's hosting of the 2002 Miss World Pageant, a range of participating individuals and committees spoke out in strong terms against the Sharia. Genevieve de Fontenay, head of the Miss France committee, asserted that the Sharia-base sentences "are barbaric and unacceptable." Sandrine Agbopke, the pageant delegate from Togo, echoed the views of many of her competitors in saying, "Stoning this woman is not right. The authorities and all of society should rise up to end this sort of practice."[21]

Hundreds of networks of women activists, ranging from academic communities such as the Canadian Social Research links[22] to major organizations like the Feminist Majority Foundation and the National Organization for Women (NOW), to small cultural groups, such as the ecofeminist Thrice Round Pagan Community, assumed that when their petitions were presented as a voice of protest, the Muslim jurists and northern politicians would be obliged to consider their demands. They depicted the two women as dependent on "Western" assistance, presuming that the only means of securing their freedom would be intervention by the Nigerian Federation precipitated by international human rights agitation. The internal reform of a new and flawed Islamic justice system was not explored as an option neither in the popular-culture media nor among mainstream international human rights NGOs. These latter groups, some of whom work with feminist NGOs, are engaged in the brokering of particular conceptions of justice, democracy, and free-market liberalism enabled through legal practices.[23] As we have seen in earlier chapters, their members – otherwise referred to as members of "civil society" – are law students, lawyers, activists, policy makers, development workers, and human rights activists, most of whom are invested in the spread of human rights and less constrained by the obligations of a sovereign nation than they might once have been.

In an effort to "save Amina and Safiya," many critics engaged in the circulation of images and texts that were blatantly offensive to many Muslims. Some of the media conjured images of indigent women being sacrificed by barbaric male Muslim jurists. The most common narratives in the anti-Sharia campaigns reflected a public critique of the Islamic crime of *zina* as unacceptable and of the authority to punish it as therefore illegitimate. The petitions circulated among networks of feminist NGOs – examples of a popular technique developed as part of secular democratic governance as a means of symbolizing the strength and authority of the outraged "global" voice to respond to civil-society issues "elsewhere" – expressed outrage but failed to acknowledge the efforts of the defense team. Discourses of the Nigerian Sharia as embodying cruel and unusual punishment became the popular protest refrain, and as increasing numbers positioned Islam against the "West," and the "Third World" against the "First World," many untruths made the rounds in an effort to demonize Islam.

By early 2003, after key Internet postings had been circulating for over a year, various NGOs began calling on the Nigerian administration to stop the Sharia punishment by declaring it a cruel and unusual form of punishment. Presuming the absence of a relevant appeals process in the country, they represented the urgency as if the international community represented the last resort for Amina. E-mails such as the

219

following, allegedly written by a member of Amnesty International–Latin America, circulated widely and without censorship.

> Subject: Amnesty campaign against stoning Amina Lawal
>
> The Nigerian supreme court has upheld the death sentence for Amina Lawal, condemned for the crime of adultery on August 19th 2002, to be buried up to her neck and stoned to death.
>
> Her death was postponed so that she could continue to nurse her baby and is now set for June 3rd. If you haven't been following this case, you might like to know that Amina's baby is regarded as the "evidence" of her adultery. The father denied everything when he realised the trouble he was in. . . .
>
> This case is being handled by the Spanish branch of Amnesty International, which is attempting to put together enough signatures to make the Nigerian government rescind the death sentence. A similar campaign saved another Nigerian woman, Safiya, condemned in similar circumstances. By March 4th the petition had amassed over 2,600,000 signatures. It will only take you a few seconds to sign Amnesty's online petition. . . .
>
> Please sign the petition now, then copy this message into a new email and send it to everyone in your address book. . . . [24]

Despite the suggestion that this intervention was initiated by Amnesty International, a press release issued by Amnesty on May 6, 2003, disavowed the e-mail campaign and its "misleading information falsely attributed to one of the web pages of the Spanish section of Amnesty International." The organization reaffirmed that the case of Amina Lawal was "of the highest priority" and noted, "Our public material mentions 3 June 2003 not as the date for carrying out a sentence of death, but as the new date set by the Sharia Court of Appeal of Katsina State for the hearing against her sentence."[25]

Not only was some of the central information in the e-mail quoted above false, but by disrespecting the religious principles of Islam on which the Sharia is built, by regarding it as only a barbaric practice, this petition had the effect of insulting jurists of the lower courts, consequently compromising the defense team's safety.[26] By asserting the power and legitimacy of a global petition to force change, the e-mail also dismissed the Nigerian system of jurisprudence as insignificant and unable to address its own domestic affairs. In fact, unbeknownst to the authors and signers of the global petition, a multilayered legal process guaranteed under the Nigerian Constitution was already unfolding. Within the Sharia and Nigerian system of appeals, the predominantly Muslim legal team of Nigerian attorneys and consultants were applying locally relevant legal strategies to pursue their client's case. However, the international activists opposing Sharia (whom I call the anti-Sharia activists) apparently failed to educate themselves on the rules of procedure and levels of legal engagement in northern Nigeria.[27] As a result, they took action that further angered Muslim fundamentalists – who were already uninterested in the struggles of "Western" feminism, which to them seems inappropriately preoccupied with worldly and individualist concerns that only superficially address the purpose of life – and created an even more hostile environment for the defense team.

Members of the Nigerian Coalition for the International Criminal Court, many non-Muslims, also pondered the relevance and possibilities of using international law standards to override aspects of the Sharia as unconstitutional. Yet from a trajectory of Muslim modernist perspectives, the Sharia and its punishments make provisions for redemption of the body from sins committed in life, and for the soul after the death – although a violent one – of the body as a domain of sovereign being.

At the core of secular state authority are democratic norms enshrined in the force of law. As such, the symbolism of violent punishment by the secular state (such as capital punishment) is embedded in these foundations of state authority and not in explicit adherence to religious doctrine. Religiously driven punishments, such as those of the Sharia, represent differences in both the basis of authority and in the execution of order.

For various Muslim jurists, the legitimate basis on which people ought to act, as women or men following a righteous path, is derived from Allah and not from "the people" or from a dictum of the state. In keeping with other text-based religious traditions, Islam regards the text and laws derivable from the Qur'an as living documents, the interpretations of which afford believers the power to apply core principles to changing social contexts. Practitioners use Qur'anic religious texts to engage in traditions of reading, reasoning, justification, and negotiation. These actions on the part of religious readers make them active agents in the processes of interpretation within which faith is exercised and submission is possible.

Shifting the focus of punishment from the private individual (Habermas 1989) – or from the individual whose relationship is with God or Allah – to the individual who is defined by his or her relation to the state, human rights activists' opposition to Sharia practices amounts to an effort to protect the sanctity of the rights-endowed body from the specter of violence made possible by the confessing and submitting body.[28] Their forms of mobilization are part of the policing and judgment of Muslims whose practices, from a liberalist perspective, desecrate the new order of rights. Drawing their mandate from the symbolism of the violated body, such activists speak for and on behalf of the state as well as new suprastate forms of sovereignty. Acting in this capacity, their efforts do not always anticipate, accommodate, or even register the complexities that emerge when a variety of institutions and ideologies compete for legitimacy and power. The issue to consider here is that those agents are intervening to protect not only the rights-endowed body but also the gendered body. Such protections involve a moral economy driven by the presumed authority of the state to administer punishment, accompanied by an implicit disregard of the epistemological concerns of a Muslim believer – all while reserving for the state the right to declare the legitimacy and legality of the practices of its believers.

Note that institutions such as treaties, constitutions, and states index a parallel rather than a fundamentally different process of making meaning and consolidating power. These sites legitimize corporal punishment or prison sentences as representative of the authority of lawmaking and law enforcement. Civil society participates in these regimes of rationality and interpretation by making, enforcing, challenging, and deploying them for its own purposes. The important point here is that, like religious thought, secular thought and its related logic of punishment entail multiple levels of practice and meaning production; these give coherence to various social interpretations and provide "ordering agents" through which people conceive of the world in manageable ways.

One of the consequences of the widespread – and ill-informed – response to the Amina Lawal case was an uncomfortable alignment between women's rights groups and the conservative Right over a shared demand for a constitutional intervention irrespective of proper legal channels. Concerned that these alignments and methods were spinning out of control, the founding director of BAOBOB, Ayesha Imam, in May 2003 finally called for a halt to the international campaign for Ms. Lawal's immediate release, as indicated by the following broadcast e-mail circulated within the same women's and human rights networks:

> Because of the circumstances in Nigeria today, which are very volatile, we felt that having a big international campaign and protest letters that were based on inaccurate information and not very carefully worded, would actually be more damaging than helpful. In fact, it was detrimental since

they [Western human rights activists] had to put out an appeal to the international community in order to clarify the situation and ask people to not participate in these international protest campaigns.[29]

Although international campaigns are seen by many as being extremely productive, this one, waged with misinformation and degrading representations, was deemed inappropriate. "We're not against all international campaigns, but they're not necessarily suited to every single situation," Imam said. Moreover,

> If pardons come as a result of international political pressure, then it's hard to say to people it was their right all along – what they feel is that somebody stronger than you forced you to back down. . . . That doesn't help to build a culture with the respect of human rights.[30]

In addition to alluding to the counterproductiveness of certain interventions, Imam also highlighted the ambitions of Islamic reform from within, and not through international initiatives or laws. Her own intervention thus reflected her hope for the reform of problematic aspects of Sharia jurisprudence.

The following excerpts from another e-mail sent by Imam and BAOBAB Executive Director Sindi Maedar-Gould on May 2, 2003, to her international contacts further delineates the factual errors circulating around the case and explains the need for the international community to respect internal Sharia judiciary procedures:

> Contrary to information being widely circulated, Amina Lawal's conviction has NOT been upheld by Nigeria's Supreme Court. . . . In other words, the process is a long way from immediate stoning to death. . . .
>
> Contrary to the statements in many of the internationally originated appeals for petitions and protest letters, none of the victims received a pardon as a result of international pressure. None of them has received a pardon at all – or needed to, so far.
>
> None of the sentences of stoning to death have been carried out. Either the appeals were successful or those convicted are still in the appeals process.
>
> However, if there is an immediate physical danger to Ms. Lawal and others, it is from vigilante and political further (over)reaction to international attempts at pressure. . . .
>
> Dominant colonialist discourses and the mainstream international media have presented Islam (and Africa) as the barbaric and savage Other. Please don't buy into this. Accepting stereotypes that present Islam as incompatible with human rights not only perpetuates racism but also confirms the claims of right-wing politico-religious extremists in all of our contexts. . . .

> Using local structures and mechanisms (as a means of resisting retro-
> gressive laws or interpretations of laws and the forces behind them) is the
> priority. It strengthens local counter-discourses and often carries greater
> legitimacy than "outside" pressure.[31]

In the postscript of this letter, the authors reminds readers that

> BAOBAB for Women's Human Rights has been closely involved with
> defending the rights of women, men and children in Muslim, customary and
> secular laws – and, in particular, of those convicted under the new Sharia
> Criminal legislation acts passed in Nigeria since 2000. In fact, BOABAB
> was . . . the first, and again for some time the only NGO to actually find the
> victims and support their appeals, raising funds for the costs and putting
> together a strategy team of women's and human rights activists, lawyers and
> Islamic scholars contributing their expertise and time voluntarily.[32]

After making evident the goals and work of BAOBAB, they then
indicate that anyone who wants to support this work should send a
contribution to BAOBAB/Women Living Under Muslim Laws International Solidarity Network-Africa and Middle East (WLUML-AME)
Rights Advocacy Fund, Legal Defense Fund, or Core Funding.[33] Thus,
it was monetary support, not proactive protests, that was needed.

VERNACULAR KNOWLEDGES: NIGERIAN
CONSTITUTIONALISM FROM THE GROUND UP

Hauwa Ibrahim, a Muslim human rights lawyer, was the legal architect
behind the defense of Amina Lawal and a critical advisor for Safiya's
defense. In addition to collaborating with attorney Aliyu Musa Yawuri
on the Lawal case, she provided pro bono representation for more than
seventy-nine Sharia defendants during 2001–8[34] Many of these defendants have already been marginalized members of society for whom
access to a legal defense is often fleeting.

Ibrahim, like many of her clients, was raised in a small village: Hinnah
in Gombe State, northern Nigeria. Her work provides one example
of the strategy to reform Islam from within. Admittedly, this is not
necessarily easy in northern Nigeria where, as in other parts of the
world, increasingly fundamentalist forms of Islamic practices are taking
shape. In providing her legal defense of Lawal, Ibrahim, a woman,
was not actually allowed to speak before the court. Instead, she passed
notes to her junior magistrate, Yawuri, who, as a man, was permitted
to stand before the judges. This limitation on her participation did

not, however, prevent her from leading the defense, both within and outside of the courtroom. Following the successful appeal of both cases, Ibrahim refused a generous offer of funding from both international and national NGOs. Insisting on setting her own agenda and not wanting to follow the dictates of international donors, she began to work steadily on Islamic legal reform of various sections of the Sharia penal code.

Ibrahim's reform team has been engaged in what she called a "bottom-up approach" in which they locate their intervention in the context of accepting the religious and cultural value of traditional understandings of Islam, while also working creatively to harmonize its laws and regulations with Nigerian constitutional structures. Since 2001, Ibrahim has been engaged in working to clarify Nigerian constitutional positions that will lead to the revision of the newly adopted SPC. She describes this reform project as a necessarily multi-tiered approach engaging a variety of institutions and actors – locally, nationally, and internationally – in which other constitutional codes are being studied and other Islamic reform projects analyzed. The American Bar Association's African Law Initiative has been working alongside Lawyers without Borders (Paris, France, and Québec, Canada) to collaborate with Ibrahim and her team and to assist local attorneys in providing legal and professional services to those indicted under the Sharia. Ibrahim hopes that these initiatives will ultimately make possible the delivery of what she hopes will be seen to all as a "fair" Islamic justice system. They have involved investigations of the sites of reform necessary within the new Sharia – specifically, its rules of procedure and evidence requirements – and work will be conducted toward reviewing and reforming these laws where and when necessary.

While Ibrahim and her colleagues are willing to work in partnership with international donors such as the United Nations, the World Bank, and various other international governmental and nongovernmental organizations, they also believe strongly that Islamicists must take the lead in producing culturally sensitive approaches to reform. In an effort to render compatible Islamic jurisprudence and Nigerian constitutionalism, Ibrahim's team of lawyers, law students, and researchers has been investigating various key issues in relation to the promotion and protection of rights under the new Sharia legal system. Their goal is to create a center for the progressive implementation of new Islamic reforms. These reforms highlight the desire for the possible complementarity of not only Islam and national constitutionalism, but also when micropractices that lead to change are seen as acceptable, reform is possible not only in Islam, but also in rethinking the basis upon which the rule of law operates.

In working for reform, Ibrahim cites those sections of the Nigerian Constitution that provide for its supremacy, specifically the following stipulations in Section 1:

> 1(1) This Constitution is supreme and its provisions shall have binding force on the authorities and persons throughout the Federal Republic of Nigeria.... (3) If any other law is inconsistent with the provisions of this Constitution, this Constitution shall prevail, and that other law shall, to the extent of the inconsistency, be void.

The Constitution further provides that "The Government of the Federation or of a State shall not adopt any religion as State Religion" (sec. 10). Section 277 creates room under federal jurisdiction for the implementation of Islamic law:

> (1) The Sharia Court of Appeal of a State shall, in addition to such other jurisdiction as may be conferred upon it by the law of the State, exercise such appellate and supervisory jurisdiction in civil proceedings involving questions of Islamic personal law.

The central problem today is that, in various instances, the Sharia penal code conflicts with the Nigerian Federal Constitution. Before outlining that problem and some of Ibrahim's strategies for solving it, I turn first to an overview of the Nigerian federalist legal system.

As discussed in Chapter 5, the Nigerian system of jurisprudence has been greatly influenced by English law and exists in relation to several subsystems and constitutional provisions.[35] Although Sharia and customary laws are applicable at the local level in some states, at the federal level, the Nigerian legal system is applicable throughout the country. In the hierarchy of the Nigerian legal system, the Supreme Court is the highest-level court in Nigeria and serves as the ultimate authority on all legal matters. Below the Supreme Court is the Federal Court of Appeal, which has jurisdiction to hear and determine appeals from the following lower courts: Federal High Court, the High Court of the Federation Capital Territory (Abuja), High Court of a state (Sharia), Court of Appeal of the Federal Capital Territory (Abuja), Sharia Court of Appeal of a state, and Customary Court of Appeal of a state (with appellate and supervisory jurisdiction in civil proceedings involving questions of customary law).[36]

At the lower levels of Nigeria's courts, each state (including Abuja) has its own legal system, permitted to coexist insofar as it is willing to defer to the higher judiciaries. For example, the Sharia Courts of Appeal have jurisdiction over any issues that "may be conferred upon [them] by the law of the State" but are specifically established to deal with "questions of Islamic personal law." Courts in states that administer Islamic personal law are deemed competent to hear related appeals. However, as late as 2005, there remained questions regarding whether the Sharia Courts of Appeal have jurisdiction to hear such cases. This is because it is believed by some that these courts still do not have legitimate jurisdiction to hear criminal cases. Below the appeals courts are the Magistrate Courts, which every state possesses. These courts are "divided into a number of classes, and the classification determines the level of jurisdiction and the powers" possessed by each magistrate.[37] In southern Nigeria, Customary Courts prevail and deal with issues that are covered in customary law, with unlimited civil jurisdiction in cases of family law and criminal jurisdiction in a few areas. The parallel courts in northern Nigeria states are the Area and District Courts.[38] Since 1999, twelve states have converted their Area Courts into Sharia courts that, beyond claiming jurisdiction over civil cases dealing with monetary issues within a certain value as well as unlimited civil jurisdiction in cases of family law, now claim criminal jurisdiction in much of northern Nigeria.

The problem with this conversion has been that, in almost all cases, the penal codes advocated by the twelve northern states were hastily drafted, with many incorrect cross-references, defective wording, omissions, and contradictions (Peters 2001). This was in part due to a dilemma of the new legal order, which lacked the legal resources to recruit the judges, court officials, and police officers that could effectively administer it. As a result, almost all the defendants in the many Sharia cases with which Hauwa Ibrahim has been involved were unaware of the provisions of the law before they were brought to court. Ibrahim has also called for better education of the officers of the court and has outlined in detail the need for judicial reform:

> Generally speaking, reform should address issues of strict standards of proof and evidence in all offences, especially the offences carrying the death penalty. Second, offences and their punishment must be founded in written law and not the discretion of the judge (as suggested in some of the provisions of the [SPC]). Third, there should be separation of powers between the

executive and the judiciary to respect the independence of the judiciary and allow it to serve justice. Fourth, the laws should be certain and respect the principle of fundamental human rights and human dignity. Fifth, the law should not be repugnant to natural justice, equity, and good consciousness. Sixth, in the quest for dispensing quick justice, the law should have a clear and written procedural process.[39]

All of these issues are important to the reform process. One specific issue that has attracted a great deal of interest from international donors, and here serves as an illustration of the kind of strategy Ibrahim deploys, involves the burden of proof of adultery or fornication required to convict the accused properly. The Islamic school of thought known as classical Maliki,[40] used in the twelve states that adopted the Sharia legal system, indicates that the pregnancy of an unmarried woman is in itself proof of *zina*. This rule was applied in the cases of Amina Lawal and Safiya Hussaini, but the pregnancy proof was not considered sufficient to hold up on appeal. One form of the further proof of *zina* under both the Kano and Niger SPC laws is the testimony of four male witnesses. This, Ibrahim argues, needs attention because of its fundamental incompatibility with constitutionally mandated gender equality – a basic tenet for which she has struggled all her life.

In calling for change, Ibrahim points to the many protections of the accused provided by the Nigerian Constitution's right to a fair hearing, including that "Every person who is charged with a criminal offence shall be presumed to be innocent until he [or she] is proved guilty" (sec. 36 (5)) and to "carry out the examination of witnesses to testify on his [or her] behalf before the court or tribunal on the same conditions as those applying to the witnesses called by the prosecution" (sec. 36 (6) (d)). In citing these provisions, Ibrahim demonstrates that the Sharia's special provision to weigh the testimony of male witnesses more heavily than that of female witnesses undermines the accused's constitutional right, as a Nigerian citizen, to equal access to witness testimony.

As this example suggests, Ibrahim's legal strategy was developed as part of her larger reform project mentioned earlier in this section, involving the application of the best constitutional principles to Sharia procedural and evidentiary rules. It also reflects an example of strategies of vernacularization, as well the spaces of incommensurability that exist in seemingly divergent domains of practice.

Moving from a further look at her team's approaches and priorities, I end this chapter by recounting the interplay between international and more circumscribed justice processes mobilized through different strategies for the opposition or reform of religious law. In so doing, I attempt to frame the growth of Islamic revivalisms and related controversies connected to Islam's system of jurisprudence and punishment in relation to the globalization of feminist human rights networks. As we shall see, local justice conceptions are made through complex and contested relationships not only to the state and to paramilitary actors but also to extrastate, international apparatuses – including those championed by global rights activists sometimes unable or unwilling to acknowledge the detrimental effects of their own power (or violence) in trying to apply "universal" norms.

ISLAMIC REFORM IN RELATION TO OTHER KINDS OF REFORM

The constructive approach to legislative reforms engaged in by Ibrahim's team of collaborators has ranged from reviewing existing laws to writing new ones. Beyond their basic strategy of harmonizing the Sharia legal system with the Nigerian Constitution, Ibrahim's team has outlined a nineteen-point list of approaches and priorities, including cooperating with Nigerian legislators and with "civil society" as part of a domestic program; "devising principles and mechanisms to guide ... humanitarian intervention" and the distribution of human rights materials; engaging in media debates to spark dialogue with skeptics, those practicing "moderate" Sharia, and other religious and cultural communities who have experienced similar challenges; and "[p]romoting research and discussion on issues of Islam in areas such as marriage, divorce, modesty, submission, physical abuse, security, etc."[41]

Claiming that "In Nigeria, the rule of Shari'a law has violated legal due process and the basic human rights of many," Ibrahim offers that

> The legal reforms we propose will rely upon Nigerian constitutional law as well as international human rights standards (to which Nigeria is a signatory) as the basis for legal reform. Furthermore, we hope to encourage the legislatures in other "moderate" Islamic countries to follow the rule of law and due process....
>
> The easiest and most effective way to implement human rights is through action within each country's own legal system. If domestic law provides an effective system of remedies for violations of international human rights obligations, the authority of a nation's own legal system can be mobilized to support compliance with international norms. Most human rights treaties

229

require that parties incorporate relevant obligations into their domestic law and that they provide appropriate local remedies. This in turn provides the rationale for the common requirement that domestic remedies be exhausted before an international body will investigate a complaint of human rights violation.

By accepting the conventions, treaties, protocols and optional protocols, states commit themselves to undertake a series of measures to end problems that are linked closely to gender, cultural, religious, and other equality related problems like poverty, illiteracy, and traditional dogma.[42]

These goals for reform reflect those of the world human rights provisions. With the 1948 Universal Declaration of Human Rights (UDHR) and the establishment of the United Nations, the development of human rights for all – the right to share entitlements to the social heritage of a "civilized" society – became part of modern citizenship.[43] The UDHR begins by asserting in its Preamble the "inherent dignity and . . . the equal and inalienable rights of all members of the human family."[44] It makes clear that human rights cannot be protected by state civil and political laws alone – a claim that Ibrahim's reformist (and to date successful) approach challenges. Many global feminists have strategically aligned themselves with such documents as the UDHR to bolster their construction of a notion of universal sisterhood. As detailed in the earlier analysis of the feminist movement's mobilization in support of Safiya Hussaini and Amina Lawal,[45] it was the liberalist human rights epistemologies that provided the cultural imperative for action. These cosmologies were predicated on human rights doctrine and treaties that laid the groundwork for articulating their intervention as appropriate. Indeed, these forms of "justice talk"[46] represent an aspect of the structural organization of both international and national power – and as such are connected to various forms of violence built into the widespread relations of global and neocolonial inequality. In relating these structural violences, obscured by the rhetoric of peace and justice, to the specter of violence shrouding the Sharia, it is essential that we understand inequality not only in relation to unequal targets of crime but also in relation to the recognition of how the form and structure of the Sharia either subverts or reinforces the core values of religious power, the right to execute punishment, and presumptions about sovereignty at the heart of these forms of Islamic modernist vernacular meaning making.

As we have seen throughout this book, the power inequality between neoliberal "Western" democracies and other "rogue" states manifests, in part, through the workings of the international human rights regime, in which Western democracies are able to enforce their own moral, ethical, and political frameworks, using extreme violence where they deem necessary. That is, neoliberal regimes use many kinds of force to provide rationales for the laws they make and to ensure the conditions for their enforcement. Liberalism's justification for violence derives from its key tenet of universality, which can be referenced to explain the deploying of overt, even military, violence when other means do not suffice to achieve neoliberal priorities.[47] The differentials in power among segments of a state's population offer similar potential for deploying violence through the ways state brokers rationalize and implement the life of the law. Thus, the contemporary secular state and the international human rights regime share a semantic framework that characterizes Islamic violence (such as amputations, floggings, or deaths by stoning) as "barbaric," whereas the violence of the modern secular state (e.g., its power to imprison, kill, and even to commence war) is normalized and even celebrated as "civilized" – and, thus, as a legitimate form of governance. Both Islamic and the secular governance forms engage in the management of life and death based on their various epistemologies for determining proof, punishment, and the appropriate basis for classifying individual rights – and both require reform.

To echo Ibrahim, what is needed is not the eradication of religious laws that contravene human rights principles but legal reform in both Islamic and non-Islamic spheres of knowledge through which various inequalities can be addressed and seemingly illegible domains of knowledge understood in their own terms. The aggressively universalizing and dominating tendencies of secularism and liberalism call for a radical rethinking of human rights frameworks in terms of a power analysis of their aims, alliances, and effects. In a range of religious Islamic judicial contexts in northern Nigeria, Islamic reformists such as Ibrahim engaging in the vernacularization of disparate knowledge domains are calling for legal reform to "promote respect for human rights and human dignity"[48] in their own terms. This involves encouraging a form of good governance and due process that is recognizable to all those who participate in its principles. For Ibrahim, it also means the vernacularization of the best of international law standards to find ways to "create a stable and predictable legal system, that will provide the proper climate for investment."[49]

Shying away from legal reform that seeks to import "models" inconsistent with national legal and religious and traditional contexts, Ibrahim insists that comprehensive and sustainable approaches involving the drafting of laws by local experts will produce "best practice principles and international standards." Ultimately, "fostering public understanding and ownership of proposed laws ensures that they are suitable for the economic, social, and legal environment, and facilitate understanding by the public at large."[50]

As we have seen, then, anti-Sharia adherents are differently engaged in forming alliances with international institutions and discourses than are those who respect the existence of the system while emphasizing the need for reform. Global feminists and other human rights organizations, such as members of the Coalition for the International Criminal Court, are working from a vantage point of power to ensure widespread implementation of international instruments (conventions, treaties, protocols) through which new forms of vernacular justice are taking shape. "Local" actors such as Ibrahim, sometimes using different conceptual strategies, are working to combine an internationalist language and set of priorities with various vernacular models and discourses. Their aim is to effect practical and achievable change in specific national and regional contexts.

The current human rights literature has long documented both the forms of pluralism through which to understand alternative forms of justice and the various ways that agents creatively invoke human rights norms with the goal of adapting them strategically (see, e.g., Niezen 2003; Merry 2006b). However, these various justice-making processes exist in relation to, and in competition with, international and humanitarian interventions. They represent the dialogues and processes, discussions and debates, through which the basis for justice is established by means of the "victim" – a problematically necessary figure that seemingly makes international intervention all the more urgent.

VIOLENCE AS CENTRAL TO THE PRACTICE OF THE EVERYDAY

One of the problems with human rights discourses that have been imported into the growing rule of law regime has been their tendency to universalize the structure and meaning of the human condition. This is often done without taking into account the range of diverse histories, contexts, and practices within which particular meanings of violence and ethnocentrism take shape. I am not advocating a relativist response to such conditions of violence – far from it. I am arguing that we need a critical approach to studies that deal with the discursive practices around which fictions are made real; we need a critical approach that attends to the ways that those meanings are entrenched in historical and epistemic contemporary sociopolitical orders – that examine the strategic vernacularization of various hegemonic regimes. Such an approach would explore the causes of violence and the structuring of international spheres of justice making so as to recognize that justice mechanisms incorporated *after* violence attest to the impossibility of achieving justice itself. In this way, we can explore how the process of securing rights can be both products of strategic translations (Merry 2006a) and attempts to recast those knowledge forms rendered illegible to international standards and rearticulated in relation to the spheres of logic and power within which they are imbricated.

Anthropology has long been criticized for its historical complicity with colonizing projects, for having played a significant role in rapidly rendering local knowledge legible to imperial institutions and participating in the construction of notions of "tradition." Since the early twentieth century, anthropologists have been attempting to understand the logic of cultural norms that are central to the life of the law. These early anthropological approaches to understanding human societies were often based on a view of cultural practices as self-contained and expressed within "primitive" social organizations. This was intended as a corrective to "Western" schemas of progress that tended to see "other" societies as chaotic, despotic, and incapable of progressing into modernity. Over the past twenty-five years, anthropologists have responded to these often self-generated critiques through a range of reflexive and engaged investigations into how, and for what purpose, knowledge of sociocultural processes is produced. Against this disciplinary backdrop, things are changing again. Perhaps more than during even colonial periods, events during the mid-twentieth to the early twenty-first centuries have resulted in profoundly altered social worlds for those communities historically taken as appropriate "subjects" for anthropological inquiry.

The anthropologists' alternative view – motivated by a discourse of cultural relativism and, later, legal pluralism in the United States, as well as cultural translation in the United Kingdom – called these universalist schemas into question (Herskovits 1990 [1941]; Goodale and Merry 2007; Goodale 2008). Such research has since moved from concerns with the political organization of the "primitive" embedded in particular evolutionary schemes used to measure progress, to the function of politicolegal systems in authority mechanisms or dispute resolution, to the processes by which cultural meanings are embedded in institutions of power. These approaches to understanding the life of the law – and how meanings of justice and power travel, and are interrogated and made sense of, and at times are not made sense of at all – represent one of the most complicated yet exciting areas of legal studies today. The challenge has been how to address critically the reemergence of various neoliberal uses of individualism, freedom, liberty, and "universality" as they have been taken up in the scholarship. In our various Sharia-related *zina* case studies in this chapter and Chapter 5, the basis for inquiry has involved understanding which practices are made acceptable (understood in vernacular forms) and which are seen as criminal, as well as how those classifications are created, defended, made sense of, and resisted. The basis for inquiry has also allowed us to understand how people's conceptions of the presumed "justice" of a conviction is based on the constructed criminalization of consensual sex when the defendants themselves have willingly confessed to the "crime" and submitted to the resultant punishment – death by stoning – yet still maintain that their prosecution may have been politically motivated. These seemingly contradictory processes are actually far from contradictory; rather, they are at once locally performative within fields of acceptability yet critical of that which represents the human and interpretive aspect of religious meaning making. Importantly, it is not their micropractices that make them incommensurate with various "rule of law" assignments of criminal responsibility and rights-endowed subjectivity. It is the inability of some norms and practices embedded in alternative trajectories of knowledge to make sense within other, more hegemonic domains of liberalist power.

TOWARD A CRITICAL TRANSNATIONAL LEGAL PLURALISM

This book has explored the challenges of liberalism's cultural life that have come into play through new rule of law regimes and religious practices, the contemporary mobilizations of which extend beyond the borders of the nation state. It also considers how best to address concerns over international jurisdiction alongside the emergence of new forms of criminal responsibility and different notions of crime and justice in more circumscribed contexts. This has involved making sense of the ways that key liberal tenets are taking shape through the cultivation of the liberal subject (see, e.g., Rose, 2003; Coleman, 2006) and how they are alternatively mapped in different epistemological trajectories. As I demonstrated, this making of the individual subject is expressed within the cultural logics of various institutional mechanisms that establish private property, the rule of law, and individual liberty and freedoms as key features for defining justice (Rose 2003; Coleman 2006). A wide range of conceptions of justice exist alongside a notion of the individual and selfhood through which liberalist views of agency and free will thrive in particular moral and institutional economies and through which the language of the tribunal as triumphant and morally shaped takes shape, while the intelligibility of other trajectories or rationalities is negated. In this regard, understanding the ways that people create cultural meanings of justice – how notions of what constitutes "crime" are influenced by executors of the state; how religious, political, and historical institutions are called on to legitimize definitions of crime; how notions of the appropriateness of "punishment" are both produced and contested; and how international norms encroach upon local

235

practices – must involve broadening our understanding of the human rights–rule of law movement in relation to the complex play of power on various scales. Accordingly, these processes must also highlight how the triumph of the tribunalization of African violence is playing out alongside the specters of death and victimhood, as well as through various other conceptualizations of justice.

The growth of various NGOs, religious organizations, and international institutions; the revisions to legal texts and constitutional provisions; the spread of arms deployed in sub-Saharan Africa and consequent violence; and the development of new humanitarian and transnational networks discussed in the foregoing pages reflect domains of contemporary governance playing out in uneven relations of power. The development of these transnational regimes reflects the relationship between the legitimization of human rights and rule of law discourses and local agents' attempts to compete for and uphold particular regimes of knowledge and replicate their social worlds in their own terms. In this regard, what has become the hegemony of the rule of law and its alliance with what Mariella Pandolfi (2003) has called the humanitarian–military apparatus represent the spectacularity of justice talk engaged in by members of the NGO elite, international institutions, and humanitarian organizations. However, as I have shown, local political actors (such as Islamic devotees, victims, and rebel fighters) also articulate their own models of worship, confession, piety, and criminal punishment within other spheres of social power. These various domains of international and more localized forms of social production reflect competing formations that have moved well beyond the purview of the postcolonial and liberal state and are engaged in new tenets that are productive of the management of violence, not its disappearance.

Clearly, international justice tribunals, such as the International Criminal Court's Lubanga trial, represent spectacular performances in which a new language of responsibility and a new moral economy of protecting the victim – the rationale for just intervention – are articulated and displayed through the existence of a violation yet are often represented as rooted in age-old principles of law. Similarly, various Islamic articulations – themselves representative of a spectacularity of Islamic authorial divinity – are also products of social change over time. Thus, this book, while showing how certain Islamic conceptual practices may not always map easily onto Western constitutionalism and forms of liberal rationalism, ends with a case study of *strategic translation*.

Building on Sally Merry's application of the ways that vernacular practices are made real in human rights contexts, I have shown how in the context of conceptually incommensurate practices divided by uneven power relations, the work of translation and innovation are necessary to create new fictions around which regimes of truth that produce justice can be strategically translated. I have shown that victims of systematic violence address their social location through practices that strategically place them in conditions of possible empowerment. Sometimes this means that actors engage in vernacularization; other times, however, they engage in praxeological forms that entail demonstrations of praiseworthiness within their own sociocultural, religiolegal contexts.

This book thus articulates a theory of "victims" that shows them as clearly agential – even though they are often rendered by the human rights apparatus as powerless, occupying bare life, and in need of humanitarian intervention. In fact, institutions such as the International Criminal Court actually draw their power from the imaginary of the victim, whose liberation is possible only through suffering; the victim figure thus remains both central and marginal to the process. Seen in this way, the work of the court is vested in a political imaginary in which the power to end violence exists more in its construction of justice than in its potentiality.

The reality is that to achieve justice in daily life is to return to the root causes that are instrumental in the conditions of possibility within which options emerge. This is the space of justice – the space for the return of the political, the space opened up for eradicating the need for international juridical intervention. However, what I show in Chapter 6 is that the informal processes of negotiating life-producing possibilities before the existence of an injury, infraction, or death represents the critical life-preserving difference that is desperately needed in the world today.

Clearly, liberal legalism is not the sole model for articulating justice in the world. In fact, in various examples in the second half of the book, there often exists a lack of loyalty to the symbolic meanings that propel secular legalisms and their related international institutionalisms. My efforts to understand when and how particular legal practices are seen as legitimate, or when they travel, show the importance of exploring the workings of transnational circulations through the life of the law. They further show how meanings of justice and power travel and assume new forms despite the hegemony of liberal articulations of justice. This area

237

of exploring the preconditions of transnational legitimacy represents one of the most methodologically complicated yet exciting areas of legal studies today. Mapping out a new methodology for asking critical questions about the making of justice in transnational alliances involves understanding why some particular concepts and cultural practices are not easily incorporated into human rights standards, whereas others are more readily vernacularized. Given the diversity in the ways that social norms gain force through various institutions of knowledge and power, it is important to detail and clearly articulate how particular norms are institutionally systematized, made natural, and produced as "legitimate." With this goal, I ask how particular values cross-cut multiple regimes of knowledge and authority, class groups, and forms of alliance that are productive of insurgencies and inequalities. How, for example, are we to understand the justice of a conviction based on the criminalization of consensual sex when the defendants themselves have willingly confessed to the "crime" and submitted to the resultant punishment – death by stoning – yet still maintain that their prosecution may have been politically motivated? This and other problematics central to this book are best explored through both pragmatic and analytic approaches.

In pragmatic terms, it is important to recognize that culture is dynamic and always in contexts of change. In this regard, to make the good life viable for those who live in regions of poverty, postcolonial dismay, and institutional limitations, agents of international human rights principles need to recast the goals of such a life to take seriously the plight of political and economic concerns. Similarly, in various faith-based domains, in which there remain political and social disparities, similar active forms of creative reform are needed. In analytic terms, what is needed is a critical approach to legal pluralist methods that takes up epistemology and translations in ways that unfold the language of justice and push us to denaturalize those sociopolitical institutions that often presume control over justice-granting power. It involves recognizing the ways that domains of "political justice" are actually also sites for struggle over the control of which knowledge and authorial regimes count as legitimate domains of practice and purpose. It is also important to explore these struggles in their related transnational orbits of power because today, more than ever, these are the domains within which various struggles over "justice" are being waged between postcolonial states and those states and institutions associated with the Global North.

Committed to both the pragmatic and the analytic, I have taken seriously my role in disclosing the ways that knowledge-making practices are deployed and become hegemonic. I have denaturalized those relations that are taken as "natural" and highlighted the existence of hierarchies of politicoeconomic power that reproduce inequalities, especially in the Global South. As I have made clear, the use of courts, tribunals, or informal regulatory mechanisms as means for dispute settlement cannot possibly address the magnitude of the social injustice under scrutiny in and of themselves. Ideally, justice is the absence of a need for "justice-making" mechanisms. It represents the conditions in which the social constructions of equality, dignity, and fairness, can be presumed and expressed through the "good life."

A critically engaged transnational legal pluralism, therefore, must be shaped by the use of particular methodologies that allow us to document how people succeed in producing fictions constituted as "authentic" and "legitimate," that which is justice producing. This involves paying attention to the ways that facts are made and not found and highlighting the presence and absence, the silences and specters, of transnational interrelationships. It means uncovering the political economies that undergird violence and bringing to the fore both the conditions that sustain violence and those that enable change.

This approach to critical legal pluralism starts with an exploration of the metacultural contexts within which justice making operates in the international realm and a microcultural detailing of the cultural presumptions through which people deploy socially relevant relationships. This entails exploring which frames are used to explore the effects of particular meanings of justice and asking how one translates across difference. Such processes involve detailing the models of justice being used and the frameworks within which legal spheres operate, as well as rethinking the relevance of epistemology and interrogating its limits. They involve delineating the cultural contexts operative within particular fields of power and understanding how translation operates across different fields of power, foreclosing or opening up strategies for inclusion.

If this book attempts to reorient international law scholarship in any way, it is by bringing culturalist approaches to bear on otherwise normative and often unquestioned presumptions about justice. At minimum, it shows that not everyone uses the same concepts everywhere – that there is a difference in the culture of conceptual applications that must be addressed in the ways we understand the expansion of the rule of law as a liberatory regime. The more expansive questions have to do with exploring how we parse cultural forms in different places in relation to hierarchies of difference.

The related challenge of this book has been to explore the ways that various justice-making institutions share deep structures through their search for certainty, discursive processes of finding legal truth, and authorial texts by which legal determinations are made. Yet, in the contexts of these parallelisms, it is important to recognize that the failure of liberal legalism in sub-Saharan Africa and the overthrow of national judiciaries with the ICC is not simply because of the existence of "weak states" that are unable to operationalize democratic regimes and are in need of intervention. At root are questions about how to develop legal certainty out of uncertainty, how to produce commensurability out of sometimes incommensurate relationships. In this regard, focusing on legal language, strategies of power, and epistemological logic allows us to consider how notions of the rule of law look to those operating from the African continent. For although linguistic micropractices are manifest in a range of legal and political spheres, if we can start by understanding how agents create meanings in a range of domains of power and inequality – and, as a result, they both reinforce particular power relations and attempt to undermine them – we can begin to map the fictions that are part of the practices of "justice in the making" in relation to the possibilities of their undoing.

NOTES

Preface

1. Pseudonym used here.
2. Although 120 states signed the Rome Statute in 1998, for the ICC to enter into force, 60 states had both to sign and ratify the statute. This occurred on April 11, 2002, and it legally came into force on July 1, as noted.
3. The *Rule of Law* is often capitalized in the literature as a way to emphasize its force and importance. In this book, it does not appear in caps. Instead, it is described akin to any other legal formations and, to signal its parallels with all others, I remove the capitalization and represent them all in the same way.
4. In 1998, eighty-four nation-states still had the death penalty without qualification (although a number of countries have since abolished it to gain entry to the EU). In 1998, there were 1,625 known executions in 37 countries, 76 percent of which took place in China (1,067), the Democratic Republic of the Congo (100), or the United States (68). (By comparison, Iran had 66 and Nigeria had 6.) I am interested here in locating issues related to how crimes are classified as justifying the sentence of death through an engagement with "the Other." I posit analyses toward a critical reflection of the anthropology of human rights as a denaturalization project.

Introduction

1. Hearing, Pre-Trial Chamber I, open session, November 9, 2006, transcript ICC-01/04-01/06-T-30. This and numerous other transcripts of hearings in this case are online at http://www.icc-cpi.int/cases/RDC/c0106/c0106 _hs.html. Accessed June 2008. [The ICC has recently restructured its

Web site and many, if not all, of the ICC links provided herein have been superseded. However, the reader should still be able to find each document cited by using the country and document number on the new site.]

2. Hearing, Pre-Trial Chamber I, open session, November 10, 2006, transcript ICC-01/04-01/06-T-32, pp. 49–50. Accessed June 5, 2007.

3. Ibid., 48–51.

4. Ibid., 53.

5. See *The Prosecutor v. Thomas Lubanga Dyilo*, case no. ICC-01/04-01/06, Public Court Records – Trial Chamber I, online at http://www.icc-cpi.int/cases/RDC/c0106/c0106_docTrial1.html (accessed September 9, 2008).

6. This concept is described in Chapter 2, § "Command Responsibility and the Spectrality of Justice"; see also Chapter 4, § "The ICC and the Concept of Intention."

7. The Iraqi Special Tribunal is discussed later in this Introduction; see § "U.S. Contestations of the ICC."

8. See § "Regular Budget" among the ICTY's "General Information," online at http://www.un.org/icty/glance-e/index.htm (accessed September 2, 2008).

9. The court's earlier *Tadic* decision (in *Prosecutor v. Duško Tadic*, case no. IT-94-1) reinforced the jurisdictional basis for its authority to litigate alongside the developing corpus of international criminal law.

10. Two critical legal concepts have transformed the terrain within which international criminal law has taken shape: (1) the *individualization of responsibility*, in which "command responsibility" (see Chapter 4, § "The ICC and the Concept of Intention") has imputed the responsibility of violence not simply on those who commit the violence physically but also on those who enable or do not prevent such violence, and (2) the *transformation of territoriality*, in which the principle of "complementarity" (see § "Jurisdictional Friction" later in this Introduction) between national and international bodies is being renegotiated on the world stage.

11. The most common jurisdictional principles have traditionally been established on the basis of territory. The control of crime in a territory, in its narrowest sense, refers to people being tried and punished either under the relevant national laws of the territory in which the crime occurred or according to relevant local laws. In contrast, the most recent expansions in international governance have produced a wider conception of jurisdiction that leaves open the possibility of including acts that occur *outside* the state territory in question yet have a direct effect on that territory. The extranational reach of criminal jurisdiction, expanded during the Nuremberg Trials, was further developed through the landmark decisions of the ICTY.

12. See "Statute of the International Criminal Tribunal for the former Yugoslavia," art. 7(3), UNSCR 827, U.N. SCOR, 48th Sess., 3217th mtg.,

U.N. Doc. S/RES/827 (1993), *amended by* UNSCR 1166, U.N. SCOR, 53rd Sess., 3878th mtg., U.N. Doc. S/RES/1166 (1998) [hereinafter ICTY Statute], online at http://www.un.org/icty/legaldoc-e/basic/statut/statute-feb08-e.pdf.

13. See Chapter 1, § "Moral Economies and Praxeology."

14. The mass violence was sparked by the death of the Rwandan president Juvénal Habyarimana, an ethnic Hutu, when his plane was shot down above Kigali airport on April 6, 1994. The media blamed Paul Kagame, leader of the Rwandese Patriotic Front (RPF), for giving direct orders for the rocket attack, although ethnic strife among the minority Tutsis and majority Hutus was not new. The two groups share a common language, regional development, and traditions, but the Belgian colonial powers classified them as having distinct identities. During Belgian colonial rule, the Tutsis were hierarchicalized as eugenically superior to Hutus and granted better career opportunities, education, and economic privileges. This had led to growing political resentment among a range of ethnic Hutus, and in 1962, when Belgium granted Rwanda independence, various Hutus had taken control of governance.

15. See "Statute of the International Criminal Tribunal for Rwanda," UNSCR 955, U.N. SCOR, 49th Sess., 3453th mtg., U.N. Doc. S/RES/955 (1994) [hereinafter ICTR Statute], online at http://www.un.org/ictr/statute.html (accessed January 20, 2008). The crimes enumerated were "Genocide" (art. 2). "Crimes against humanity" (art. 3), and "Violations of Article 3 common to the Geneva Conventions and of Additional Protocol II." For the Geneva Conventions and Protocols, see "1949 Conventions & Additional Protocols" online at http://www.icrc.org/ihl.nsf/CONVPRES?OpenView (accessed September 2, 2008).

16. Akayesu was convicted on nine counts, including Genocide, seven counts of Crime against humanity (three of murder, plus extermination, torture, rape, and other inhumane acts), and Incitement to Commit Genocide. See the judgment in *The Prosecutor v. Jean-Paul Akayesu*, case no. ICTR-96-4-T, available online through the "Cases" link at the ICTR Web site: http://69.94.11.53/default.htm (accessed September 2, 2008).

17. ICTR Statute, art. 6(1).

18. See "Status of Cases," available online through the "Cases" link at the ICTR Web site: http://69.94.11.53/default.htm (accessed September 2, 2008).

19. Interview data on file with author.

20. UN Security Council Resolution 1315 of August 14, 2000, requested "the Secretary-General to negotiate an agreement with the Government of Sierra Leone to create an independent special court consistent with this resolution." Available online at http://www.un.org/docs/scres/2000/sc2000.htm (accessed August 30, 2008). The "Agreement . . . on the

Establishment of a Special Court for Sierra Leone" of January 16, 2002, is online at http://www.sc-sl.org/Documents/scsl-agreement.html and http://www.icrc.org/ihl.nsf/WebART/605-%201?OpenDocument (both accessed September 2, 2008).

21. Johnny Paul Koroma was reported to have been killed in June 2003. As of September 2008, the Special Court has not been provided with definitive evidence of his death, and the indictment against him stands. See "Other Indictments" online at http://www.sc-sl.org/cases-other.html (accessed September 2, 2008).

22. See the SCSL's timelines for the various cases, online at http://www.sc-sl .org/index.html (accessed September 2, 2008).

23. The Taylor trial, which opened June 4, 2007, is ongoing as of this writing. Minutes of the trial are online at http://www.sc-sl.org/Taylor-minutes. html (accessed September 2, 2008).

24. For the Rome Statute of the ICC to enter into force, sixty states had to sign and ratify it. The sixtieth state party to the statute entered its ratified instrument on July 1, 2002, and the treaty entered into force that midnight. After July 1, states no longer had the option of simply signing: they had to both sign and ratify the instrument to enter the ranks of state parties that had acceded to the Rome Statute.

25. United Nations, Rome Statute of the International Criminal Court, UN Doc. A/CONF.183/9, July 17, 1998 [hereinafter Rome Statute], art. 5. Available online at http://untreaty.un.org/cod/icc/statute/romefra.htm and http://www.icc-cpi.int/about/Official_Journal.html.

26. Ibid., Preamble.

27. U.S. resistance is discussed later in the § "U.S. Contestations of the ICC." Sudan and Uganda are addressed later in the § "Jurisdictional Friction" (see also Chapter 3 for Uganda).

28. "ICC Prosecutor Presents Case against Sudanese President, Hassan Ahmad AL BASHIR, for Genocide, Crimes against Humanity and War Crimes in Darfur," ICC press release, July 14, 2008. Available online at http://www.icc-cpi.int/press/pressreleases/406.html (accessed August 24, 2008).

29. For a discussion of fatwas, see Chapter 4, § "The Response of Religious Revivalism."

30. Paul Zeleza, "The 2007 Kenyan Elections: Holding a Nation Hostage to a Bankrupt Political Class," *The Zeleza Post*, December 31, 2007. Available online at http://zeleza.com/blogging/african-affairs/2007-kenya-elections-holding-nation-hostage-bankrupt-political-class (accessed January 13, 2008).

31. This is in sharp contrast to earlier tribunals, such as the ICTY and the ICTR, in which the sphere of the international simply claims primacy over the national. (See further Brown 1998; Holmes 1999.)

32. "Warrant of Arrest Unsealed against Five LRA Commanders," ICC press release, October 14, 2005, online at http://www.icc-cpi.int/pressrelease _details&id=114&l=en.html (accessed January 12, 2008). Re: Otti's death: Noel Mwakugu, "Obituary: LRA Deputy Vincent Otti," January 23, 2008, *BBC News*, online at http://news.bbc.co.uk/2/hi/africa/7083311.stm (accessed February 13, 2008). See also Luis Moreno-Ocampo, "Submission of Information Regarding Vincent Otti," ICC-02/04-01/05-258, November 8, 2007, available online for download at http://www.icc-cpi.int/ cases/UGD/c0105/c0105_docOTP.html (accessed February 14, 2008). Official confirmation of Lukwiya's death came three months after he was killed: "Statement by the Chief Prosecutor Luis Moreno-Ocampo on the Confirmation of the Death of Raska Lukwiya," November 7, 2006, online at http://www.icc-cpi.int/cases/UGD/c0105/c0105_pr.html (accessed January 12, 2008).

33. "Statement of the Prosecutor of the International Criminal Court Mr. Luis Moreno Ocampo to the Security Council on 29 June 2005 Pursuant to UNSCR 1593 (2005)" (quotations on pp. 2–3); available for download at http://www.icc-cpi.int/press/pressreleases/108.html (accessed January 12, 2008).

34. Elizabeth Rubin, "If Not Peace, Then Justice," *New York Times*, April 2, 2006, online at http://www.nytimes.com/2006/04/02/magazine/ 02darfur.html (accessed January 12, 2008). Resolution 1593, "while recognizing that States not party to the Rome Statute have no obligation under the Statute," also "*Decides* that the Government of Sudan . . . shall cooperate fully with and provide any necessary assistance to the Court and the Prosecutor pursuant to this resolution" (op. ¶2) and "encourages . . . the creation of institutions, involving all sectors of Sudanese society, such as truth and/or reconciliation commissions, in order to complement judicial processes" (op. ¶5). United Nations, Security Council, Resolution 1593 (2005), online at http://www.un.org/News/Press/docs/ 2006/sc8627.doc.htm or for download via http://www.un.org/Docs/ sc/unsc_resolutions05.htm (accessed January 12, 2008).

35. Structural Adjustment Programs are discussed in Chapter 1, § "Mortgaging Africa's Future: The Fine Print on Loans."

36. The very international treaties that African nations have signed to express their commitment to membership in the world community (see Hathaway 2007) serve only as governmental expressions of international compliance. However, in the midst of unsettled postcolonial disputes with long histories in colonial restructuring, violent *intranational* clashes have erupted with consequences that have placed them under the scrutiny of the ICC. This is the case in Uganda, the Sudan, the Central African Republic, and the DRC, as is discussed in Part One of this book. Nevertheless, there are other reactions to the restructuring of

African states that have led to attempts to level power using pluralist legal systems.

37. Although the United States signed the statute in 2000, at the time of this writing it has not ratified it, thereby not subjecting itself to the jurisdiction of the ICC. To fall under the subject matter jurisdiction of the ICC, states must both sign and ratify the treaty.

38. See, e.g., Human Rights News, "United States Efforts to Undermine the International Criminal Court," September 2002, online at http://www .hrw.org/campaigns/icc/docs/art98analysis.htm (accessed September 3, 2008).

39. This does not include an obligation by the United States to subject those persons to investigation or prosecution.

40. The "American Service-members' Protection Act" is Title II of P.L. 107-206, online in context at http://frwebgate.access.gpo.gov/cgi-bin/getdoc .cgi?dbname=107_cong_public_laws&docid=f:publ206.107 or on its own at http://www.state.gov/t/pm/rls/othr/misc/23425.htm (both accessed January 12, 2008). For the nickname, see, e.g., "U.S.: 'Hague Invasion Act' Becomes Law," Human Rights News, August 3, 2002, online at http://www .hrw.org/press/2002/08/aspa080302.htm (accessed January 12, 2008).

41. The amendment, titled "Limitation on Economic Support Fund Assistance for Certain Foreign Governments That Are Parties to the International Criminal Court," became sec. 574 of P.L. 108-447, online at http://frwebgate.access.gpo.gov/cgi-bin/getdoc.cgi?dbname=108_cong _public_laws&docid=f:publ447.108 (accessed January 12, 2008).

42. This was later renamed the Supreme Iraqi Criminal Tribunal by the "Law of the Supreme Iraqi Criminal Tribunal," art. 37, in Al-Waqa'i Al-Iraqiya: Official Gazette of the Republic of Iraq, no. 4006 (October 18, 2005).

43. See Ian Fisher and John F. Burns, "The Reach of War: The Tribunal; Court Hands Legal Custody of Saddam Hussein to Iraq," New York Times, July 1, 2004, online at http://www.nytimes.com/2004/07/01/ international/middleeast/01IRAQ.html; John F. Burns, "First Case against Hussein, Involving Killings in 1982, Is Sent to a Trial Court," New York Times, July 18, 2005, online at http://www.nytimes.com/2005/ 07/18/international/middleeast/18saddam.html (both accessed September 3, 2008).

44. Marc Santora, James Glanz, and Sabrina Tavernise, "Dictator Who Ruled Iraq with Violence Is Hanged for Crimes against Humanity," New York Times, December 30, 2006, online at http://www.nytimes. com/2006/12/30/world/middleeast/30hussein.html (accessed September 3, 2008). (The hanging was at 6:10 a.m., so it was already December 31 in Iraq.) "In a statement written in advance, Mr. Bush said . . . 'Bringing Saddam Hussein to justice will not end the violence in Iraq, but it is an important milestone on Iraq's course to becoming a democracy that

can govern, sustain and defend itself, and be an ally in the war on terror.'"

Chapter 1

1. David Stout, "U.S. to Create a Single Command for Military Operations in Africa," *New York Times*, February 7, 2007.
2. On donor capitalism, see the subsequent sections titled "Reconfigurations of State Practices" and "Donor Capitalism to the Rescue?"
3. On these three precursor courts, see the Introduction (§ "Antecedents to the ICC").
4. On the UDHR, see Chapter 4, § "Genealogies of 'Secularism' and the Politics of Constitutive Power." The International Covenant, which was intended to build on the UDHR, was adopted by General Assembly Resolution 2200A (XXI) of December 16, 1966 (download available at http://www.un.org/documents/ga/res/21/ares21.htm) and entered into force on March 23, 1976; the ICCPR is online at http://www2.ohchr.org/english/law/ccpr.htm (accessed September 2, 2008).
5. On circulation models, see the Introduction (§ "Modeling the Spread of 'Human Rights' and the 'Rule of Law'").
6. See Chapter 4, § "The ICC: A Movement in the Making," regarding the establishment of the ICC.
7. Rome Statute, arts. 5 and 12. Clauses of immunity have in the past protected governmental officials from being prosecuted for crimes against humanity committed while in office. The International Law Commission structured the Rome Statute in such a way that eradicated protections against immunity; see ibid., art. 27.
8. Rome Statute, art. 5(1).
9. The text of the Rome Statute of the ICC contains a preamble and 128 articles, which are grouped into thirteen parts. It delineates the court's subject matter and jurisdiction, both temporally and substantively; it codifies the crimes and appropriate sentences. Procedural rules are set forth and means are noted for the development of procedural norms in conjunction with the general principles of criminal law that are to serve in the operation of the ICC.
10. Yearbook of the International Law Commission 1951, vol. II. Second Report on a Draft Code of Offences Against the Peace and Security of Mankind by Mr. J. Spiropoulos, Special Rapporteur (Part I). UN document A/CN.4/44. Online at http://www.un.org/law/ilc/index.htm (accessed January 7, 2009).
11. UN General Assembly Resolution 36/108 of December 10, 1981. Accessed January 9, 2009, from http://daccessdds.un.org/doc/RESOLUTION/GEN/NR0/407/32/IMG/NR040732.pdf?OpenElement.

12. Yearbook of the International Law Commission 1994, vol. II (2). "Report of the International Law Commission on the Work of Its Forty-Sixth Session, 2 May–22 July 1994, Official Records of the General Assembly, Forty-ninth session, Supplement No. 10," online at http://untreaty.un.org/ilc/documentation/english/A_49_10.pdf (accessed January 8, 2009).

13. "Report of the Preparatory Commission for the International Criminal Court." United Nations Preparatory Commission for the International Criminal Court, UN Document PCNICC/2000/INF/3 July 6, 2000, online at http://documents-dds-ny.un.org/doc/UNDOC/GEN/N00/519/95/pdf/N0051995.pdf?OpenElement (accessed January 5, 2009).

14. Yearbook of the International Law Commission 1991, vol. II (2). "Report of the International Law Commission on the work of its forty-third session, 29 April–19 July 1991, Official Records of the General Assembly, Forty-sixth session, Supplement No. 10. Vol. II A/46/10," online at http://untreaty.un.org/ilc/documentation/english/A_46_10.pdf (accessed November 10, 2008).

15. See p. 10, § 27, in "Report of the International Law Commission on the Work of Its Forty-Seventh Session (1995). Topical summary of the discussion during its fiftieth session prepared by the Secretariat." UN document A/CN.4/472, February 16, 1996, online at http://daccessdds.un.org/doc/UNDOC/GEN/N96/038/77/PDF/N9603877.pdf?OpenElement (accessed January 7, 2009).

16. Ibid., p. 10, § 28.

17. Ibid., p. 11, § 32.

18. Ibid., p. 9, § 23.

19. Ibid., p. 11, § 31.

20. Ibid., p. 12, § 34.

21. Ibid., p. 11, § 32.

22. Ibid., p. 31, § 122.

23. Preparatory Committee on Establishment of International Criminal Court, First Session, 6th Meeting (PM) March 27, 1996, UN doc. L/2766 "Terrorism Should Be 'Core Crime' of Proposed International Court," India Tells Preparatory Committee.

24. However, because of diplomatic controversies over which acts constitute "aggression," the crime of aggression remains undefined in the corpus of crimes under the statute.

25. For more on this problematic argument, see Chapter 2, § "The ICC and the Tribunalization of African Violence."

26. For Foucault (1978), *biopower* relates to the government's concern with fostering the life of the population and centers on the poles of disciplines ("an anatomo-politics of the human body") and regulatory controls ("a biopolitics of the population"). As a technology of power and a way to exercise various techniques into a single technology of power, it allows

for the control of entire populations. It has the power to achieve the subjugation of bodies and the control of populations (1978:140).

27. United Nations, Rome Statute of the International Criminal Court, UN Doc. A/CONF.183/9, July 17, 1998 (hereafter Rome Statute), art. 117, "Assessment of Contributions," online at http://untreaty.un.org/ cod/icc/statute/romefra.htm and http://www.icc-cpi.int/about/Official _Journal.html.Rome Statute: "The contributions of States Parties shall be assessed in accordance with an agreed scale of assessment, based on the scale adopted by the United Nations for its regular budget and adjusted in accordance with the principles on which that scale is based" (accessed October 1, 2008).

28. Participation and cooperation with international institutions and courts are not necessarily voluntary because states engage in what Hazan (2006) refers to as "strategic bargaining" or "cheque book diplomacy." In his example, he highlights "the granting of a loan of US$10 billion conditional on the former Serbian president's transfer to the ICTY prison" (2006:26).

29. Stephanie Nieuwoudt, "Slow Progress at Rwandan Tribunal," Global Policy Forum, July 27, 2006, online at http://www.globalpolicy.org/ intljustice/tribunals/rwanda/2006/0727slow.htm (accessed September 3, 2008). Pierre Hazan, "Measuring the Impact of Punishment and Forgiveness: A Framework for Evaluating Transitional Justice," *International Review of the Red Cross* 88 (2006): 19–47, cites "[t]he US$700 million which the ICTR has cost to date." He continues, "The US$700 million which the ICTR has cost to date would doubtless have been better invested in rebuilding the judicial system and the rule of law in Rwanda, thus curbing the government's drift towards authoritarianism."

30. See the § "Regular Budget" among the ICTY's "General Information," online at http://www.un.org/icty/glance-e/index.htm (accessed September 2, 2008).

31. Security Council Report, "International Criminal Tribunals," June 2007, online at http://www.securitycouncilreport.org/site/c.glKWLeMTIsG/ b.2776107/k.9DA/June_2007BRInternational_Criminal_Tribunals.htm (accessed September 3, 2008). http://www.securitycouncilreport.org/site/ pp.aspx?c=glKWLeMTIsG&b=2776107&printmode=1.

32. See http://www.icc-cpi.int/press/pressreleases/311.html (accessed September 11, 2008).

33. See "Global appeal for EUR10 million to assist 1.7 million victims of sexual violence launched," ICC Press Release, ICC-CPI-20080910-PR353_ENG, September 10, 2008, online at http://www.icc-cpi.int/press/ pressreleases/420.html (accessed September 11, 2008).

34. "International Court Seeks Funds for Women Victims," Associated Press, September 10, 2008, online at http://www.iht.com/articles/ap/2008/09/10/ europe/EU-International-Court-Victims.php.

35. Hazan notes, "[t]he government did not begin paying compensations to victims until December 2003, more than five years after the TRC had presented its findings. A fund of 660 million rand (US$100 million) was set aside to make one-off payments of 30,000 rand to 22,000 victims – considerably less than the fund of 3 billion rand recommended by the TRC" (2006:44).

36. Hannerz (1990:244) holds that most are "extensions or transformations of the cultures of western Europe and North America."

37. In regard to whether tourists, exiles, businesspeople, and labor migrants are cosmopolitans, Hannerz asserts that being mobile is not enough to turn one into a cosmopolitan: quoting Paul Theroux (1996:104–5), tourists, for example, experience foreign lands as "home plus" some unaccustomed feature, "but the 'plus' has nothing to do with alien systems of meaning" (Hannerz 1990:239–40).

38. See Rantanen's (2007) interview with Ulf Hannerz. See also Hannerz (1990), who argues that although "some transnational cultures are more insulated from local practices than others," globalization has brought a "large number of people" together and that their territorial cultural practices "are entangled with one another" (1990:244). Employees of international NGOs, activists, legal advisers, and consultants represent a particular type of cosmopolitanism engaged in the globalization of a culturally particular form of international criminal law, although one that is packaged in the language of universal human rights.

39. To conduct their human rights work, CBO staff must rely much more on funding from external sources. As a result, CBOs – what some call "indigenous NGOs" – compete with international organizations for grants to administer services within their countries but also form occasional alliances with various international NGOs in an attempt to collaborate, ultimately with the goal of accessing donor funding for the purpose of "capacity building," a strategy that has increased since the 1990s.

40. Research data on file with author. Note that the translations of this and subsequent parts of this exchange, originally in Arabic, were provided by CICC staff.

41. Research data on file with author.

42. Research data for this and the following quotation are on file with author.

43. Tsing's concept of friction was described in the Introduction (§ "Modeling the Spread of 'Human Rights' and 'Rule of Law'"). U.S. contestation of the ICC was also discussed in the Introduction (§ "U.S. Contestations of the ICC").

44. CICC, "States Parties to the Rome Statute of the ICC," July 18, 2008, online at http://www.iccnow.org/documents/RatificationsbyUNGroup _18_July_08.pdf, and Human Rights Watch, "Rome Statute Ratifications,"

online at http://www.hrw.org/campaigns/icc/ratifications.htm (both accessed September 5, 2008).

45. Research data on file with author.

46. The majority of states have constitutions that require legislative incorporation. In the United States, for example, treaties are made with the
consent of the U.S. Senate; however, in giving consent, the Senate does
not enact constituent power. Rather, it is the president, who works through
international executive agreements, who has constituent power to enforce
international treaties. Interestingly, the U.S. Constitution excluded the
House of Representatives from treaty making. Congress enacts bills that
are constituted as domestic law, and the Executive, alongside the Senate
and the House of Representatives, participates in the process of autho-
rizing constituent power. Historically, the United States established a
Supremacy Clause that privileges the integrity of treaties. This was developed with the 1783 Treaty of Paris, following the American Revolutionary
War, that guaranteed British rights and made them binding on all states.
The non-self-executing treaty model was developed to maintain the nonparticipation of the House of Representatives in the treaty-making process.
It stands to reason that using this route ensures the ordinary legislative
process, for if the treaty involves amendments of domestic law, then the
House will want to ensure that there is the potential for implementing constitutional amendments through the ordinary legislation process. In the
late 1970s, the Carter administration's goal was to commit to human rights
treaties and to bind the United States to the UN process, but not necessarily to make changes in U.S. human rights law through the treaty route
alone. The administration wanted to ensure that the House was brought
into the process so as not to commit to laws that extend beyond existing
U.S. law. (Summary of 2005 e-mail correspondence, Arthur Rovine, former U.S. assistant legal advisor for Treaty Affairs, Carter administration,
1975–1981.)

47. See § "Challenges and Contestations to the ICC in Uganda."

48. The Victims Trust Fund is an independent fund of donations for states and
donor companies that represents some of the innovative steps taken by the
ICC to acknowledge the rights of victims. As documented in the Rome
Statute (art. 75), provisions are to be made to provide financial resources
(and even relocation if necessary) for victims so that they can participate
in the criminal justice process and claim reparations. See CICC, "Victims
Trust Fund," online at http://www.iccnow.org/?mod=trustfund (accessed
September 5, 2008).

49. On this process, see Chapter 3, § "Challenges and Contestations to the
ICC in Uganda."

50. United Nations Environment Programme and Mryka Hall-Beyer, "Mining and Oil Extraction in Africa," in *Encyclopedia of Earth*, ed. Cutler

J. Cleveland (Washington, DC: Environmental Information Coalition, National Council for Science and the Environment); posted November 21, 2006, online at http://www.eoearth.org/article/Mining_and_oil _extraction_in_Africa (accessed September 5, 2008).

51. Ibid. Some African governments have grown warier of the long-term environmental results of the extraction industries (ibid.): "Due to the long-lasting impact of mining, many governments have, since the 1990s, enacted environmental impact assessment (EIA) policies and laws."

52. Ibid., which also states: "In 2003, Africa produced 8.7 million barrels per day (bbl/d) of oil with the top producers being Nigeria, Algeria, Libya, Angola, and Egypt. Total African oil consumption in 2003 was 2.7 million bbl/d and the top oil consumers were Egypt, South Africa, Nigeria, Libya and Algeria."

53. Ibid.

54. "Partnership for African Universities," *Africa Recovery* 14.2 (July 2000):17, online at http://www.un.org/ecosocdev/geninfo/afrec/vol14no2/univbx .htm (accessed September 8, 2008).

55. NEPAD is now a program of the African Union (AU), which superseded the OAU in July 2002. For more on NEPAD, see Edozie (2004). In April 2008, a NEPAD Review Summit, comprising five heads of state (from Algeria, Egypt, Nigeria, Senegal, and South Africa), met to discuss furthering organizational goals; Bathandwa Mbola, "Summit to Discuss Global Challenges Facing Africa," *BuaNews*, April 15, 2008, online at http:// www.buanews.gov.za/view.php?ID=08041510451001&coll=buanew08 (accessed September 8, 2008).

56. "Volkswagen Community Trust invests R1.2 Million in Education in 2008," February 4, 2008 (accessed September 6, 2008).

57. "Research in Sub-Saharan Africa: Funding for Six New Projects," December 6, 2006, online at http://www.volkswagenstiftung.de/funding/ international-focus/knowledge-for-tomorrow-cooperative-research- projects-in-sub-saharan-africa/bewilligungen-2008.html?L=1 (accessed September 6, 2008).

58. Vangelis Vitalis, "Official Development Assistance and Foreign Direct Investment: Improving the Synergies," presented at Organisation for Economic Co-operation and Development's Global Forum on International Investment: Attracting Foreign Direct Investment for Development, Shanghai, December 5–6, 2002 (p. 3), online at http://www.oecd.org/ dataoecd/54/61/2764550.pdf (accessed May 26, 2008).

59. Data on file with author.

60. Foundation Center, "Foundation Growth and Giving Estimates: Current Outlook," 2007 (p. 6), online at http://www.foundationcenter.org/ gainknowledge/research/pdf/fgge07.pdf (accessed May 25, 2008).

61. Data collected through annual reports on file with author.
62. Centre for Democracy and Development, "Annual Report, 1997–1999," online at http://www.cdd.org.uk/pdf/ar01final.pdf (accessed September 8, 2008).
63. Amnesty International, "The History of Amnesty International," online at http://www.amnesty.org/en/who-we-are/history (accessed September 8, 2008).
64. Amnesty International, "Annual Review, March 2005–April 2006," online at http://www.amnesty.org/en/library/info/ORG10/006/2007/en (originally accessed November 20, 2007). Total resources expended are shown as £30,983,000 for fiscal year ending March 31, 2006, at which point the exchange rate was 1.7393 (per http://www.x-rates.com/cgi-bin/hlookup.cgi).
65. Human Rights Watch, "Financial Statements, Year Ended June 30, 2006," online at http://www.hrw.org/annual-report/finStmt2006.pdf (p. 6; accessed November 20, 2007).
66. Human Rights First, "Annual Report 2005–2006," online at http://www.humanrightsfirst.org/pdf/07221-hrf-ar-05-06.pdf (accessed November 20, 2007). This shows "$8.38 million in total organizational expenditures" but "total expenses" of $31,480,886 (p. 29 and overleaf).

Chapter 2

1. Pre-Trial Chamber I, "Document Containing the Charges," ICC-01/04-01/06-356-Anx2, August 28, 2006, p. 24, online at http://www.icc-cpi.int/cases/RDC/c0106/c0106_docOTP5.html (accessed October 25, 2007). (All of the public documents of the Lubanga case (no. ICC-01/04-01/06) are available and retrievable by date through the links found at http://www.icc-cpi.int/cases/RDC/c0106/c0106_doc.html; direct links to specific documents are included herein when possible.)
2. Ibid.
3. On the use of this term, see Chapter 1, § "Moral Economies and Praxeology."
4. The Redress Trust, "Victims, Perpetrators or Heroes?: Child Soldiers before the International Criminal Court," September 2006, online at http://www.crin.org/docs/redress_cs.pdf, p. 26, citing UN Doc. S/2000/915 (October 4, 2000) (accessed October 25, 2007).
5. United Nations, Rome Statute of the International Criminal Court, UN Doc. A/CONF.183/9, July 17, 1998 [hereinafter Rome Statute], art. 8 (2(b)(xxvi)); online at http://untreaty.un.org/cod/icc/statute/romefra.htm and http://www.icc-cpi.int/about/Official_Journal.html.
6. See the Introduction, § "Antecedents to the ICC," for a discussion of the SCSL.

7. In each case, the wording of the pertinent charge was "Conscripting or enlisting children under the age of 15 years into armed forces or groups, or using them to participate actively in hostilities."

8. Other charges that stuck include murder (as both a crime against humanity and a war crime) and rape. The judgment in the case, *Prosecutor v. Brima, Kamara and Kanu*, online at http://www.sc-sl.org/AFRC.html (accessed December 7, 2007).

9. This is the date that the sealed arrest warrant of February 10, 2006, was unsealed and announced publicly; it also the date Thomas Lubanga was transferred to the ICC: "First Arrest for the International Criminal Court," press release, March 17, 2006, online at http://www.icc-cpi.int/ pressrelease_details&id=132.html. Pre-Trial Chamber I, Warrant of Arrest, doc. ICC-01-04-01-06-2, online at http://www.icc-cpi.int/cases/ RDC.html (both accessed January 5, 2008).

10. Kofi Annan, "Children and Armed Conflict: Report of the Secretary General," October 26, 2000, UN Security Council Report S/2006/826, online via http://www.un.org/Docs/sc/sgrep06.htm (accessed December 7, 2007).

11. The pretrial hearing was the initial hearing held by the ICC to determine whether the prosecutor had enough evidence to proceed to trial with Lubanga before the ICC.

12. November 9, 2006 of ICC pretrial hearings.

13. In these enactments, the prosecution is not inherently the moral victor. Rather, rule of law spectacles not only do the work of providing a language of moral fortitude in which justice making becomes fundamentally allied with a moral imaginary of goodness but also represent that which opposes it as insufficient, substandard, and underdeveloped.

14. The text of the Rome Statute contains a preamble and 128 articles, which are grouped into thirteen parts. It delineates the court's subject matter and jurisdiction, both temporally and substantively; it also codifies the crimes and appropriate sentences. Procedural rules are set forth, and means are noted for the development of procedural norms in conjunction with the general principles of criminal law that are to serve in the operation of the ICC.

15. As determined by the statute (art. 126), this was sixty days after its ratification by 60 of the 120 (Schabas 2004:18). As of September 2008, there were 146 signatories and 108 ratifications. Coalition for the International Criminal Court, "States Parties to the Rome Statute of the ICC," July 18, 2008, online at http://www.iccnow.org/documents/RatificationsbyUNGroup_ 18_July_08.pdf, and Human Rights Watch, "Rome Statute Ratifications," online at http://www.hrw.org/campaigns/icc/ratifications.htm (both accessed September 5, 2008). See Chapter 4, § "The ICC: A

Movement in the Making," for more regarding the establishment of the ICC.

16. Rome Statute, art. 1.

17. Ibid., arts. 5, 12. Clauses of immunity have in the past protected governmental officials from being prosecuted for crimes against humanity committed while in office. The International Law Commission structured the Rome Statute in such a way that eradicated protections against immunity; see ibid., art. 27.

18. Ibid., arts. 5, 12.

19. "Affirming that the most serious crimes of concern to the international community as a whole must not go unpunished and that their effective prosecution must be ensured by taking measures at the national level and by enhancing international cooperation."

20. Ibid., Preamble and art. 1.

21. International Bar Association, *IBA Monitoring Report*, "Balancing Rights: The International Criminal Court (ICC) at a Procedural Crossroads," May 2008, pp. 19–20, online at http://www.ibanet.org/humanrights/ICC _Monitoring.cfm (accessed September 20, 2008). International Bar Association, *IBA Monitoring Report*, "International Criminal Court," September 2006, p. 5, online at http://www.ibanet.org/iba/article.cfm?article=94 (accessed October 25, 2007).

22. This was to distinguish it from the new (and neighboring) Republic of the Congo, formerly known as French Congo.

23. International Rescue Committee (IRC), "Mortality in the Democratic Republic of Congo: Results from a Nationwide Survey (April–July 2004)," pp. 3, 11, online at http://www.theirc.org/resources/DRC_ MortalitySurvey2004_RB_8Dec04.pdf (accessed October 27, 2007). The vast majority of these deaths (80%–90%) were from easily preventable diseases and malnourishment resulting from the disruption of health service, agriculture, and infrastructure and from refugee displacement (p. 3). The 2004 IRC report also includes death toll estimates of 3.3 million and 4.4 million (pp. 11–12), a range reflecting changes in basic assumptions in the model. A more recent IRC report states: "Based on the results of the five IRC studies, we now estimate that 5.4 million excess deaths have occurred between August 1998 and April 2007. An estimated 2.1 million of those deaths have occurred since the formal end of war in 2002." See IRC, "Mortality in the Democratic Republic of Congo: An Ongoing Crisis," 2007, p. ii, online at http://www.theirc.org/ resources/2007/2006–7_congomortalitysurvey.pdf (accessed September 10, 2008).

24. See the Introduction, § "Prologue: The International Criminal Court and the Democratic Republic of Congo."

25. The Nuremberg Tribunal recognized that "a person who committed an act which constitutes a crime under international law" was not relieved of responsibility by having "acted as Head of State or responsible Government official" or "pursuant to order of his Government or of a superior." See Principles III and IV in "Principles of International Law Recognized in the Charter of the Nuremberg Tribunal and in the Judgment of the Tribunal, 1950," online at http://www.icrc.org/ihl.nsf/FULL/390?OpenDocument (accessed January 18, 2008). Relevant cases at the ICTY are *The Prosecutor v. Zejnil Delalić* et al. (case no. IT-96-21-T); *The Prosecutor v. Timohir Blaškić* (IT-95-14-T); *The Prosecutor v. Zlatko Aleksovksi* (IT-95-14/1-T); *The Prosecutor v. Dario Kordić and Mario Čerkez* (IT-95-14/2); and *The Prosecutor v. Dragoljub Kunarac and Radomir Kovač* (IT-96-23). See Eugenia Levine, "Command Responsibility: The *Mens Rea* Requirement," *Global Policy Forum* (February 2005), n. 36, online at http://www.globalpolicy.org/intljustice/general/2005/command.htm (accessed December 14, 2007).

26. It is worth noting that children – even those over age fifteen – are not, in fact, under the ICC's jurisdiction: "The Court shall have no jurisdiction over any person who was under the age of 18 at the time of the alleged commission of a crime" (art. 26).

27. The four Geneva Conventions and their agreements are as follows: First, "for the Amelioration of the Condition of the Wounded and Sick in Armed Forces in the Field" (1864; last revised 1949); Second, "for the Amelioration of the Condition of Wounded, Sick and Shipwrecked Members of Armed Forces at Sea" (1949; succeeding the 1907 Hague Convention X); Third, "relative to the Treatment of Prisoners of War" (1929; last revised 1949); Fourth, "relative to the Protection of Civilian Persons in Time of War" (1949, drawing on the 1907 Hague Convention IV). See, e.g., "1949 Conventions & Additional Protocols," online at http://www.icrc.org/ihl.nsf/CONVPRES?OpenView (accessed September 2, 2008).

28. Foreign Affairs and International Trade Canada, "ICC Signatory and Ratification Status (as of December 11, 2006)," online at http://www.international.gc.ca/court-cour/list-ratification-liste.aspx?lang=eng (accessed September 10, 2008).

29. Human Rights Watch, "Rome Statute Ratifications," online at http://www.hrw.org/campaigns/icc/ratifications.htm (both accessed September 5, 2008).

30. Pre-Trial Chamber I, Warrant of Arrest, doc. ICC-01-04/01-06-2, online at http://www.icc-cpi.int/cases/RDC.html (accessed November 1, 2007).

31. Pre-Trial Chamber I, Thursday, November 9, 2006, open session, transcript ICC-01/04-01/06-T-30-EN, online at http://www.icc-cpi.int/cases/RDC/c0106/c0106_hs.html (accessed November 1, 2007). The

Pre-Trial Chamber I comprised Judge Claude Jorda (France), Judge Akua Kuenyehia (Ghana), and Judge Sylvia Steiner (Brazil).

32. Ibid., 76–82. Mr. Walleyn was reading text provided by Mr. Mulenda, who was unable to attend that day (p. 4). The anonymous victims they represented were known as a/0001/06 to a/0003/06 (or a1–a3); the fourth participant, called a/0105/06, was represented by Ms. Carine Bapita Buyangandu. *ICC Newsletter*, November 2006, no. 10, p. 7; online at http://www.icc-cpi.int/library/about/newsletter/10/en_11.html (accessed November 1, 2007).

33. Pre-Trial Chamber I, Tuesday, November 14, 2006, open session, transcript ICC-01/04-01/06-T-34-EN, beginning on p. 52; online via http://www.icc-cpi.int/cases/RDC/c0106/c0106_hs.html (accessed October 30, 2007). Subsequent pages are noted in the text.

34. Interviewed by the author in The Hague, November and December 2006.

35. BBC TV, *Panorama: The New Killing Fields*, aired November 14, 2004.

36. ICC, "Victims and Witness Protection," online at http://www.icc-cpi.int/victimsissues/witnessprotection.html (accessed November 1, 2007).

37. ICC, "Participation of Victims in Proceedings," online at http://www.icc-cpi.int/victimsissues/victimsparticipation.html (accessed November 1, 2007).

38. ICC, "Victims Trust Fund," online at http://www.icc-cpi.int/vtf/vsfmeetings.html (accessed November 1, 2007).

39. The ICTY concluded that "had reason to know" under Article 7(3) of its Statue of the Tribunal requires the commander to have "had in his possession information which at the least, would put him on notice of the risk of . . . offences by indicating the need for additional investigation in order to ascertain whether . . . crimes were committed or were about to be committed by his subordinates." Notably, the Trial Chamber commented that it made no findings on the present state of customary law, which may have changed following the adoption of the Rome Statute of the International Criminal Court.

40. See case no. IT-96-21-T, "Judgement," ICTY Trial Chamber, November 16, 1998; online at http://www.un.org/icty/Supplement/supp1-e/celebici.htm (accessed November 1, 2007). For an overview of the ICTY, see the Introduction, § "Yugoslavia: Milošević and the ICTY."

41. Y. Sandoz, C. Swinarski, and B. Zimmerman, eds. (1987), *Commentary on the Additional Protocols of 8 June 1977 to the Geneva Conventions of 12 August 1949*, ¶3560 (Geneva: ICRC and Dordrecht: Martinus Nijhoff). Quoted in Levine, "Command Responsibility."

42. Contemporary stereotypes of Africa as, say, incapable of self-management and inherently poor – despite the fact that the material sources of conflicts are in fact diamonds, gold, and other rich mineral resources, such as

coltan – continue to plague conceptions of Africa's potential, including its youth.

43. See, e.g., Chapter 1, § "Extraction and the 'Public Good.'"
44. This document, ICC-ASP/1/3, is online at http://www.icc-cpi.int/about/ Official_Journal.html (accessed November 1, 2007).
45. On these formations, see Chapter 1, § "Biopolitics and Necropolitics."
46. Based, clearly, on Derrida's (1992) notion of the "mystical foundations of authority," described in the Introduction, § "Limits to the Models."
47. Here I am referring to the specter of victims whose death haunts legal proceedings.

Chapter 3

1. United Nations, Rome Statute of the International Criminal Court, UN Doc. A/CONF.183/9, July 17, 1998 (hereinafter Rome Statute), art. 53; online at http://untreaty.un.org/cod/icc/statute/romefra.htm and http://www.icc-cpi.int/about/Official_Journal.html.
2. Richard Dicker, director of Human Rights Watch's International Justice Program, quoted in [Hannah Gaertner,] "Uganda: No Amnesty for Atrocities," *Human Rights News*, July 28, 2006, online at http://hrw .org/english/docs/2006/07/27/uganda13863.htm (accessed February 12, 2008).
3. Daniel Wallis (for Reuters), "Uganda Aims to Formalise Peace Rites, Boost LRA Talks," August 6, 2006, online at http://en.epochtimes.com/news/ 6-8-6/44657.html (accessed September 11, 2008). This was excerpted by the Coalition for the ICC and cited as http://www.alertnet .org/thenews/newsdesk/L06749187.htm in "Uganda (Part 2): Parliament to Discuss Reconciliation; Kony Shifts," online at http://www.iccnow .org/?mod=newsdetailnews=1898 (accessed December 5, 2007).
4. Tim Allen, "War and Justice in Northern Uganda: An Assessment of the International Criminal Court's Intervention," London: Crisis States Research Centre, Development Studies Institute, London School of Economics, 2005, online at http://www.crisisstates.com/download/ others/AllenICCReport.pdf (accessed September 15, 2008).
5. A particularly unique aspect of Museveni's democracy was the prohibition of party campaigning, put in place in 1986 to avoid political-party building along ethnic lines. However, this provision seems to have resulted in disadvantaging contenders to the presidency – a result to which a range of groups objected. Under the nonparty democratic system, candidates for both presidential and parliamentary elections were expected to campaign as individuals, not as representatives of a party, although parties could exist. In this context, candidates were not to commence their electoral campaign by engaging as a permanent opposition party;

rather, once potential candidates succeeded in achieving nominations, they could compete in the elections. This and other aspects of governmental policies inspired violent resistance struggles against the Museveni government. After nineteen years, the nonparty system was replaced by a multiparty one through a constitutional referendum held on July 28, 2005. "Uganda Backs Multi-Party Return," *BBC News*, August 1, 2005, online at http://news.bbc.co.uk/2/hi/africa/4726419.stm (accessed February 13, 2008).

6. The intermittent talks, held in Juba – the capital of what since 2005 has been the autonomous region of Southern Sudan – are still ongoing as of this writing (September 2008).

7. For in-depth statistics and further context regarding the abduction of Ugandan youths, as well as their return to and "reintegration" into society, see Jeannie Annan, Christopher Blattman, and Roger Horton, "The State of Youth and Youth Protection in Northern Uganda: Findings from the Survey of War Affected Youth – A Report for UNICEF Uganda" (September 2006), online at http://www.sway-uganda.org/SWAY.Phase1.FinalReport.pdf (accessed April 13, 2008). The report, which focuses on abductees and the needs of those who manage to return, notes that "the UN has estimated that 20,000 to 25,000 children have been abducted" (p. 55) but also that "Youth not only face a significant risk of abduction into the LRA, but also forcible recruitment into the Ugandan army as well.... Once with the LRA, not all abductees become fighters, and relatively few are forced to kill" (p. vi).

8. The suggestion that if the LRA was in power, religion rather than law would represent the new order is part of a larger rhetoric strategy being used by various spokespeople. However, there is widespread agreement throughout the country that such articulations of Christianity point to the political and not spiritual motives of LRA leaders.

9. Agence France-Presse, "War in Northern Uganda World's Worst Forgotten Crisis: UN," November 11, 2003, online at http://www.reliefweb.int/rw/rwb.nsf/AllDocsByUNID/e1f176894430fdeec1256ddb0056ea4c. See also Jeffrey Gettleman and Alexis Okeowo, "Ugandan Rebels Delay Peace Deal," *New York Times*, April 11, 2008, online at http://www.nytimes.com/2008/04/11/world/africa/11uganda.html (both accessed September 11, 2008).

10. Human Rights Watch, *Abducted and Abused: Renewed War in Northern Uganda*, Uganda 15.12(A) (New York: HRW, July 2003), online at http://www.hrw.org/reports/2003/uganda0703/ (accessed February 13, 2008). It is worth noting that, following its section on "Human Rights Abuses by the Lord's Resistance Army," the report has another on "Human Rights Violations by Ugandan Government Forces." See also Foundation

for Human Rights Initiative, *The Bi-annual Human Rights Reporter*, 2004, Kampala, Uganda.

11. "Assembly of States Parties: Uganda (African States)," online at http://www.icc-cpi.int/asp/statesparties/countryid=20.html (accessed February 13, 2008).

12. "President of Uganda Refers Situation Concerning the Lord's Resistance Army (LRA) to the ICC," online at http://www.icc-cpi.int/pressrelease_detailsid=16l=en.html (accessed February 13, 2008).

13. This is the date on which the Rome Statute came into force and thus the temporal jurisdiction of the ICC commenced. Documentation on Moreno-Ocampo's concern obtained through personal conversation at Yale University on December 6, 2006. Data on file with author.

14. ICC, "Prosecutor of the International Criminal Court Opens an Investigation into Northern Uganda," July 29, 2004, online at http://www.icc-cpi.int/press/pressreleases/33.html (accessed February 14, 2008).

15. The warrants are available online at http://www.icc-cpi.int/cases/UGD.html (accessed February 14, 2008). See also "Warrant of Arrest Unsealed against Five LRA Commanders," ICC press release, October 14, 2005, online at http://www.icc-cpi.int/pressrelease_detailsid=114l=en.html (accessed January 12, 2008).

16. See "Amnesty Act 2000 (Ch 294)," commenced January 21, 2000 (hereinafter Amnesty Act 2000), online at http://www.c-r.org/our-work/accord/northern-uganda/additional-keytexts.php (accessed February 14, 2008) and http://www.saflii.org/ug/legis/consol_act/aa2000294120/ (accessed September 12, 2008). See also Mallinder (2007).

17. See Apollo Mubiru and Cyprian Musoke, "Kony Denied Amnesty," *New Vision* (Kampala), April 20, 2006, online at http://www.newvision.co.ug/D/8/13/494054, and "UGANDA: LRA Leaders Not Entitled to Amnesty – Minister," *IRIN Africa*, April 21, 2006 (both accessed September 12, 2008). See also Mallinder (2007).

18. See "Ugandan Rebel Leader Kony Offered Amnesty," *Independent* (London), July 5, 2006, online at http://findarticles.com/p/articles/mi_qn4158/is_20060705/ai_n16511071, and Frank Nyakairu, "Uganda: Museveni Amnesty to Kony Illegal – ICC," *Monitor* (Uganda), July 6, 2006, online at http://www.afrika.no/Detailed/12493.html (both accessed September 12, 2008). For the quotations, see "Uganda LRA Rebels Reject Amnesty," *BBC News*, July 7, 2006, online at http://news.bbc.co.uk/2/hi/africa/5157220.stm (accessed February 14, 2008). The creation of an autonomous Southern Sudan, coming with the official ending of the twenty-two-year-long Second Sudanese Civil War (1983–2005), may also affect the peace process in northern Uganda: "Diplomats in the region say [this]... is a 'completely new element in this process, which might successfully push [the Ugandan authorities] into peace talks'." Janet

Anderson, "World Court Faces Biggest Challenge," Institute for War
& Peace Reporting, "Africa Reports," no. 67, June 16, 2006, online at
http://iwpr.net/?p=acrs=fo=321675apc_state=henh (accessed January 9,
2007).

19. Nyakairu, "Uganda: Museveni Amnesty to Kony Illegal – ICC." See
    also Emmy Allio, "Uganda: UN Stalls on Kony," New Vision (Kam-
    pala), August 8, 2006, online at http://www.publicinternationallaw.org/
    warcrimeswatch/archives/wcpw_vol01issue14.html (both accessed April
    14, 2008).
20. Bill No. 13. See *Uganda Government Gazette* no. 58, vol. XCL, September
    22, 1998.
21. Barney Afako, "Reconciliation and Justice: 'Mato Oput' and the Amnesty
    Act," *Accord: An International Review of Peace Initiatives*, no. 11 (*Pro-
    tracted Conflict, Elusive Peace: Initiatives to End the Violence in North-
    ern Uganda*, ed. Okello Lucima), online at http://www.c-r.org/our-work/
    accord/northern-uganda/reconciliation-justice.php (accessed February
    14, 2008).
22. Afako, "Reconciliation and Justice." The Amnesty Act of 2000 was inten-
    ded, in part, to "Fill the vacuum left by the expiry of the Amnesty Statute
    of 1987"; Ugandan Parliament, House, "Second Reading, The Amnesty
    Bill, 1999," November 30, 1999, online at http://www.parliament.go
    .ug/hansard/hans_view_date.jsp?dateYYYY=1999dateMM=11dated=30
    (accessed September 12, 2008); the bill passed two months later, in
    January 2000.
23. See the untitled preamble of the Amnesty Act 2000.
24. Ibid., Part II, sec. 3(1).
25. Ibid., Part II, secs. 4(1)(d) and 4(1)(b).
26. Ibid., Part I, sec. 2.
27. See the 1995 Ugandan Constitution, art. 25 (10), available for
    download at http://www.ugandaonlinelawlibrary.com/files/constitution/
    constitution_1995.pdf (accessed February 14, 2008). The UAC is the
    statutory body set up by the Ugandan government to give a blanket
    amnesty to surrendering rebels.
28. "Amnesty Act, 2000," Part III, sec. 9 (c).
29. See also Erin K. Baines, "Roco Wat I Acoli/Restoring Relationships in
    Acholi-land: Traditional Approaches to Justice and Reconciliation,"
    Conflict and Development Programme, Liu Institute for Global Issues,
    September 2005, online at http://www.erinbaines1.moonfruit.com/#/
    reports/4516056074 (accessed June 17, 2008); Baines, "Accountability,
    Reconciliation and the Juba Talks: Beyond the Impasse," Justice and Rec-
    onciliation Project, Gulu District NGO Forum, *Field Notes* no. 3 (October
    2006), online at http://northern-uganda.moonfruit.com/#/fieldnotes/
    4516577115 (accessed June 16, 2008); Baines, "The Cooling of Hearts:

Community Truth-Telling in Acholi-land," Justice and Reconciliation Project, Gulu District NGO Forum, Liu Institute for Global Issues, 2007, online at http://www.ligi.ubc.ca/sites/liu/files/Publications/JRP/July2007_JRP_CoolingofHearts.pdf (accessed June 17, 2008); and Stephen Arthur Lamony, "Approaching National Reconciliation in Uganda: Perspectives on Applicable Justice Systems," Uganda Coalition for the International Criminal Court, working paper, 2006, online at http://www.iccnow.org/documents/ApproachingNationalReconciliationInUganda_07aug13.pdf (accessed June 17, 2008).

30. Thomas Harlacher et al., "Traditional Ways of Coping in Acholi: Cultural Provisions for Reconciliation and Healing from War," Kampala, Uganda: Intersoft Business Services, Ltd., 2006, online at http://www.chrisblattman.org/TraditionalWaysOfCopingInAcholi.pdf, pp. 78–81 (accessed June 18, 2008).

31. Ibid., 59–60. "In cases where someone has killed an enemy or a foreigner in a war, the cleansing would typically take place in the form of '*kwero merok*,' an elaborate ritual for 'cleansing the enemy.' If a person has killed someone from a friendly clan, the cleansing would be performed in a '*mato oput*' ritual" (59).

32. Patrick Tom, "The Acholi Traditional Approach to Justice and the War in Northern Uganda," August 2006, online at http://www.beyondintractability.org/case_studies/acholi_traditional_approach.jsp?nid=6792, quoting from "Uganda: Traditional Ritual Heals Communities Torn Apart by War," *IRIN Africa*, June 9, 2005, online at http://www.irinnews.org/report.aspx?reported=54858 (both accessed September 12, 2008).

33. Afako, "Reconciliation and Justice."

34. This is the case even though the guilt and submission implied by the term *kica* are resented by the LRA.

35. Afako, "Reconciliation and Justice."

36. Harlacher et al., "Traditional Ways of Coping in Acholi," 80–2.

37. Anderson, "World Court Faces Biggest Challenge."

38. Gulu respondents thought that nothing had changed as a result of the ICC's arrest warrants, but a few Amuru respondents noted that the warrants were causing a stall in the talks.

39. Victims Rights Working Group, "Ugandan Peace Talks: Victims' Rights Must Be Respected," statement of August 3, 2006, online at http://www.iccnow.org/documents/VRWG_Statement_3Aug06.pdf (accessed February 15, 2008).

40. Uganda is not the only country in this situation. Rwanda has become famous for its recourse to tradition-inspired *gacaca* courts alongside international and national justice options in its path to reconstruction. *Gacaca* is geared toward facilitating and expediting the trials of the more than a

hundred thousand people imprisoned since the Rwandan genocide. It is used as a form of "reconciliation and healing." Rather than serving prison sentences, those convicted are being called on to confess before elected judges. In these meetings, entire communities gather to give testimony. The judges are then asked to give testimony to what they saw, heard, and experienced during the genocide. In another example, the African Union has recommended incorporating traditional forms of reconciliation to resolve the Darfur crisis in the Sudan.

41. On February 20, 2008, the two sides signed an agreement that "severe crimes committed by the rebels during the war will be tried under 'a special division of the High Court in Uganda,'" although it did "not mention in which court Mr. Kony could face trial." Reuters, "Rebels and Ugandan Government Agree to Terms of Prosecutions of War Crimes," *New York Times*, February 20, 2008, online at http://www .nytimes.com/2008/02/20/world/africa/20uganda.html (accessed September 13, 2008). Four days later, a cease-fire agreement was signed, one that "formalizes a 2006 cessation of hostilities and creates a six-mile buffer zone around rebel territory." Reuters, "Uganda and Rebels Sign Cease-Fire," *New York Times*, February 24, 2008, online at http://www .nytimes.com/2008/02/24/world/africa/24uganda.html (accessed September 13, 2008). A final peace agreement, however, has yet to be signed, and the ICC's arrest warrants are proving to be a sticking point: "Mr. Kony . . . has said he will not surrender until the indictments are lifted. Uganda has said it will not push for the indictments to be lifted until he surrenders. The plan then is to try Mr. Kony in Ugandan courts – if the International Criminal Court lets go of the case. Officials of the International Criminal Court . . . said this week that the indictments still stood but added that judges were reviewing them." Jeffrey Gettleman and Alexis Okeowo, "Warlord's Absence Derails Peace Effort in Uganda," *New York Times*, April 12, 2008, online at http://www .nytimes.com/2008/04/12/world/africa/12uganda.html (accessed September 13, 2008).

42. "Government of Uganda's Position at the Government of Uganda–Lord's Resistance Army Talks," July 19, 2006, online at http://www.ugpulse .com/articles/daily/homepage.asp?ID=458 (accessed February 15, 2008).

43. Charles Ariko, "Amnesty Act Extended for Two Years," August 6, 2008, online at http://www.newvision.co.ug/D/8/13/643331 (accessed September 13, 2008). This was the third renewal of this law since its enactment in 2000.

44. Amnesty International, "Uganda: Concerns about the International Criminal Court Bill 2004," AI index no. AFR 59/005/2004, July 27, 2004, http://www.amnesty.org/en/library/info/AFR59/005/2004 (originally accessed November 19, 2007).

45. Amnesty International, "International Criminal Court: The Failure of States to Enact Effective Implementing Legislation," AI Index no. IOR 40/019/2004, September 1, 2004, http://www.amnesty.org/en/library/info/IOR40/019/2004 (originally accessed November 19, 2007).

46. "Uganda: Cabinet through with Draft Law on Kisanja," Asia Africa Intelligence Wire, November 23, 2004, online at http://allafrica.com/stories/200411221726.html and http://www.accessmylibrary.com/coms2/summary_0286-14585205_ITM (accessed September 13, 2008). The second quotation is from field data collected by the author.

47. Field data on file with the author. It is not unusual that contemporary state legal systems contain parallel and often contradictory internal and international commitments to legal norms and their execution, extending across international, state, and customary law.

48. That is, under ICC guidelines for initiating an investigation; see Rome Statute, art. 53(1)(c).

49. As noted earlier, in April 2008, the ICC stated "that the indictments still stood but . . . that judges were reviewing them"; Gettleman and Okeowo, "Warlord's Absence Derails Peace Effort in Uganda."

50. ICC, Office of the Prosecutor, "The Interests of Justice," September 2007, p. 5, online at http://www.icc-cpi.int/library/organs/otp/ICC-OTP-InterestsOfJustice.pdf (accessed April 14, 2008).

51. Ibid., p. 7. A draft, "Internal OTP Discussion Paper" version of this document, circulated in June 2006 (and on file at Yale University, Department of Anthropology), noted: "in practice it is conceivable that . . . the interests of the victims may weigh against ICC action, especially when the victims themselves voice these concerns. . . . There is rarely a homogenous reaction among victims to atrocities: reactions and priorities vary for many different reasons."

52. Rome Statute, art. 53 (1). The article continues: "In deciding whether to initiate an investigation, the Prosecutor shall consider whether: (a) The information available to the Prosecutor provides a reasonable basis to believe that a crime within the jurisdiction of the Court has been or is being committed; (b) The case is or would be admissible under article 17; and (c) Taking into account the gravity of the crime and the interests of victims, there are nonetheless substantial reasons to believe that an investigation would not serve the interests of justice."

53. The two OTP documents of June 2006 were ICC, Office of the Prosecutor, "Criteria for Selection of Situations and Cases," draft policy paper; and the aforementioned "The Interests of Justice: Internal OTP Discussion Paper." Copies of these are on file at Yale University, Department of Anthropology.

54. ICC, OTP, Luis Moreno-Ocampo, "Statement by the Chief Prosecutor on the Uganda Arrest Warrants," The Hague, October 14, 2005, online at

http://www.icc-cpi.int/cases/UGD/c0105/c0105_pr.html (accessed February 16, 2008).

55. ICC, OTP, "Interests of Justice," p. 3.

56. See UN Security Council, "Security Council, Following Day-Long Debate, Underscores Critical Role of International Law in Fostering Global Stability, Order," press release, June 22, 2006, on 5474th meeting, http://www.un.org/News/Press/docs/2006/sc8762.doc.htm (accessed February 16, 2008): "Touching on another issue highlighted in today's debate, Nicolas Michel, under-Secretary-General for Legal Affairs and United Nations Legal Counsel, said that ending impunity for perpetrators of crimes against humanity was one of the principal evolutions in the culture of the world community and international law over the past 15 years. 'Justice should never be sacrificed by granting amnesty in ending conflicts,' he said, adding that justice and peace should be considered as complementary demands and that the international community should 'consider ways of dovetailing one with the other.'" The trend was confirmed in the statement of that month's president of the Security Council, Per Stig Møller of Denmark, that "the Council intends to continue forcefully to fight impunity with appropriate means and draws attention to the full range of justice and reconciliation mechanisms to be considered, including national, international and 'mixed' criminal courts and tribunals, and as truth and reconciliation commissions" (ibid.).

57. Report by Diane Orentlicher, "Report of the Independent Expert to Update the Set of Principles to Combat Impunity – Addendum: Updated Set of Principles for the Protection and Promotion of Human Rights through Action to Combat Impunity," UN Economic and Social Council, Commission on Human Rights E/CN.4/2005/102/Add.1, 61st Session, February 8, 2005, online at http://ap.ohchr.org/documents/alldocs.aspx?doc_id=10800 (accessed February 16, 2008). See, in particular, Principle 19, "Duties of States with Regard to the Administration of Justice": "States shall undertake prompt, thorough, independent and impartial investigations of violations of human rights and international humanitarian law and take appropriate measures in respect of the perpetrators, particularly in the area of criminal justice, by ensuring that those responsible for serious crimes under international law are prosecuted, tried and duly punished" (para. 1).

58. ICC, OTP, "Interests of Justice," 5: "In order for a case to be admissible, not only do the crimes have to be within the jurisdiction of the Court, but they must also meet the higher threshold of being of 'sufficient gravity to justify further action' of the Court in terms of Article 17(1)(d)."

59. ICC, OTP, "Criteria for Selection of Situations and Cases," draft policy paper.

60. [Hannah Gaertner,] "Uganda: No Amnesty for Atrocities," *Human Rights News*, July 28, 2006; online at http://hrw.org/english/docs/2006/07/27/uganda13863.htm (accessed February 12, 2008).
61. Ibid.
62. Ibid.
63. Documents on file with author.
64. Documents on file with author.
65. This and the following two quotations are from Zachary Lomo and James Otto, "Not a Crime to Talk: Give Peace a Chance in Northern Uganda," joint statement dated July 24, 2006, Kampala, online at http://www.refugeelawproject.org/resources/papers/others/press.Juba.pdf (accessed February 16, 2008).
66. Many of the legal documents generated for the production of the Rome Statute were the result of heated negotiations during the United Nations Conference of Plenipotentiaries (June 15–July 17, 1998), held in Rome. During 1996–8, ten sessions of the UN Preparatory Committee had been held in at the UN headquarters in New York to work on a draft statute that would create the legal authority to establish a permanent International Criminal Court. The UN's International Law Commission had produced a first draft. A working draft followed and was presented and debated by representatives from more than one hundred countries at the 1998 Rome Conference.
67. See the § "International NGOs and the Cosmopolitan Elite."
68. These relations have been further developed through the notion of the *homo sacer* developed in the context of the history of European state formation by Agamben (1998). Thus, the *homo sacer* (see next paragraph in the text) and changing forms of sovereignty can be applied to the new global order to explain struggles between national and traditional jurisdiction over Uganda's LRA in relation to the contradictory ascendance of the victims on the world stage.
69. Agamben (2005:1): "The essential contiguity between the state of exception and sovereignty was established by Carl Schmitt in his book *Politische Theologie* (1922)." The phrase "he who decides on the state of exception" is Schmitt's.
70. See Hansen and Stepputat (2005), and in particular Simon Turner's contribution, "Suspended Spaces – Contesting Sovereignties in a Refugee Camp," in that volume (312–32).
71. See § "Child Soldiers: Specters of International Justice."
72. See also Chris Dolan, "Inventing Traditional Leadership? A Critical Assessment of Denis Pain's 'The Bending of the Spears,'" COPE Working Paper 31, London and Nairobi: ACORD, online via http://www.acord.org.uk/b-resources.htm (accessed September 16, 2008).
73. See Introduction, § "Fictions and Specters of Justice."

Chapter 4

1. See, e.g., "Déclaration des droits de l'Homme et du citoyen," August 26, 1789 (hereinafter Rights of Man), art. 3; online in French at http://www .conseil-constitutionnel.fr/textes/d1789.htm and in English at http://www .hrcr.org/docs/frenchdec.html (both accessed January 16, 2008).
2. See United Nations, Rome Statute of the International Criminal Court, UN Doc. A/CONF.183/9, July 17, 1998 (hereafter Rome Statute), art. 12; online at http://untreaty.un.org/cod/icc/statute/romefra.htm and http://www.icc-cpi.int/about/Official_Journal.html (accessed November 2, 2007).
3. "Principles of International Law Recognized in the Charter of the Nuremberg Tribunal and in the Judgment of the Tribunal, 1950," online at http://www.icrc.org/ihl.nsf/FULL/390?OpenDocument (accessed January 18, 2008).
4. Laws of the Federation of Nigeria, Criminal Code Act, chap. 77 (1990; revised edition), online at http://www.nigeria-law.org/Criminal% 20Code%20Act-Tables.htm (accessed January 19, 2008).
5. Much of this section, like parts of other sections of this chapter, derives from Clarke (2006).
6. These sectarian clashes represented the protestors' disagreement with the pageant. They argued that the allowances for female nudity produced a situation in which contestants were not only vulgar and indecent but also insulting to Islamic precepts of modesty. The initial violence represented both a reaction to that irreverence and a defense of the Prophet. Interviews by Kamari Maxine Clarke, in Abuja, Nigeria (December 2002).
7. Jessi Herman, "A Divided Nigeria," Institute for Global Engagement, November 30, 2001, at paras. 2–3, http://www.globalengagement.org/ issues/2001/11/nigeria.htm (accessed January 5, 2006).
8. "Muslims Condemn Nigerian 'Fatwa,'" BBC News, November 29, 2002, at paras. 4–6, http://news.bbc.co.uk/2/hi/africa/2525573.stm; "Writer's Anger over Miss World Deaths," BBC News, January 18, 2003, at para. 8, http://news.bbc.co.uk/2/hi/africa/2671229.stm (both accessed January 5, 2006).
9. "Muslims Condemn Nigerian 'Fatwa,'" at para. 6; "Writer's Anger over Miss World Deaths," at para. 7.
10. Research by Kamari Maxine Clarke, in Abuja, Nigeria (December 2002) (on file with author).
11. Ibid.
12. Ultimately, the pageant organizers moved the pageant to London, England. As a result, contracts were broken and millions of investment dollars lost to these violent protests. See "Muslims Condemn Nigerian 'Fatwa,'" at para. 5. However, these protests were connected to long histories of strife

between Christians and Muslims in the Nigerian north and to ongoing political instability in the region. See "Africa's Press Reflect on Miss World Riots," *BBC News*, November 29, 2002, at paras. 10–11, http://news.bbc .co.uk/2/hi/africa/2527339.stm (accessed January 4, 2006).

13. "Writer's Anger over Miss World Deaths," at para. 5. Kaduna is a city with a predominantly Muslim majority of more than two million residents. See Herman, "Divided Nigeria," at para. 4.

14. Interviews by Kamari Maxine Clarke, in Abuja, Nigeria (December 2002). Surely as people were fleeing, others were also capitalizing on the opportunity to vandalize stores and market stalls, engaging in the theft of valuable goods (ibid.).

15. See "Nigeria: Over 200 Killed in 'Miss World' Pageant Riots," *Facts on File World News Digest*, November 21, 2002 (accessed January 8, 2006); "Miss World Abandons Nigeria," *Mail & Guardian*, January 1, 2002 [*sic*], http://www.mg.co.za/articledirect.aspx?area=mg_flat&articleid=12535 (accessed January 8, 2006); U.S. Dept. of State, Bureau of Democracy, Human Rights, and Labor, *International Religious Freedom Report 2003* (December 18, 2003), "Nigeria," http://www.state.gov/g/drl/rls/irf/2003/ 23745.htm (accessed January 8, 2006).

16. See CIA World Factbook, "Nigeria," online at https://www.cia.gov/ library/publications/the-world-factbook/geos/ni.html (accessed May 24, 2008).

17. Although there continue to be disputes over the actual population breakdown, the figures given are those of the CIA World Factbook, "Nigeria," online at https://www.cia.gov/library/publications/the-world-factbook/geos/ni.html (accessed January 19, 2008). Regions are per *International Religious Freedom Report 2003*, "Nigeria."

18. *Sharia* is an Arabic word that means "the way to the watering place." It highlights "the way" – that is, the path or road that every Muslim has to follow to earn the pleasures of life and to avoid the wrath of wrongdoing. The Sharia, also referred to as Islamic law, is considered to be a divine law, the authority of which depends on the revealed word of Allah, or God. Its formal structure is embedded in the complex of divinely revealed rules to which the Muslim faithful are expected to submit. Because it is a code for living for Muslims, a major feature of the Sharia is that it draws no distinction between the religious and the secular; between legal, ethical, and moral questions; or between the public and private aspects of a Muslim's life. Unlike the popular technical definition of Western law, which highlights written and unwritten rules that are enforced by coercive powers of the state, the validity of Sharia is located in the manifest will of Allah, and its principles represent a broader sphere that encompasses outward conduct, moral value, and cultural principles.

19. See also Michael Gallagher, "The Many Faces of Sharia," *BBC News*, June 21, 2000, http://news.bbc.co.uk/2/hi/africa/621126.stm (accessed January 19, 2008).

20. Hauwa Ibrahim and Princeton N. Lyman, "Reflections on the New Shari'a Law in Nigeria," June 2004, Africa Policy Studies Program at the Council on Foreign Relations, online at http://www.cfr.org/content/ publications/attachments/Reflections_on_the_New_Sharia_in_Nigeria.pdf (accessed January 19, 2008).

21. See also Herman, "Divided Nigeria," 5–6.

22. The basic principle of the everlasting life of the soul after the death of the body is found not in only Islam but also in Christianity, Hinduism, and Buddhism.

23. Here the modern concept of death and one strand of Islamic concepts of death can be argued as being divergent.

24. It has been suggested that Islamic faith requires that those who defy the authority of the state because of contravening faith-based convictions should be treated with indulgence.

25. Research by Kamari Maxine Clarke, in Abuja, Nigeria (December 2002) (on file with author).

26. Ibid.

27. A fatwa is issued in response to a question posed to a mufti by an individual or court of law. The religious jurist's authoritative legal interpretation provides the basis for a court decision or government action on issues not covered by the *fiqh* (Islamic jurisprudence) literature and, therefore, is neither binding nor enforceable in secular state contexts. Often the authority of the fatwa is determined by the mufti's level of education and status within the community.

28. Cf. Rome Statue, at art. 6, and "Convention on the Prevention and Punishment of the Crime of Genocide," art. 2, UN General Assembly resolution 260 A (III), adopted December 9, 1948 (entered into force January 12, 1951), 78 U.N.T.S. 277; online at http://www.unhchr.ch/html/menu3/b/p_genoci.htm (accessed January 20, 2008).

29. International Law Commission, "Draft Code of Crimes against the Peace and Security of Mankind," art. 17, U.N. GAOR, 51st Sess., U.N. Doc. A/CN.4/532 (1996); online at http://untreaty.un.org/ilc/texts/ instruments/english/draft%20articles/7_4_1996.pdf (accessed January 20, 2008).

30. See "Statute of the International Criminal Tribunal for the Former Yugoslavia," art. 4, UNSCR 827, U.N. SCOR, 48th Sess., 3217th mtg., U.N. Doc. S/RES/827 (1993), *amended by* UNSCR 1166, U.N. SCOR, 53rd Sess., 3878th mtg., U.N. Doc. S/RES/1166 (1998) (hereafter ICTY Statute), online at http://www.un.org/icty/legaldoc-e/basic/ statut/statute-feb08-e.pdf; see also *Prosecutor v. Goran Jelisić*, Case

No. IT-95-10-T, Judgment (December 14, 1999), at http://www.un. org/icty/jelisic/trialc1/judgement/index.htm (both accessed January 20, 2008). Mr. Jelisic was convicted by the Trial Chamber for "violations of the laws or customs of war and crimes against humanity, committed in May 1992 in Brčko, a town... in north-eastern Bosnia and Herzegovina.... The Trial Chamber imposed a single sentence of 40 years' imprisonment, the harshest sentence handed down by a Trial Chamber of the Tribunal at the time." ICTY Statute, Judicial Supplement 26; *Prosecutor v. Goran Jelisić*, Case No. IT-95-10-A (July 5, 2001), at http://www.un .org/icty/Supplement/supp26-e/jelisic.htm (accessed January 20, 2008).

31. See "Statute of the International Criminal Tribunal for Rwanda," art. 2, UNSCR 955, U.N. SCOR, 49th Sess., 3453th mtg., U.N. Doc. S/ RES/955 (1994), at http://www.un.org/ictr/statute.html (accessed January 20, 2008).

32. Professor Whitley Kaufman (2003) has shown that there has been significant criticism against this doctrine because some critics have felt that judges do tend to consider motive. By showing the mischaracterization of the role of motive, he attempts to uphold the orthodox assumption that motive is irrelevant.

33. Rome Statute, at art. 28 (a).

34. Schabas 2004:38 ("What sets genocide apart from crimes against humanity and war crimes is that the act... must be committed with the specific intent to destroy in whole or in part a national, ethnical, racial or religious group as such"); see also *American Jurisprudence 2d*, vol. 21: *Criminal Law*, §§ 127–8 (St. Paul, MN: Thomson West, 1981).

35. Ibid., at §127.

36. Specific intent is defined as the "intent to accomplish the precise criminal act that one is later charged with." Bryan A. Garner, ed., *Black's Law Dictionary*, 8th ed., 826 (St. Paul, MN: Thomson West, 2004). The most common usage of specific intent is to designate a special mental element that is required above and beyond any mental state required with respect to the *actus reus* (lit.: "bad act") of the crime. Common law larceny, for example, requires the taking and carrying away of the property of another, and the defendant's mental state as to this act must be established, but in addition it must be shown that there was an "intent to deprive the possessor of [the property] permanently" (ibid.:896). Similarly, common law burglary requires a breaking and entry into the dwelling of another, but in addition to the mental state connected with these acts, it must also be established that the defendant acted "with the intent to commit a felony therein" (ibid.:211). Ultimately, a defendant must not only intend the act as charged but also intend to violate law (ibid.:825).

37. Rome Statute, art. 6.

38. *Mens rea* – i.e., intent (lit.: "guilty mind") – means that a person knowingly engages in conduct in which he or she means to cause the consequence or is aware that the consequence will occur as a result of his or her actions. See *Black's Law Dictionary*, 825, 1006.

39. Ibid., at 826.

40. The reality is that where genocide is concerned, often the principle actor, the person who carries out the murder, lacks genocidal intent. Instead, the tendency is that subordinates are incited by leaders who possess the intent to "destroy the group, in whole or in part." It is the leader, as accomplice, who possesses the intent required in Article 6 of the Rome Statute. Thus, according to international criminal law, it is likely that the said party would be found culpable, despite the fact that the subordinate lacks special intent. The principle offenders would therefore be guilty of murder, not genocide, because they were unaware of genocidal intent. In an attempt to classify criminal action, the prosecution must look for narrowly tailored conduct and the intended results of action. See Schabas 2004:29–30.

41. Ibid., at 38. The elements of the crime of genocide enumerated in Rome Statute, art. 6 – and with the same wording in the Genocide Code et al. – are the following: "(a) Killing members of the group; (b) Causing serious bodily or mental harm to members of the group; (c) Deliberately inflicting on the group conditions of life calculated to bring about its physical destruction in whole or in part; (d) Imposing measures intended to prevent births within the group; (e) Forcibly transferring children of the group to another group."

42. Rome Statute, art. 25 (3) (f).

43. However, in the absence of proof that actual orders were given, the statute outlines two approaches. The first, undermining the common law presumption of innocence, is to presume that the commander ordered his or her subordinate to commit the crimes. The second is to prosecute the commander not for ordering the commission of the crime but for negligence in failing to prevent it from happening. See Rome Statute, art. 28.

44. Article 28 (b) of the Rome Statute is concerned with the superior responsibility of civilian leaders.

45. This is derived from a range of orthodox interpretations in which the following Qur'anic verses were cited by northern Nigerian jurors: "And fight in the way of Allah against those who fight against you, but be not aggressive surely Allah loves not the aggressors" (Qur'an,2:190); "And if they break their oaths after their agreement and revile your religion, then fight the leaders of disbelief" (Qur'an, 9:12).

46. See § "The Response of Religious Revivalism" earlier in the chapter.

47. See, e.g., Rome Statute, arts. 27 and 28.

48. This point should be seen in relation to the political process that produced member states that are legally obliged to concede to the jurisdiction of the state. For even in this realm of victim's rights and democratic commitments by Northern states to the rule of law, the majority of member states to the UN Security Council are not ratified member states to the Rome Statute of the ICC. This circumscribes the political possibilities for pursuing genocide everywhere – thus its concentration on cases in Africa).

49. For example, whereas some previous tribunals have held primary or concurrent jurisdiction, the ICC follows the *principle of complementarity*, according to which national courts hold jurisdictional primacy. The ICC may take jurisdiction if a state is deemed unable or unwilling to investigate an allegation that the prosecutor for the ICC identifies as a possible violation consistent with crimes of the types the court is authorized to pursue. See Rome Statute, art. 1.

50. Talcott Parsons (1968) used the idea of "modernization" as a lens through which to view all developments in "non-Western" societies, further highlighting a decrease, not an increase, in religion in public life.

51. In the Preamble to France's current constitution, "The French people solemnly proclaim their attachment" (*proclame solennellement son attachement*) to the 1789 Rights of Man. "Constitution de la Cinquième République Constitution" (June 3, 1958), in French at http://www.solon.org/Constitutions/France/French/cons58.html and in English at http://www.assemblee-nationale.fr/english/8ab.asp (both accessed January 16, 2008).

52. These, of course, comprise Amendments I–X of the U.S. Constitution; online at http://www.archives.gov/national-archives-experience/charters/bill_of_rights_transcript.html (accessed January 16, 2008).

53. The Covenant of the League of Nations, a component of the 1919 Treaty of Versailles, entered into force January 10, 1920 (Howard-Ellis 1929, 98–9). The failure of the League set precedence for the gap between universal moral pursuits of liberalism and the ability to follow through domestically as well as on a global scale. Exemplary of this is the United States' refusal to ratify the covenant, as well as the nation's policies of racial segregation, which dominated its domestic policy well into the late 1960s. For the covenant itself, see http://www.firstworldwar.com/source/leagueofnations.htm (accessed January 10, 2008).

54. The United Nations was set up with five permanent members of the Security Council having veto power and many states still under colonial rule; it was the General Assembly that became the organ for the public expressions of common interests and the diplomatic "will" of the international community (Schachter 1991/2000: 246). For example, the General Assembly considered the most fundamental principles of law – that there

can be no punishment of crime without a preexisting law (*nullum crimen sine lege, nulla poena sine lege*) – to reconsider the authority of the newly formed UN to punish German acts ex post facto (Steiner and Alston 2000:116–18).

55. "A Universal Declaration of Human Rights," G.A. Res. 217A (III), at 71, U.N. GAOR, 3d Sess., 1st Plen. Mtg., U.N. Doc A/810 (Dec. 10, 1948) (hereafter UDHR), available for download (in six languages) at http://www.un.org/Docs/asp/ws.asp?m=A/RES/217%20(III) or for reading online at http://www.un.org/Overview/rights.html (both accessed January 10, 2008). A verbatim record of the UDHR's adoption at the Hundred and Eighty-third Plenary Meeting, Palais de Chaillot, Paris, may be downloaded from http://www.un.org/Depts/dhl/landmark/amajor.htm (accessed January 10, 2008).

56. "Convention for the Protection of Human Rights and Fundamental Freedoms," Rome, November 4, 1950; available at http://conventions.coe.int/Treaty/en/Treaties/Html/005.htm (accessed January 10, 2008).

57. Organization of American States Inter-American Specialized Conference on Human Rights, "American Convention on Human Rights," San José, Costa Rica, November 22, 1969; available at http://www.cidh.org/Basicos/English/Basic3.American%20Convention.htm (accessed January 10, 2008).

58. Organisation of African Unity, "African (Banjul) Charter on Human and Peoples' Rights," Nairobi, Kenya, adopted June 27, 1981, OAU Doc. CAB/LEG/67/3 rev. 5, 21 I.L.M. 58 (1982); available for download at http://www.africa-union.org/root/au/Documents/Treaties/treaties.htm (accessed January 10, 2008).

59. "Charter of the United Nations" (hereafter UN Charter), adopted June 26, 1945 (entered into force October 24, 1945), 59 Stat. 1031, T.S. 993, 3 Bevans 1153; available at http://www.un.org/aboutun/charter/ (accessed January 18, 2008). Security Council authorization is covered by arts. 39–50, self-defense by art. 51.

60. "Iraq: Resolution 1441," advice (marked Secret) of British Attorney General Lord Goldsmith to Prime Minister Blair regarding UNSCR 1441 and the legality of the Iraq War, March 7, 2003, para. 4; available at http://cms.isn.ch/public/docs/doc_10669_290_en.pdf (accessed January 18, 2008). This third criterion was the justification for the handling of the Kosovo crisis of the 1990s, as well as for No-Fly Zones (ibid.).

61. Highlighting that which appears outside of the norm for legitimate violence, Goldsmith's report makes clear that the argument of self-defense is justified only "if there is an actual or imminent threat of an armed attack" (ibid., para. 3). In other words, the use of force must be seen as necessary and deployed as a means of averting an attack – and thus a proportionate response in the context of imminent danger. Cf. UN Charter, which

allows for self-defense only "if an armed attack occurs" (art. 51), with no mention of imminence.

62. UDHR, Preamble.

Chapter 5

1. In particular, my research was conducted in such Nigerian states as Zam-fara, Kaduna, and Niger. As a non-Nigerian, non-Muslim woman traveling with a research entourage of male research assistants, undergraduate and graduate students, as well as Nigerian legal scholars and defense attorneys, gaining clearance to observe court hearings was not always easy. When-ever I found myself traveling without the company of a male Muslim, gaining access was all the more difficult.

2. Interview data on file with author. Dan Isaacs, "Nigerian Woman Fights Stoning," July 8, 2002, BBC News, World Edition, online at http://news .bbc.co.uk/1/hi/world/africa/2115278.stm (accessed December 3, 2007).

3. U.S. Dept. of State, Bureau of Democracy, Human Rights, and Labor, *International Religious Freedom Report 2001* (October 26, 2001), "Nige-ria," http://www.state.gov/g/drl/rls/irf/2001/5687.htm (accessed February 18, 2008).

4. Terms such as *thief* and *recompense* require interpretation as to who and what they pertain to and when they should be applied.

5. David Bamford, "Hand Amputation in Nigeria," *BBC News*, July 7, 2001, online at http://news.bbc.co.uk/2/hi/africa/1428159.stm (accessed Febru-ary 19, 2008).

6. CIA World Factbook, "Nigeria," online at https://www.cia.gov/library/ publications/the-world-factbook/geos/ni.html (accessed February 19, 2008).

7. Robert Lalasz, "In the News: The Nigerian Census," April 1, 2006, online at http://www.prb.org/Articles/2006/IntheNewsTheNigerianCensus.aspx (accessed February 19, 2008).

8. See Chapter 4, § "Islam and Sharia, Duties and Obligations."

9. See Chapter 1, § "Moral Economies and Praxeology."

10. The emir was the person who initially heard such land and finance matters. The title *emir* referred both to head of state and supreme judge. Preoccupied with executive matters, the emir increasingly delegated most of the judicial work to trusted officials who had made a specialty of law. These officials, each known as an alkali (*plural*: alkalai), served as professional judges: they did not have an executive or administrative function, which meant there was a separation of agencies discharging executive and judiciary functions.

11. Islamic personal law was first referred to as the "law of the com-munity"; the basis for jurisdiction in British common law was

known as the "law of the territory." See also Joy Ngozi Ezeilo, Muhammed Tawfiq Ladan, and Abiola Afolabi-Akiyode, eds., *Shari'a Implementation in Nigeria: Issues & Challenges on Women's Rights and Access to Justice* (Enugu, Nigeria: Women's Aid Collective/Lagos: Women's Advocates Research and Documentation Centre, 2003), online at http://www.boellnigeria.org/documents/Sharia%20Implementation% 20in%20Nigeria.pdf (accessed April 11, 2008).

12. Native Court Ordinance, 1933, sec. 10 (2).

13. British Colonial Office (1958) (the so-called Willink Report), 66–9.

14. Four of the jurists were Muslim: Sayad Mohammed Abu Ranat (chief justice of the Sudan), who was panel chairman; Justice Mohammed Sherif (chairman of the Pakistan Law Commission); Shettima Kashim (waziri of Bornu); and M. Musa (chief alkali of Bida). Two of the jurists were Christian: Mr. Peter Achimugu (a member of the "minority" ethnic groups in the northern region) and Professor J. N. D. Anderson (professor of Oriental law at the University of London). Chairman Abu Ranat, Sherif, and Anderson were all experts in common law and Islamic law.

15. This was modeled on the Sudan Penal Code. Obi N.I. Ebbe, "Nigeria," 1993, in *World Factbook of Criminal Justice Systems*, online at http://www .ojp.usdoj.gov/bjs/pub/ascii/wfbcjnig.txt (accessed February 19, 2008).

16. The leader's response to this trend was the implementation of a punishment for apostasy that restricted the ability of people to change their religion. This innovation, however, presented a challenge to the federal system, which protected the rights of citizens to religious freedom. It also accorded legal freedoms to the accused that state officials felt should have been authorized by government alone. Even when this law was abolished in 1961, thereby restricting Muslims from such freedoms, Muslim judges continued to exercise personal jurisdiction over all citizens within its state.

17. For background see § "Islam and Sharia, Duties and Obligations" in Chapter 4.

18. United Nations, Rome Statute of the International Criminal Court, UN Doc. A/CONF.183/9, July 17, 1998 (hereafter Rome Statute), art. 7, online at http://untreaty.un.org/cod/icc/statute/romefra.htm and http://www.icc-cpi.int/about/Official_Journal.html.

19. U.S. Dept. of State, Bureau of Democracy, Human Rights, and Labor, *International Religious Freedom Report 2001* (October 26, 2001), "Nigeria," online at http://www.state.gov/g/drl/rls/irf/2001/5687.htm; and "Nigerian Flogging Condemned," *BBC News*, January, 23, 2001, online at http://news.bbc.co.uk/2/hi/africa/1132168.stm (both accessed February 18, 2008).

20. See Asifa Quraishi, "Her Honor: An Islamic Critique of the Rape Laws of Pakistan from a Woman-Sensitive Perspective," online at http://www .karamah.org/articles_quraishi.htm (accessed April 11, 2008).

21. The term *muhsan* is variously defined, but two good working definitions are "a free person – male or female – who is in a position to enjoy lawful wedlock" (Sidahmed 2001:190) and "a free person (i.e., someone not a slave) with no prior conviction of illicit sex" (Peirce 2003:134). A stricter legal definition is found, e.g., in Pakistan's "The Offence of Zina (Enforcement of Hudood) Ordinance, 1979," sec. 2: "(d) 'Muhsan' means (i) a Muslim adult man who is not insane and has had sexual intercourse with a Muslim adult woman who, at the time he had sexual intercourse with her, was married to him and was not insane, or (ii) a Muslim adult woman who is not insane and has had sexual intercourse with a Muslim adult man who, at the time she had sexual intercourse with him, was married to her and was not insane." Online at http://www.pakistani.org/pakistan/legislation/zia_po_1979/ord7_1979.html (accessed February 20, 2008).

22. This case is covered in some detail in BAOBAB for Women's Human Rights, "Sharia Implementation in Nigeria: The Journey So Far," Lagos: BAOBAB, 2003, 15–17, online at http://www.baobabwomen.org/publications_womenshr.htm (accessed February 21, 2008); and in Human Rights Watch [Carina Tertsakian et al.], "Political Shari'a"? "Human Rights and Islamic Law in Northern Nigeria," *HRW Report* 16.9(A) (September 2004), 25–30, online at http://www.hrw.org/reports/2004/nigeria0904/index.htm (accessed February 20, 2008).

23. Initially, before taking the matter to court, the father had demanded a bride price of 10,000 naira (c. US$70/GBP 50), but Ahmadu could afford only 5,000. Human Rights Watch, *"Political Shari'a"?*, 25, and Dennis Elam, "I Fell in Love with a Married Man and Am Having a Baby . . . and Now," *Sunday Mirror (London)*, December 22, 2002, online at http://findarticles.com/p/articles/mi_qn4161/is_20021222/ai_n12852602 (accessed February 21, 2008).

24. This sequence of events in the case are the result of the Upper Area Court judge being advised at Minna that he had erred in his judgment, having failed to act on the revisions to the recently Sharia-ized penal code, in which secs. 387 and 388 of the Sharia Code of Niger State had been amended to death by stoning. As a result, both defendants, having already been convicted of *zina*, were newly sentenced to death – while already serving their time in jail. Human Rights Watch, *"Political Shari'a"?*, 26–7; BAOBAB, "Sharia Implementation in Nigeria," 16. Such a procedural error is an example of the internal politics of Sharia-ization as criticized in public discourse.

25. Contrary to particular secular dismissals of preparing for the conditions of life after death, various forms of Nigerian Islamic reverence for the sacredness of life encompasses this sacredness even in "death" (see Chapter 4, § "Islam and Sharia, Duties and Obligations"). Views on this matter highlight key tenets for which human relationships with "God" are sustained,

and thus justice procured. Therefore, detailing the particular ways that individuals cultivate the self in relation to submission to God are important for making assessments about how to understand various paths to justice.

26. Data on file with author.

27. Author interview with Ahmadu Ibrahim and Fatima Usman, July 15, 2005 (hereafter cited in text as Interview 7/15/05).

28. See "Court Transcript for the Upper Area Court New Gawu – Judge: Abdulrahaman Alhassan; Plaintiff: Commissioner of Police Niger State; Defendants: (1) Ahmadu Ibrahim; (2) Fatima Usman Lambata; Court Adjourned until May 28, 2002."

29. BAOBAB, "Sharia Implementation in Nigeria," 16.

30. See also Chapter 4, § "Radical Islam and Its Spaces of Power."

31. Interview on file with author.

Chapter 6

1. This case is outlined in Human Rights Watch [Carina Tertsakian et al.], *"Political Shari'a"? Human Rights and Islamic Law in Northern Nigeria,* HRW Report 16.9(A) (September 2004), 34, online at http://www.hrw.org/reports/2004/nigeria0904/index.htm (accessed February 20, 2008), as well as in BAOBAB for Women's Human Rights, "Sharia Implementation in Nigeria: The Journey So Far," Lagos: BAOBAB, 2003, 13–14, online at http://www.baobabwomen.org/publications_womenshr.htm (accessed February 21, 2008). See also Chikodi Okerecha, "Should Safiya Die," online at http://www.onlinenigeria.com/safiya.asp (accessed February 21, 2008).

2. As noted in Chapter 5 (§ "Politics, Agency, and the Crime of *Zina*"), the term *zina* covers not only adultery but also fornication.

3. Because Safiya was pregnant, however, her sentence had been delayed until after the two-year period necessary for weaning the infant. This and other details of the application of Sharia law in this case are given in Women's Aid Collective (WACOL), "Safiyyatu's Case," 2002, online at http://www.wacolnigeria.org/Safiyyatu_case.doc (accessed February 23, 2008).

4. "Nigerian Woman Condemned to Death by Stoning Is Acquitted," *New York Times*, March 26, 2002, online at http://query.nytimes.com/gst/fullpage.html?res=9F05E4DF123BF935A15750C0A9649C8B63 (accessed February 21, 2008). Although she had already been divorced for two years, there is precedent under Islamic law that "a woman can be divorced while pregnant and carry that pregnancy for 5 years before delivery"; WACOL, "Safiyyatu's Case," 26. This idea of the "sleeping embryo" is addressed further below in the § "Case Study: Amina Lawal."

5. See Chapter 5 (§ "Politics, Agency, and the Crime of *Zina*").
6. By this time, the United States had been at war for five and a half months with Afghanistan, where the impact on women of the Taliban's enforcement of Sharia law had already drawn international attention. Also by then, 170 nation-states had either ratified or acceded to the 1979 Convention on the Elimination of All Forms of Discrimination against Women.
7. "Amina was convicted based on the fact that she had this baby without a husband and that she confessed. Her confession from the trial court record was that, when they ask her, 'You have this baby and you are not married?' And she said, 'Yes,' and that was what was termed as a confession." "Nigerian Women Speak Out: Hauwa Ibrahim, Amina Lawal's Attorney," *FRONTLINE World*, January 2003, online at http://www.pbs.org/frontlineworld/stories/nigeria/voice01.html (accessed February 26, 2008).
8. Regarding the pageant controversy, see Chapter 4 (§ "The Response of Religious Revivalism").
9. The proceedings were postponed on three separate occasions: on March 25, 2003, it was adjourned until June 3, 2003, then again until August 27, 2003, at which time her appeal was entertained; the case was then reserved for judgment until September 25, 2003.
10. Note that the International Criminal Court had come into force on July 1, 2002, providing new means to pursue such issues on an international level.
11. On erroneous or inflammatory online campaigns, see the § "Good-Willed Democracy: Feminist NGOs and the Errors of Protest" later in this chapter.
12. See § "Islam and Sharia, Duties and Obligations."
13. The *mazhab* (or *madh'hab*) Maliki, named for the famed eighth-century Imam Malik, is one of several extant schools of Islamic jurisprudence.
14. "Court Record from the Upper Sharia Court of Katsina State; Holden at Funtua. Appeal No. 1/2002; Between Appellant, Amina Lawal Kurami and Respondent, The State."
15. The word *muhsinat* is an alternative spelling of *muhsanat*, the feminine plural of *muhsan* (a Muslim now or ever married), which we encountered in Chapter 5 (see § "Politics, Agency, and the Crime of *Zina*").
16. SWT is the abbreviation for the phrase *Subhanahu wa ta'ala* ("glorious and exalted is He [Allah]"), used when invoking Allah's name. Likewise, SAW abbreviates *Sallallahu 'alayhi wasallam* ("Peace be upon him"), often used when invoking the name of the Prophet Muhammad.
17. See "Constitution of the Federal Republic of Nigeria," 1999, esp. sec. 15 (2), "discrimination on the grounds of . . . sex . . . shall be prohibited"; and sec. 42 (1), "A citizen of Nigeria of a particular . . . sex . . . shall not, by reason only that he is such a person: (a) be subjected either expressly by, or in the practical application of, any law in force

in Nigeria." Available at http://www.nigeria-law.org/ConstitutionOfThe
FederalRepublicOfNigeria.htm (accessed February 24, 2008).

18. In both Safiya's and Amina's court cases, BAOBAB for Women's Human
Rights provided legal defense teams comprising professionals who understood the issues of civil and political human rights. Economic support was
also accepted from donor agencies that offered it in the interest of promoting progress toward democratization in Nigeria, increasing transparency
in governance and law, and working to eliminate discrimination against
women.

19. See, e.g., Dr. Ayesha Imam of BAOBAB: "I don't know how [the reports]
originated – they're all over the Internet. It has been suggested that they
might come from mistranslations of appeals for international petitions.
All I know is that there are far too many of them." "Amina Lawal Campaign 'Unhelpful'," *BBC News*, May 13, 2003, online at http://news.bbc
.co.uk/2/hi/africa/3024563.stm (accessed February 23, 2004).

20. See, e.g., the press release "Amnesty International Welcomes Decision
to Spare Amina Lawal's Life," September 25, 2003, in which Curt Goer-
ing, Senior Deputy Executive Director for Amnesty International USA,
was recorded as saying, "We congratulate the millions of activists ... who
voiced their opposition to such a cruel and unusual punishment." Online
at https://lists.resist.ca/pipermail/project-x/2003-September/004465.html
(accessed February 25, 2004).

21. Chidi 'Uzor et al., "Aftermath of Death Sentence on Amina Lawal: France,
Belgium Pull Out of Miss World Contest," *This Day Online*, September 7, 2002, online at http://www.thisdayonline.com/archive/2002/09/
07/20020907news03.html and http://www.ccadp.org/aminalawal-news/
2002.htm (both accessed February 25, 2008).

22. See their Web page "Internet Petitions and Letter-Writing Campaigns –
Yes or No?: The Story of Amina Lawal," online at http://www
.canadiansocialresearch.net/petition.htm (accessed February 25, 2004).

23. Unlike the modern state system of the seventeenth to twentieth century, in which interstate relations were guided by internal legal norms
and principles of subjecthood and citizenship, today the norms that are
being mobilized are working through the engine of global capital and are
leveling the ideological principles of exclusion that were once embodied
in relationships to the state alone.

24. "Amina Lawal Petition," http://urbanlegends.about.com/library/blamina
-lawal.htm (accessed February 24, 2004).

25. Amnesty International, "Nigeria: False Information about Amnesty
International's Campaign on Amina Lawal," press release, May 6,
2003, online at http://www.amnestyusa.org/document.php?lang=e&id=
80256AB9000584F680256D1E005C0314 (accessed February 25, 2008).

26. I was told that many of the defense team members' lives were threatened.

27. Many did not understand that even if the Sharia Court of Appeal affirmed the lower court's holding, there were still levels of recourse for relief from execution by the Federal Court of Appeal as well as the Supreme Court of Nigeria.

28. See also the related discussion in Chapter 5 (§ "Sharia-ization in Nigeria, post-1999").

29. Imam's concerns were also expressed to BBC World Service's *Everywoman* program: "Amina Lawal Campaign 'Unhelpful'," *BBC News*, May 13, 2003, online at http://news.bbc.co.uk/2/hi/africa/3024563.stm (accessed February 23, 2008).

30. Ibid.

31. Ayesha Imam and Sindi Medar-Gould, "How Not to Help Amina Lawal: The Hidden Dangers of Letter Campaigns," *CounterPunch*, May 15, 2003, online at http://www.counterpunch.org/iman05152003.html (accessed February 26, 2003).

32. Ibid.

33. WLUML-AME stands for Women Living under Muslim Laws International Solidarity Network – Africa and Middle East.

34. Data on file with author.

35. See § "Changes in Colonial Governance: Vernacularizing the Judicial Reach of Courts."

36. See, e.g., Motherland Nigeria, "Legal," online at http://www.motherlandnigeria.com/legal.html (accessed February 26, 2008). The third highest level is the Federal High Court, which has jurisdiction over civil matters as well as matters relating to revenue/taxation of the government of the Federation. Civil or criminal jurisdiction may be conferred upon it by an act of the National Assembly. After the Federal High Court are the State High Courts, which have jurisdiction to hear civil proceedings as well as any criminal proceedings involving or relating to any penalty, forfeiture, punishment, or other liability related to an offense committed by any person.

37. Ibid.

38. See the diagram in § "Judicial Precedents," Yemisi Dina, John Akintayo, and Funke Ekundayo, "Guide to Nigerian Legal Information" (February 2005), online at http://www.nyulawglobal.org/globalex/nigeria.htm (accessed April 11, 2008).

39. Hauwa Ibrahim and Princeton N. Lyman, "Reflections on the New Shari'a Law in Nigeria," June 2004, Africa Policy Studies Program at the Council on Foreign Relations, 21, online at http://www.cfr.org/content/publications/attachments/Reflections_on_the_New_Sharia_in_Nigeria.pdf (accessed January 29, 2008).

40. This *fiqh* was introduced earlier in this chapter (§ "Case Study: Amina Lawal").

41. Ibrahim and Lyman, "Reflections on the New Shari'a Law in Nigeria," 30–1.
42. Ibid., 33.
43. See the discussion of the UDHR in Chapter 4 (within § "Genealogies of 'Secularism' and the Politics of Constitutive Power").
44. "A Universal Declaration of Human Rights," adopted and proclaimed by General Assembly resolution A/RES/217 (III) of December 10, 1948, available for download (in six languages) at http://www .un.org/Docs/asp/ws.asp?m=A/RES/217%20(III) or for reading online at http://www.un.org/Overview/rights.html (both accessed January 10, 2008).
45. See § "Good-Willed Democracy: Feminist NGOs and the Errors of Protest."
46. Regarding "justice talk," see Chapter 1 (§ "Moral Economies and Praxeology").
47. For more on this use of universality, see the Introduction (§ "The ICC and Competing Notions of Justice in Africa") and Chapter 4 (§ "Secular versus Nonsecular Forms of Violence").
48. Ibrahim and Lyman, "Reflections on the New Shari'a Law in Nigeria," 25.
49. Ibid.
50. Ibid., 26.

BIBLIOGRAPHY

Abdel Haleem, M. A. S., trans. 2004. *The Qur'an*. Oxford: Oxford University Press.

Abdullah, Ibrahim, ed. 2000. *Between Democracy and Terror: The Sierra Leone Civil War*. Dakar, Senegal: Codesria.

Abou El Fadl, Khaled. 1998a. "Political Crime in Islamic Jurisprudence and Western Legal History." *U.C. Davis Journal of International Law and Policy* 4.1: 1–28.

1998b. "Striking a Balance: Islamic Legal Discourses on Muslim Minorities." In *Muslims on the Americanization Path?* ed. Yvonne Yazbeck Haddad and John L. Esposito, 47–64. Atlanta: Scholars Press.

2003. *Reasoning with God: Rationality and Thought in Islam*. Oxford: Oneworld.

Adriani, John. 1961. "Some New Anesthetic Agents." *American Journal of Nursing* 61.5: 60–2.

Agamben, Giorgio. 1998. *Homo Sacer: Sovereign Power and Bare Life*. Trans. Daniel Heler-Roazen. Stanford, CA: Stanford University Press.

2005. *State of Exception*. Trans. Kevin Attell. Chicago: University of Chicago Press.

Ahdar, Rex J., ed. 2000. *Law and Religion*. Aldershot, UK: Ashgate/Burlington, VT: Dartmouth Press.

Ake, Claude. 1996. *Democracy and Development in Africa*. Washington, DC: Brookings Institution.

Aldana-Pindell, Raquel. 2002. "In Vindication of Justiciable Victims' Rights to Truth and Justice for State-Sponsored Crimes." *Vanderbilt Journal of Transnational Law* 35.5: 1399–502.

Alder, Ken. 2002. "A Social History of Untruth: Lie Detection and Trust in Twentieth-Century America." *Representations* 80: 1–33.

Allen, Chris. 1999. "Warfare, Endemic Violence and State Collapse." *Review of African Political Economy* 26.81: 367–84.

Allen, Jonathan. 1999. "Balancing Justice and Social Unity: Political Theory and the Idea of a Truth and Reconciliation Commission." *University of Toronto Law Journal* 49.3: 315–53.

Allen, R. E. 1980. *Socrates and Legal Obligation*. Minneapolis: University of Minnesota Press.

Allen, Tim. 2006. *Trial Justice: The International Criminal Court and the Lord's Resistance Army*. London: Zed Books.

Altman, Andrew. 1990. *Critical Legal Studies: A Liberal Critique*. Princeton: Princeton University Press.

Anderson, Kenneth. 2000. "After Seattle: Public International Organizations, Non-Governmental Organizations (NGOs), and Democratic Sovereignty in an Era of Globalization: An Essay on Contested Legitimacy." Unpublished monograph.

Anderson, Kenneth, and David Rieff. 2005. "'Global Civil Society': A Sceptical View." In *Global Civil Society 2004/5*, ed. Helmut Anheier, Mary H. Kaldor, and Marlies Glasius, 26–39. London: Sage Publications.

An-Na'im, Abdullahi A. 1995. "Toward an Islamic Hermeneutics for Human Rights." In *Human Rights and Religious Value: An Uneasy Relationship?* ed. Abdullahi An-Na'im, Jerald D. Gort, Henry Jansen, and Hendrik M. Vroom, 229–42. Grand Rapids, MI: William B. Eerdmans Publishing/Amsterdam and New York: Rodopi.

1999. "Universality of Human Rights: An Islamic Perspective." *Japan and International Law: Past, Present and Future*, ed. Nisuke Ando, 311–25. The Hague: Kluwer Law International.

2005. "Globalization and Jurisprudence: An Islamic Law Perspective." *Emory Law Journal* 54: 25–51.

An-Na'im, Abdullahi A., and Francis Deng, eds. 1990. *Human Rights in Africa: Cross-Cultural Perspectives*. Washington, DC: Brookings Institution.

Appleby, R. Scott. 2001. "Review of *Religion, Beliefs, and International Human Rights*, by Natan Lerner." *Journal of Law and Religion* 16.2: 605–8.

Apraku, Kofi Konadu. 1991. *African Emigres in the United States: A Missing Link in Africa's Social and Economic Development*. New York: Praeger.

Apter, Andrew. 2005: *The Pan-African Nation: Oil and the Spectacle of Culture in Nigeria*. Chicago: University of Chicago Press.

Arendt, Hannah. 1970. *On Violence*. New York: Harcourt, Brace & World.

2000. "Stateless Persons." In *The Portable Hannah Arendt*, ed. Peter Baehr, 23–72. New York: Penguin Putnam.

Asad, Talal. 1993. *Genealogies of Religion: Discipline and Reasons of Power in Christianity and Islam*. Baltimore: Johns Hopkins University Press.

2003. *Formations of the Secular: Christianity, Islam, Modernity*. Stanford, CA: Stanford University Press.

Avruch, Kevin. 2006. "Culture, Relativism and Human Rights." In *Human Rights and Conflict: Exploring the Links between Rights, Law, and Peacebuilding*, ed. Julie A. Mertus and Jeffrey W. Helsing, 97–120. Washington, DC: United States Institute of Peace.

Bahnassi, Ahmad Fathi. 1982. "Criminal Responsibility in Islamic Law." In *The Islamic Criminal Justice*, ed. M. Cherif Bassiouni, 171–93. London: Oceana Publications.

Baines, Erin K. 2007. "The Haunting of Alice: Justice and Reconciliation in Northern Uganda." *International Journal of Transitional Justice* 1.1: 91–114.

Balewa, B. A. T. 2002. *Common Law and Sharia in Nigeria*. Enugu, Nigeria: Fourth Dimension.

Barnes, Sandra T. 2005. "Global Flows: Terror, Oil, and Strategic Philanthropy." *African Studies Review* 48.1: 1–22.

Barnett, Larry D. 1993. *Legal Construct, Social Concept: A Macrosociological Perspective on Law*. New York: A. de Gruyter.

Barry, Andrew, Thomas Osborne, and Nikolas Rose, eds. 1996. *Foucault and Political Reason: Liberalism, Neo-Liberalism, and Rationalities of Government*. Chicago: University of Chicago Press.

Bass, Gary Jonathan. 2001. *Stay the Hand of Vengeance: The Politics of War Crimes Tribunals*. Princeton: Princeton University Press.

Bassiouni, Cherif. 2006. "International Recognition of Victims' Rights." *Human Rights Law Review* 6.2: 203–79.

Bastian, Misty. 2005. "'Terror against Terror': 9/11 or 'Kano War' in the Nigerian Press?" In *Terror and Violence: Imagination and the Unimaginable*, ed. Andrew Strathern, Pamela J. Stewart, and Neil L. Whitehead, 40–60. London and Ann Arbor, MI: Pluto Press.

Bate, Barney. In press. *Kavitha's Love: Tamil Oratory, the Dravidian Aesthetic, and Democratic Practice in South India*. New York: Columbia University Press.

Baucom, Ian. 2005. *Specters of the Atlantic: Finance Capital, Slavery, and the Philosophy of History*. Durham, NC: Duke University Press.

Bauman, Richard W. 1996. *Critical Legal Studies: A Guide to the Literature*. Boulder, CO: Westview Press.

Bauman, Zygmunt. 2001. *Community: Seeking Safety in an Insecure World*. Cambridge: Polity & Blackwell.

Bayart, Jean-François, Stephen Ellis, and Béatrice Hibou. 1999. *The Criminalisation of the State in Africa*. Oxford: James Currey.

Beer, Lawrence W., and C. G. Weeramantry. 1979. "Human Rights in Japan: Some Protections and Problems." *Universal Human Rights* 1.3: 1–33.

Beirne, Pier. 1982. "Ideology and Rationality in Max Weber's Sociology of Law." In *Marxism and Law*, ed. Piers Beirne and Richard Quinney, 44–62. New York: Wiley.

Bellah, Robert, ed. 1973. *Emile Durkheim on Morality and Society*. Chicago: University of Chicago Press.

Benjamin, Walter. 1986. "Critique of Violence." In *Reflections: Essays, Aphorisms, Autobiographical Writings*, ed. Peter Demetz, trans. Edmund Jephcott, 277–300. New York: Random House.

Berman, Paul S. 2007a. "A Pluralist Approach to International Law." *Yale Journal of International Law* 32.2: 301–29.

2007b. Global Legal Pluralism. Southern California Law Review. Volume 80, September 2007, Number 6.

Berry, Sara. 1993. *No Condition Is Permanent: The Social Dynamics of Agrarian Change in Sub-Saharan Africa*. Madison: University of Wisconsin Press.

Bienen, Henry. 1985. *Political Conflict and Economic Change in Nigeria*. London and Totowa, NJ: Frank Cass.

Billon, Philippe Le. 2001. "The Political Ecology of War: Natural Resources and Armed Conflicts." *Political Geography* 20: 561–84.

Binder, Guyora. 2002. "The Rhetoric of Motive and Intent." *Buffalo Criminal Law Review* 6.1: 1–96.

Bivar, A. D. H., and M. Hiskett. 1962. "The Arabic Literature of Nigeria to 1804: A Provisional Account." *Bulletin of the School of Oriental and African Studies* 25.1–3: 104–48.

Bloom, Allan. 1975. "Justice: John Rawls vs. the Tradition of Political Philosophy." *American Political Science Review* 69.2: 648–62.

Bohannan, Paul. 1957. *Justice and Judgment among the Tiv*. London and New York: Oxford University Press.

Borradori, Giovanna. 2003. *Philosophy in a Time of Terror: Dialogues with Jürgen Habermas and Jacques Derrida*. Chicago and London: University of Chicago Press.

Bourdieu, Pierre. 1987. "The Force of Law: Toward a Sociology of the Juridical Field." *Hastings Law Review* 38: 805–53.

Bourdieu, Pierre, and Loïc Wacquant. 1999. "On the Cunning of Imperialist Reason." *Theory, Culture & Society* 16.1: 41–58.

1977. *Outline of a Theory of Practice*. Cambridge: Cambridge University Press.

Bowen, J. R. 2003. *Islam, Law and Equality in Indonesia: An Anthropology of Public Reasoning*. Cambridge: Cambridge University Press.

2004. "Does French Islam Have Borders? Dilemmas of Domestication in a Global Religious Field." *American Anthropologist* 106.1: 43–55.

British Colonial Office. 1958. *Report of the Commission Appointed to Enquire into the Fears of Minorities and the Means of Allaying Them* (Sir Henry Willink, Chair). Cmnd. 505. London: HMSO.

Brockopp, Jonathan. 2000–1. Review of *Islamic Law: Theory and Practice*, ed. Robert Gleave and Eugenia Kermeli. *Journal of Law and Religion* 15.1–2: 417–19.

Brooks, Daphne. 2006. *Bodies in Dissent: Spectacular Performances of Race and Freedom 1850–1910*. Durham, NC: Duke University Press.

Brown, Bartram S. 1998. "Primacy or Complementarity: Reconciling the Jurisdiction of National Courts and International Criminal Tribunals." *Yale Journal of International Law* 23: 383–436.

Brown, Philip Marshall. 1943. "Law and Religion." *American Journal of International Law* 37.3: 505–7.

Brown, Wendy. 1995. *States of Injury: Power and Freedom in Late Modernity*. Princeton: Princeton University Press.

2001. *Politics out of History*. Princeton: Princeton University Press.

2004. "'The Most We Can Hope for . . .': Human Rights and the Politics of Fatalism." *South Atlantic Quarterly* 103.2–3: 451–63.

ed. 2002. *Left Legalism/Left Critique*. Durham, NC: Duke University Press.

Brysk, Alison, ed. 2002. *Globalization and Human Rights*. Berkeley and Los Angeles: University of California Press.

Butler, Judith 2006. *Precarious Life: The Power of Mourning and Violence*. London: Verso.

Byang, Danjuma. 1988. *Sharia in Nigeria: A Christian Perspective*. Jos, Nigeria: Challenge Press.

Cahn, Jonathan. 1993. "Challenging the New Imperial Authority: The World Bank and the Democratisation of Development." *Harvard Human Rights Journal* 6: 159–94.

Cain, Patricia. 1991. "Feminist Jurisprudence." In *Feminist Legal Theory: Readings in Law and Gender*, ed. Katharine T. Bartlett and Rosanne Kennedy, 263–80. Boulder, CO: Westview Press.

Caudill, David S. 2001. Review of *Faith and Order: The Reconciliation of Law and Religion*, by Harold J. Berman. *Journal of Law and Religion* 16.2: 713–17.

Chaplin, Jonathan. 2001. Review of *Religious Human Rights in Global Perspective*, 2 vols., ed. John Witte Jr. and Johan van der Vyver. *Journal of Law and Religion* 16.2: 617–21.

Chapman, John W. 1975. "Rawl's Theory of Justice." *American Political Science Review* 69.2: 588–93.

Chatterjee, Partha 2005. "Empire and Nation Revisited: 50 Years after Bandung." *Inter-Asia Cultural Studies* 6.4: 487–96.

Chayes, Abram, and Antonia Handler Chayes. 1995. *The New Sovereignty: Compliance with International Regulatory Agreements*. Cambridge, MA: Harvard University Press.

Chege, Michael. 1999. "Politics of Development: Institutions and Governance." Background paper prepared for World Bank's "Africa in the 21st Century" project. Washington, DC: Global Coalition for Africa.

Clark, Berry, and Herbert Gintis. 1978. "Rawlsian Justice and Economic Systems." *Philosophy and Public Affairs* 7.4: 302–25.

Clarke, Kamari M. 2004. *Mapping Yorùbá Networks: Power and Agency in the Making of Transnational Communities*. Durham, NC: Duke University Press.

——— 2006. "Internationalizing the Statecraft: Genocide, Religious Revivalism, and the Cultural Politics of International Law." *Loyola of Los Angeles International and Comparative Law Review* 28.2: 279–333.

——— ed., 2005. "Local Practices, Global Controversies: Islam in Sub-Saharan African Contexts." Working Paper. New Haven: Macmillan Center for International and Area Studies, Yale University.

Clarke, Kamari M., and Mark Goodale. 2009. *Mirrors of Justice: Law and Power in the Post-Cold War Era*. Cambridge: Cambridge University Press.

Clarke, Kamari M., and Deborah Thomas, eds. 2006. *Globalization and Race: Transformations in the Cultural Production of Blackness*. Durham, NC: Duke University Press.

Cocks, Raymond. 2004. *Sir Henry Maine: A Study in Victorian Jurisprudence*. Cambridge: Cambridge University Press.

Cohen, Jean L. 2004. *Regulating Intimacy: A New Legal Paradigm*. Princeton: Princeton University Press.

Cohen, Stanley. 1972. *Folk Devils and Moral Panics: Creation of Mods and Rockers*. London: MacGibbon & Kee.

Coicaud, Jean-Marc, Michael W. Doyle, and Anne-Marie Gardner, eds. 2003. *The Globalization of Human Rights*. Tokyo and New York: United Nations University Press.

Coleman, Gabriella. 2006. Paper presented at the WISER Johannesburg Summer School. Johannesburg, South Africa.

Collier, Jane F., Bill Maurer, and Liliana Suarez-Navaz. 1995. "Sanctioned Identities: Legal Constructions of Modern Personhood." *Identities* 2.1–2: 1–27.

Collier, J[ohn] G. 2001. *Conflict of Laws*, 3d ed. Cambridge: Cambridge University Press.

Collier, Paul, and Anke Hoeffler. 1998. "On Economic Causes of Civil War." *Oxford Economic Papers* 50.4: 563–73.

Comaroff, Jean, and John Comaroff. 2004a. "Criminal Obsessions, After Foucault: Postcoloniality, Policing, and the Metaphysics of Disorder." *Critical Inquiry* 30.4: 800–24.

——— 2004b. "Policing Culture, Cultural Policing: Law and Social Order in Postcolonial South Africa." *Law and Social Inquiry* 29.3: 513–45.

Comaroff, John L., and Simon Roberts. 1981. *Rules and Processes: The Cultural Logic of Dispute in an African Context*. Chicago: University of Chicago Press.

Conley, John M., and William M. O'Barr. 1990. *Rules versus Relationships: The Ethnography of Legal Discourse*. Chicago: University of Chicago Press.

Conrad, Joseph. 1999 [1902] *Heart of Darkness*. New York: Penguin.

Cornell, Vincent J. 1999. "Fruit of the Tree of Knowledge: The Relationship between Faith and Practice in Islam." *The Oxford History of Islam*, ed. John L. Esposito, 63–105. Oxford and New York: Oxford University Press.

Cotran, Eugene, and Mai Yamani, eds. 2000. *The Rule of Law in the Middle East and the Islamic World: Human Rights and the Judicial Process*. London: I. B. Tauris.

Coughlin, John J. 2003–4. "Canon Law and the Human Person." *Journal of Law and Religion* 19.1: 1–58.

Coutin, Susan Bibler, Bill Maurer, and Barbara Yngvesson. 2002. "In the Mirror: The Legitimation Work of Globalization." *Law and Social Inquiry* 27.4: 801–43.

Cowan, Jane K. 2006. "Culture and Rights after 'Culture and Rights.'" *American Anthropologist* 108.1: 9–24.

Coward, Harold, ed. 1997. *Life after Death in World Religions*. Maryknoll, NY: Orbis Books.

Cowen, Jane K., Marie-Bénédicte Dembour, and Richard A. Wilson, eds. 2001. *Culture and Rights: Anthropological Perspectives*. Cambridge: Cambridge University Press.

Cryer, Robert. 2005. *Prosecuting International Crimes: Selectivity and the International Criminal Law Regime*. Cambridge: Cambridge University Press.

Danesh, Roshan. 2003–4. "Internationalism and Divine Law: A Baha'i Perspective." *Journal of Law and Religion* 19.2: 209–42.

Das, Veena. 2006. "Review Essay: Poverty, Marginality, and Illness." *American Ethnologist* 33.1: 27–32.

Davidson, Basil. 1998. *The African Past and Present: West Africa before the Colonial Era: A History to 1850*. London: Longman.

Deflem, Mathieu. 1998. "The Boundaries of Abortion Law: Systems Theory from Parsons to Luhmann and Habermas." *Social Forces* 76.3: 775–818.

——— ed. 1996. *Habermas, Modernity and Law*. London: Sage Publications.

Derrida, Jacques. 1992. "Force of Law: The 'Mystical Foundations of Authority.'" Trans. Mary Quittance. In *Deconstruction and the Possibility of Justice*, ed. Drucilla Cornell, Michel Rosenfeld, and David Gray Carlson, 3–67. New York and London: Routledge.

——— 1994. *Specters of Marx: The State of the Debt, the Work of Mourning, & the New International*. Trans. Peggy Kamuf. London: Routledge.

——— 2002. *Acts of Religion*. Ed. Gil Anidjar. New York: Routledge.

——— 2004. "The Last of the Rogue States: The 'Democracy to Come,' Opening in Two Turns." Trans. Pascale-Anne Brault and Michael Naas. *South Atlantic Quarterly* 103.2–3: 323–41.

Dezalay, Yves, and Bryant G. Garth. 1995. "Merchants of Law as Moral Entrepreneurs: Constructing International Justice from the Competition for Transnational Business Disputes." *Law & Society Review* 29: 27–64.

2002. *The Internationalization of the Palace Wars: Lawyers, Economists, and the Contest to Transform Latin American Studies*. Chicago: University of Chicago Press.

Dotan, Yoav. 2001. "Global Language of Human Rights." In *Cause Lawyering and the State in a Global Era*, ed. Austin Sarat and Stuart Scheingold, 244–63. Oxford: Oxford University Press.

Dudley, B. J. 1968. *Parties and Politics in Northern Nigeria*. London: Frank Cass.

Duffield, Mark. 2001. *Global Governance and the New Wars: The Merging of Development and Security*. London: Zed Books.

Durham, W. Cole, Jr., and Troy J. Beatty. 2001. *Review of Religious Liberty and International Law in Europe*, by Malcom D. Evans. *Journal of Law and Religion* 16.2: 623–34.

Durkheim, Emile. 1964 [1893]. "Organic Solidarity Due to the Division of Labor." Trans. G. Simpson. In *Division of Labor in Society*, 111–32. New York: Free Press.

   1992 [1957]. *Professional Ethics and Civic Morals*, 2d ed. Trans. Cornelia Brookfield. London: Routledge.

Dworkin, Ronald. 2000. *Sovereign Virtue: The Theory and Practice of Equality*. Cambridge, MA: Harvard University Press.

Edozie, R. K. 2004. "Promoting African 'Owned and Operated' Development: A Reflection on the New Partnership for African Development (NEPAD)." *African and Asian Studies* 3.2: 145–173.

Ekechi, F. K. 1972. *Missionary Enterprise and Rivalry in Igboland 1857–1914*. London: Frank Cass.

Elias, Norbert. 1994 [1939]. *The Civilizing Process*. Trans. E. Jephcott. Oxford: Basil Blackwell.

Emon, Anver M. 2001a. Review of *The Principles of Islamic Jurisprudence*, vol. 1: *The Command of the Shari'ah and Juridical Norm*, by Ahmad Hasan. *Journal of Law and Religion* 16.2: 645–6.

   2001b. Review of *Rethinking Tradition in Modern Islamic Thought*, by Daniel W. Brown. *Journal of Law and Religion* 16.2: 647–52.

Englund, Harri. 2006. *Prisoners of Freedom: Human Rights and the African Poor*. Berkeley: University of California Press.

Erikson, Kai T. 1966. *Wayward Puritans: A Study in the Sociology of Deviance*. New York: John Wiley & Sons.

Esposito, John L., ed. 2003. *The Oxford Dictionary of Islam*. Oxford and New York: Oxford University Press.

Esposito, John L., and Francois Burgat, eds. 2003. *Modernizing Islam: Religion in the Public Sphere in the Middle East and Europe*. New Brunswick, NJ: Rutgers University Press.

Evans, Malcolm D., and Rachel Murray, eds. 2001. *Documents of the African Commission on Human and People's Rights*. Oxford: Hart Publishing.

Everett, Robinson O. 1959. "New Procedures of Scientific Investigation and the Protection of the Accused's Rights." *Duke Law Journal* 1.2: 32–77.

Ewing, Sally. 1987. "Formal Justice and the Spirit of Capitalism: Max Weber's Sociology of Law." *Law and Society Review* 21.3: 487–512.

Falola, Toyin, et al. 1989. *History of Nigeria.* Ikeja: Longman Nigeria.

Faier, Lieba. 2009. *Intimate Encounters: Filipina Migrants Remake Rural Japan* [working title]. Berkeley: University of California Press.

Feldman, Joe. 1973. "Some Features of Justice and 'A Theory of Justice.'" *California Law Review* 61.6: 1463–78.

Ferguson, James. 1999. *Expectations of Modernity: Myths and Meanings of Urban Life on the Zambian Copperbelt.* Berkeley: University of California Press.

2002. "Of Mimicry and Membership: Africans and the 'New World Society.'" *Cultural Anthropology* 17.4: 551–69.

2006. *Global Shadows: Africa in the Neoliberal World Order.* Durham, NC: Duke University Press.

Fernández Olmos, Margarite, and Lizabeth Paravisini-Gebert. 2003. *Creole Religions of the Caribbean: An Introduction from Vodou and Santería to Obeah and Espiritismo.* New York: New York University Press.

Finkel, David. 2002. "Crime and Holy Punishment: In Divided Nigeria, Search for Justice Leads Many to Embrace Islamic Code." *Washington Post,* November 24, A01.

Finnström, Sverker. 2004. "'For God & My Life': War and Cosmology in Northern Uganda." In *No Peace No War: An Anthropology of Contemporary Armed Conflicts,* ed. Paul Richards, 98–116. Athens: Ohio University Press; Oxford: James Currey.

2006. "Wars of the Past and War in the Present: The Lord's Resistance Movement/Army in Uganda." *Africa* 76.2: 200–20.

2008. *Living with Bad Surroundings: War, History, and Everyday Moments in Northern Uganda.* Durham, NC: Duke University Press.

French, Jan Hoffman. 2002. "Dancing for Land: Law-Making and Cultural Performance in Northeastern Brazil." *Political and Legal Anthropology Review (PoLAR)* 25.1: 19–36.

Ford, Richard. 1999. "Law Territory (A History of Jurisdiction)." *Michigan Law Review* 97.4: 843–930.

Foucault, Michel. 1977. *Discipline and Punish: The Birth of the Prison.* Trans. Alan Sheridan. London: Penguin.

1978. *The History of Sexuality: An Introduction.* Volume 1. Trans. Robert Hurley. New York: Vintage.

1980. "Two Lectures." In *Power/Knowledge: Selected Interviews and Other Writings, 1972–1977,* ed. Colin Gordon, 78–108. New York: Pantheon.

1994. "Governmentality." Trans. R. Hurley et al. In *Power: The Essential Works of Michel Foucault, 1954–1984,* vol. 3, ed. J. D. Faubion, 201–24. New York: New Press.

1995. *Discipline and Punish: The Birth of the Prison.* New York: Random House.

Friedman, Lawrence. 2001. "Erewhon: The Coming Global Legal Order." *Stanford Journal of International Law* 37: 347–64.

Friedrich, Carl J., and John W. Chapman, eds. 1963. *Nomos VI: Justice.* New York: Atherton Press.

Gabel, Peter, and Jay Feinman. 1982. "Contract Law as Ideology." In *The Politics of Law: A Progressive Critique,* ed. D. Kairys, 172–84. New York: Pantheon.

Gallagher, Nancy E. 1989. "Islam v. Secularism in Cairo: An Account of the Dar al-Hikma Debate." *Middle Eastern Studies* 25.2: 208–15.

Ganesan, Arvind, and Alex Vines. 2004. "Engine of War: Resources, Greed, and the Predatory State." In Human Rights Watch, *World Report 2004: Human Rights and Armed Conflict,* ed. Joseph Saunders and Iain Levine, 301–24. New York: Human Rights Watch.

Ganguly, Keya. 2001. *States of Exception: Everyday Life and Postcolonial Identity.* Minneapolis: University of Minnesota Press.

Garland, David. 1986. "Foucault's Discipline and Punish: An Exposition and Critique." *American Bar Foundation Research Journal (Law and Social Inquiry)* 4: 847–80.

1997. "Governmentality and the Problem of Crime: Foucault, Criminology, Sociology." *Theoretical Criminology* 1.2: 173–214.

Geertz, Clifford. 1984. "Distinguished Lecture: Anti Anti-Relativism." *American Anthropologist* 86.2: 263–278.

Geis, Gilbert. 1959. "In Scopolamine Veritas: The Early History of Drug-Induced Statements." In *Journal of Criminal Law, Criminology, and Political Science* 50.4: 347–57.

Geo-Jaja, Macleans A., and Garth Mangum. 2003. "Economic Adjustment, Education, and Human Resource Development in Africa: The Case of Nigeria." *International Review of Education* 49.3–4: 293–318.

Gessner, Volkmar. 1995. "Global Approach in the Sociology of Law: Problems and Challenges." *Journal of Law and Society* 22.1: 85–104.

Gluckman, Max. 1965. *Custom and Conflict in Africa.* Oxford: Basil Blackwell.

1973 [1955]. *Judicial Process among the Barotse of Northern Rhodesia,* 2d ed. Manchester: Manchester University Press, for Institute for African Studies, University of Zambia.

Goodale, Mark. 2006a. "Ethical Theory as Social Practice." *American Anthropologist* 108.1–2: 25–37.

2006b. "Introduction to 'Anthropology and Human Rights in a New Key.'" *American Anthropologist* 108.1–2: 1–8.

2007. "The power of right(s): tracking empires of law and new modes of social resistance in Bolivia (and elsewhere). In *The Practice of Human*

Rights: Tracking Law between the Global and the Local, ed. Mark Goodale and Sally Engle Merry, 130–162. Cambridge: Cambridge University Press.

2008a. *Human Rights: An Anthropological Reader*. Oxford: Blackwell.

2008b. *Dilemmas of Modernity: Bolivian Encounters with Law and Liberalism*. Chapter 5. Stanford: Stanford University Press.

Goodale, Mark, and Sally Engle Merry. 2007. *The Practice of Human Rights: Tracking Law between the Global and the Local*. Cambridge: Cambridge University Press.

Green, S. J. D. 1989. "Emile Durkheim on Human Talents and Two Traditions of Social Justice." *British Journal of Sociology* 40.1: 97–117.

Greenhouse, Carol J. 1986. *Praying for Justice: Faith, Order, and Community in an American Town*. Ithaca: Cornell University Press.

1998. *Democracy and Ethnography: Constructing Identities in Multicultural Liberal States*. Albany: State University of New York Press.

2005. "Nationalizing the Local: Comparative Notes on the Recent Restructuring of Political Space." In *Human Rights in the War on Terror*, ed. Richard Ashby Wilson, 184–208. New York: Cambridge University Press.

Gregory, Sam. 2006. "Transnational Storytelling: Human Rights, WITNESS, and Video Advocacy." *American Anthropologist* 108.1–2: 195–204.

Gurule, Jimmy. 2001–2. "United States Opposition to the 1998 Rome Statute Establishing an International Criminal Court: Is the Court's Jurisdiction Truly Complementary to National Criminal Jurisdictions?" *Cornell International Law Journal* 35.1: 1–45.

Haas, Peter M. 1989. "Do Regimes Matter: Epistemic Communities and Mediterranean Pollution Control." *International Organization* 43.3: 377–403.

1992a. "Introduction: Epistemic Communities and International Policy Coordination." *International Organization* 46.1: 1–35. Reprinted in *Knowledge, Power and International Policy Coordination*, ed. Peter M. Haas, 1–35. Columbia: University of South Carolina Press, 1997.

1992b. "Banning Chlorofluorocarbons: Epistemic Community Efforts to Protect Stratospheric Ozone." *International Organization* 46.1: 187–224. Reprinted in *Knowledge, Power and International Policy Coordination*, ed. Peter M. Haas, 187–224. Columbia: University of South Carolina Press, 1997.

Habermas, Jürgen. 1986. "Law as Medium and Law as Institution." In *Dilemmas of Law in the Welfare State*, ed. Gunther Teubner, 203–20. Berlin: W. de Gruyter.

1988. "Law and Morality: How Is Legitimacy Possible on the Basis of Legality?" (Lecture I). Trans. Kenneth Baynes. In *The Tanner Lectures on Human Values*, vol. 8, ed. Sterling M. McMurrin, 219–79. Salt Lake City: University of Utah Press.

1989. *The Structural Transformation of the Public Sphere: An Inquiry into a Category of Bourgeois Society.* Trans. Thomas Burger with Frederick Lawrence. Cambridge, MA: MIT Press.

1998. *Between Facts and Norms: Contributions to a Discourse Theory of Law and Democracy.* Trans. William Rehg. Cambridge, MA: MIT Press.

2006. "Religion in the Public Sphere." Trans. Jeremy Gaines. *European Journal of Philosophy* 14.1: 1–25.

Habermas, Jürgen, and Jacques Derrida. 2005. "February 15; or, What Binds Europeans Together: Plea for a Common Foreign Policy, Beginning in Core Europe." In *Old Europe, New Europe, Core Europe: Transatlantic Relations after the Iraq War*, ed. Daniel Levy, Max Pensky, and John Torpey, 3–13. London and New York: Verso Books.

Hackett, Rosalind I. J. 2005. "Rethinking the Role of Religion in Changing Public Spheres: Some Comparative Perspectives." *Brigham Young University Law Review* 2005.3: 659–82.

Hall, Stuart, ed. 1997. *Representation: Cultural Representations and Signifying Practices.* London: Sage Publications.

Hallaq, Wael B. 2003–4. "Juristic Authority vs. State Power: The Legal Crises of Modern Islam." *Journal of Law and Religion* 19.2: 243–58.

Hannerz, Ulf. 1990. "Cosmopolitans and Locals in World Culture." In *Theory, Culture and Society* 7.2: 237–51; reprinted in *Global Culture: Nationalism Globalization and Modernity*, ed. Mike Featherstone, 237–51. London: Sage, 1990.

Hansen, Thomas Blom, and Finn Stepputat, eds. 2005. *Sovereign Bodies: Citizens, Migrants, and States in the Postcolonial World.* Princeton: Princeton University Press.

Harvey, David. 2003. *The New Imperialism.* Oxford: Oxford University Press.

Hathaway, Oona. 2007. "Why Do Countries Commit to Human Rights Treaties?" *Journal of Conflict Resolution* 51.4: 588–621.

Hazan, Pierre. 2006. "Measuring the impact of punishment and forgiveness: a framework for evaluating transitional justice." *International Review of the Red Cross* 88.861:19–47.

Held, David. 1980. *Introduction to Critical Theory: From Horkheimer to Habermas.* Berkeley: University of California Press.

Henkin, Louis. 1989. *International Law: Politics, Values and Functions*, chap. X, "State Values and Other Human Values," 168–83. Dordrecht, The Netherlands: Martinus Nijhoff. Excerpted in Steiner and Alston (2000: 127–30).

1990. *The Age of Rights.* New York: Columbia University Press.

2000. "Protecting the World's Exiles: The Human Rights of Non-Citizens." *Human Rights Quarterly* 22.1: 280–97.

Henkin, Louis, Gerald Neuman, Diane Orentlicher, and David Leebron. 1999. *Human Rights.* New York: Foundation Press.

Herman, Judith. 2005. "Justice from the Victim's Perspective." *Violence against Women* 11.5: 571–602.

Herskovits, Melville J. 1990 [1941]. *The Myth of the Negro Past*. Boston: Beacon Press.

Hirsch, John L. 2001. *Sierra Leone: Diamonds and the Struggle for Democracy*. Boulder, CO: Lynne Rienner.

Hirsch, Susan F. 1998. *Pronouncing and Preserving: Gender and the Discourses of Disputing in an African Islamic Court*. Chicago: University of Chicago Press.

2008. *In the Moment of Greatest Calamity: Terrorism, Grief, and a Victim's Quest for Justice*. Princeton, NJ: *Princeton University Press*.

Hobbes, Thomas. 1958 [1651]. *Leviathan*, ed. Michael Oakeshott. Oxford: Basil Blackwell.

Hobsbawm, Eric, and Terence Ranger, eds. 1983. *The Invention of Tradition*. Cambridge: Cambridge University Press.

Holland, Nancy J. 2002–3. "'Truth as Force': Michel Foucault on Religion, State Power, and the Law." *Journal of Law and Religion* 18.1: 79–97.

Holmes, J. 1999. "The Principle of Complementarity." In *The International Criminal Court: The Making of the Rome Statute – Issues, Negotiations, Results*, ed. R. S. Lee, 41–78. The Hague: Kluwer Academic.

Howard, A. E. Dick. 1998. *Magna Carta: Text and Commentary*, rev. ed. Charlottesville: University Press of Virginia.

Howard-Ellis, Charles. 1929. *The Origin, Structure & Working of the League of Nations*. Boston and New York: Houghton Mifflin.

Hunt, Alan. 1978. "Emile Durkheim: Towards a Sociology of Law." In *The Sociological Movement in Law*. London: Macmillan.

Ibrahim, Hauwa. 2004. Speech before the World Coalition against the Death Penalty, Montréal, Canada. October 6. [Copy on file with present author.]

Ignatieff, Michael. 1994. *Blood and Belonging: Journeys into the New Nationalism*. New York: Farrar, Straus & Giroux.

2001. "Human Rights as Idolatry." In *Human Rights as Politics and Idolatry*, ed. Amy Guttman, 53–98. Princeton: Princeton University Press.

Jackson, Sherman A. 1996. *Islamic Law and the State: The Constitutional Jurisprudence of Shihab al-Din al-Qarafi*. Leiden: Brill.

Jailed, M. L., ed. 2006. "Democratic Republic of Congo: Kinshasa Clashes." *Africa Research Bulletin: Political, Social and Cultural Series* 43.8: 16757B–16758B.

Jamar, Steven D. 2001. Review of *Religion and International Law*, by Mark W. Janis and Carolyn Evans. *Journal of Law and Religion* 16.2: 609–12.

Jessop, Bob. 1980. "On Recent Marxist Theories of Law, the State and Juridico-Political Ideology." *International Journal of the Sociology of Law* 8.4: 339–68.

Joseph, Richard A. 1988. *Democracy and Prebendal Politics in Nigeria: The Rise and Fall of the Second Republic.* Cambridge: Cambridge University Press.

Jurgensmeyer, M. 1993. *The New Cold War? Religious Nationalism Confronts the Secular State.* Berkeley: University of California Press.

Kahn, Paul W. 1999. *The Cultural Study of Law: Reconstructing Legal Scholarship.* Chicago: University of Chicago Press.

Kasfir, Nelson. 1976. *The Shrinking Political Arena: Participation and Ethnicity in African Politics, with a Case Study of Uganda.* Berkeley: University of California Press.

Kaufman, Whitley R. P. 2003. "Motive, Intention, and Morality in the Criminal Law." *Criminal Justice Review* 28.2: 317–35.

Keck, Margaret, and Kathryn Sikkink. 1998. *Activists beyond Borders: Advocacy Networks in International Politics.* Ithaca: Cornell University Press.

Kennett, Austin. 1968. *Bedouin Justice: Law and Customs among the Egyptian Bedouin.* London: Frank Cass.

Knauft, Bruce. 2002. *Critically Modern: Alternatives, Alterities, Anthropologies.* Bloomington: Indiana University Press.

Kogacioglu, Dicle. 2004. "The Tradition Effect: Framing Honor Crimes in Turkey." *Journal of Feminist Cultural Studies* 15.2: 118–51.

Koh, Harold H. 1996. "Transnational Legal Process." *Nebraska Law Review* 75: 181–207.

——— 1997. "Why Do Nations Obey International Law?" *Yale Law Journal* 106.8: 2599–659.

——— 1998. "The 1998 Frankel Lecture: Bringing International Law Home." *Houston Law Review* 35.3: 623–81.

——— 1999. "How Is International Human Rights Law Enforced?" *Indiana Law Journal* 74.4: 1397–1417.

Kriksciun, Alex K. 2007. "Uganda's Response to International Criminal Court Arrest Warrants: A Misguided Approach?" *Tulane Journal of International and Comparative Law* 16.1: 213–41.

Lacey, Marc. 2005. "Atrocity Victims in Uganda Choose to Forgive." *New York Times*, April 18.

Laplante, Lisa J. 2007. "Entwined Paths to Justice: The Inter-American Human Rights System and the Peruvian Truth Commission." In *Paths to International Justice: Social and Legal Perspectives*, ed. Marie-Bénédicte Dembour and Tobias Kelly, 216–42. Cambridge: Cambridge University Press.

Laslett, Barbara, Johanna Brenner, and Yesim Arat, eds. 1995. *Rethinking the Political: Gender, Resistance, and the State.* Chicago: University of Chicago Press.

Lasswell, Harold D. 1946. "The Interrelations of World Organization and Society." *Yale Law Journal* 55.5: 889–909.

Lerner, Natan. 1999–2000. "Review Essay: A Secular View of Human Rights." *Journal of Law and Religion* 14.1: 67–76.

Lewis, Bernard, ed. 1992. *The World of Islam: Faith, People, Culture.* London: Thames & Hudson.

Llewellyn, Karl N., and E. Adamson Hoebel. 1941. *Cheyenne Way: Conflict and Case Law in Primitive Jurisprudence.* Norman: University of Oklahoma Press.

Locke, John. 1988 [1689]. *Two Treatises of Government,* ed. Peter Laslett. Cambridge: Cambridge University Press.

Luban, David. 1994. *Legal Modernism.* Ann Arbor: University of Michigan Press.

Lugard, Frederick John Dealtry. 1907. *Northern Nigeria (Report for the Period from 1st January, 1906, to 31st March, 1907, By the High Commissioner of Northern Nigeria).* London: HMSO.

MacIntyre, Alasdair C. 1988. *Whose Justice? Which Rationality?* Notre Dame: University of Notre Dame Press.

MacKinnon, Catherine. 1991. "Difference and Dominance: On Sex Discrimination." In *Feminist Legal Theory,* ed. Katherine Bartlett and Rosanne Kennedy, 81–94. Boulder, CO: Westview Press.

McGowan, Randall. 1989. "Punishing Violence, Sentencing Crime." In *The Violence of Representation: Literature and the History of Violence,* ed. Nancy Armstrong and Leonard Tennenhouse, 140–56. New York: Routledge.

McLagan, Meg. 2006. "Introduction: Making Human Rights Claims Public." *American Anthropologist* 108.1: 191–220.

Macpherson, C. B. 1962. *The Political Theory of Possessive Individualism: Hobbes to Locke.* Oxford: Clarendon Press.

Mahmood, Saba. 2005. *Politics of Piety: The Islamic Revival and the Feminist Subject.* Princeton: Princeton University Press.

Malinowski, Bronislaw. 2006 [1926]. *Crime and Custom in Savage Society: An Anthropological Study of Savagery.* New York: Home Farm Books.

Mallinder, Louise. 2007. "Can Amnesties and International Justice Be Reconciled?" *International Journal of Transitional Justice* 1.2: 208–30.

Mamdani, Mahmood. 1988. "Uganda in Transition: Two Years of the NRA/NRM." *Third World Quarterly* 10.3: 1155–81.

    1995. "The Politics of Democratic Reform in Contemporary Uganda." *East African Journal of Peace and Human Rights* 2.1: 91–101.

    1996. *Citizen and Subject: Contemporary Africa and the Legacy of Late Colonialism.* Princeton: Princeton University Press.

    2000. *Beyond Rights Talk and Culture Talk: Comparative Essays on the Politics of Rights and Culture.* New York: St. Martin's Press; London: Palgrave Macmillan.

    2001. *When Victims Become Killers: Colonialism, Nativism, and the Genocide in Rwanda.* Princeton: Princeton University Press.

Martin Shaw, Carolyn. 1995. *Colonial Inscriptions: Race, Sex, and Class in Kenya.* Minneapolis: University of Minnesota Press.

Marx, Karl. 1869. "Report of the General Council on the Right of Inheritance." Internet Archive. Marxists.org.

Marx, Karl, and Friedrich Engels. 1978 [1859]. "Preface to Contribution to the Critique of Political Economy." In *The Marx-Engels Reader*, ed. Robert Tucker, 3–6. New York: W. W. Norton.

   1985 [1846]. "The Relation of State and Law to Property." In *The German Ideology*, ed. C. J. Arthur. New York: International Publishers.

Mattei, Ugo, and Laura Nader. 2008. *Plunder: When the Rule of Law Is Illegal*. Oxford: Blackwell.

Maurer, Bill. 1995. "Writing Law, Making a 'Nation': History, Modernity, and Paradoxes of Self-Rule in the British Virgin Islands." *Law & Society Review* 29.2: 255–86.

   2004. "On Divine Markets and the Problem of Justice: *Empire* as Theodicy." In *Empire's New Clothes: Reading Hardt and Negri*, ed. Paul Passavant and Jodi Dean, 57–72. New York: Routledge.

Mbembe, Achille. 2003. "Necropolitics." Trans. Libby Meintjes. *Public Culture* 15.1: 11–40.

Merry, Sally Engle. 1990. *Getting Justice and Getting Even: Legal Consciousness among Working-Class Americans*. Chicago: University of Chicago Press.

   1992. "Anthropology, Law and Transnational Processes." *Annual Reviews in Anthropology* 21: 357–79.

   1998. "Global Human Rights and Local Social Movements in a Legally Plural World." *Canadian Journal of Law and Society* 12.2: 247–71.

   2000. *Colonizing Hawaii: The Cultural Power of Law*. Princeton: Princeton University Press.

   2006a. *Human Rights and Gender Violence: Translating International Law into Local Justice*. Chicago: University of Chicago Press.

   2006b. "Transnational Human Rights and Local Activism: Mapping the Middle." *American Anthropologist* 108.1–2: 38–51.

Mertus, Julie A., and Jeffrey W. Helsing, eds. 2006. *Human Rights and Conflict: Exploring the Links between Rights, Law, and Peacebuilding*. Washington, DC: United States Institute of Peace.

Messick, Brinkley M. 2001. "Indexing the Self: Expression and Intent in Islamic Legal Acts." *Islamic Law and Society* 8.2: 151–78.

Meyjes, P. 1961. "Scientific Criminal Investigation Techniques under Dutch Law, with Special Consideration of Scientific Lie Detection and Blood Alcohol Tests." *Journal of Criminal Law, Criminology, and Police Science* 51.6: 653–60.

Michael, Sarah. 2004. *Undermining Development: The Absence of Power among Local NGOs in Africa*. Bloomington: Indiana University Press.

Milligan, Heather L. 2002. "The Influence of Religion and Morality Legislation on the Interpretation of Second-Parent Adoption Statutes: Are the

California Courts Establishing a Religion?" *California Western Law Review* 39.1: 137–62.

Moenssens, Andre A. 1962. "Narcoanalysis in Law Enforcement." *Journal of Criminal Law, Criminology, and Political Science* 52.4: 453–8.

Montesquieu, Charles deSecondat. 1952 [1748]. *The Spirit of the Laws*. Trans. Thomas Nugent. (Published in one volume with Jean-Jacques Rousseau's *On the Origin of Inequality, On Political Economy, and The Social Contract*, trans. G.D.H. Cole, as vol. 38 of Great Books of the Western World.) Chicago: William Benton/Encyclopaedia Brittanica.

Moore, Sally Falk. 2005. *Law and Anthropology: A Reader*. Boston and Oxford: Blackwell.

Muehlberger, C. W. 1951. "Interrogation under Drug Influence: The So-Called 'Truth Serum' Technique." *Journal of Criminal Law, Criminology, and Political Science* 42.4: 513–28.

Murithi, Timothy. 2002. "Rebuilding Social Trust in Northern Uganda." *Peace Review* 14.3: 291–5.

Mutua, Makau. 2002. *Human Rights: A Political and Cultural Critique*. Philadelphia: University of Pennsylvania Press.

Nader, Laura. 1972. "Up the Anthropologists: Perspectives Gained from Studying Up." In *Reinventing Anthropology*, ed. Dell H. Hymes, 284–311. New York: Pantheon Books.

1979. "Disputing without the Force of Law." *Yale Law Journal* 88.5: 998–1021.

1990. *Harmony Ideology: Justice and Control in a Zapotec Mountain Village*. Stanford, CA: Stanford University Press.

1999. "The Globalization of Law: ADR as 'Soft' Technology." *American Society of International Law, Proceedings* 93: 304–11.

2002. *The Life of the Law: Anthropological Projects*. Berkeley: University of California Press.

Nader, Laura, and Harry F. Todd Jr., eds. 1978. *Disputing Process: Law in Ten Societies*. New York: Columbia University Press.

Nash, June. 1989. "A Redistributive Model for Analyzing Government Mediation and Law in Family, Community, and Industry in a New England Industrial City." In *History and Power in the Study of Law: New Directions in Legal Anthropology*, ed. June Starr and Jane F. Collier, 81–112. Ithaca: Cornell University Press.

Nelson, Diane M. 1999. "A Transnational Frame-Up: ILO Convention 169, Identity, Territory and the Law." In *A Finger in the Wound: Body Politics in Quincentennial Guatemala*, 283–347. Berkeley: University of California Press.

Niezen, Ronald. 2003. *The Origins of Indigenism: Human Rights and the Politics of Identity*. Berkeley and Los Angeles: University of California Press.

Nmehielle, Vincent O. 2004. "Sharia Law in the Northern States of Nigeria: To Implement or Not to Implement, the Constitutionality Is the Question." *Human Rights Quarterly* 26.3: 730–59.

Nnaemeka, Obioma, ed. 2005. *Female Circumcision and the Politics of Knowledge: African Women in Imperialist Discourses.* Westport, CT: Praeger.

Nnoli, Okwudiba. 1978. *Ethnic Politics in Nigeria.* Enugu, Nigeria: Fourth Dimension.

Obe, Ayo. 2005. "The Relationship between Divine and Human Law: Shari'a Law and The Nigerian Constitution." In *Local Practices, Global Controversies: Islam in Sub-Saharan African Contexts*, ed. Kamari M. Clarke, 103–44. Working Paper. New Haven: Macmillan Center for International and Area Studies, Yale University.

Okafor, Obiora Chinedu. 2000. *Re-defining Legitimate Statehood: International Law and State Fragmentation in Africa.* The Hague: Martinus Nijhoff.

2007. *African Human Rights System, Activist Forces and International Institutions.* Cambridge: Cambridge University Press.

Okereafoezeke, Nonso. 2002. *Law and Justice in Post-British Nigeria: Conflicts and Interactions between Native and Foreign Systems of Social Control in Igbo.* Westport, CT: Greenwood Press.

Oloka-Onyango, Joe. 1991. "The National Resistance Movement, Grassroots Democracy, and Dictatorship in Uganda." In *Democracy and Socialism in Africa*, ed. Roberta Cohen and Harry Goulbourne, 125–41. Boulder, CO: Westview Press.

Orentlicher, Diane F. 2007. "Settling Accounts: Revisited: Reconciling Global Norms with Local Agency." *International Journal of Transitional Justice* 1.1:10–22.

Pain, Dennis. 1997. *"The Bending of Spears": Producing Consensus for Peace and Development in Northern Uganda.* Report commissioned by International Alert and Kacoke Madit. London: Kacoke Madit.

Pandolfi, Mariella. 2003. "Contract of Mutual (In)Difference: Governance and the Humanitarian Apparatus in Contemporary Albania and Kosovo." *Indiana Journal of Global Legal Studies* 10.1: 369–81.

Parsons, Talcott. 1954. "A Sociologist Looks at the Legal Profession." *Essays in Sociological Theory*, 370–85. New York: Free Press.

1962. "The Law and Social Control." In *Law and Sociology*, ed. William M. Evan, 56–72. New York: Free Press.

1968. "Law and Sociology: A Promising Courtship." In *The Path of the Law from 1967: Proceedings and Papers at the Harvard Law School Convocation Held on the One-Hundred Fiftieth Anniversary of Its Founding*, ed. Arthur E. Sutherland, 47–54. Cambridge, MA: Harvard Law School.

1978. "Law as an Intellectual Stepchild." In *Social System and Legal Process*, ed. Harry M. Johnson, 11–58. San Francisco: Jossey–Bass.

Parsons, Talcott, and Edward A. Shils, eds. 1965. *Toward a General Theory of Action*. New York: Harper & Row, Harper Torchbooks.

Pashukanis, E. B. 1978. *Law and Marxism: A General Theory*. London: Ink Links.

Peluso, Nancy Lee, and Michael Watts, eds. 2001. *Violent Environments*. Ithaca: Cornell University Press.

Perry, Michael. 1998. *The Idea of Human Rights: Four Inquiries*. Oxford: Oxford University Press.

Peters, Ruud. 2001. *The Reintroduction of Islamic Criminal Law in Northern Nigeria*. Study Conducted on Behalf of the European Commission. Lagos, Nigeria: European Commission.

Peterson, Paul A. 1954. "Evidence: Character of the Criminally Accused: Admissibility of Psychiatric Testimony." *California Law Review* 42.5: 880–5.

Philips, Susan Urmston. 1998. *Ideology in the Language of Judges: How Judges Practice Law, Politics, and Courtroom Control*. Oxford: Oxford University Press.

Pogge, Thomas W. 2001. "Rawls on International Justice." *Philosophical Quarterly* 51.203: 246–53.

Pollis, Adamantia, and Peter Schwab, eds. 2000. *Human Rights: New Perspectives, New Realities*. Boulder, CO: Lynne Rienner.

Pospisil, Leopold J. 1958. *Kapauku Papuans and Their Law*. New Haven: Yale Department of Anthropology.

1971. *Anthropology of Law: A Comparative Theory*. New York: Harper & Row.

Poulantzas, Nicos. 1978. *State, Power, Socialism*. London: New Left Books.

Povinelli, Elizabeth A. 2002. *The Cunning of Recognition: Indigenous Alterities and the Making of Australian Multiculturalism*. Durham: Duke University Press.

2001. "Radical Worlds: The Anthropology of Incommensurability and Inconceivability." *Annual Review of Anthropology* 30.1: 319–334.

Powelson, John P. 1998. *The Moral Economy*. Ann Arbor: University of Michigan Press.

Previn, Matthew P. 1996. "Assisted Suicide and Religion: Conflicting Conceptions of the Sanctity of Human Life." *Georgetown Law Journal* 84.3: 589–616.

Proulx, Vincent-Joel. 2004. "Rethinking the Jurisdiction of the International Criminal Court in the Post-September 11th Era: Should Acts of Terrorism Qualify as Crimes against Humanity?" *American University International Law Review* 19.5: 1009–89.

Rachels, James. 1997a. "Punishment and Desert." In *Ethics in Practice*, ed. Hugh LaFollette, 466–74. Malden, MA: Blackwell.

1997b. *Can Ethics Provide Answers? And Other Essays in Moral Philosophy*. Totowa, NJ: Rowman & Littlefield Publishers.

Rantanen, Terhi. 2007. "A Transnational Cosmopolitan: An Interview with Ulf Hannerz." *Global Media and Communication* 3.1: 11–27.

Ratner, Steven R., and Jason S. Abrams. 2001. *Accountability for Human Rights Atrocities in International Law: Beyond the Nuremberg Legacy*, 2d ed. Oxford: Oxford University Press.

Rawls, John. 1958. "Justice as Fairness." *Philosophical Review* 67.2: 164–94.

1963. "The Sense of Justice." *Philosophical Review* 72.3: 281–305.

1971. *A Theory of Justice.* Cambridge, MA: Harvard University Press.

2001. *Justice as Fairness: A Restatement.* Cambridge, MA: Harvard University Press.

2005. *Political Liberalism*, 2d ed. New York: Columbia University Press.

Reasons, Charles E., and Robert M. Rich, eds. 1978. *The Sociology of Law: A Conflict Perspective.* Toronto: Butterworths.

Reisman, W. Michael. 2004. "Learning to Deal with Rejection: The International Criminal Court and the United States." *Journal of International Criminal Justice* 2.1: 17–18.

Reisman, W. Michael, Mahnoush H. Arsanjani, Siegfried Wiessner, and Gayl S. Westerman. 2004. *International Law in Contemporary Perspective*, 2d ed. New York: Foundation Press.

Riches, David, ed. 1986. *The Anthropology of Violence.* Oxford: Blackwell.

Riles, Annelise. 2006. "Anthropology, Human Rights, and Legal Knowledge: Culture in the Iron Cage." *American Anthropologist* 108.1–2: 52–65.

Robertson, A. H., and J. G. Merrills. 1997. *Human Rights in the World: An Introduction to the Study of the International Protection of Human Rights*, 4th ed. Manchester: Manchester University Press.

Rose, Nikolas. 2003. "Neurochemical Selves." *Society* 41.1: 46–59.

Rosen, Lawrence. 1989. *The Anthropology of Justice: Law as Culture in Islamic Society.* Cambridge: Cambridge University Press.

2006. *Law as Culture: An Invitation.* Princeton: Princeton University Press.

Ross, Michael L. 2004. "How Do Natural Resources Influence Civil War? Evidence from Thirteen Cases." *International Organization* 58.1: 35–67.

Sands, Philippe. 2003. *From Nuremberg to The Hague: The Future of International Criminal Justice.* Cambridge: Cambridge University Press.

Santos, Boaventura DeSousa. 1980. "Law and Community: The Changing Nature of State Power in Law Capitalism." *International Journal of the Sociology of Law* 8.4: 379–97.

Schabas, William A. 2001. *An Introduction to the International Court.* Cambridge: Cambridge University Press.

Schachter, Oscar. 1991. *International Law in Theory and Practice*, chap. VI, "Resolutions and Political Texts," 84–105. Dordrecht, The Netherlands: Martinus Nijhoff. Excerpted in Steiner and Alston (2000: 130–4).

Schlesinger, Stephen C. 2003. *Act of Creation: The Founding of the United Nations – A Story of Superpowers, Secret Agents, Wartime Allies and Enemies, and Their Quest for a Peaceful World.* Boulder, CO: Westview Press.

Schoenfeld, Eugen, and Stjepan G. Mestrovic. 1989. "Durkheim's Concept of Justice and Its Relationship to Social Solidarity." *Sociological Analysis* 50.2: 111–27.

Scott, Alan. 1997. *The Limits of Globalization: Cases and Arguments.* London: Routledge.

Scott, David G. 2001. Book Essays and Reviews; *War and Peace: Cross, Crescent, and Sword: The Justification and Limitation of War in Western and Islamic Tradition,* ed. by James Turner Johnson and John Kelsay. *Journal of Law and Religion* 16.2: 999–1005.

Scott, James C. 1976. *The Moral Economy of the Peasant: Subsistence and Rebellion in Southeast Asia.* New Haven: Yale University Press.

Scott, Joan Wallach. 2007. *The Politics of the Veil.* Princeton: Princeton University Press.

Shaw, Malcolm N. 2003. *International Law,* 5th ed. New York: Cambridge University Press.

Sherry, Michael S. 1995. *In the Shadow of War: The United States since the 1930s.* New Haven: Yale University Press.

Sidahmed, Abdel Salam. 2001. "Problems in Contemporary Applications of Islamic Criminal Sanctions: The Penalty for Adultery in Relation to Women." *British Journal of Middle Eastern Studies* 28.2: 187–204.

Silving, Helen. 1956. "Testing of the Unconscious in Criminal Cases." *Harvard Law Review* 69.4: 683–705.

Simmel, George. 1950. "Custom, Law, Morality." In *The Sociology of George Simmel,* ed. Kurt H. Wolff, 99–104. New York: Free Press.

Simon, Jonathan. 1992. "'In Another Kind of Wood': Michel Foucault and Sociolegal Studies." *Law & Social Inquiry* 17.1: 49–55.

Slaughter, M. M. 1993. "The Salman Rushdie Affair: Apostasy, Honor, and Freedom of Speech." *Virginia Law Review* 79.1: 153–204.

Smith, M. G. 1964. "Historical and Cultural Conditions of Political Corruption among the Hausa." *Comparative Studies in Society and History* 6.2: 164–94.

Smith, T. B. 1951. "Mental Abnormality and Responsibility in International Criminal Law." *Transactions of the Grotius Society* 37: 99–125.

Speed, Shannon. 2006. "At the Crossroads of Human Rights and Anthropology: Toward a Critically Engaged Activist Research." *American Anthropologist* 108.1: 66–76.

Spiro, Melford. 1978. "Culture and Human Nature." In *The Making of Psychological Anthropology,* ed. G. D. Spindler (pp. 330–360). Berkeley: University of California Press.

Spiro, Peter J. 2009. "NGOs and Human Rights: Channels of Power." Paper presented at the Yale Law School Law and Globalization Seminar, February 9 in New Haven, CT.

Spitzer, Steven. 1983. "Marxist Perspectives in the Sociology of Law." *Annual Review of Sociology* 9: 103–24.

Starr, June. 1992. *Law as Metaphor: From Islamic Courts to the Palace of Justice.* Albany: State University of New York Press.

Starr, June, and Jane F. Collier, eds. 1989. *History and Power in the Study of Law: New Directions in Legal Anthropology.* Ithaca: Cornell University Press.

Steiner, Henry J., and Philip Alston, eds. 2000. *International Human Rights in Context: Laws, Politics and Morals,* 2d ed. Oxford: Oxford University Press.

Stoler, Ann L. 1995. *Race and the Education of Desire: Foucault's History of Sexuality and the Colonial Order of Things.* Durham and London: Duke University Press.

Strathern, Marilyn. 2004 [1991]. *Partial Connections, Updated Edition.* Walnut Creek, CA: Altamira Press.

Strauss, Leo. 1950. "Natural Right and the Historical Approach." *Review of Politics* 12.4: 422–42.

    1953. *Natural Right and History.* Chicago: University of Chicago Press.

Sturm, Douglas. 1989. "Human Rights and Political Possibility: A Religious Inquiry." *Criterion* 28.1: 2–8. Reprinted in *Journal of Religion and Law* 13.1 (1996–9): 43–6.

Suárez-Orozco, Marcelo. 2005. *The New Immigration: An Interdisciplinary Reader,* ed. Marcelo M. Suárez-Orozco, Carola Suárez-Orozco, and Desirée Baolian Qin, 3–20. New York: Routledge.

Sunder, Madhavi. 2003. "Piercing the Veil." *Yale Law Journal* 112.6: 1399–1472.

Sura al-Furqaan. 1996. "The Meaning and Explanation of the Glorious Qur'an" 6.25:68–70.

Tabiu, Muhammed. 2001. "Sharia, Federalism, and Nigerian Constitution." Paper presented at the International Conference on Sharia, organized by the Nigerian Muslim Forum, April 14, London, England.

Tay, Alice, with Eugene Kamenka. 1985. "Marxism, Socialism and the Theory of Law." *Columbia Journal of Transnational Law* 23: 217–49.

Taylor, Charles. 1989. *Sources of the Self: The Making of the Modern Identity.* Cambridge, MA: Harvard University Press.

Teubner, Gunther, ed. 1996. *Global Law without a State: Studies in Modern Law and Policy.* Hanover: Dartmouth Publishing Group.

Tronto, Joan. 1984. "Law and Modernity: The Significance of Max Weber's Sociology of Law," Review of *Max Weber,* by Anthony Kronman. *Texas Law Review* 63.4: 565–77.

Trouillot, Michel-Rolph. 2003. *Global Transformations: Anthropology and the Modern World.* New York: Palgrave Macmillan.

Trubek, David M. 1984. "Where the Action Is: Critical Legal Studies and Empiricism." *Stanford Law Review* 36.1–2: 575–622.

2006. "The 'Rule of Law' in Development Assistance: Past, Present, and Future." In *The New Law and Economic Development: A Critical Appraisal*, ed. David M. Trubek and Alvaro Santos, 74–94. Cambridge: Cambridge University Press.

Trubek, David, Yves Dezalay, Ruth Buchanan, and John Davis. 1994. "Global Restructuring and the Law: Studies of the Internationalization of Legal Fields and the Creation of Transnational Arenas." *Case Western Reserve Law Review* 44: 407–98.

Tsing, Anna L. 2005. *Friction: An Ethnography of Global Connection.* Princeton: Princeton University Press.

Turkel, Gerald. 1996. *Law and Society: Critical Approaches.* Boston: Allyn & Bacon.

Twist, Susan. 2006. "Rethinking Retrospective Criminality in the Context of War Crimes Trials." *Liverpool Law Review* 27.1: 31–66.

Umar, Muhammad S. 2005. *Islam and Colonialism: Intellectual Responses of Muslims of Northern Nigeria to British Colonial Rule.* Leiden: Brill.

Urdal, Henrik. 2005. "People vs. Malthus: Population Pressure, Environmental Degradation, and Armed Conflict Revisited." *Journal of Peace Research* 42.4: 417–34.

Vago, Steven. 1994. *Law and Society*, 4th ed. Englewood Cliffs, NJ: Prentice–Hall.

Venkatraman, Bharathi Anandhi. 1995. "Islamic States and the United Nations Convention on the Elimination of All Forms of Discrimination against Women: Are the Shari'a and the Convention Compatible?" *American University Law Review* 44: 1949–2027.

Waldman, Marilyn Robinson. 1965. "The Fulani Jihad: A Reassessment." *Journal of African History* 6.3: 333–55.

Ward, Kevin. 2001. "'The Armies of the Lord': Christianity, Rebels and the State in Northern Uganda, 1986–1999." *Journal of Religion in Africa* 31.2: 187–221.

Watts, Michael J. 1992. "The Shock of Modernity: Petroleum, Protest and Fast Capitalism in an Industrializing Society." In *Reworking Modernity: Capitalisms and Symbolic Discontent*, ed. Allan Pred and Michael John Watts, 21–63. New Brunswick, NJ: Rutgers University Press.

ed. 1987. *State Oil and Agriculture in Nigeria.* Berkeley: University of California, Institute of International Studies.

Weber, Max. 1951. *Religion of China.* Trans. and ed. Hans H. Gerth. New York: Free Press.

1954. "Basic Concepts of Sociology: The Formal Qualities of Modern Law." Trans. Edward Shils. In *Max Weber on Law in Economy and Society*, ed. Max Rheinstein, 1–10, 301–21. New York: Simon & Schuster.

1978 [1925]. "Economy and Law (The Sociology of Law)." Trans. E. Shils. In *Economy and Society*, ed. Guenther Roth and Claus Wittich, 641–900. Berkeley: University of California Press.

2001 [1904–5]. *The Protestant Ethic and the Spirit of Capitalism*, 3d ed. Trans. Stephen Kalberg. Chicago: Roxbury Publishing.

Whitaker, Mark P. 1996. "Relativism." *Encyclopedia of Social and Cultural Anthropology*, ed. Alan Barnard and Jonathan Spencer, 478–82. London: Routledge.

Williams, Frieda-Nela. 1991. *Precolonial Communities of Southwestern Africa: A History of Owambo Kingdoms*, 1600–1920. Windhoek: National Archives of Namibia.

Williams, Gavin. 1991. *Capitalists, Peasants and Land in Africa: A Comparative Perspective*. Johannesburg: University of the Witwatersrand, African Studies Institute.

Williams, Michael W. 1991. "Pan-Africanism and Zionism: The Delusion of Comparability." *Journal of Black Studies* 21.3: 348–71.

Wilson, Richard A. 2001. *The Politics of Truth and Reconciliation in South Africa: Legitimizing the Post-Apartheid State*. Cambridge: Cambridge University Press.

2005. *Human Rights and the War on Terror*. New York: Cambridge University Press.

2006. "Afterword to 'Anthropology and Human Rights in a New Key': The Social Life of Human Rights." *American Anthropologist* 108.1: 77–83.

ed. 1996. *Human Rights, Culture and Context: Anthropological Perspectives*. London: Pluto Press.

Woodiwiss, Anthony. 2003. *Making Human Rights Work Globally*. London: GlassHouse.

Yadudu, Auwalu Hamsxu. 1991. "Colonialism and the Transformation of the Substance and Form of Islamic Law in the Northern States of Nigeria." *Journal of Law and Religion* 9.1: 17–47.

Yakubu, John Ademola. 2005. "Colonialism, Customary Law and Post-Colonial State in Africa: The Case of Nigeria." *Africa Development* 30.4: 201–20.

Zachariah, K. C., and Julien Conde. 1981. *Migration in West Africa: Demographic Aspects*. Oxford: Oxford University Press, for the World Bank.

Zeitlin, Jonathan, and David M. Trubek, eds. 2003. *Governing Work and Welfare in a New Economy: European and American Experiments*. Oxford: Oxford University Press.

Žižek, Slavoj. 2004. "From Politics to Biopolitics . . . and Back." *South Atlantic Quarterly* 103.2–3: 501–21.

2005. "Against Human Rights." *New Left Review* 34: 115–31.

INDEX

Continued from page iii

Constituting Democracy:
Law, Globalism and South Africa's Political Reconstruction
Heinz Klug

The Ritual of Rights in Japan:
Law, Society, and Health Policy
Eric A. Feldman

The Invention of the Passport:
Surveillance, Citizenship and the State
John Torpey

Governing Morals:
A Social History of Moral Regulation
Alan Hunt

The Colonies of Law:
Colonialism, Zionism and Law in Early Mandate Palestine
Ronen Shamir

Law and Nature
David Delaney

Social Citizenship and Workfare in the United States and Western Europe:
The Paradox of Inclusion
Joel F. Handler

Law, Anthropology and the Constitution of the Social:
Making Persons and Things
Edited by Alain Pottage and Martha Mundy

Judicial Review and Bureaucratic Impact:
International and Interdisciplinary Perspectives
Edited by Marc Hertogh and Simon Halliday

Immigrants at the Margins:
Law, Race, and Exclusion in Southern Europe
Kitty Calavita

Lawyers and Regulation:
The Politics of the Administrative Process
Patrick Schmidt

Law and Globalization from Below:
Toward a Cosmopolitan Legality
Edited by Boaventura de Sousa Santos and Cesar A. Rodriguez-Garavito

Public Accountability:
Designs, Dilemmas and Experiences
Edited by Michael W. Dowdle

Law, Violence and Sovereignty among West Bank Palestinians
Tobias Kelly

Legal Reform and Administrative Detention Powers in China
Sarah Biddulph